D0934617

INTRODUCING NEW GODS
The Politics of Athenian Religion

INTRODUCING NEW GODS

The Politics of Athenian Religion

Robert Garland

Cornell University Press

Ithaca, New York

First published 1992 Cornell University Press.

Library of Congress Cataloging-in-Publication Data
Garland, Robert.
 Introducing new gods : the politics of Athenian
religion / Robert Garland.
   p.   cm.
 Includes bibliographical references and index.
 ISBN 0-8014-2766-5   (alk. paper)
  1. Athens (Greece)—Religion   2. Religion and
politics–Greece–Athens.   I. Title.
BL793.A76G37   1992
292'.08'09385—dc20   91–35672

Printed in Great Britain

Photo credits

The author and publisher are grateful to the following for
supplying and giving permission to reproduce photo-
graphs: British Museum: Plates 14, 16, 24, 28; Alison
Frantz: 1, 5, 6, 7, 8, 9, 19, 20, 21, 29, 30; German
Archaeological Institute, Rome: 13, 23, 27; Gustavianum,
Uppsala: 2; Louvre: 22; Martin von Wagner Museum,
University of Würzburg: 12; Metropolitan Museum of Art,
New York: 3, 4; Museum of Fine Arts, Boston: 10; Ny
Carlsberg Glyptothek, Copenhagen: 25; Staatliche Museen
zu Berlin: 18.

Contents

Preface   vii
List of illustrations   xi
Abbreviations   xiii

Introduction: Others and the Other   1

1.   Ancestral Rites   23

2.   Pheidippides and the Magic Mountain   47

3.   Themistokles and the Cult of the Intellect   64

4.   Theseus' Old Bones   82

5.   Transfiguration and the Maiden   99

6.   Asklepios and his Sacred Snake   116

7.   Sokrates and the New *Daimonia*   136

8.   The World of the Athenian *Aition*   152

Conclusions   171

Chronology of Athenian Religion   174
Glossary   180
Notes   183
Bibliography   210
Index Locorum   226
Index of Gods and Heroes   229
General Index   231

For my father and my godfather, Benjamin Drewery

βίος ἀνεόρταστος μακρὴ ὁδὸς ἀπανδόκευτος

Demokritos (DK 68 F 230)

The physicist Leo Szilard once announced to his friend Hans Bethe that he was thinking of keeping a diary: 'I don't intend to publish it; I am merely going to record the facts for the information of God.' 'Don't you think God knows the facts?' Bethe asked. 'Yes,' said Szilard. 'He knows the facts, but He does not know *this version of the facts*' (quoted by Freeman Dyson, *Disturbing the Universe* [New York 1979] xi).

Preface

In the evening I went very unwillingly to a society in Aldersgate Street,
where one was reading Luther's preface to the epistle of the Romans. About
a quarter before nine, while he was describing the change which God works
in the heart through faith in Christ, I felt my heart strangely warmed. I felt
I did trust in Christ, Christ alone, for salvation; and an assurance was given
me, that He had taken away *my* sins, even *mine*, and saved me from the law
of sin and death.

> John Wesley, entry in his *Journal* for 24 May 1738

My aim in this book is to ask some very down-to-earth questions. How did
a new god or hero succeed in gaining acceptance into the highly
competitive structure of Athenian polytheism? How did one recognise a
god whom one did not know? Or to put it in the language of the Greeks, its
purpose in the first instance is to identify everything that is implied by
'*nomizein theon*', the technical term, as I take it, for the recognition or
formal acknowledgement of a deity's presence in the community through
the traditional apparatus of cultus, including votive offerings, sacrifices,
prayers, and the like.[1]

But in addition to being a study of what we might aptly describe today
as the marketing or promotional aspects of Athenian cult, it is also a
search for a pattern of association between politics and religion. Greek
religion is sometimes treated as a kind of abstraction, independent of the
complex reality surrounding it and sustaining it. The truth is far
different. Nilsson (*GGR* I³, 713) once remarked in regard to the Archaic
period that religion and politics were 'one and the same'. That is
something of an oversimplification. Though it would be wrong to regard
the popularity enjoyed by the gods and heroes of Athens as a simple
consequence of the manipulation of public opinion, they were certainly
dependent upon and vulnerable to public opinion. By subtitling this book
'the politics of Athenian religion' I am using a form of shorthand for the
invisible network which made possible the introduction of a new cult.
Greek religion positively simmers with the passions of those who created
it. It possesses the dimensions of their dreams, their illusions and,

---

[1] Here and elsewhere I adopt the translation of *nomizein theous* which was proposed by J.
Burnet, *Plato's Apology* (Oxford, Clarendon), 104, viz. 'acknowledge the gods by giving
them the worship prescribed by *nomos* ('law, custom').

ultimately, as one watches cults decline and decay, their disillusionments too. It also happens to supply us with a map to chart the not always visible currents that turn the course of history in one direction rather than another, not least because the introduction of a new god, as I shall try to demonstrate, often furnishes us with his supporters' explanation of why events turned out the way they did. So far as I am aware, no previous attempt has been made to align Athenian religion with Athenian politics for the four-hundred-year period covered by this survey.

By restricting our investigation to a single polis, we have the best chance of discovering why a particular deity gained entry into the community at a particular moment in history. In addition, a limited focus enables us to contemplate how and in response to what set of pressures the rules of procedure regarding the introduction of new gods altered, as I believe they did, over the course of time. The cults which form the centrepiece to this investigation – Pan, Artemis Aristoboule, Theseus, Bendis, Asklepios and Sokrates' *daimonion* – could not be more diverse in the differing perspectives which they offer on religious innovation. Far from being a handicap, however, this is rather an asset, since viewed overall the series affords an invaluable insight into the collective religious mentality of the Athenians in the period from the Persian Wars to the trial of Sokrates, with the important qualification that it was a mentality which evolved radically in the course of those ninety-odd years.

My inquiry ends with the trial of Sokrates not, I wish to point out at the beginning, because Athens' canon of gods and heroes had effectively stabilised by the beginning of the fourth century. On the contrary, the period from 399 onwards witnessed further innovation, and in so far as the epigraphical data gains in richness, there is more, not less, to investigate. But the year 399 does mark an important watershed in Athenian religion, for the following reasons: first, because of the implications of Sokrates' trial and condemnation for the restored authority of the Athenian Demos; and secondly because an important review of Athens' sacred calendar was completed just before the trial, which also had profound consequences for the organisation and practice of Athenian religion. It is because this inquiry is essentially constructed around a number of highly individual case-studies that I have largely ignored the studies of anthropologists working in the field of Greek religion, significant though their work has been for the investigation of more general problems.

Since no first-person reports have come down to us from the individuals who took it upon themselves to be the champion of a new cult, we are dealing with testimony in which the interpretations of the leading participants rarely intervene. Does that matter? The question is patently absurd. We might just as well ask: 'Do individuals matter in history?' Emphatically they do, as the presence of Mikhail Gorbachev on the world stage has categorically proved, notwithstanding the fact that we need to be reminded from time to time of the obvious folly of writing history 'arbitrarily reduced to the role of quintessential heroes' (Braudel 1980, 10). I should like to acknowledge that a major source of inspiration came from teaching the Book of Exodus to first-year undergraduates at Colgate University in courses entitled 'Roots of Western Civilization' and 'The Birth of Ancient Religion', which led me to become engrossed in the figure and personality of Moses. God's election of this feeble, violent, irascible and self-deprecating old man to be the leader of a dynamic Judaic revival movement is for me a sublime paradox. In the whole of Greek literature there is no comparable emphasis upon the personality of the instigator of a new cult. And this fact is no less paradoxical and, in its own curious way, no less sublime.

While I was a Ph.D. student at University College London I happened to have lunch one day with a fellow called Vic who worked just off the Tottenham Court Road. He was courteous enough to ask me about the subject of my research and having listened to an account of my fascination with Greek burial customs, smiled with brutal geniality and said: 'So what?' His question has stuck with me over the years. Like Vic, I do not believe that scholarship is an end in itself. Fifty years ago my father, a prisoner of war on board a Japanese freighter, was torpedoed by an American submarine. He managed to survive eighteen hours in the water and was eventually picked up by a Japanese boat because he had insisted on allowing a Japanese sailor to take refuge on his raft as well. Had he not done so, he and the other men on the raft would have been left to die in the water. Some time earlier my father had met my future godfather, with whom he spent the rest of the war as a POW. Both were moved from Nagasaki a few days before the atomic bomb fell in the mainly Christian district of the city, killing 40,000 with a flash of light which lasted only seconds. If they had been Greeks they would have erected shrines to the gods who had miraculously preserved their lives. But my father is a Protestant and my godfather, Benjamin Drewery, a Methodist minister. Forty-four years later I heard Ben preach a sermon about the birth of the Methodist movement. I had not previously known the story about John Wesley's conversion, in particular the detail of feeling his heart 'strangely warmed' with the realisation that he was saved, which came upon him at a quarter to nine one Thursday evening in Aldersgate Street. The prosaic, circumstantial, Anglo-Saxon exactitude of his report – did Wesley check his timepiece at the instant of his conversion? – made a profound impression upon me. His experience of Christ's saving grace seemed worlds apart from, say, the blinding flash of light that appeared to St Paul on the road to Damascus, and I wanted to know why. I wanted to know how and in what frame of mind my father and godfather would have gone about setting up a cult to their saviour gods if they had been Greeks, let's say on the morning after Nagasaki.

An early version of Chapter 1 was given as a seminar to the Classics

Department at Princeton University in April 1990 and to the Classics
Department at Union College in October of the same year, and of Chapter
7 to the Colgate Humanities Colloquium in September 1990. I am most
grateful to all those who participated in these events for their valuable
comments and suggestions. This study has greatly benefited from grants
from Colgate University, including those associated with the Roy D. and
Margaret B. Wooster chair. Much of the research was undertaken in the
spring semester of 1990 at the Institute for Advanced Study in Princeton,
to which I am greatly indebted. In particular I would like to express my
gratitude to Glen Bowersock, Christian Habicht, and above all to Homer
and Dorothy Thompson, for the pleasure of their company and for sharing
their ideas. Jacob Neusner, a colleague during my time at the Institute,
has stimulated me to see beyond the boundaries of my discipline. Not for
the first time Jon Mikalson has saved me from overstatement and error,
by reading through two chapters when I had reached an advanced stage
in the preparation of the manuscript. Although our approaches to
Athenian religion are by no means identical and although he is likely to
have (not for the first time) reservations about my *Quellenforschung*, the
rigour of his criticism has induced me to reflect longer and, I hope, more
profoundly. Colleagues and friends at Colgate University have nourished
the progress of this work in diverse ways, and I wish to thank especially
Anthony Aveni, Gary Urton and John Rexine. I also wish to express my
gratitude to the students on whom I first tried out my ideas four years
ago, notably Ronald Pollett and Alicia Price. My sincere appreciation is
also due to the two anonymous readers of Cornell University Press for
their helpful and generous criticism. No one is responsible for my errors
or my opinions: this has been a personal undertaking. Finally, I wish to
thank my wife Roberta, for helping me to innovate in more ways than I
can count.

Hamilton, New York   R.G.

Illustrations

Plates

(between pages 112 and 113)

1. The Acropolis from the northwest
2. Black-figure *hydria* depicting Athena as an owl
3. Attic *kylix* showing Nike acclaiming the winner of a lyre-playing contest
4. Panathenaic prize amphora
5. & 6. The 'Olive Tree' pediment
7. The 'Bluebeard' pediment
8. Pediment depicting Herakles wrestling with a Triton
9. Pediment showing the apotheosis of Herakles
10. Bell krater depicting Pan pursuing a goatherd
11. The cave of Pan on the northwest slope of the Acropolis
12. Black-figure *kylix* depicting Pan as a runner
13. Portrait herm of Themistokles
14. *Oinochoê* showing Boreas abducting Oreithyia
15. *Kratêriskoi* as used in the cult of Artemis
16. Red-figure *kylix* depicting Theseus killing the Minotaur
17. The shrine of Artemis Aristoboule
18. Red figure *lêkythos* depicting Herakles and Theseus
19. The Athenian Treasury at Delphi
20 & 21. Metopes from the Athenian Treasury at Delphi
22. Red-figure *kylix* showing Amphitrite welcoming Theseus
23. Roman copy in marble of the Tyrannicides
24. Roman copy in marble of a portrait of Perikles
25. Votive relief from the Piraeus depicting Asklepios
26. Votive relief in honour of Bendis
27. Roman copy in marble of a portrait of Sokrates
28. Head of Asklepios from Milo
29. Athena's sacred olive tree beside the Erechtheion
30. The place where Poseidon is said to have struck the Acropolis with his trident

Figures

1. Map of Attica   xvi
2. Plan of the Mycenaean *megaron* at Eleusis   26
3. Possible shrine of Phrontis at Sounion   33
4. Drawing of the Altar of the Twelve Gods in the Agora   41
5. Drawing of the monument to the eponymous heroes of the
    ten Attic tribes   44
6. Reconstruction of the placing of figures in the picture of the
    Battle of Marathon in the Stoa Poikile   56
7. Map of the plain of Marathon   56
8. Plan of the northwest slope of the Acropolis   59
9. Plan of the shrine of Artemis Aristoboule in Melite   77
10. The northwest corner of the Agora   104
11. The Periklean telesterion   108
12. The Telemachos monument   119
13. The sanctuary of Asklepios on the south slope of the Acropolis   127
14. The Stoa Basileos on the west side of the Agora   137

Abbreviations

Ancient authors and their works

Aes(chylus) *Eum(enides), Pers(ai), P(rometheus) V(inctus)*
Ail(ian) *V(aria) H(istoria)*
Aischin(es)
A(nthologia) P(alatina)
Apollod(oros)
Aristeides *Panath(ênaïkos)*
Ar(istophanes) *Acharn(ians), Lys(istratê), Plout(os)*
Arist(otle) *Ath(ênaiôn) Pol(iteia), Poet(ics), Pol(itics), N(ikomachean) E(thics)*
Arr(ian) *Kynêget(ikos)*
Ath(enaios) *Deipn(osophistai)*
Bacchyl(ides) *Dith(yramb)*
Cic(ero)
Dem(osthenes)
D(iodoros) S(iculus)
D(iogenes) L(aertios)
Et(ymologicum) M(agnum)
Eur(ipides) *Ba(cchai), El(ektra), H(ercules) F(urens), Hipp(olytos), I(phigeneia at) T(auris), Med(ea), Rhes(os), Supp(liants)*
H(ymn to) Dem(eter)
H(ymn to) Her(mes)
H(ero)d(o)t(os)
Hes(iod) *Th(eogony)*
Hom(er) *Il(iad), Od(yssey)*
Isok(rates)
Joseph(os) *(Against) Ap(ion)*
Jul(ian) *Or(ationes)*
Li(vy)
Luk(ian) *(pro) Laps(u inter salutandum), Pisc(ator)*
Lykourg(os) *(Against) Leok(rates)*
Lys(ias) *Epitaph(ios)*
Macrob(ius) *Sat(urnalia)*
Men(ander)
Ov(id) *Metam(orphoses)*

Paus(anias)
Phil(ostratos) *V(ita) A(pollonii), V(itae) S(ophistarum)*
Pi(ndar) *Pyth(ian)*
Pl(ato) *Apol(ogy), Euthyd(êmos), Euthyph(ro), Ph(ai)d(o), Ph(ai)dr(os), Rep(ublic), Theait(êtos)*
Pl(i)n(y) *H(istory of)N(atural Phenomena)*
Plu(tarch) *Alk(ibiades), Arist(eides), Kim(on), Mor(alia), Per(ikles), Sol(on), Them(istokles), Thes(eus)*
Polyain(os)
P(apyri) Oxy(rhynchus)
Porph(yry) *(On) Abst(inence)*
S(ophokles) *O(edipus) T(yrannos)*
Str(abo) *Geog(raphy)*
Sud(a)
Suet(onius) *J(ulius) C(aesar)*
Th(eo)phr(astos) *Char(acters)*
Thuk(ydides)
Val(erius) Max(imus)
Xen(ophon) *Anab(asis), Apol(ogy), Hell(ênika), Hipp(archikos), Mem-(orabilia)*

Periodicals

AA = Archäologischer Anzeiger
A&A = Antike und Abendland
AAA = Archaiologika Analekta ex Athênôn
ABSA = Annual of the British School at Athens
AC = L'Antiquité Classique
AD = Archaiologikon Deltion
AHB = Ancient History Bulletin
AJA = American Journal of Archaeology
AJAH = American Journal of Ancient History
AJP = American Journal of Philology
AK = Antike Kunst
AncW = Ancient World
ARW = Archiv für Religionswissenschaft
ASAA = Annuario della Scuola Archeologica di Atene
BABesch = Bulletin Antieke Beschaving
BCH = Bulletin de Correspondance Hellénique
BICS = Bulletin of the Institute of Classical Studies
CJ = Classical Journal
CP = Classical Philology
CQ = Classical Quarterly
CR = Classical Review
CSCA = California Studies in Classical Antiquity

G&R = Greece and Rome
GRBS = Greek, Roman and Byzantine Studies
HSCP = Harvard Studies in Classical Philology
HThR = Harvard Theological Review
JDAI = Jahrbuch des Deutschen Archäologischen Instituts
JHPh = Journal of the History of Philosophy
JHS = Journal of Hellenic Studies
JTS = Journal of Theological Studies
MDAI(A) = Mitteilungen des Deutschen Archäologischen Instituts (Athen. Abt.)
MH = Museum Helveticum
PAA = Praktika tês Akadêmias Athênôn
PCPhS = Proceedings of the Classical Philological Society
PP = La Parola del Passato
RA = Revue Archéologique
REA = Revue des Études Anciennes
REG = Revue des Études Grecques
Rev. Phil. = Revue Philologique
RH = Revue Historique
RhM = Rheinisches Museum
TAPA = Transactions of the American Philological Association
TLS = Times Literary Supplement
YCS = Yale Classical Studies
ZPE = Zeitschrift für Papyrologie und Epigraphik

Other abbreviations can be found in the Bibliography.

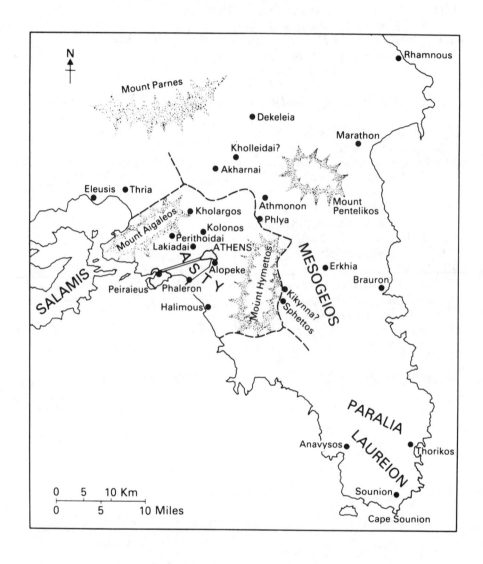

Fig. 1. Map of Attica. From J.W. Roberts, *City of Sokrates*.

Introduction:
Others and the Other

A polytheistic system by definition offers a plurality of choices to those who subscribe to the belief that god is not one but many. That much is self-evident. The specific corollary is sometimes overlooked that polytheism also imposes a heavy burden of choice upon its subscribers. The Athenian pantheon, like every other Greek pantheon, was in a state of permanent flux. New cults came into being while old cults waned. Radical re-evaluations most commonly took place at moments of crisis, since a crisis provided the most favourable conditions for the introduction of new gods. Typically it was when the Greeks won a spectacular military victory, experienced a natural disaster such as drought, famine or plague, or re-defined their social and political identity, that they responded either by endorsing a new cult or enhancing the prestige of an already existing one. For this reason the successes of the Persian wars wholly transformed the face of Athenian religion, since these not only were achieved against all odds but also contributed to the radicalisation of Athens' political system. By the same token Athens' lacklustre performance in the Peloponnesian War was deficient in stimulating religious change.

Greek religion was votive in essence; that is to say, it operated on the principle that the gods responded to gifts by giving gifts in return, and votive religion, as Burkert (1987, 14) has observed, is experimental by definition. There was no point in doing altar-curtsey before a god who merely sat on his hands. Votives were not vouched to deities afflicted with sclerotic immobility. Numerous examples prove the general point. While waging war against Athens, the Thebans appealed to the Aiginetans for military assistance, and the latter responded by forwarding cult statues of their national heroes, the Aiakidai, as helpers. The Aiakidai proved useless, however, and were promptly returned to their owners like defective merchandise bought on approval from a mail order catalogue with a request for the genuine article – men – instead (Hdt. 5.80.1-81.1). Similarly in Aristophanes' *Wasps* (ll. 119-23), when initiation into Korybantic rites fails to bring Philokleon to his senses, the old reprobate is shipped across to Aigina to spend a night in Asklepios' sanctuary in the hope that the Epidaurian god will be able to succeed where the Mother of the Gods had failed.

One problem was that the goodwill of the gods could never be counted upon, however dutiful their worshippers. In the *Iliad* Trojan women place a robe on the knees of Athena and promise to sacrifice twelve heifers in her temple if she will take pity on their city, themselves and their little children (6.309-11). But the goddess studiously averts her gaze and instead favours the Greeks. Even more poignant is Ajax's outburst of gratitude in Sophokles' *Ajax*. 'How well you stood beside me!' he exclaims in pitiful delusion to his supposed ally Athena just after she has caused him to butcher a herd of cattle in the mistaken belief that he was venting his rage upon the captains of the Greek army (l. 92). In sum, the gods did not see themselves as members of a caring profession, to use the current cant term. Given the fact that the Greeks found themselves adrift in a world dangerously subject to interventions by hidden forces which they could only sometimes identify, rarely predict and never wholly control, we can only applaud the prudence of the Athenians (among others) in eventually taking out an all-risk insurance policy by erecting an altar in the Agora 'To the Unknown God' (Acts 17:23).

Multiplicitous polytheism

'Everything divine is envious and meddlesome,' Solon observed at his celebrated meeting with the Lydian king Kroisos (Hdt. 1.32.1), and the evidence of mythology fully backs up his claim. Mount Olympos was neither egalitarian nor democratic, and the Greek gods were no less competitive than their human counterparts.

To understand just how envious and meddlesome they could be, we have only to consider the fate of Hippolytos in Euripides' play of that name. The young man devotes himself exclusively to the worship of Artemis, a chaste goddess who rigorously shuns sexual intercourse, and publicly snubs Aphrodite, whom he contemptuously brands as 'a goddess who is adored by night' (l. 106). In revenge for Hippolytos' rejection of her, Aphrodite engineers the violent destruction of his entire family. Let it be emphasised that there was nothing inherently sacrilegious in favouring one deity before another. On the contrary, the superabundance of choice made it almost inevitable. Favouritism, moreover, worked both ways: from gods to men (which was called *theophilia*) as well as from men to gods (*philotheia*). As Hippolytos himself uncontentiously observed (l. 104), 'Everyone has his preferences, in gods and men alike'. Artemis, too, not only acknowledges that she is Hippolytos' greatest friend among the gods (l. 1394), but also that he is her greatest friend among mortals (ll. 1333, cf. 1398). We might also reflect upon the bond between Odysseus and Athena in the *Odyssey*, a pair who are united in their joint aptitude for cunning (13.296-9). One could even with impunity identify one's favourite deity openly, as Odysseus does in the case of Athena in Sophokles' *Ajax* (l. 14). Mere favouritism, however, is manifestly not what is at stake in Euripides' play. What *is* at stake is exclusiveness. Judged by the standards of acceptable religious behaviour, Hippolytos' action represents a wholly unacceptable, fanatical extreme.[1] For not only does he boast of enjoying a depth of intimacy with Artemis which she denies the rest of humanity (1. 84-6), but he also has the temerity to make it a matter of public record that he holds her rival in complete contempt. The correct posture towards a hostile deity would appear to have been a diplomatic silence of the kind which Odysseus scrupulously maintains towards his mortal enemy Poseidon throughout the *Odyssey*.

The legend surrounding Hippolytos' name explores a source of anxiety which is embedded in all polytheistic systems. How could a pious Greek honour deities as diverse and mutually antagonistic as Artemis and Aphrodite? How was it possible for him to display his devotion to Aphrodite without denying the legitimacy of the claims of her personified antithesis? The answer surely has to do with the fact that mutual regard was not a necessary condition which determined whether men and gods did business together. Divided allegiance constituted the hallmark of polytheism and no man (or god) could be all things to all gods (or men). The very complexity of human life militated strongly against exclusive attachments.

The animosity which existed between Artemis and Aphrodite exemplifies the warring element that lay at the core of polytheism itself, riven as it was with competing and self-contradictory obligations. The rivalry between Athena and Poseidon in the *Odyssey*, or the division among the Olympians in the *Iliad*, which mirrors the Trojan War itself, are examples of the same phenomenon. Although the Greeks would have never put it in these terms, the envy of their gods thus serves as a metaphor for opposing tendencies in human nature. Being sensible to the contradictions which reside in every human personality, they perhaps worshipped Artemis alongside Aphrodite, albeit subconsciously, in part to reconcile the turbulence of their own psyches.

While on one level Euripides' treatment of the legend of Hippolytos served as an object lesson which no Greek needed to be taught, the play's conclusion, where we are treated to the unedifying spectacle of Artemis vowing to avenge Hippolytos' death by slaying the next mortal to whom her rival takes a fancy (ll. 1416-22), reminded him that even innocent bystanders might become victims caught up in the crossfire between deities who embodied natural opposites. Except in the pathologically unbalanced mind of a Hippolytos, however, the very comprehensiveness

---

[1] Festugière's (1954, 14-18) characterisation of Hippolytos as the exemplar of a type of 'personal piety' is surely unacceptable. Far from being pious in any sense of the term which would have been recognisable to the average Greek, Hippolytos is actually the embodiment of the complete opposite. Cf. also Burkert (*GR*, 274): 'The bond between a man and a god never becomes so close that it could be expressed by a possessive pronoun. Greeks do not pray "my god!", as Hittites and Hebrews do.'

of polytheism set a natural ceiling upon the degree of involvement which a worshipper might properly be allowed with one deity. Hence piety could be defined as 'participating on an annual basis in the state sacrifices (*thusias dêmoteleis poieisthai*) and not neglecting any festival or *heortê*' (cf. Theopompos *FGrH* 115 F344 in Porph. *Abst.* 2.16). Being endemically unstable, the system actively fostered diversity.

With few exceptions the phenomenon of conversion, in the sense of an exclusive and abiding attachment to a single god or goddess, had little place in mainstream Greek religion. A god entered the community as a 'useful supplement', not as a 'substitute' demanding complete rejection of that community's previous religious experience, to use Nock's (1933, 7 and 12) helpful terminology. The evidence to the contrary is unimpressive. When Sokrates in Aristophanes' *Clouds* agrees to accept the elderly Strepsiades as his pupil on condition that the latter renounce his belief in all the gods except Chaos, the Clouds and Tongue, the audience would have been expected to interpret such an outrageous demand as a sign of Sokrates' eccentricity, presumptuousness and irreligiosity (ll. 423-6). Likewise when we read in a fourth-century inscription from Sardis in Lydia that worshippers of Zeus are debarred from participating in the mysteries of Sabazios, Angdistis and Ma, we would surely be justified in suspecting more than a trace of oriental influence (*SEG* XXIX.1205.8-11).

As proof of the foregoing, let us note that the enjoyment of a special relationship with a single deity guaranteed neither immunity in battle nor prosperity in peace. To give an obvious and striking example, the love which Zeus professes towards certain supposedly privileged mortals in the *Iliad* is virtually the kiss of death. His doomed favourites include Achilles, Hektor, Sarpedon and Patroklos. Whom the gods loved died young, and the few exceptions prove the rule. Athena's affection for Odysseus does, it is true, secure her favourite's homecoming after an unconscionable delay on the part of the cumbrous Olympian bureaucracy, yet it can do nothing to neutralise the hostility of Poseidon, who will terminate the hero's life in a watery embrace (*Od.* 11.134-6).

The human factor

Hippolytos ignores Aphrodite not, of course, because he questions the reality of her divinity but because of a temperamental opposition to her claims upon his behaviour. Polytheism not only required its adherents to make choices between publicly acknowledged gods, however. It also laid upon them an obligation to distinguish genuine gods from either fraudulent or worthless ones. Greek religion offered profits and emoluments to its organisers and managers, and like all human enterprises it was surely tainted by greed, nepotism and graft. A charge of corruption is already made in the *Odyssey* (2.178-86), when

Eurymachos, one of the suitors, accuses the seer Halitherses of prophesying Odysseus' return merely in the hope of receiving a reward from his son Telemachos. Inevitably, too, it is easier to identify the worldly motives for introducing new gods than it is the 'religious' ones. The setting up of a new cult was never without economic consequences, first for those promoting it, secondly for the neighbouring community, and thirdly for already established cults, particularly those whose sphere of influence had close affinities with the new entrant and which henceforth might be in direct competition with it for goodwill and financial support.

A sanctuary with a Panhellenic reputation such as Delphi, Eleusis, Epidauros or Olympia not only received a large income in the form of gifts and fees, but also provided immense wealth for its local community, notably those who supplied board and lodging or who manufactured and sold votive offerings. It is the frightening prospect of the bottom falling out of the market in miniature silver shrines of Artemis throughout the Roman province of Asia as a result of the Christian claim that 'gods made with human hands are not gods' which induced the Ephesian silversmith Demetrios and his fellow craftsmen to instigate a riot when St Paul preached in their city (Acts 19:23-40). Even a small and insignificant foundation might provide its management with limited income and remuneration, as is suggested by an inscription from the sanctuary of the river god Kephissos in Phaleron which states that anyone who wished could sacrifice on its altar 'on the appropriate terms' (*epi telestôn agathôn*), which perhaps means after paying the requisite fee. (*IG* II² 4548 = *LSGS* 17.6f.)²

Charismatic religious figures of the kind who pioneered the introduction of new cults were suspected of venality throughout Greek history. Since many of them depended for their income upon charitable gifts, the charge was easy to make and virtually impossible to refute. Thus the Theban king Pentheus castigates the seer Teiresias in Euripides' *Bacchai* (ll. 255-7):

By introducing (*espherôn*) yet another new *daimôn* or divinity to the human race you hope to make a profit by examining flights of birds and interpreting burnt offerings.

In his account of the beliefs of a Thracian tribe known as the Getai who lived along the north shores of the Black Sea, Herodotos tells a fascinating anecdote about an otherwise unknown spiritual guru called Salmoxis who was credited by his followers with having evaded death. Herodotos' Greek informants, who occupied territory adjoining the Getai, were sceptical to say the least and provided the historian with a rather

---

² Other interpretations are, however, possible. Guarducci (1974, 59) would transcribe *epitelestôn agathôn*, i.e. after having received (i.e. from the gods) good things.

different explanation for his popularity. Though his informants do not spell out in detail what motivated Salmoxis to start his own cult, the fact that he was enamoured of a sophisticated lifestyle suggests that greed figured prominently in his calculations. Herodotos writes (4.95-6):

> I have been told ... that this Salmoxis was a human being who lived in Samos and was a slave of Pythagoras, the son of Mnesarchos. Later he became free and acquired a considerable fortune. He then returned to his native country. As the people there were both poor and ignorant, Salmoxis, who had become accustomed to a more sophisticated lifestyle and attained greater awareness than was common among his compatriots ... built an *andrôn* (banqueting room) to which he invited the chief men among the townsfolk. While he was entertaining them he proceeded to teach them that neither he nor his fellow drinking-companions nor their descendants would die, but instead they would go to a place where they would live for ever in the enjoyment of every blessing. While he was doing all this and making these pronouncements, Salmoxis set about constructing an underground chamber. When the chamber was completed, he disappeared from sight of the Thracians and descended to his underground chamber, where he lived for three years. In the meantime his friends sorely missed him and grieved for him as if dead. In the fourth year he appeared (*ephanê*) to the Thracians, thereby persuading them of the truth of his teaching.

Herodotos concludes his account with exemplary evenhandedness:

> I for my part neither disbelieve in Salmoxis and his underground chamber nor do I completely believe the story either .... Whether this Salmoxis was a human being or a local *daimôn* or divine spirit among the Getai, let's leave him be.

The charge of religious fraud persisted throughout antiquity, a notorious late example being the infamous Alexander of Abonoteichos who was mercilessly pilloried by the satirist Lukian for having established a lucrative oracular shrine in his home town in the second century AD.

A seer like Teiresias who provided mantic support for a new cult presumably commanded fees which were commensurate with his own reputation. The sky, so to speak, was his limit. The priest of a new cult also stood to benefit, albeit more modestly, since his office entitled him to a small salary and a portion of the sacrifices performed in its sanctuary, and, from the fourth century onwards, possible exemption from taxation. In the Classical period the most lucrative Athenian priesthood is likely to have been that of the Two Goddesses, Demeter and Kore, whose ministers received a portion of each sacrifice, a fee from every initiate, and a proportion of the proceeds from the sale of the harvest from the Rarian field (*IG* I^2 1672). In some parts of the Greek world, though never to our knowledge in Athens, priesthoods were used as a bargaining chip in the wheelings and dealings of self-seeking politicians. On Samos, for instance, a certain Maiandrios, successor to the tyrant Polykrates, offered to surrender his power in favour of democracy on condition that he could keep six talents of his predecessor's fortune and be appointed priest of the cult of Zeus Eleutherios, which he intended to introduce in commemoration of the restoration of constitutional rule (Hdt. 3.142.4). The move was apparently designed to secure his immunity from prosecution for the crimes and illegalities which he had committed as a tyrant. Likewise at Gela on Sicily a certain Telines, ancestor of the future tyrant Gelo, agreed to reinstate a party of exiles on condition that the hierophancy of the established cult of Demeter and Kore be henceforth reserved within his family (Hdt. 7.153.3). Since the person of a hierophant was sacrosanct, Telines evidently saw this as his best safeguard against threats to his life.

The introduction of a new cult also served to promote the interests of aspiring political leaders. *Philotimia*, love of honour, was evidently perceived to be a legitimate and powerful incentive behind the introduction of a new god, as Plutarch's use of the term to explain Kimon's motive for retrieving Theseus' bones from Skyros indicates (below p. 83). It was an incentive, however, which might not invariably have been exercised in the public interest. Certainly Euripides entertained the theoretical possibility that the motivation of supporters of new cults occasionally left something to be desired. In the *Bacchai* the elderly Kadmos tells his grandson Pentheus not to tax his conscience overmuch with the theological niceties of Dionysos' claim to godhead, but instead to concentrate his mind upon the honour that will accrue to the family name from the public avowal that his sister Semele has given birth to a god (ll. 333-6):

> For even if this person is not a god, as you say, let it be alleged by you that he is. Lie in this seemly fashion so that Semele shall appear to have sired a god and so that family honour (*timê*) shall descend on us and our whole *genos*.

Founders of new cults might also be suspected of seeking to extract sexual favours from female devotees, particularly if the rituals which they instigated involved initiation. This in Pentheus' judgement is the chief reason why the Stranger, who is Dionysos in disguise, entices women up on to the mountains outside Thebes (Eur. *Ba*. 222f., 237f., 260f., 353f., 487 and 957f.). Pentheus, of course, makes a fatal misjudgement, and one which tells us much about his own disturbed psychology. Dionysos and his adherents were manifestly not fraudulent, even if the status-conscious Kadmos did jump on their bandwagon. As Euripides well understood, motives are never pure and rarely simple. The king's subsequent dismemberment at the hands of the enraged maenads reminds us, too, just how high the stakes could be for both petitioning deity and petitioned community.

Even allowing for the fact that self-interest was an important element in many decisions to sponsor a hitherto unacknowledged deity, however, it is wholly unwarranted to assume that innovators were merely in the business of advancing their political careers or lining their own pockets. To charge a Peisistratos, a Themistokles or a Kimon with religious manipulation on the grounds that they inaugurated cults to celebrate their own achievements is in fact to evade one of *the* central intellectual challenges of Athenian religion. As Connor (1987, 50) rightly points out: 'The successful politician is closely linked to his community and shares many of its values ... . His success derives not so much from his intellectual or emotional distance from the community or his cleverness at seeking his own advantage at the expense of the community, as from his attunement to civic needs and aspirations, and his ability to give them form and expression.'

In his discussion of the complex mixture of motives which prompted the pious Nikias to fund expensive celebrations in honour of Apollo on Delos, Plutarch writes (*Nik.* 4.1):

> It is clear that in what he did there was an element of ostentatiousness (*doxa*) and love of honour (*philotimia*) which were intended to confer on him visibility and popularity, though from his disposition and character in other ways you would say with confidence that this sort of currying popular favour was rather a corollary of his piety (*eusebeia*).

In other words, the impetus behind Nikias' behaviour was primarily *eusebeia*, aided and abetted by *doxa* and *philotimia*. While illuminating up to a point, this analysis yet fails to provide us with a sense of what I would define as the inner compulsion which fired Nikias to act in this way. Inner compulsion hardly ever surfaces in our sources, though it can occasionally be deduced, as in Pausanias' description (6.9.6-8) of the mysterious death of Kleomedes, whose elevation to heroic status constituted a response on the part of the traumatised Astypalaieans to being victims of what was surely one of the most horrendous and disturbing crimes perpetrated in antiquity:

> At the previous Olympiad (i.e. 495 BC) Kleomedes of Astypalaiea is said to have killed Ikkos of Epidauros in a boxing match. On being found guilty of unfair play by the judges and deprived of his victory, he went mad because of grief. Returning to Astypalaiea, he attacked a school with sixty pupils inside and tore down a pillar supporting the roof. The roof collapsed on top of the children, and while he was being stoned by the townsfolk, he fled to the sanctuary of Athena. He entered a chest that was lying in the temple and pulled down the lid. The Astypalaieans laboured in vain to open it. When they eventually succeeded in breaking it into pieces, they did not find

Kleomedes either alive or dead. They sent some men to Delphi to inquire about what had happened to Kleomedes and, according to the report, received this reply: 'Kleomedes of Astypalaiea is the last of the heroes. Honour him with sacrifices, since he is no longer a mortal.'

'A land most dear to the gods'

The sneering late-fifth-century pamphleteer who goes under the title of the Old Oligarch claims that Athens had twice as many festivals as any other Greek city (3.2), and Perikles, too, in the Funeral Speech makes a point of mentioning that 'the contests and sacrifices held throughout the year' provided 'plentiful relaxation for the spirit'. Perikles was implicitly contrasting Athens with Sparta, whose serious-minded citizenry evidently possessed far fewer pleasing diversions of this kind (Thuk. 2.38.1). Even allowing for rhetorical exaggeration, such remarks provide powerful testimony to the complexity of Athens' sacred calendar (cf. Mikalson *SCCAY*, 201), and incidentally as well to the size of her pantheon. Foreigners also acknowledged that there was something distinctive about the religious practices of the Athenians. The indefatigable second-century AD traveller Pausanias, whose breadth of experience made him as well qualified as anyone to pronounce upon the subject, praised the Athenians because 'they are more pious than other people' (1.17.1) and because 'they exhibited more zeal (*spoudê*) in religious matters than any other people' (1.24.3). During his abortive attempt to convert Athens to Christianity in *c.* AD 65 St Paul uncharitably observed that the city was 'infested with idols (*kateidôlos*)' (Acts 17:16, cf. 16:22). Large and small, official and unofficial, shrines were everywhere. The densest concentrations were on the summit of the Acropolis, on its northern and southern slopes and western approaches, on the neighbouring Areopagus, and in the Agora below. In the suburbs of Athens an important cluster of ancient cults was located on the banks of the Ilissos River southeast of the Acropolis, and another in the Academy to the northwest. In the Piraeus, too, where there was a very large settlement of metics of divers ethnic backgrounds, sanctuaries proliferated.

In the course of this investigation I shall seek to demonstrate that Athens not only took a significant part in promoting new cults throughout the Greek world, but also gave them a prominence which greatly facilitated their subsequent elevation to the rank of Panhellenic deities. Such elevation happened in the case of both Pan and Asklepios who, before entry, were localised deities with no evident intent of spreading outside Arkadia and the northeast Peloponnese respectively. Athens' influential role was not overlooked by other Greeks. Diodorus Siculus (4.39.1), for instance, says of the worship of the divine Herakles: 'The Athenians first of all people honoured Herakles with sacrifices as a god and held up as an example to all other men their own piety towards the

god. Thereby they induced first all the Greeks and then all men in the
inhabited world to worship Herakles as a god.'

As in other Greek communities, the acceptance of a new deity was by no
means automatic or guaranteed. The *Homeric Hymn to Delian Apollo*
lists some thirty communities, Athens among them, which refused Leto
permission to give birth to Apollo on their soil before she finally found a
warm welcome on the humble island of Delos (ll. 30-50). As a metaphor
for the rough road which had to be travelled by supporters of a new cult
seeking a permanent home for their god, the hymn bears eloquent
witness to the strength of opposition which even the cult of a major
Olympian deity was believed to have faced in its infancy. It is regrettable
that the Athenians did not keep statistics on the acceptance-rate of
petitioning deities: it would be fascinating to know what proportion of
them met the same fate as Apollo.

We do not know how many gods, heroes and other supernatural beings
received worship within the confines of any ancient Greek community.
What is incontestable, however, is that their number was such that no
worshipper, however devout, would have been able or indeed permitted to
perform cult in connection with more than a fraction of the total. In
fifth-century Athens the state supported at public expense at least forty
deities whom it referred to collectively as 'The Other Gods' – other, that
is, than Athena Polias, the foremost state deity, and the two Eleusinian
Goddesses, Demeter and her daughter Persephone or Kore.[3] In addition,
there were cults which were recognised by, and in many cases exclusive
to, a variety of sub-divisions of the citizen body, in particular the four
Ionian and ten Kleisthenic tribes into which all its members were
divided, the aristocratic kin-groups or *genê* of which there are some 60
known to us by name, the unknown number of phratries or brotherhoods,
and the 139 demes. One could even make religious duties at the lowly
deme level a full-time occupation, as we see from a contemptuous remark
made by Sostratos in Menander's *Dyskolos* (ll. 260-3): 'My mother is going
to make a sacrifice to some god or other. She does this every day,
wandering around the whole deme in a circle, sacrificing.' The deme of
Erkhia, which has furnished us with the only sacred calendar that has
survived complete, conducted sacrifices in honour of forty-three different
deities and heroes (*SEG* XXI.541, *c.* 375-350). Though Erkhia was
above-average in size, it was by no means one of the largest demes. If we
assume that its demesmen were neither more nor less religious than any

---

[3] The term 'state cult' eludes exact definition. S. Aleshire, *The Athenian Asklepieion*
(Amsterdam 1989), 14 n. 5, proposes simply 'one where the Athenian dêmos and boulê ...
exercise some supervision over the presence and disposition of the votives dedicated in a
sanctuary.' Supervision would presumably have varied in individual instances, quite aside
from the fact that this would have been only one of many areas in which the state made its
influence felt. As Mikalson (*GRBS* 23.3 [1982] 215) points out, in the fifth century 'virtually
all Athenian *heortai* (i.e. festivals) had some administrative control and financial support
from the state.'

others, there must have been literally thousands of such cults throughout Attica. From the fourth century onwards there was also a multitude of deities worshipped by privately-constituted religious associations known as *orgeônes, thiasôtai, eranistai* and the like, many of which were sponsored by one or other of Athens' numerous ethnic minorities.

To the Athenian people themselves the size of their pantheon afforded palpable proof that they inhabited 'a land most dear to the gods' (Aes. *Eum.* 847; cf. *Pers.* 347; Pi. fr. 75.4 Maehler *T*). Their *theophilia* was also demonstrated by the famous legend of the contest between Athena and Poseidon for the guardianship of the land, as Sokrates remarks in Plato's *Menexenos* (237c), although we should note that Athens was not the only territory privileged to have aroused divine jealousy (cf. Plu. *Mor.* 741a with Loeb notes *ad loc.*; Parker [1986, 199]; and E. Wüst in *RE* 22 [1953] cols. 460-1). From a more critical perspective, however, the same phenomenon was merely a symptom of her people's insatiable appetite for novelty. Alluding to the failure of St Paul's mission to Athens, the author of Acts disdainfully comments, 'All the Athenians and foreigners living among them passed their time either speaking or hearing of something new' (17:21).

More objectively, the size of Athens' pantheon was in part a reflection of the complexity of her social and political structures and of her availability to foreign influence, especially from the middle of the fifth century onwards when metics began settling within her borders in very large numbers. This basic principle is neatly illustrated by Herodotos' claim (5.7) that the politically backward Thracians worshipped only three deities, Ares, Dionysos and Artemis, while a fourth, Hermes, was exclusive to their kings. Even allowing for Herodotos' undoubted ignorance of the finer points of Thracian religion, the comparative lack of religious choice was a feature of conservative and culturally backward communities.

The majority of Athens' gods were localised variants of the Olympian twelve around whose first name (Athena, Artemis, Zeus, etc.) clustered a multiplicity of 'surnames' or *epiklêseis*, by which each deity was distinguished from others on the basis of an extensive set of criteria which included function, appearance, affiliation, place of worship and so on. Athena Nike, for instance, was associated with Victory, Artemis Leukophryene was distinguished by her white brow, Zeus Kronion was venerated as the son of Kronos, and Athena Polias resided on the Acropolis. We know the identity of at least a dozen Athenas who were worshipped in the Asty (or city of Athens) and twenty others who received cult in the countryside. There is no warrant for assuming that such diversity was fostered by dissident elements seeking to establish their own brand of Athena-worship. In the absence of any theology as such, the concept of 'schism' was alien to the ancient world. Polyonomy had the obvious benefit of enabling a Greek community to innovate at will, because there could in theory be any number of different deities bearing the name of Athena, while remaining strictly within the bounds of Olympian (i.e. Panhellenic) religion, because the divine family constituted a fixed unit of twelve. In other words, it permitted each community to combine stability with flexibility – by endowing its own Olympians with certain local characteristics.[4]

Faced with a daunting *embarras de richesse*, on what grounds did an individual elect to perform cult on behalf of deities A, B and C, while paying only scant attention to deities D through Z? Even a man of such exemplary piety as the Athenian general Nikias, who reputedly 'sacrificed to the gods every day and invariably kept a seer in the house' (Plu. *Nik.* 4.2), presumably had to choose which gods to honour, not least because Greek cult, which primarily entailed sacrifice, could properly be conducted only inside a sanctuary. Any decision concerning which deities to worship must therefore have been made on the basis of an extensive set of criteria, of which two of the most important were proximity to a sanctuary and family tradition. This said, except in the case of cults which designated an exclusive body of worshippers, such as those connected with the family, deme or tribe, many religious communities perhaps met only once a year, to celebrate the birthday of the deity or the anniversary of his entry into the community. It is obvious therefore that Greek cults did not have followings which resembled those attracted by Judaism or Christianity.

Gods and heroes worshipped by one's father or ancestors were known as *theoi patrôöi*, and attachment towards a *patrôös* would have been strengthened by the belief that the worshipping group was descended from an eponymous god or hero. Eponymism has been appropriately described as 'the projection of the group ... onto the plane of myth or cult or both' (Kearns, *AH* 83), and it is not unlikely that the members of such a group would have been encouraged to emulate the deeds and personalities of their eponym. Foremost among the *theoi patrôöi* of the Athenians was Apollo Patroös, so named because he was the father of Ion, the legendary founder of the Ionian race who was himself father of the four eponymous heroes of the original, pre-Kleisthenic tribes (cf. Hdt. 5.66.2; Eur. *Ion* 1575-81; Pl. *Euthyd.* 302cd). The Greek family, no less than the community of which it constituted a fractional entity, was in a very real sense defined by the cults which it chose to honour (cf. Davies 1988, 369). Of Kleisthenes' rival Isagoras Herodotos writes (5.66.1): 'He was a man of distinguished family although I cannot say who his forebears are. His kinsfolk sacrifice to Karian Zeus.'[5]

---

[4] See W. Burkert, *Structure and History in Greek Mythology and Ritual* (Berkeley 1979), 125-32, on the striking differences between Demeter of Eleusis and the black Demeter of Phigalia in Arkadia.

[5] As Jon Mikalson points out to me, Isagoras' devotion was clearly something of an oddity and it is evidently for this reason that Herodotos singles it out as noteworthy.

Other factors which influenced choice of allegiance were social status and means of livelihood. Every trade or profession had its own divine patron. Asklepios represented physicians, the Anakes (known also as the Dioskouroi) safeguarded sailors and shipowners, Hephaistos metalworkers, Prometheus potters, and so on.[6] It can hardly be fortuitous that a cult of Hephaistos, the god of metalworkers, was established in the Agora on Kolonos Agoraios where human labourers plied the same craft. Though evidence about the social and economic status of a worshipping community is hard to come by, it is not inconceivable that some cults were particularly favoured by persons of similar background and wealth (cf. Osborne *Demos*, 159f.). There were also deities who had to be placated by particular age-groups, as for instance Artemis Brauronia, who posed a threat to female adolescents. Last but by no means least, as we have already seen, there was temperamental preference. Certain personalities are compatible, others are not, whether the personalities in question are human or divine.

Only within the sphere of domestic religion was religious conformity implicitly enjoined upon the citizenry, since before taking up the archonship an elected candidate was required to undergo public scrutiny at which he was asked: 'Do you have in your home an Apollo Patroös and a Zeus Herkeios (Of the enclosure), and if so where are their shrines located?' ([Arist.] *AP* 55.3). Though the worship of these deities was not prescribed by law, the failure to provide a satisfactory answer debarred a candidate from assuming public office and so effectively resulted in partial disenfranchisement. Apart from Apollo Patroös and Zeus Herkeios, however, a family would have had considerable freedom of choice, given the fact that in the domestic no less than in the public sphere there was a variety of deities available.

Athenians were also under a civic obligation to participate in the major festivals of state such as the Panathenaia and City Dionysia, since the safety and security of the community were judged to be dependent upon the goodwill of its gods, which in turn depended upon the honours (*timai*) and attention (*epimeleia*) that those gods received from the community. In time of war, indifference to state religion on the part of an individual was regarded almost as a form of betrayal, while active participation constituted evidence of patriotism. In 403, for instance, after the defeat of

---

[6] As the second century AD historian Arrian states (*Kyn.* 35): 'Those who travel by sea ... make thank-offerings to ... Poseidon, Amphitrite and the Nereids. Those who till the land turn to Demeter and Kore, and Dionysos. Those who practise crafts to Athena and Hephaistos. Those who are concerned with education to the Muses, Apollo Mousagetes, Mnemosyne and Hermes. Those who are occupied with love affairs to Aphrodite, Eros, Peitho (Persuasion) and the Charites (Graces). Those who are engaged in hunting must not neglect Artemis Agrotera (Huntress), Apollo, Pan, the Nymphs, Hermes Enodios (Of the wayside) and Hegemonios (Leader), nor such mountain gods as there are. Otherwise their pursuits will only half succeed. The dogs are hurt, the horses become lame, and the men meet with accidents.'

the army of the Spartan-backed Thirty Tyrants who had abolished Athens' democratic constitution, the herald of the Eleusinian Mysteries made an impassioned plea for reconciliation on the grounds that they, the demo-crats, had shared with the supporters of oligarchy 'in the most holy religious services, in sacrifices (*thusiai*) and in splendid festivals (*heortai*)' (Xen. *Hell.* 2.4.20). I shall seek to demonstrate that the accusation of 'not acknowledging the gods whom the state acknowledges', which constituted part of the religious charge against Sokrates, may have been based in part on his poor attendance record on such occasions (below p. 142).

How to introduce a new god

With the noticeable exception of Athena almost all the cults which we shall be investigating were thought to have originated outside Attica; that is to say, almost all were conceived of as imports from abroad. Migration from without, not emergence from within, was the predominant image which those seeking to promote a new cult primarily fostered among their supporters. The gods, and hence by implication the instigators of their cults, were constantly on the move. The most notable exception to this rule is the Two Goddesses, who seem not to have tried to export their mysteries outside Eleusis (cf. Burkert 1987, 36f.). The image of a deity arriving from elsewhere conveniently explained why that deity had not previously manifested himself to the community, while also relieving the community from anxiety at having neglected a potential benefactor in the past.[7]

It was the responsibility of the god to signal his readiness to be incorporated into the community by commissioning a private individual to speak on his behalf rather in the manner that a proxenos was delegated to look after the interests of foreigners in any city-state. This he did, most conveniently perhaps, by means of an epiphany. Thus in Euripides' *Bacchai* the Stranger claims to have received the secret rites or *orgia* from Dionysos 'face to face' (ll. 465-74). Epiphanies are a standard feature of battle narratives in all but two of the Greek historians, Thukydides and Polybios, a circumstance which suggests that they enjoyed widespread belief throughout the Greek world (cf. Pritchett *GSW* III, 42). From the evidence of tragedy it seems that a deity might also communicate by voice alone, as Athena does to Orestes when giving instructions about the establishment of a cult in honour of his sister Iphigeneia (Eur. *IT* 1446-74; cf. *Hipp.* 86). Likewise the eccentric Sokrates claimed to have heard but never to have seen his personal guiding-spirit or *daimonion*, which he appropriately designated his 'voice' or *phônê*. A no less eccentric figure, Theophrastos' *Superstitious Man*,

---

[7] It is noteworthy, too, that at least three Olympian deities, namely Aphrodite, Dionysos and Hephaistos, have origins which lie outside Greece proper (cf. Burkert, *GR*, 152, 162f. and 167).

'immediately builds a hero shrine if he sees a snake', evidently in the belief that he has encountered a chthonic being in theriomorphic form (*Char.* 16.4, cf. 8).

An illuminating instance of the way in which a sponsor was commissioned is Hellenistic in date and comes from Delos. A priest called Apollonios recorded on a column in the First Sarapieion on Delos how the Egyptian god Sarapis had declared to him in his sleep 'that a Sarapieion must be consecrated to him personally, that he must not live in rented accommodation as before, and that he himself would find a place where the sanctuary should be established and that he would reveal (*sêmainein*) it' (*IG* XI.4 1299.14-18). Occasionally, it seems, the deity left behind physical traces of his visit: a certain Xenainetos of Opos received a nocturnal communication from Sarapis who informed him that he had placed a letter under his pillow which he was to deliver to a fellow-citizen named Eurynomos, containing the instruction 'that he should receive (*hupodexasthai*) Sarapis and his sister Isis' (*IG* X.2.1 255.5f.).

In Greek literature epiphanies constitute a literary topos, the standard elements of which are the deity's unearthly beauty, supernatural stature, luminous clothing and divine fragrance. Often there is a reference to the amazement (*thambos*), sometimes even to the terror, of those experiencing the *mysterium tremendum* of divinity. The self-revelation of Demeter before her departure from Eleusis in the Homeric *Hymn to Demeter* is one of the earliest and most elaborate examples in the genre (ll. 275-83):

> When she had spoken, the goddess sloughed off her old age and changed her stature and her form. Beauty surrounded her, a delightful fragrance emanated from her perfumed robes, a radiance shone afar from the goddess' immortal flesh, golden tresses of hair fell down her shoulders, and the well-built palace was filled with splendour equal to that of lightning. She went forth from the palace. Metaneira's knees gave way under her and she remained speechless for a long time, failing to remember to pick up her latest-born son from the floor ... .

Odysseus' reaction to the sight of the beautiful Nausikaa when he emerges naked from the bushes on the shores of Scheria affords us a rare first-person description of the impact of an epiphany upon the recipient (Hom. *Od.* 6.149-161), though it is doubtful whether the fluent Odysseus really believes in Nausikaa's divinity:

> Lady, I beg you, are you a goddess or a mortal? If you are a goddess, one of those who dwell in the wide heavens, you are most like Zeus' daughter Artemis in form and stature and appearance ... . For I have never before seen anyone like you, neither man nor woman, and rapture (*sebas*) seizes me as I gaze upon you.

Later Odysseus is himself mistaken for a god by Telemachos who, in consequence of his father's sudden revitalisation at the touch of Athena's golden wand, is also seized with amazement and fear. Telemachos petitions his father to be gracious so that he can offer him 'pleasing sacrifices and gifts of gold' (16.184f.), a form of words which reveals that he intends to establish a cult in his honour. So in the *Hymn to Aphrodite* (ll. 100-2), when Aphrodite appears to Anchises the latter promises to 'construct an altar on a high rock, plainly visible, and sacrifice fair offerings at all seasons'. Likewise it was while Moses was tending his flock of sheep in the Sinai wilderness that he was commissioned by the Lord to be his spokesman at the court of Pharaoh.[8]

The impact of an epiphany upon the observer depended somewhat upon the majesty of the divinity. The informality of the rustic goat-god Pan is evident from the fact that he was worshipped in caves not temples. Perhaps he merely jogged beside the flagging Pheidippides up on Mount Parthenion when commissioning him to be his messenger. Though nothing is recorded with respect to his entry into Athens, the divine healer Asklepios regularly adopted a more imposing way to announce his presence. A paian (*IG* IV² 128.64-77) composed in his honour by an Epidaurian called Isyllos describes how the god 'shining in golden armour' appeared to Isyllos as a boy when sick:

> Beholding you, the boy prayed, stretching forth his arms in suppliant fashion, and spoke as follows: 'I have no portion in your gifts, Asklepios Paian, but have pity on me.' You replied to me in accents clear: 'Be of good cheer. I shall be with you in due season – wait here – once I have warded the fates of death from the Spartans ... .' And so he departed for Sparta. But he stirred me to announce to the Spartans that the god was coming, all in due order. They harkened as I uttered tidings of salvation, Asklepios, and you saved them. And they bade everyone receive you with gifts of friendship, pronouncing you the *sôtêr* or saviour of broad Lakedaimon.

The awesome consequences of a full revelation by Zeus are revealed in the celebrated myth of Semele who yearned to see her lover in all his glory and who fatally consummated her desire by being incinerated with his thunderbolt.

In the Archaic period the Athenians seem not to have been less credulous of epiphanies than any other Greeks. That at least is the impression which we receive from Herodotos (1.60.3-5) whose celebrated account of Peisistratos' staging of a pseudo-epiphany to recover the

---

[8] In antiquity generally, nothing better epitomises the fact that the burden of commissioning an appropriate representative who could speak on his behalf lay foremost with the deity than Moses' extreme reluctance to present himself before Pharaoh, as indicated by his repeated protests, 'Who am I that I should go to Pharaoh?', 'Who are you?', 'What if the Egyptians don't believe me?', 'I am slow of speech and slow of tongue' – culminating with the plaintive cry, 'Please, O Lord, make someone else Your agent' (Exodus 3).

tyranny after his first exile is one of the most blatant instances of religious manipulation in all Greek history. Peisistratos dressed up an exceptionally tall woman called Phye – her name, appropriately, means Growth – in a suit of armour so as to resemble the goddess Athena. He then made a dramatic entry into Athens mounted on a chariot with Phye at his side 'in a suitably striking pose'. Although the historian is profoundly scornful of the ruse, contemptuously dismissing it as 'a most stupid device', he accepts its authenticity uncritically and does not doubt that the Athenians as a whole, notwithstanding their reputation for intellectual sophistication, were totally fooled by it. Whether historical or not, the anecdote thus presupposes the existence of a mentality which in the mid-sixth century accepted the reality of epiphanies.

This mentality persisted into the Persian War period, to judge from reports of various deities and heroes who were sighted before or during battle. A critical question for the present inquiry is whether Athenians of the later-fifth century were as credulous of epiphanies as their ancestors or whether, partly as the result of the intellectual movement associated with the sophists, belief in such phenomena had begun to wane. Though numerous epiphanies are recorded in connection with the Persian Wars, the evidence is much harder to come by for the period following. In the funeral oration which he delivered in honour of the dead in the Samian War Perikles (Stesimbrotos *FGrH* 107 F9 in Plu. *Per.* 8.6) reportedly declared, 'We cannot see the gods but we believe them to be immortal from the honours which we pay to them and the blessings we receive from them.' But how typical was Perikles of his contemporaries? Somewhat confusingly the same authority informs us (Plu. *Per.* 13.8) that Perikles once saw Athena Hygieia in a dream urging a course of medical treatment for one of his key workmen who had been injured in a fall, though the anecdote is prefaced with the words 'so they say'.

When Asklepios arrived in the Piraeus in 420 in the form of a snake, who can say what percentage of the population regarded this reptile as the god's physical representative and what percentage as the symbol of his healing power and presence? The dividing line between credulity and suspension of disbelief is impossibly fine.

In the Greek world at large belief in epiphanies certainly persisted into the Christian era, as we see, for instance, from the amusing description in Acts (14:8-18) of the visit of St Barnabas and St Paul to the Greek town of Lystra in Lykaonia. After witnessing St Paul's miraculous healing of a cripple, the local people instantly hailed the pair as Zeus and Hermes, claiming, 'The gods in human form have come down among us' (14:11). Barely could the apostles restrain the hastily summoned priest of Zeus from sacrificing a herd of garlanded oxen to their godhead on the spot. (The author passes up a magnificent opportunity for comic relief by leaving the priest's discomfiture to his readers' imagination.) But was Athens typical of the rest of Greece?

On *a priori* grounds we can readily appreciate that the Athenian Demos as a collective body would have been extremely mistrustful of individuals who professed to have been singled out for a personal encounter with a deity, since such claims implied privileged access to the divine, were ultimately unverifiable, and could easily be turned to political advantage. It cannot have repudiated experiences of the divine altogether, however, without also raising doubts about the legitimacy of those cults whose credentials rested in part upon attestations of this kind. The situation may not have been unlike that which prevails in the Roman Catholic Church today, where an alleged vision is treated as a mere delusion unless proof to the contrary can be supplied. It may have been the case, too, that whereas a reported encounter with an Olympian god in central Athens would have been greeted with incredulity by the majority, the reported sighting of a minor deity in the Attic countryside through the haze of a hot summer's afternoon raised few eyebrows. So, again, it is in the Church, where reported epiphanies of saints or the Blessed Virgin Mary are accepted far more readily than those of the Risen Lord.

We know precious little about the identity of the instigators of new cults, though as a group they needed to be persons of stolid conviction, restless energy and exceptional charisma. Indeed we are lucky when merely a name has survived. Nothing is recorded of Pegasos of Eleutherai who brought the cult of Dionysos to Athens, of Pheidippides who championed Pan, or of Telemachos who installed Asklepios beside the Acropolis. Similarly we know little about the social organisation which underpinned the spread of a cult. Some were clearly more aggressive than others, one such being the cult of the Mother of the Gods whose dissemination was in the grasping hands of itinerants known as *mêtragyrtai* or 'beggars of the Mother', held by many in contempt.

Accounts of epiphanies tell us little about the affective state of the recipient of the vision before, during or after. We are not entitled to infer that Pheidippides, for instance, was 'a changed man' as a result of his encounter with Pan before the battle of Marathon. Nor do we know anything about his relationship with the god before this event. We certainly cannot assume that Pheidippides was 'holy' in our sense of the word – indeed the notion of a holy man is strikingly absent from Greek thought in this period (cf. Humphreys 1975, 110). But the point is precisely this: the experience of an epiphany was a *privilege*, not a consequence of any particular personality trait, far less the result of anything resembling the Christian state of grace. It is the conspicuous refusal on the part of the Greeks to acknowledge the existence of a distinctively spiritual outlook which is manifested only by certain select or selected individuals, that creates a seemingly impermeable wall around their religious experience. Insofar as the gods chose their human sponsors according to some kind of criteria, those criteria appear to have been wholly practical (cf. p. 50).

A convenient forum in which to advertise the benefits of a new god and hence to drum up popular support would have been a public meeting place such as the Agora, the civic, administrative and commercial heart of the city and a popular venue for all those who wished to exchange ideas on a wide range of topics. We are told that St Paul, for instance, when he visited Athens, 'argued in the synagogue with the Jews and devout persons, and in the Agora every day with those who chanced to be there' (Acts 17:17). Subsequently the apostle was invited to present his case more formally on the hill known as the Areopagus – or alternatively before the administrative body of that name (below p. 100). A more intimate locus for theological debate was provided by symposia or drinking parties, which enabled the proponents of a new cult to expound their doctrine to a select few. As we have seen, it was in just such a context that the Thracian mystic Salmoxis lectured his adherents on how to escape death. Interestingly, too, it is the symposium, or its Levantine equivalent, which in the Gospels is the preferred setting for many of Christ's most important teachings.

What kind of strategy could a sponsor use to advertise the merits of the deity whose admission he was advocating? In other words, what kind of arguments would induce the Boule, which set the agenda for the Ekklesia, to decide that a petitioning cult already enjoyed sufficient grass-roots support among the populace to justify putting its claims to a democratic vote? Although we have no direct evidence about the nature of the debate which would take place in either an informal gathering of friends or an assembly of citizens, the sponsor presumably had to be able to demonstrate first that he was the god's representative; secondly, that the god was eager to establish residence within the community; and thirdly, that some benefit had already accrued to the state which could be construed as proof (*marturion*) or a sign (*sêmeion*) of his goodwill.[9] It must never be overlooked that the entry of one god effectively meant the diminution, possibly even the ultimate demise of another. According to Diodoros Siculus (4.39.4) this was in fact the reason why Herakles is said to have graciously declined the invitation to be admitted into the ranks of the Olympian twelve. 'It would,' he pointed out, 'be ridiculous for me to receive an honour which meant depriving another god of his honour.'

From *c.* 460 onwards the authorisation for introducing new gods lay chiefly in the hands of the Boule and Demos, which alone had the right to recommend and implement religious change. The success or failure of any petition must have depended largely on the amount of support which the promotors of a new cult could elicit from those whose needs and concerns the new deity particularly addressed. To give a banal example, it would have been useless to make application on behalf of a god who presided over leather manufacturing without mobilising the support of the

[9] Cf. also Exodus 3.12: 'And He said, 'I will be with you; that shall be your sign that it was I who sent you', where the 'sign' in question takes the form of the Lord's constant presence at Moses' side.

tanning community. The support of religious personnel was also critical. Faced with the prospect of a newcomer inserting himself alongside their own cult, some would be fearing that their status and livelihood might be threatened by the new applicant, whereas others would be hoping for a substantial increase in wealth and prestige. It is a fair assumption that the sponsors of Pan, for instance, enjoyed the support of the priesthood of his mythical relatives the Nymphs and Artemis Agrotera, Artemis Aristoboule that of her namesake Artemis Mounychia, Theseus that of his father Poseidon, and Asklepios that of his co-workers the Eleusinian Goddesses. In each case the established priesthoods evidently made careful calculation at the time of application by the new deity and decided that the potential benefits to themselves outweighed the risks. Although the entry of a new cult was perhaps invariably a co-operative enterprise requiring vigorous support from several sectors of society, it is never possible to do more than speculate about the precise identity of the community of interests which promoted it both formally and informally.

Although in the Classical period the Demos strictly regulated the introduction of previously unknown gods, it is not clear whether it would have interfered with the right of any Athenian citizen, whether male or female, to establish a sanctuary to an already acknowledged deity on private land. The inscription from Phaleron alluded to previously, which records the erection of a shrine to Kephissos by Xenokrateia, makes no mention of the fact that the founder had sought and obtained permission from the Demos, as it surely would have done if Xenokrateia's action had required official approval (*IG* II² 4548 = *LSGS* 17; above p. 5).[10]

In the interval between recommendation and implementation the approval of the gods had to be obtained in consultation with an oracle (cf. Pl. *Rep.* 4.427bc). Religious innovation was thus the consequence of a strictly bilateral enterprise involving a recommendation from the state on the one hand and authorisation from an oracular source on the other, as this passage in Demosthenes (21.51) clearly demonstrates:

> You surely know that you perform all these choruses of yours and hymns to the god not only in accordance with the laws pertaining to the Dionysia, but also in accordance with oracles, in all of which, whether from Delphi or Dodona, you will discover that the god's response (*anêirêmenon*) to the city is to establish choruses in accordance with ancient practice and to let smoke from the sacrificial offerings circulate through the streets and to wear garlands upon one's head.

Oracular authority was, however, curtailed by a number of provisos. First, although there were some exceptions, oracles usually operated on the principle of petition response. The god could sanction; less frequently

---

[10] Guarducci (1974, 58), however, proposes that the inscription in question commemorates not the establishment of a *hieron* to the god but simply the dedication of a hallowed gift (*hieron ... to dôron*) to Kephissos.

did he propose. The Panhellenic oracular shrines no doubt owed their authority in part to the fact that they scrupulously avoided all suspicion of interfering in the internal affairs of the autonomous city-state. Apollo's non-interventionist attitude is epitomised in a remark ascribed to Sokrates by Xenophon (*Mem.* 4.3.16): 'You know that the god of Delphi, whenever anyone asks him, "How can I do what is pleasing to the gods?", replies, "In accordance with state law." ' A further proviso was that the god did not issue commands; he merely recommended. Hence the customary response to any question involving innovation was that it would be 'preferable and better (*lôion kai ameinon*)' for the Demos to implement, or refrain from implementing, a proposed change (e.g. *SEG* XXI.519.5f.). Finally, although Delphi was the oracle which the Athenians consulted most frequently in the fifth century, it did not exercise a monopoly. When, for instance, it became impractical to reach Delphi during the Peloponnesian War, the oracles of Zeus at Dodona in northern Greece and Zeus Ammon in the Libyan desert were consulted instead.

Setting up a new cult could be an extremely costly undertaking. From earliest times the two chief requirements were the purchase of consecrated ground (*temenos*), which was set apart for the use of the deity or hero, and the construction of an altar on which to kindle a fire and conduct a sacrifice (cf. Hom. *Il.* 8.48, 23.148; *Od.* 8.363). A temple and a cult-statue were common but not obligatory accessories. In addition, many sanctuaries contained ancillary buildings such as *hestiatoria* or dining rooms, and presumably all used sacred vessels made of costly metals such as gold and silver. The services of various professionals were required in the initial stages, including that of a poet to write a hymn in the god's honour. Larger and more prestigious cults needed to draw on interest from a capital investment in order to help defray the cost of their sacrifices, the maintenance and upkeep of their sanctuaries, the payment of temple officials, and so on. We gain some insight into the sums involved from the fact that Nikias, who was one of the richest Athenians of his day, paid out ten thousand drachmas to purchase a piece of land on Delos, which he subsequently consecrated (*kathierôse*) to Apollo so that its revenue could be used to fund sacrificial banquets in the god's honour (Plu. *Nik.* 3.6). It follows from this that the sponsor of a new cult had to be a man of substance or at least be able to call upon friends and well-wishers who were themselves persons of substance.

As the pressure on land in urban centres like Athens grew, it must have become increasingly difficult for a new cult to establish itself in a prime location. One solution was to persuade an already established god or hero to share his sanctuary with a new entrant. There are numerous examples of this practice from the fifth century. Pan, for instance, seems to have owed his entry in part to the willingness of the Nymphs to provide accommodation for him in their caves. Asklepios was given temporary lodgings in the City Eleusinion before establishing himself on the south slope of the Acropolis. Theseus' gratitude to Herakles was such that he allegedly made over all but four of his consecrated precincts to Herakles (below p. 92). The most striking example of temple-sharing, however, is in connection with the Erechtheion on the Acropolis, which accommodated sanctuaries of Athena Polias and Pandrosos, altars of Hephaistos, Zeus Herkeios (Of the enclosure), Zeus Hypatos (Highest), Poseidon and the hero Boutes, and tombs of Erechtheus and Kekrops – not to mention the fact that it also housed a sacred snake. Though the precise reason for the proximity of so many shrines within the same precinct is unclear, it is probable that its complex layout and architectural structure reflects an attempt to give spatial definition and unity to a cluster of closely related cults.

The picture I have so far drawn lacks any suggestion of the fever of excitement which was generated by a god's entry. Obviously enthusiasm ran high, but how high? We are told, for instance, that when Kimon brought Theseus' bones back to Athens, the people rejoiced and greeted them 'as though Theseus himself were returning to the city'. Was Theseus an exception? We cannot assume so. All the gods and heroes who gained entry into Athens were keenly desired by some section of her populace, if not by the entire citizenry. Although we know little about the specific ritual employed at the inauguration of a new cult, it can hardly be doubted that a god's entry constituted a moment of supreme tension and drama in the life of the community, comparable in intensity to the strength of the community's yearning for his presence in its midst.

1

Ancestral Rites

Once upon a time, according to the reactionary fourth-century orator Isokrates, Athens had possessed a time-hallowed and static religious system which adequately served all her needs. Recently, however, new-fangled observances had been introduced into the canon which were not only costly but also, to judge from Athens' conspicuous lack of success in both domestic and foreign policy, largely ineffective. Isokrates' belief in a golden era of religious stability was fuelled in part by the observation that in his day the level of funding provided by the state for new gods often exceeded that allowed for old ones. The crisis was so acute that some of the most venerable rites, if we are to take him at his word, were virtually bankrupt. In a pamphlet entitled the *Areiopagitikos*, composed in *c.* 355 shortly after the end of the disastrous Social War which saw the final extinction of Athens as a major military power in the Greek world, Isokrates wrote (29-30):

> First of all, in regard to matters pertaining to the gods ... our ancestors did not worship them or celebrate their rites irregularly or erratically. They did not on a whim send 300 oxen to be sacrificed while omitting the ancestral sacrifices (*tas patrious thusias*). Nor did they celebrate supplementary festivals (*tas epithetous heortas*) which incorporated a banquet (*hestiasis*) in an extravagant manner, while doing sacrifices on the cheap [literally, 'from contracts'] when it came to the most sacred of their holy rites. Their principal concern was not to omit any of the ancestral practices (*ta patria*) and not to add anything that was not traditional (*exô tôn nomizomenôn*). For they recognised that piety (*eusebeia*) consists not in paying out large sums of money but in preserving unchanged the rites which their ancestors had handed down to them. In corresponding manner the assistance which they received from the gods came not irregularly and in fits and starts (viz. as it does today), but at the right moment for the working of the land and the harvesting of the fruits.

The premiss underlying Isokrates' complaint should not be interpreted as a manifestation of his own personal eccentricity. On the contrary, the distinction between what constituted ancestral rites (usually referred to as *ta patria*) and supplementary ones (*ta epitheta*) was fundamental to

Athenian religious thinking. We see this from the fact that Nikomachos was elected in 410 to head a commission empowered to undertake a review of Athens' lawcode, including the task of transcribing (*anagraphein*) what are called *ta patria* (Lys. 30.29; cf. Sud. *s.v. epithetous heortas*; see below p. 145). It follows that Nikomachos must have been required to exclude, or at any rate list separately, everything which he identified as *ta epitheta*.[1]

We cannot establish the exact date when the distinction between ancestral and supplementary rites first emerged in analyses of Athenian religion, but it was certainly in common use before the middle of the fifth century, being implicit in a decree dated *c.* 460 relating to the religious duties of the Praxiergidai *genos* (below p. 100). Without providing any definition of the terms, [Aristotle] in his *Athenaiôn Politeia* or *Constitution of Athens* utilised the distinction to prove the relative antiquity of the offices of archon basileus, polemarchos and eponymous archon, the three most venerable magistracies in the Athenian state. He writes (*AP* 3.3):

> Evidence that this (i.e. the post of eponymous archon) was the last of the magistracies to be instituted is provided by the fact that the archon does not supervise any of the *patria*, as do the basileus and the polemarchos, but only the *epitheta*. It is for this reason that this office only became important in recent times, being magnified by the *epitheta*.

Later in the same work the author provides a summary account of the religious duties of these three magistrates. He tells us that the archon basileus supervised the Eleusinian Mysteries and the festival of Lenaia in honour of Dionysos, and directed 'virtually all the ancestral sacrifices' (57.1). The polemarch conducted a sacrifice to Artemis Agrotera (Wild or Huntress) and to Enyalios (the personification of the war shout), arranged the annual funeral on behalf of the war dead, and made offerings (*enagismata*) to the so-called Tyrannicides Harmodios and Aristogeiton (58.1). [Aristotle's] testimony is not as helpful as it might be, however, for after asserting that the eponymous archon supervised 'only the *epitheta*', he goes on to tell us (56.4-6) that these incorporated the City Dionysia, a festival almost certainly introduced around the time of

---

[1] Although it is impossible to test the proposition, it is hardly to be doubted that the term 'ancestral' resonated with something of the same vibrancy as it does in certain quarters today. 'Let us practise the religion of our fathers' was the rallying cry of the outlawed Roman Catholic Archbishop Marcel Lefebvre when he illegally celebrated the mass in Lille on 29 August 1976 according to the rites established by Pope Pius V in the mid-sixteenth century, having earlier condemned what he called 'the neo-modernist and neo-Protestant tendency clearly manifested during Vatican II'. Cf. also K. Rasmussen, *Intellectual Culture of the Iglulik Eskimos* (Copenhagen 1929), 55, citing an Eskimo informant: 'Our fathers have inherited from their fathers all the old rules of life which are based on the experience and wisdom of generations. We do not know how, we cannot say why, but we keep those rules in order that we may live untroubled.'

Peisistratos; the Thargelia, which is also likely to have been of considerable antiquity; the quadrennial *theôria* or religious embassy to Delos, revived in 426/5 though ancient in origin; and, finally, the processions in honour of Asklepios and Zeus Soter, instituted in 420 and *post* 493/2 respectively. However we interpret his claim, therefore, it would seem that the eponymous archon presided over both *patria* and *epitheta*. And this in turn strongly suggests that the Athenians themselves did not necessarily know the relative chronology of their cults.[2] But even if they had possessed the means to do so with some accuracy, vested interest and propaganda would have further obscured the distinction, given the fact that cults which were recognised as 'ancestral' would inevitably have enjoyed superior prestige and distinction.

We, of course, know better than the Greeks. Or with the aid of archaeology, we should do. But even so, we find it difficult to escape the influence of their peculiarly truncated picture of history, specifically their belief in uninterrupted cultural continuity from the end of the Bronze Age (Late Helladic III) through to the beginning of the Geometric era – a period of about four hundred years – and their tendency to attribute historical process to the genius of a single individual. What follows is, at best, an artist's impression of the origins of Athens' ancestral rites.

The problem of continuity from the Bronze Age

Thanks to the decipherment of baked clay tablets in the Linear B script from Bronze Age sites such as Pylos and Knossos, we know that the Mycenaeans subscribed to a polytheistic system of belief which, superficially at least, resembled that of the Greeks of the historical period. Thus the names of most of the Olympian deities have been identified on the tablets, the notable exceptions being Apollo and Aphrodite. Some names appear in a form which exactly corresponds to later Greek usage, such as Zeus, Hera and Poseidon; others, like 'Atanapotnija', 'For the mistress of At(h)ana', which was found on an inscribed tablet from Knossos, leave little room for interpretive doubt.[3] By contrast, the three primary elements of a Greek sanctuary, which from the eighth century onwards consisted of an altar at which sacrifice was performed, a temple facing the altar, and a cult statue housed inside

[2] The study of the topography of Athens can serve as a rough guide to relative chronology, as Thukydides (2.15.3-5) noted, the most ancient sanctuaries being those located on the Acropolis and 'the part below it chiefly facing south'. The attempt to provide Athenian cults with an era-date does not demonstrably pre-date the fifth century and has little if any basis in historical fact (see further p. 152).

[3] Though the origins of the Olympian family as such are not my concern here, it is generally agreed that some of them belong to a pre-Hellenic Aegean substratum, that others are decidedly of Indo-European background, and that a third group were imported from abroad, notably from the East.

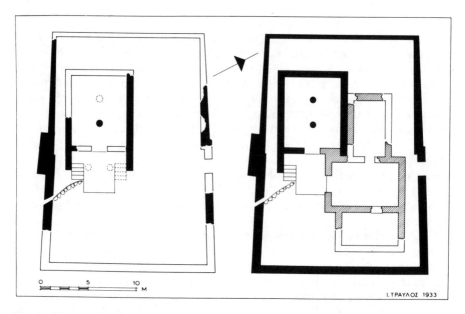

Fig. 2. Plan of the Mycenaean *megaron* at Eleusis (Late Helladic II and IIIB). From J. Travlos, *BTAA*.

the temple, has not as yet been found anywhere in Bronze Age Greece.

Suggestive and alluring though the evidence may be, we can only speculate about the extent to which the religious practices of Mycenaean times formed part of a continuous thread into the Geometric period, through the intervening, still very imperfectly understood Dark Age. It is for this reason that the investigation of a distinctively Attic brand of religion properly has to take as its point of departure the beginning of the eighth century, the period which also sees the emergence of the great Panhellenic sanctuaries at Olympia, Eleusis, Delphi and Delos, as well as the composition of the Panhellenic epics of Homer and Hesiod. Whichever Attic sanctuary we turn to, the problem is virtually identical. At Eleusis, for instance, the home of the Mysteries of Demeter and Kore, a structure identified as a *megaron* or palace dating to Late Helladic II has been discovered on the site of the future Telesterion or Hall of Initiation (Fig. 2). What is crucially lacking, however, is evidence to connect it with the later worship of the Two Goddesses. Travlos (*BTAA*, 92) believes that the *megaron* survived intact to the beginning of the sixth century 'and was consecrated to the Two Goddesses and used for cultic purposes'. Maybe so. But even if we concede this point, there is nothing to prove that it was originally constructed with this purpose in mind; nothing, in other words, to prove that the Mycenaeans worshipped Demeter and Kore in the form that they were later worshipped on this site. Even uninterrrupted continuity of worship does not prove continuity of cult, as the later erection of Christian temples on pagan sites strikingly proves. The earliest unambiguous evidence for the cult of the Two Goddesses at Eleusis dates to *c*. 750 when a structure identified as the Sacred House was erected, probably as a residence for the Eumolpidai *genos*, who exercised exclusive control over the Mysteries before the Athenian state became involved in their administration (see below p. 36).

At Brauron in northeast Attica pottery finds indicate the presence of a sanctuary of late-eighth-century date on a site whose earliest occupation belongs to the Early Helladic period, but again there is no proven continuity between the two periods. On Mount Hymettos a tenth-century sanctuary of Zeus Ombrios (Showery) has produced evidence of occupation from the Late Protogeometric period onwards. Although exiguous traces of Bronze Age material have also come to light here, it has not been demonstrated that they have any connection with the later worship of the Olympian deity (Paus. 1.32.2; cf. Langdon 1976, 74). Even on the Acropolis itself there is little evidence of post-Bronze Age religious activity which pre-dates the eighth century. All this is not to deny that a number of sanctuaries were constructed, with apparent deliberateness, on the ruins of their Bronze Age predecessors, perhaps even with the intention of presenting a picture of continuity. But this in itself tells us nothing beyond the plain and self-evident fact that the Greeks were eager to preserve their own myths.

The synoecism

What form Greek religion assumed in the Dark Age is unclear, but the dearth of archaeological data does not entitle us to assume that cultic activity itself played little part in the lives of the people. Perhaps, as de Polignac (1984, 25) has suggested, it had a quality of expression 'too close to everyday life to leave identifiable traces in the record'. From the second half of the eighth century onwards, however, a number of dramatic changes are detectable in the archaeological record including a rise in the number and quality of dedications made in sanctuaries, the beginnings of temple construction, and the earliest secure evidence of hero-cult. The reasons for these changes, which are by no means confined to Attica, are not fully understood, but they surely reflect profound upheavals which were taking place in Greek society itself. Camp (1979, 403f.) has suggested that that the eighth century was a period of dire climatic hardship and that a number of new cults were introduced in order to avert the effects of a prolonged drought which brought in its wake famine and plague. Although the evidence for such a catastrophe is controversial and problematic, it is striking that many foundation legends incorporate reference to some natural disaster. Although the majority of these legends in the form in which they have come down to us postdate this era by several centuries, one at least, namely that relating to the Two Goddesses, is sixth-century in date at latest and may indeed preserve the memory of some cataclysmic event (below p. 154).

Another reason for the growth in religious activity is the synoecism, the name given to the process by which the inhabitants of Attica agreed to recognise Athens as their political and administrative centre. If the later constitutional reforms of Kleisthenes are anything to go by, we are surely justified in seeking evidence at this date of a radical transformation in the structure of Athenian worship in line with profound changes in her political and social structure. Certainly the Athenians themselves later regarded the synoecism as an era of intense religious fervour, as the cluster of cults introduced in the name of Theseus, the legendary architect and instigator of the synoecism, amply demonstrates (see below p. 91).

In religious terms one of the most significant developments which now took place was that deities and heroes who previously had been exclusive to a specific *genos* were henceforth required to transcend the boundaries of their particular kin-group and represent the interests of the entire citizen body. The end product, so to speak, was a community with common gods as well as common political institutions. It is no exaggeration to state that the synoecism was predicated as much on the unification of the religious life of a number of previously separate communities, as it was on the integration of their disparate political processes. Although we do not know what difference, if any, state involvement made to the religious outlook of the inhabitants of the newly formed Attic community, it is evident that their religious rituals were now required to assume a civic dimension. At the basic level prayers had to be reformulated in order to include reference to the entire citizen body, and sacrifices had to be enlarged so as to enable the entire community to partake in the banquet which followed. Many important sanctuaries which were situated in the countryside probably acquired separate shrines or branch establishments in the Asty, in part to symbolise their newly acquired civic status and in part to give unity to the religious experience of the newly-formed citizen body. Had this new religious perspective not evolved, in particular had the numerous *genê* out of which Attica was born jealously treated their own gods and heroes as their exclusive property, the unification could never have come about. It may have been at the time of the synoecism that the population of Attica was for the first time divided into four tribes, the Argadeis, Aigikoreis, Geleontes and Hoplites, which in later times at least were believed to have been founded by the four eponymous sons of Ion. These so-called Ionian tribes functioned as both religious and military affiliations, as did their later, Kleisthenic counterparts (see pp. 43-5).

It is to this period, too, that we should assign the elevation of Athena to the rank of Athens' foremost state deity with the title Polias (Of the Acropolis) or Poliouchos (Acropolis-guarding), an event which, as much as any other, may be taken to mark the completion of the transition to a unified Attica. Henceforth all Attica was sacred to the goddess, a form of divine possession or *katalêpsis* which is commemorated in the Attic myth of the contest between Athena and Poseidon. Though *katalêpsis* was a fairly common phenomenon in the Greek world, the bond which existed between Athena and her chosen people was unusually close. Curiously no *aition* or foundation legend has survived relating to the goddess's entry into Athens. Perhaps its absence can be interpreted as a reflection of the city's patriotic conviction that Athena belonged to Athens from the start; that her cult, like her people, was an autochthonous creation and not, like others, an import from abroad.

Athena's deep and abiding commitment to the fortunes of her state is powerfully caught in the following lines composed by the early-sixth-century lawgiver Solon (*IEG* 4.1-4), which incidentally contain the earliest reference to the goddess in Athenian literature:

> Our city shall never fall by the doom of Zeus nor by the contriving of the blessed gods. Pallas Athena, great of heart, our overseer (*episkopos*), born of the thunder-father, holds up her hands to guard us.

Solon seems to be suggesting here that the bond between goddess and community was so strong that Athena's protective influence was judged to be capable of shielding the city from the two most serious threats known to the human race, namely an otherwise irresistible pronouncement of doom by the chief of the gods on the one hand and collective malevolence on the part of the entire Olympian régime on the other. His poem also intimates that Athena exercised her guardianship over Athens not primarily by demonstrations of brute force but by intercession with her father, in much the same way as the Blessed Virgin Mary intercedes with the Son.[4]

Precisely what form the worship of Athena on the Acropolis had taken before the synoecism is impossible to determine, but it may be that her elevation occasioned a compromise with the so-called chthonic or underworld beings, who had probably been worshipped on this rocky eminence since time immemorial. The investigation of chthonic religion is complicated by the fact that with the notable exception of the dramatist Aeschylus our literary sources pay it only scant attention. The chthonic gods themselves have left equally few traces in the archaeological record since they were not usually worshipped in temples. Even so there can be no doubt that they represented a vital and enduring strand in Greek religion. Despite her miraculous birth from the head of her father Zeus,

---

[4] The lines uttered by the Delphic oracle to the Athenian ambassadors when Xerxes' army invaded Attica in 480 – 'Pallas Athena cannot propitiate Olympian Zeus, even though she prays with many utterances and profound wisdom' – may have been intended as a timely warning to Athens against placing too much reliance upon the extent of the goddess' influence with her father in the forthcoming conflict (cf. Herington 1963, 66). See further below p. 64.

as later dramatically depicted on the east pediment of the Parthenon, Athena herself was intimately linked to these dark forces and perhaps came as close as any Olympian towards achieving a synthesis between these two opposing tendencies in the Greek religious impulse. The evidence for her attachment to them is manifold. The symbol *par excellence* of chthonic religion, the snake, appeared on her aegis or breastplate, and the inside rim of the shield belonging to the chryselephantine statue of Athena Parthenos designed by Pheidias, which was housed inside the Parthenon, had a snake coiled around it. The Erechtheion, where Athena Polias received worship, was a sanctuary consecrated in part to chthonic religion. Most striking of all it is Athena who in Aeschylus' *Eumenides* successfully mediates between Olympians and chthonic forces in the form of the Furies or Erinyes, defining for the latter a completely new identity as beneficent deities of the Athenian state.

Other cults of Athena which were very ancient include that of Pallenis who was worshipped in the deme of Pallene about five miles north of Athens, and of Hellotis who belonged to the deme of Marathon. The fact that Athena received cult on the summit of Mount Pentelikon may also be taken as evidence of her primacy in Attica at a very early date, since mountain peaks were usually consecrated to Zeus (cf. Paus. 1.32.2). A question which may never be answered with certainty is whether her promotion to the rank of Polias was the result of the dispersal of the goddess' cult from the Acropolis into the countryside or of its convergence thither from regions which already possessed a localised Athena before the synoecism. On balance, however, it seems more likely that the worship of Athena existed on the Acropolis before her elevation to the rank of Polias than that a number of widely dispersed cults banded together to produce a centralised version of Athena on a site where she was hitherto unknown. This, however, is not to deny the possibility that the cult of Athena in the Attic countryside may well have been as ancient as that on the Acropolis. According to the testimony of Pausanias (1.26.6) Athena's wooden image, which is said to have dropped on to the Acropolis 'from out of the sky', was regarded as sacred 'many years before the demes united together'.

It is striking that the newly-constituted polis did not assume direct control over the cult of Athena Polias but left its management in the hands of its original priesthood, whose members were drawn exclusively from the ranks of the Eteoboutadai *genos* (Aischin. 2.147). The state's role henceforth became purely supervisory, a function which was entrusted to the archon basileus who perhaps at the same time assumed the priestly offices once invested in the old kings of Athens. An entirely separate branch of the Eteoboutadai administered the cult of Poseidon, a circumstance which may hint at a rift within the *genos* itself ([Plu.] *Mor.* 843e; cf. Paus. 1.26.5). It is tempting to detect traces of genuine rivalry between these two priesthoods for prime position in the new state in the myth of the divine contest between Athena and Poseidon. Although the absence of any representation of Poseidon in Attic art before the fifth century has raised doubts about the antiquity of his cult in Athens (cf. L.H. Jeffery in Binder 1984, 21f.), he is likely to have been worshipped on the north face of the Acropolis from very early times, perhaps near the cleft above the Mycenaean well, as the god who presided over sources of underground water (cf. Jeppesen 1979, 393).

Finally, as Plato (*Rep.* 3.414c-e) well understood, there was no better way of founding a polis and forging a spirit of national identity than by furnishing its citizens with a convenient assemblage of ready-made myths to explain their origins as a united and unified people. Many of Athens' most celebrated myths undoubtedly date from the time of the synoecism, among them that relating to the birth of their king Erichthonios in whose reign allegedly the inhabitants of Attica were first called 'Athenians' (Hdt. 8.44.2) and who is said to have founded the Panathenaia (Hellanikos *FGrH* 323a F2; Androtion *FGrH* 324 F2). Since Erichthonios was conceived from the seed which Hephaistos spilled in over-eager desire for Athena on the occasion when the god attempted unsuccessfully to rape her (e.g. Eur. fr. 925 N^2), he may be regarded, in a manner of speaking, as Athena's offspring through parthenogenesis. Thus the myth of Erichthonios' conception, no less than that of the divine contest, afforded further evidence of the indissolubility of the ties between the Polias and her polis (cf. Loraux 1981, 204).

Hero-cult

The earliest conclusive evidence for the presence of hero-cult in Attica and Greece generally also dates from the time of the synoecism (*c.* 750-700). Less potent than a god or a goddess, a hero had the special advantage of being the exclusive property of the community in which he lodged, whether tribal, local or national. Unlike his divine counterparts, therefore, he was not subject to any possible conflict of interests when his community went to war. Hero-cult, too, seems to have had a major hand in the formation of the polis, though there is disagreement as to what precise form that took. The phenomenon was largely inspired by the excavation of Mycenaean tholos and chamber tombs, whose size and architectural elaboration, together with the quality and costliness of their burial goods, powerfully stirred the Greek imagination (cf. Coldstream 1977, 346f. and fig. 110). Such excavations, accidental in some cases, were in others the result of deliberate archaeological forays. Eventually the impulse to pay homage to a heroic past was no longer confined to the occupants of Mycenaean tombs but came to include more recent burials as well.

As a branch of chthonic religion, hero-cult formed a counterpart to the worship of the Olympian deities and was characteristically attended by blood sacrifice and libations. Typical offerings of suitably heroic flavour include miniature terracotta horses and shields, bronze tripods and cauldrons of the kind that would have served as prizes at funeral games, and drinking cups or *kantharoi* such as might have been used for pouring libations to the dead (cf. Abramson 1979, 11; Blegen, *AE* 39 [1937] 377-90). These tended to be deposited neatly in one corner of the tomb. In later times such offerings, known as *enagismata*, were normally made to a hero once a year on his appointed festal day. In Attica objects of late Geometric or early Archaic date have been discovered in a number of Mycenaean tombs notably in Aliki Glyphada, Menidi, Thorikos and Eleusis. The Agora, which served as an important burial ground from *c.* 1450 to 700 BC, has also produced evidence for possible hero-cult in this period. A walled burial precinct erected *c.* 725 in the vicinity of the later Tholos on the west side is perhaps to be connected with the worship of Strategos, the eponymous hero of the Strategeion or headquarters of the generals (cf. Young 1939, 1ff.; Thompson 1978, 99f.). About a century later very rich votive deposits were made at the north foot of the Areopagus in connection with an earlier burial (cf. Burr 1933, 636-40).

Until recently it was generally believed that hero-cult owed its origins and promotion to the circulation of epic poetry. The argument ran as follows: the outstanding deeds performed by the heroes of the Argonautika, the Thebaïka, and the Trojan War had generated an unprecedented level of interest among Greeks in their own legendary past, which induced them to place offerings in or on top of Mycenaean tombs on a recurrent basis as a way of linking themselves imaginatively to that past. Yet the theory that hero-cult was actually subsequent to the spread of epic and inspired by it leaves awkwardly unexplained both why the practice is unknown in regions such as Crete and Thessaly, which are known to have played a leading part in the transmission of epic poetry throughout the Greek world, and also why it chose as objects of devotion mainly anonymous heroes, instead of the well-known figures of the *Iliad* and the *Odyssey*.

More recently, therefore, scholars have sought to link the rise of hero-cult to the process of polis-formation, though the precise nature of the connection remains a matter of continuing controversy. Snodgrass (1982, 117), for instance, sees hero-cult as a reflection of endemic lawlessness in the Attic countryside at the time of the synoecism, claiming that the hero was in origin a powerful local figure who, in return for the protection which he offered during his lifetime, was rewarded after his death with modest offerings at his tomb, and who attained the status of a true hero 'many years afterwards'. Conversely Whitley (1988, 176-8) regards the promotion of hero-cult as the action of a reactionary rural élite which sought to immortalise local magnates as a way of opposing the rising tide of synoecism and countering the growing

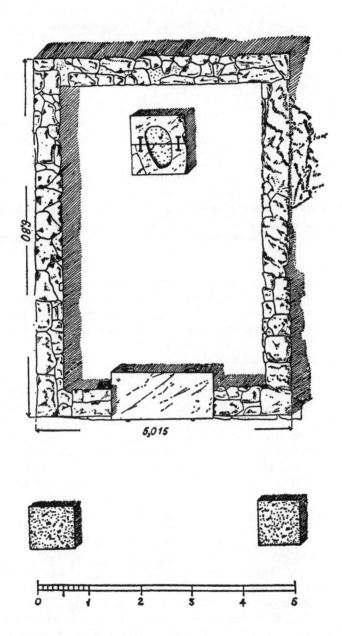

Fig. 3. Classical remains of a possible shrine of Phrontis at Sounion. From S. Meletzis & H. Papadakis, *Sounion* (Munich 1976).

tendency towards centralised control. Whatever the true facts, it can hardly be denied that hero-cult served a propagandist aim, 'justifying land ownership by creating sacred ties with its ancient inhabitants' (de Polignac 1984, 132).

The only Attic hero known to us by name whose cult can definitely be assigned to the late-eighth century is Erechtheus, of whom Homer (*Il.* 2.547-51; cf. *Od.* 7.80f.) says:

> Athena, daughter of Zeus, once fostered him and the grain-giving earth bore him. She settled (*heise*) him in Athens in her own wealthy sanctuary. There, as the years revolve, the youth of Athens propitiate (*hilaontai*) him with sacrifices of bulls and rams.

It is uncertain how best to interpret the claim that Athena 'settled' Erechtheus in her sanctuary. One possibility is that she made it temporarily available for his cult, just as the Eleusinian Goddesses later provided lodging for Asklepios while a permanent sanctuary was being prepared for him elsewhere (see below p. 123). More likely, however, we have here evidence that from the inception of his cult the hero was worshipped in the chief temple of Athena Polias, later known as the Erechtheion. With such a powerful advocate, Erechtheus' leading position as Attic hero would surely have been secure. Other hero-cults likely to have been of very great antiquity include those of Iphigeneia in Brauron on the northeast coast of Attica, Phrontis, the helmsman of Menelaus, in Sounion at the southeast tip (Fig. 3), and Herakles on Mount Hymettos to the east of Athens.

The promotion of hero-cult may have been accompanied by a corresponding diminution in importance in the cult of the ordinary dead (cf. Burkert *GR* 204). Certainly we have evidence from the beginning of the sixth century onwards for legislation aimed at curtailing what could be done both at the time of the funeral and during post-funerary rituals (see p. 36), and this tendency could have begun much earlier than written records indicate. Whether this was so or not, it is important to try to distinguish between hero-cult, which was conducted on a periodic basis once a year on behalf of an individual believed to be invested with supernatural power, and the placing of offerings on a strictly one-off basis in a grave whose occupant had been accidentally disturbed. In the latter case the modest appearance of the tomb and unexceptional quality of its previous grave gifts evidently precluded the assumption that this might be the resting place of a hero, although the respect accorded to even the ordinary dead still required that it be provided with some offerings when discovered. What blurs the distinction between the two kinds of tendance, however, is the fact that many heroes were venerated for only a brief period of time. The cult at the foot of the north slope of the Acropolis mentioned earlier, for instance, continued to be observed for barely a single generation (*c*. 740-715).

Finally, it is not known whether Attic hero-cult actually originated in the eighth century or was a recrudescence of something very much older which first came into being in the Dark Age. The discovery of some two hundred cups at the site of the future Academy on the western outskirts of Athens has suggested to some archaeologists that a cult of the eponymous hero Akademos (or Hekademos) already existed here at the beginning of the ninth century. If so, it would appear to have been an isolated instance of the practice, at least as far as Attica is concerned.[5]

Genê, phratries and demes

Another early manifestation of Athenian religion are the cults which gave definition to various subdivisions of the population. Most prominent and most powerful in this category were those connected with the sixty-odd *genê* or noble kin-groups whose members commonly, though not invariably, traced their descent back to an eponymous heroic ancestor. Although the evidence for the origins and composition of *genê* is vestigial, we can be confident that all were religious associations. Indeed it was the devotion of a *genos* to a particular cult (or cults) which primarily gave it its unity and identity. To give a few examples, the Eteoboutadai supervised the cults of Athena and Poseidon Erechtheus, the Bouzygai conducted a sacred ploughing festival connected with Zeus Teleios (All-powerful), and the Eumolpidai presided over the Mysteries at Eleusis.

Phratries, whose focus appears to have been an altar around which all official business was conducted, are likely to be of similar antiquity, though if anything we know less about their origins and membership than we do about those of the *genê* (cf. Hedrick 1984, 135-53).

Also likely to be very ancient were cults whose membership was limited to members of the same deme, as well as cults which represented amalgamations of neighbouring demes such as the Marathonian Tetrapolis and the Tetrakomoi of the Piraeus, these latter presumably being either the residue of an Attica once unified under Mycenaean rule or the embryonic anticipation of an Attica yet to be born.

Solon

The earliest literary evidence for intervention by the state in matters that have to do with religion dates to the beginning of the sixth century. The testimony relates to the Genesia, a festival originally celebrated privately

[5] The recent excavations conducted at Lefkandi on Euboia by the British School at Athens in connection with a building identified by some archaeologists as a hero shrine shed little light upon the origins of hero-cult, either here or elsewhere. As Calligas (1988, 232) rightly points out, properly interpreted the evidence points merely to the 'honorary burial of two important persons'.

on the birthday of the deceased, which according to the Atthidographer Philochoros (*FGrH* 328 F168; below p. 157) became under Solon a public festival (*heortê dêmotelês*) held on a fixed day of the year. Very likely, as Jacoby (1944, 70) has suggested, the intention behind the revision was to deprive the *genê* of the opportunity to exploit commemorative practices conducted at the tomb for political advantage on a recurrent basis throughout the year. The use of the word '*dêmotelês*' suggests that the Genesia was henceforth to be funded by the state – the first instance of which we have any concrete record of what was later to become common practice. Although there is no other evidence for state funding of public festivals earlier than the fifth century, it is possible that all the cults which became the concern of the state at the time of the synoecism were before long receiving public monies in order to help defray the cost of sacrifices and festivals, particularly in view of the fact that these ceremonies were now being conducted on a far more lavish and public scale than ever before.

Solon is also credited with the publication of Athens' first calendar of festivals and sacrifices (*hiera kai thusiai*), an innovation which affords powerful testimony to the complexity of her religious system by the beginning of the sixth century (Plu. *Sol.* 25.2; cf. Lys. 30.17 with Ehrenburg 1968, 396 n. 46). Assuming that this testimony is correct, it is likely that Solon ordered a review of the sacrificial calendar for the same reason that he instituted a fixed day for the Genesia; namely, to prevent rival *genê* from introducing additional feast-days into the calendar on a random basis as a way of enhancing their popularity and prestige. Since feast-days offered a rare occasion when the general populace had an opportunity to consume meat, they would have provided a useful and effective instrument by which aspiring politicians could court public favour.

It may also have been during Solon's ascendancy that the state first began to involve itself in the celebration of the Eleusinian Mysteries. Around the beginning of the sixth century Eleusis acquired a larger Telesterion or Hall of Initiation on the site of its Geometric predecessor, a clear sign of the sanctuary's increased wealth and prestige in this period (cf. Travlos *BTAA*, 92f.). The orator Andokides (1.111) further states that on the day after the Mysteries the Council was required by a 'law of Solon' to meet in the City Eleusinion in order to determine whether any malpractice had taken place during the celebrations (cf. *IG* II^2 794.4, 848.30 and 1072.3). Since the term 'law of Solon' incorporated many laws which are post-Solonic, however, the case for Athens' official involvement with Eleusis at this early date remains unproven.

In one instance at least Solon and his supporters are credited with having utilised religion in order to legitimate Athenian territorial ambitions. Throughout the seventh and sixth centuries Athens was still struggling to achieve geographical and political definition, and it was not until *c.* 506, when she annexed the coastal town of Oropos facing Eretria on the island of Euboia, that her boundaries became firmly established. One of the most significant enlargements in her territory came about as a result of the acquisition of the offshore island of Salamis, which she eventually succeeded in wresting from the neighbouring town of Megara. Her legal entitlement to the island, which was ultimately ratified by international arbitration, was bolstered by a legend concerning the hero Eurysakes, a native Salaminian and son of Aias, who was said to have handed the island over to the Athenians around the time of the Trojan War (Plu. *Sol.* 10.2). A cult of Eurysakes was duly founded on Kolonos Agoraios in the deme of Melite, probably at the same time as Athens was beginning to press her claim to the island (cf. Ferguson 1938, 16f.). Whether the Athenians instituted their own foundation to rival an already existing one on Salamis or, more likely, invented a completely new cult to complement the legend cannot be proven. At all events the establishment of the Eurysakeion in the very heart of Athens affords telling proof of the degree to which Athens' national interest was now perceived to be intimately bound up with possession of the island.

The cult of the war god Enyalios is also alleged to have gained entry into Athens at this time. Plutarch (*Sol.* 9) reports that 'according to some' Solon consulted the Delphic oracle about the capture of Salamis and received the following response:

Propitiate (*hilaso*) with sacrifices the local heroes who are its leaders, whom the plain of Asopias enfolds in its embrace and who, dead, face the setting sun.

Accordingly Solon sailed by night to Salamis and performed secret sacrifices to the heroes Periphemos and Kychreus in order to appropriate their goodwill in the forthcoming struggle. Having done so, he then launched a naval raid against the Megarians and succeeded in capturing one of their ships, which he then manned with an Athenian crew. Pretending to be still under a Megarian flag, the Athenians sailed into the harbour at Salamis and took the town by surprise. Their ruse was commemorated by a ritual act or *drômena*, which constituted a re-enactment of the most critical moment in the entire campaign:

An Athenian ship used to sail to the island in silence and then, amid shouts and screams from the attackers, a man dressed in armour would leap off the ship with a cry and run in the direction of the headland of Skiradion towards those who were re-enacting the attack by land. Nearby is the shrine of Enyalios which was built by Solon.

Whether strictly historical or not, Solon's supposed theft of the Salaminian heroes provides eloquent testimony to the close identification between religion and war. Quite aside from the fact that Periphemos and

Kychreus could now be expected to throw their weight behind the
Athenian cause, the humiliating loss sustained by the Megarians would
have gravely undermined their self-confidence for the forthcoming
struggle, by providing tangible proof of the weakness of their defences.

It is a further indication of the strategic and political importance of
Salamis that a *genos* known as the Salaminioi was given charge of a
number of Athens' most venerable cults including those of Aglauros,
Pandrosos and Ge Kourotrophos (Child-rearer) on the Acropolis,
Herakles at Porthmos near Sounion, Athena Skiras at Phaleron, and
Eurysakes in Melite. The origins of the Salaminian *genos* are wholly
obscure. A widely-held opinion is that its founder-members were
Salaminian noblemen who fled to Athens when their island was first
invaded by the Megarians and who were granted Athenian citizenship,
along with the right to constitute themselves into an artificial *genos*, by
way of compensation for being dispossessed. Whatever their exact
identity and composition, we can be confident that the Salaminioi wielded
considerable religious authority in view of the control which they
exercised over a number of Athens' ancestral rites, and further that their
rise to prominence was in some way connected with the conquest of
Salamis.

So far as it is possible to ascribe any underlying motive to Solon's
religious reforms, it seems fair to say that the lawgiver was more
concerned with the codification of existing practices than with any
extensive overhauling of the religious system. Certainly nothing took
place under his leadership on a scale to equal the religious changes
claimed for the Peisistratids.[6] The only ancient writer to supply us
with a political context for his legislation is Plutarch (*Sol.* 12), who
alleges that it was inspired by the bitter feuding which followed Kylon's
assassination by the Alkmaionid Megakles around the end of the seventh
century after a failed *coup* (see below p. 138). It would seem, therefore,
that Solon's chief concern was to prevent a repeat performance of the
bloody civil strife which Athens had witnessed in the years immediately
before he took control of the state, by weakening the ability of the *genê* to
exploit religious ritual for their own factional and divisive ends.

The Peisistratid tyranny

In *c.* 546, following two previous attempts at a *coup*, Peisistratos finally
succeeded in establishing a secure tyranny. It is generally believed that
the stability of the tyranny was due in large measure to his successful

---

[6] According to Plu. *Sol.* 16.3 Solon's famous Seisachtheia or Shaking-off-of-burdens, the
process by which those who had become enslaved through indebtedness were now liberated,
took the form of a public sacrifice. Although the ending in –eia was perhaps intended as a
conscious echo of other festivals (e.g. Chalkeia, Nemeseia), it is none the less significant that
Solon made no attempt to institute a permanent sacrifice in celebration of his reforms (cf.

deployment of religion in the cause of civic and political unity (e.g. Shear 1978, 3f., 7f.). Henceforth Athenian religious life came to be dominated by public cults exercising wide popular appeal (cf. Andrewes 1982, 415). It was the Peisistratids, so the theory goes, who gave added weight to the primacy of Athena and thus to the idea of Athens as the natural gravitational focus of the Athenian state. An increased sense of nationhood, of what it meant to be an Athenian, and of Athens' leading position in the Greek world as a religious innovator, are seen as the most abiding legacies of their rule.

Yet the evidence for all this remains tantalisingly inconclusive. It is alleged, for instance, that one of Peisistratos' foremost devices for achieving a spirit of national unity was the institution of the quadrennial Panathenaia in honour of Athena Polias (e.g. Ober 1989, 66). Although the origins of the annual or Lesser Panathenaia, like those of the cult of Athena itself, belong in Athens' distant past, it was during the archonship of Hippokleides in 566/5, and according to one late source specifically at the instigation of Peisistratos, that the Panathenaia was made to rival the Olympic, Pythian, Isthmian and Nemean games, the last three of which had been established on a Panhellenic footing only a decade or two previously,[7] by the inclusion of organised competitions of an athletic nature (Plate 4). A dedication by a board of *hieropoioi* or 'doers of sacred deeds', which was found on the Acropolis dating to the mid-sixth century, proudly records that these 'were the first to hold the contest in honour of the bright-eyed maiden' (Raubitschek *DAA*, nos. 326-8).

The problem with ascribing these innovations to Peisistratos, however, is that the tyrant did not initially seize power until 561/0, that is to say, five years after Hippokleides' archonship. So if he had any hand at all in restructuring the festival in his capacity as tyrant, he can only have done so as the continuator of a process that was already well underway. An alternative theory is that Peisistratos became involved in his capacity as magistrate or merely as a private citizen. It was perhaps in connection with the promotion of the Panathenaia that a certain Patrokles now erected an altar of Athena Nike on the Acropolis, thereby honouring a goddess who symbolised victory in sporting activities no less than victory in war (Raubitschek *DAA*, no. 329; cf. Eur. *Ion* 1528f.). Since an altar was an indispensable feature of Greek cult, the worship of Athena Nike may well have commenced in this period (Plate 3).

It is important to note that there exists no temple on the Acropolis which can confidently be assigned to the period of Peisistratos' tyranny. Fragmentary remains of pedimental sculpture dated *post* 570, which are commonly attributed to a temple of Athena on a site whose location has not been identified, antedate his rise to power by about a quarter of a

---

Connor 1987, 49).

[7] The traditional foundation dates are as follows: Olympic Games 776, Pythian Games 582, Isthmian Games 581, and Nemean Games 573.

century (Plates 5-9). As may have happened in the case of the Panathenaia, however, it is possible that Peisistratos had become involved in this project before establishing the tyranny.

Peisistratos' success may have depended in part upon his ability to mobilise priestly support from the cults of Athena Pallenis, Artemis Brauronia and the Doric Tetrapolis, all of which were located in northeast Attica where his family owned large estates. His celebrated ruse of staging a fake epiphany of Athena with the help of the statuesque Phye was doubtless facilitated by the fact that his influence in Pallene provided him with 'some call on a local manifestation of the goddess' (Davies *APF*, p. 455; above p. 17). It is generally assumed that one of the methods by which Peisistratos sought to consolidate and unify the Athenian state was by transplanting cults from the Attic countryside into the city. The most likely candidate for Peisistratid patronage is the cult of Artemis Brauronia, which was provided with a branch establishment on the Acropolis about this time, though the earliest datable evidence for its existence actually belongs to the end of the sixth century (cf. Schrader 1939, 262-4 nos. 377-8).

There is also circumstantial evidence to suggest that Peisistratos sought to identify himself with Herakles, who in this period acquired something of the status of national Attic hero, a role later taken over more comprehensively by Theseus. Many of the numerous Herakleia scattered throughout Attica may have been established during the tyranny, in particular the one at Marathon which lay close to the Peisistratid estates, where according to the claims of the Marathonians themselves Herakles was first elevated to the rank of god (cf. Paus. 1.15.3; above p. 9). Boardman (1972, 60f.) has suggested that the hero's introduction to Olympos upon the occasion of his deification, a popular theme in Attic art from the mid-sixth century onwards (cf. Plate 9), should actually be read as an allusion to the tyrant's temporary installation on the Acropolis, which was achieved, as in the case of Herakles' elevation, with the patronage of Athena. The analogy would have been particularly evocative if Peisistratos had taken up permanent residence on the Acropolis in the way that Herakles took up residence on Olympos as Boardman further suggests, but there is no evidence to prove that this is in fact what the tyrant did.

Finally, in the third quarter of the sixth century two small shrines, one for Apollo Patroös, the other for Zeus Phratrios or Agoraios, were erected on the west side of the Agora. Since these would have had the effect of 'symbolising the integration of the disparate and quarrelsome clans of Attica into the unified polis of all Athenians' (Shear 1978, 7), indubitably a Peisistratid aim, the tyrant's hand has been seen behind their promotion.

We are on somewhat firmer ground when we come to the period of the earliest surviving Attic inscriptions. In 522/1, the year of his archonship,

Fig. 4. Drawing of the Altar of the Twelve Gods in the Agora at Athens, as reconstructed at the end of the fifth century. From M.L. Lang, *Socrates in the Agora* (Princeton, New Jersey, 1978).

the tyrant's grandson, who also went under the name of Peisistratos, dedicated an altar to the Twelve Gods in the Agora (Thuk. 6.54.6; Fig. 4). Evidently a well-known landmark, the altar soon became the standard reference point from which road distances were measured to other parts of Attica (Hdt. 2.7.1; cf. *IG* II² 2640), and the choice of its location, at the spot which Pindar called 'the *omphalos* or navel of the city', can hardly be accidental. Several Olympian deities had shrines in outlying districts of Attica, notably Ares in Acharnai, Artemis in Brauron, Demeter in Eleusis, Dionysos in Eleutherai, and Poseidon in Sounion. What better way of symbolising the indissolubility of the recently expanded Athenian state than by hedging its borders with front-rank deities who were now to be bound in holy unity in the civic and political heart of Athens (cf. Long 1987, 173)? Although doubts have been voiced concerning the exact identity of the twelve, it is likely that they were identical with those who were depicted on the east frieze of the Parthenon, namely Zeus, Hera, Poseidon, Athena, Apollo, Artemis, Hephaistos, Aphrodite, Hermes, Demeter, Dionysos and Ares. The only god whose inclusion in the group is a little suspect is the perennial late-comer Dionysos, but given the fact that choruses at the City Dionysia performed dances at the altar of the Twelve Gods there are no good grounds for excluding him (Xen. *Hipp.* 3.2; cf. Lewis 1988, 296). The younger Peisistratos also dedicated an altar to

Pythian Apollo in the latter's sanctuary beside the Ilissos, in order, as he professed on the accompanying inscription, to commemorate his own archonship (*IG* I² 761 = *ML* 11; cf. Thuk. 6.54.6-7).[8]

The entry of Dionysos Eleuthereus into Athens may also be contemporary with the Peisistratid tyranny. At some point in the second half of the sixth century Eleutherai, a town situated on the borders between Athens and Thebes, voluntarily ceded its independence to Athens because of hatred and fear of Thebes, and a determination not to become enrolled in the newly expanding Boiotian League (Paus. 1.38.8; cf. Hdt. 6.108; Thuk. 3.55). In return for their loss of autonomy her people received a restricted form of Athenian citizenship. It is easy to comprehend that the bond between the two communities would have been further strengthened and consolidated by Athens' adoption of Eleutherai's foremost deity. Although we do not know the exact date of Dionysos' entry into Athens, it was probably during the Peisistratid tyranny that the cult rose to front-rank importance, thanks to the institution of a festival known as the City Dionysia which from *c.* 534 onwards provided a context for annual performances of tragedy.[9] A decade or so later a small temple of Dionysos Eleuthereus was erected in his sanctuary on the south slope of the Acropolis, perhaps in order to house the effigy of the god which was carried in procession during the festival. Like others of its kind, the procession therefore served in part as a way of symbolising and reinforcing Athenian dominance over an outlying district of Attica. Athens' overall control of the ritual was demonstrated by the fact that although the cult was a foreign importation, the procession commenced in the Asty and terminated at the regional shrine, whereupon it was then followed by another in the opposite direction. The course of the procession thus underscored Athens'

[8] As Homer Thompson (quoted in Hedrick 1988, 209 n. 224) argues, it is likely that the northwest corner of the Agora became increasingly important in this period as a centre of Athenian religious life, at the expense of the region beside the Ilissos River which had been prominent in earlier times, although the latter's continuing significance is indicated by the fact that the younger Peisistratos chose this region to dedicate the altar commemorating his archonship. Thompson's hypothesis is strengthened both by the presence of shrines to the Twelve Gods, Apollo Patroös and Zeus Phratrios in this quarter of the Agora, and by the fact that it was here that participants in the Panathenaic festival assembled before ascending to the Acropolis.

[9] Cf. *Marmor Parium* (43). In a stimulating article Connor (1989, 7-23) has recently put the date of the incorporation of Eleutherai into Athens, and hence of the establishment of the City Dionysia, at *post* 508/7 BC, partly on the grounds that Eleutherai did not figure in the deme organisation undertaken by Kleisthenes. Denying any Peisistratid involvement in the cult of Dionysos Eleuthereus, Connor interprets its entry as 'a celebration of the success of the system that had replaced the Peisistratid regime' (p. 12). As Ehrhardt (1990, 23) points out, however, there was at least one other part of Attic territory, notably Salamis, which was not represented in the new deme roster. See also Kolb (1977, 115-24) for arguments ascribing the promotion of Dionysos, whom he describes (p. 121) 'not as a god of the ordinary populace but as a protector god of the royal family and of the state', to the Peisistratid family.

status as permanent custodian of the god's favour.

Aristotle (*Pol.* 5.1313b 23) claims that it was Peisistratos' sons who began work on the temple of Olympian Zeus on the banks of the Ilissos River, though his testimony does not exclude the possibility that the plan was originally conceived by their father. The project, which was suspended after the overthrow of the tyranny in 511 and not finally completed until the reign of the Emperor Hadrian in the early second century AD, was more ambitious than anything previously undertaken in the Greek world with the single exception of the temple of Hera on Samos, which had been begun a decade earlier by the tyrant Polykrates. Indeed the Olympieion may have been intended as a pointed response by Athens' tyrants to Polykrates' blatant display of magnificence. Athena Polias' prestige was also significantly enhanced in this period. In the 520s a temple was either built or rebuilt in her honour on the Acropolis, and it was either now or after the restoration of constitutional government that a new series of Attic tetradrachms was issued bearing the goddess's head on the obverse side of the coin.

Numerous indicators suggest that it may have been during the tyranny that Athens came to acquire outright control over the Eleusinian Mysteries. Probably now the Kerykes or Heralds were established as an Athenian *genos* and assigned a major role in the staging of the Mysteries with the evident intention that their prestige should rival that of the Eleusinian Eumolpidai. In addition, an annual festival called the Lesser Mysteries was instituted at Agrai on the banks of the Ilissos in Athens and a branch establishment known as the City Eleusinion was set up close to the north slope of the Acropolis. To crown it all, a new and much enlarged Telesterion was built at Eleusis, more than double the size of its 'Solonian' predecessor. Significantly, too, the approach road to the Telesterion was for the first time oriented in the direction of the Asty, perhaps in deference to Eleusis' new attachment to Athens. Finally, the sanctuary itself acquired a defensive circuit wall and the deme of Eleusis was fortified, both developments affording proof of the prestige of the cult and the importance of its local community.

Kleisthenes

In the last decade of the sixth century the administrative apparatus of the Athenian state was radically overhauled by Kleisthenes in line with his intention of fracturing the power of the *genê*. In order to give cohesion to his bold new constitutional experiment, Kleisthenes divided the citizen body into ten tribes, each of which was assigned a mythical Attic hero as its eponymous ancestor: Hippothoön, Antiochos, Aias, Leos, Erechtheus, Aigeus, Oineus, Akamas, Kekrops and Pandion. The ten heroes were chosen by the Pythian priestess at Delphi allegedly from a short list of one hundred candidates which had been submitted by the state ([Arist.]

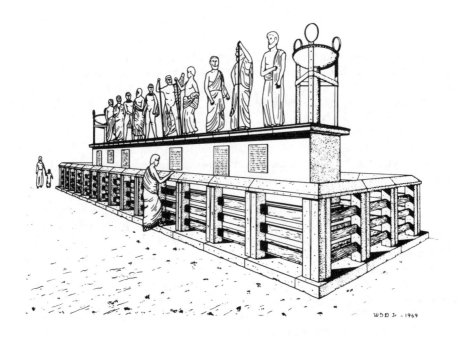

Fig. 5. Drawing of the fourth-century monument to the eponymous heroes of the ten Attic tribes. From M.L. Lang, *Socrates in the Agora* (Princeton, New Jersey, 1978).

AP 21.6). The fact that the choice could be made from such a large number of candidates, the vast majority of whom are likely to have been in receipt of cult already, affords striking proof of the vitality of hero-worship in Attica, which may well have been more plentifully supplied than any other Greek state (cf. Thompson 1978, 96).[10] Of the ten successful nominees, eight already had sanctuaries in the Asty, while the two others, Aias and Hippothoön, were worshipped on Salamis and Eleusis respectively. The election of these rank outsiders is undoubtedly a reflection of the fact that both Salamis and Eleusis were recent additions to Attic territory.

Their inclusion would have served as a way of promoting Athenian pretensions to timeless sovereignty over their birthplaces. The new tribes, which were assigned their members in a highly artificial manner, became an integral and central part of the administrative machinery of the state. The fact that they were perceived not as a sterile bureaucratic convenience, but on the contrary as vital corporate bodies each with its own distinctive identity was undoubtedly due to the status which they

[10] We know the names of approximately 300 Attic heroes and heroines in all. See Kearns (*HA*, Appendix 1). Heroines were in much shorter supply than heroes in all periods of history and throughout the Greek world, in Attica the ratio being approximately 1:5. Given the needs and presumptions of Greek society, it is unlikely that many of the one hundred nominees would have been female.

enjoyed as religious associations. And this in turn tells us much about the quality and importance of hero-cult itself in this period. Some time before 421 a monument to the eponymous heroes as a group was erected at an unknown location in the Agora (Fig. 5).[11]

Incidentally, Kleisthenes did not abolish the four pre-existing Ionian tribes but allocated to them an exclusively religious aspect. Their continuing importance is indicated by a reference to a sacrifice performed to Zeus Phratrios and Athena Phratria by the tribe Geleontes, which is recorded in Nikomachos' revised lawcode published at the end of the fifth century (*LSGS* 10.47-50). It is not known for certain whether Kleisthenes also introduced cults of the thirty *trittyes* or 'thirds' into which the new tribes were subdivided.

[Aristotle] (*AP* 21.6) tells us that Kleisthenes did not interfere with either the *genê*, the phratries or their priests, but allowed them to function 'in accordance with ancestral practice'. It is often assumed (e.g. Feaver 1957, 136f.; Ostwald 1986, 139) that the state cults which entered Athens subsequent to the reforms of Kleisthenes were invariably 'democratic'; that is to say, served by priests who were elected from the entire citizen body. But the evidence by no means supports this conclusion unquestioningly.

Finally, by around the beginning of the fifth century a cult of the Mother of the Gods had been imported from Phrygia into Athens. The goddess, one of the earliest exotic deities to be granted residence in Athens, was destined in the next century to acquire the status of tutelary deity of the bouleuterion or council chamber wherein she took up residence. The aetiology connected with her entry, which alludes to the killing of her missionary priestess and the Mother's subsequent demand for her burial, hints at the takeover by the goddess of a pre-existing hero-cult (see below p. 159).

Conclusions

As indicated at the beginning of this chapter, we do not know for certain what notional yardstick the Athenians employed to distinguish ancestral practices from supplementary ones, but certainly everything that we have examined so far would have fallen into the former category.[12] Although foundation legends in the form in which they have survived often provide the name of the king in whose reign a particular deity was

[11] The earliest example of state burial outside Attica on behalf of the war dead dates to 507/6. In the light of other reforms implemented by Kleisthenes, it is tempting to speculate whether a list of 'casualties' was now for the first time inscribed on a public war memorial with the names of the dead arranged according to tribe (cf. Clairmont *PN* I, 9 and no. 2).

[12] The term '*patrios*' seems even to have embraced certain ritual practices which were decidedly of fifth-century origin. The New Year's festival known as the *Eisitêtêria* (Entry-of-the-year), for instance, which was not established earlier than 493/2, is defined as '*patrios*' by Lysias (26.6). It would be surprising, moreover, if the rituals instituted in

believed to have entered Athens (see below p. 157), lack of consensus as to the order of their reigns prevented the Athenians from making any serious attempt to arrange *ta patria* in strict chronological sequence. When, for instance, the Atthidographers boldly took up the challenge of rationalising the monarchical period of Athenian history in the fifth century BC, the only way they could make sense of the muddle was by postulating the existence of two Attic kings called Kekrops and two called Pandion.

While genuine uncertainties on the part of the citizen body as a whole or a calculated re-writing of Athens' religious past by interested parties preclude an inquiry based on a rigorous classification along these lines, it is clear that among the most venerable cults should be numbered those which were connected with the basic structures of Athenian society, namely the *genê*, demes, tribes and phratries; those which functioned as symbols of Athens' territorial claims; and finally, those connected with natural disasters such as drought, famine and plague.

In conclusion, Isokrates' thesis that there was once a time when ancestral rites were not being supplemented by additional rites is obviously untenable. On the contrary, Athens' religious calendar was constantly being modified by new sacrifices at the expense of pre-existing ones, although the pace of religious change naturally varied according to circumstances. The belief in a golden era of religious stability enjoyed widespread acceptance largely due to the fact that, before the introduction of public records on stone from *c.* 450 onwards, it was virtually impossible to ascertain the era-date of any cult. Henceforward, however, any citizen who so desired would, by examining the inscriptions, have been able to quantify the pace of religious change. What he would not have been able to do, however, and what it will never be possible to do, is to compare the pace of religious change in Athens after *c.* 450 with that of any preceding era.

---

consequence of the return of Theseus' bones from Skyros in the 470s, one of the most momentous events in Athenian religious history, were not incorporated among *ta patria*. Possibly the term ultimately came to include all religious innovations which predated the democratic revolution of the late 460s.

2

Pheidippides and the Magic Mountain

In mid-September of 490 the Athenians, assisted by a contingent of only 1,000 Plataians and an unknown number of their own recently liberated slaves, defeated an overwhelmingly superior Persian invasion army at Marathon Bay on the northeast coast of Attica (Paus. 1.32.3). The Persian king Dareios had been conducting a war of revenge against Athens and the neighbouring island of Euboia for assisting the Ionian Greeks in their ill-fated revolt of a few years earlier, and in particular for the burning of Sardis, capital of the kingdom of Lydia, in 498. According to the testimony of Herodotos, on which this chapter mainly relies,[1] Dareios, after razing Eretria to the ground, crossed the strait which separates Euboia from Attica and landed at Marathon Bay, intending to advance on Athens by land and sea. When news of the invasion reached the city, an emergency meeting of the Assembly was held. On the urging of the general Miltiades it was decided to march out to meet the enemy rather than await his arrival in the city. Probably later the same day an army of some 9,000 citizens was therefore dispatched to Marathon. Simultaneously a long-distance runner called Pheidippides (or according to a less likely version 'Philippides') who was 'in good trim' – a delightfully vivid detail – was dispatched to Sparta with a request for military assistance (Hdt. 6.105.1). News of the decision to defend Marathon also reached the Plataians, who immediately dispatched their forces to join the Athenians.

After pitching camp in Marathon Bay, however, the Athenian war council, which consisted of ten generals plus the polemarch Kallimachos, remained undecided whether to offer battle or retire. Had it not been for the eloquence of Miltiades, faintheartedness would almost certainly have prevailed. Even so, Miltiades' speech merely succeeded in splitting the council down the middle. The decision whether to fight or withdraw thus

---

[1] Herodotos first visited Athens to gather material for his *Histories* in c. 450, returning to give recitations in 446/5. We are therefore dealing with a lapse of forty years between the events themselves and Herodotos' telling of them. For the purposes of this investigation, however, the accuracy or otherwise of his account is ultimately less important than the fact that, though seen through his eyes, it reflects a predominantly Athenian viewpoint.

ultimately rested with Kallimachos. The polemarch cast his vote in favour of battle.

The result was a resounding victory for the Athenians, and one on which they always looked back with fervent pride. Their pride is aptly symbolised by the fact that they later consecrated a temple to Eukleia, the personification of Glory, from the spoils which they captured from the Persians (Paus. 1.14.5). In addition, work was begun on two major public edifices in marble as thank-offerings for the victory, the Athenian treasury at Delphi and the predecessor to the Parthenon (Paus. 10.11.5; *ML* 19). Athenian losses – excluding, of course, an unrecorded number of their liberated slaves – amounted to 192; those on the Persian side were allegedly 6,400 (Hdt. 6.117.1). What made Marathon not merely a decisive military victory but a definitive political one as well was the fact that the invasion force was accompanied and abetted by the aged tyrant Hippias who was hoping to be reinstated in the wake of a Persian victory.

Pheidippides' mission

We can categorically affirm that the Athenians did not expect to win the battle of Marathon and that even after they had done so they could hardly believe their luck. We know that because the only way they could explain their success was by attributing it to the intervention of gods and heroes. Despite the overwhelming odds against it, their army had succeeded in administering a humiliating defeat upon their numerically vastly superior Persian adversaries. How could this have happened? How can anything happen which is so much at variance with the iron laws of statistical probability, except through supernatural agency, as the frequent appearances of gods to their favourites in the *Iliad* make abundantly clear?

Of the many supernatural occurrences connected with Marathon none is more intriguing than that involving the runner who was sent to Sparta with an appeal for military assistance (Hdt. 6.105-6). When he presented his request to the Spartans the day after he left Athens, Pheidippides was informed that although they were sympathetic in principle, they were debarred from taking immediate action owing to religious constraints. His arrival on Boedromion 10 had coincided with the Karneia, an important Doric festival held in honour of Apollo Karneios. Not until the full moon, which fell on Boedromion 16, would their army be able to take the field. Since it was about a two-day march to Marathon, this meant that the Athenians would have had to wait at least a week for their allies to arrive.

Pheidippides had no choice but to return to Marathon as the bearer of bad news. His predicament was unenviable. His run from Athens to Sparta, a distance of about 2,400 stades or 150 miles (cf. Isok. *Panath.* 24), presumably accomplished in record-breaking time, had ended in complete failure. However, on his return journey – Herodotos' narrative is vague at this point but my own conviction is that this is what he means[2] – an extraordinary event occurred. While crossing the summit of Mount Parthenion in Arkadia not far from Tegea, an isolated and inhospitable region some thirty-five miles north of Sparta, he was accosted by Pan. The goat god, we are told, 'fell in (*peripiptei*)' with him, addressed him by name, and told him to relay the following message to the Athenians: 'Why don't you pay me cult (*epimeleia*) since I am well-disposed (*eunoöu*) towards you, and have on many occasions already been useful (*chrêstou*) and will be so in the future?' (Plate 10).

Mountains are strange and wonderful places – we can appropriately use the adjective '*daimonios*' to describe them – and they were already regarded as sacred in the Early Bronze Age when worship was being conducted in peak sanctuaries on Crete. The belief in their sanctity seems to have persisted unbroken into the historical era and was certainly not confined to the Greeks. Moses' vision of the burning bush, for instance, also takes place on a mountain, the so-called 'mountain of God', variously referred to as Horeb and Sinai (Exodus 3:1). Hesiod (*Th.* 22f.) claims to have received his commission to become an epic poet from the nine Muses while pasturing his sheep in the shadow of Mount Helikon, and the gods themselves lived on Mount Olympos. So a mountainous region was a perfectly appropriate setting for an epiphany to take place, and especially one involving a rustic god like Arkadian Pan who, by virtue of his intimate association with goats, was the habitué of such terrain (cf. Borgeaud 1988, 134).

What actually happened on Mount Parthenion, assuming of course that this story is not an *ex post facto* invention either by Pheidippides himself or another interested party? It is impossible to answer that question in any precise way other than to state the obvious. According to what later became the 'official' Athenian version the herald had an almost mystical experience on a mountain – an experience which was so urgent, so intense and so compelling that he subsequently succeeded in persuading

---

[2] Borgeaud (1988, 133) takes it for granted that Pheidippides encountered Pan on his return journey, but Herodotos' narrative by no means justifies this assumption uncritically. The structure of the relevant chapters (6.105-6) is the following:

(1) The Athenian generals dispatch Pheidippides to Sparta;
(2) Pheidippides encounters Pan on the mountain;
(3) 'When their affairs had recovered', the Athenians establish a cult to Pan;
(4) Pheidippides delivers his message to the Spartans.

Thus the sole grounds for inferring that the epiphany occurred on the return journey are of a psychological nature. They are, none the less, cogent. I submit that the reason why Herodotos elects to tell the whole story at the first mention of Pheidippides' name is because he regards it as incidental to the main thrust of his narrative. It is something which he can neither omit (because it was too well-known) nor fully incorporate (because of his own reservations about it). In other words, the ancedote functions as a kind of footnote under the heading 'Pheidippides'. On Herodotos' scepticism regarding supernatural interventions, see further p. 55.

the Demos to introduce a previously ignored god into the state pantheon. From a rationalist viewpoint, it would hardly have been surprising if, exhausted, deoxygenated, isolated and utterly despondent due to the failure of a mission upon which Athens' whole survival was believed so heavily to depend and into which he had injected all his physical, emotional and spiritual energies, he thought he saw a divine being, half-god and half-man, whose natural habitat was precisely the kind of bleak and deserted landscape which he was currently traversing.

One way of interpreting Pheidippides' encounter with Pan, therefore, is to see it as a way of coming to terms with the otherwise insurmountable gap between superhuman effort and negligible result. To put it in the language of modern psychology, the god of Pheidippides' imagining compensates the runner for his wasted effort by supplying him with a positive message to offset the negative one received from the Spartans. Pan's message is thus an expression of the keenfelt desire of the runner's own ego – his desire, that is, to be the vessel of Athens' salvation. Or as Borgeaud (1988, 133) expresses it: 'The herald exteriorises as an objective fact a voice that is actually only a projection of his wish.'

We are not told how the runner reacted to his encounter nor in what frame of mind he continued upon his journey, but the indications are that the epiphany was not particularly frightening. Pan was polite, friendly and only mildly reproachful. He merely put a question to the runner which the latter was commissioned to relay but not required to answer. We can safely assume that the initial impact of his appearance would have been to restore Pheidippides' depressed spirits and flagging strength. Although we are not told why the god's choice fell on a humble and presumably otherwise insignificant individual, it was surely due in large part to the fact that as official state messenger crossing alien territory he was ideally suited to be the bearer of a petition from a god of that territory. There was, however, a further, natural affinity between the runner and the god, the latter being the son of Hermes, the patron of messengers. Pan, in other words, had carefully chosen both his man and his moment.

Herodotos does not mention either Pheidippides or Pan in his narrative again. We can be certain that the runner arrived in time for the battle, however, since in the event it did not take place until Boedromion 17. Although we are not entitled to assume that the report of the epiphany played any part in the subsequent deliberations of the Athenian war council, Miltiades at least seems to have treated it seriously, for after the battle he dedicated a statue of Pan in his sanctuary on the Acropolis and had it inscribed with lines which were later attributed to Simonides (*AP* 16.232; cf. Borgeaud 1988, ch. 7 n. 119):

> Miltiades erected me, goat-footed Pan of Arcadia, the one who fought against the Medes and with the Athenians.

It is also noteworthy that before the battle the polemarch Kallimachos took a vow to dedicate a statue of the 'imm[ortal] mess[enger]' of the gods on the Acropolis to Athena (*ML* 18 = *IG* I² 609; cf. *ABSA* 45 [1950] 140-64). His vow may be interpreted as another reference to Pheidippides' run. If that is the case, we have here persuasive evidence of the extent to which the Athenian high command pinned their hopes on the success of Pheidippides' mission.

A further piece of evidence linking Pan with the battle is the existence of a cave near Marathon sacred to the god. Located on the northeast slope of the acropolis in the deme of Oinoe, about half a mile from the modern village of Marathon, the cave contained 'rocks shaped in such a way that in many respects they resemble goats' (Paus. 1.32.7). Might it be that Pan was already present in Attica in some humble capacity before the battle was actually fought, consistent with his claim of having been useful in the past?

Herodotos' description of Pheidippides' encounter with Pan evidently constituted the explanation or *aition* for the introduction of the new cult into Athens. As such it manifests the salient characteristics of its genre: an epiphany took place at a moment of crisis, the god promised to render assistance to the beleaguered party, and the fulfilment of this promise was borne out by subsequent events. But what exactly does the foundation legend seek to explain? The answer surely is that it bridges the distance between reasonable expectation and actual result. By reasonable expectation the Athenians should have lost the battle of Marathon. In the event they won the most glorious victory in their entire history. Their numerical deficiency ought to have been redressed by the arrrival of the Spartans. In the event it was alleviated by the intervention of Pan. So the *aition* preserves the belief that Pheidippides was the medium by which the Athenians reckoned on receiving outside assistance in the form of an ally or *summachos* who would enable them to snatch victory from the jaws of defeat. And this, of course, is the identical role which the runner would have performed if his mission had met with success in the way that was originally intended.

Pan's intervention in the battle

On the level of generality the reason why the Athenians gave credence to Pheidippides' claim surely lies in the extraordinary feeling of relief generated by the victory at Marathon. But can we go further than this? Can we, in other words, discover how the runner succeeded in linking his experience on Mount Tegea to what happened at the battle in a manner which convinced the Athenians that he was indeed telling the truth? In particular, can we establish at what precise moment in the engagement Pan was supposed to have intervened? For although the god did not allude specifically to the forthcoming battle when he addressed

Pheidippides, we can hardly doubt that his promise of being useful in the future referred to the immediate crisis.

It is a curious fact that although Herodotos cites another instance of alleged supernatural intervention in connection with the battle (see below p. 54), he says nothing either to confirm or to cast doubts upon the veracity of Pan's epiphany. Since, as he testifies, the Athenians believed Pheidippides, however, it is a reasonable inference that the god was indeed assigned a specific part in the outcome of the battle, even though this may not have taken the form of a personal appearance.[3] Borgeaud (1988, 95; cf. 136) has recently proposed that Pan made his contribution only after the main battle, when the defeated Persians were scrambling back on board their ships. For after they had embarked in disorder, the latter sailed around the southern tip of Attica and headed westwards towards Phaleron Bay with the intention of capturing Athens before the victorious Athenian army returned. Instead they were forestalled by the defenders (Hdt. 6.115-16). Pan's decisive contribution, in Borgeaud's words, was 'the disarray which overtook the Persians in their retreat and momentarily disordered their manoeuvres', since it was their disarray which enabled the Athenians to race back home and take up position in advance of the enemy's arrival with only moments to spare.

Borgeaud may well be right, though a no less critical and decisive moment for the god to have intervened was at the instant when the two armies first engaged. Herodotos (6.112) gives us the following account of the opening moments of the engagement:

> After they had got into battle formation and the sacrifices had been performed with favourable outcome, the Athenians were ordered to attack. They advanced towards the barbarians at a run (*dromôi*), although the distance between them was not less than eight stades (i.e. slightly less than one mile). The Persians, seeing them come towards them at a run, prepared to receive them. They considered that it was a mad and suicidal action on the part of the Athenians in view of the fact that their forces were small – and at a run, without any cavalry or archers to support them. So that was what the barbarians imagined. But the Athenians came to close quarters

---

[3] Not much importance need be attached to Pausanias' failure to mention Pan in his description of the battle as depicted in the Stoa Poikile (see below p. 103). Perhaps the goat-god was just too unmilitary a figure to keep company with the gods and heroes of Athens. Or perhaps Pausanias simply overlooked him. For what it is worth, the second century BC historian Polemon (2.41) refers to one of the Persian ships 'being pursued by Pan', a detail which he surely did not invent. Cf. also the tabloid newspaper-style account of the battle written by Aristeides (*Panath.* 108 = 202D) in the second century AD: 'Instantly their lines were broken, the men slain, the horses captured, the ships dragged away, the money seized and the dance of Pan performed.' It is also possible that in antiquity Pan's precise role in the battle was a matter of dispute. Sud. (*s.v. Hippias*) says that he was identified by some with the *phasma* or phantom which appeared to a certain Epizelos (see below). I am grateful to Homer Thompson for discussing with me possible reasons for the omission of Pan in Pausanias' description of the painting in the Stoa Poikile. The god's inclusion in the painting is accepted by Harrison (1972, 367).

and fought in hand-to-hand combat with the enemy in a manner that was truly memorable. For they were the first Greeks that we know of who dared to gaze on Persian clothing and the men who wore it. For until that day even to hear the word Persian struck terror (*phobos*) into the Greeks.

Experiments carried out with young American males at Pennsylvania State University in 1973 have conclusively proved that Greek hoplites could not possibly have done what Herodotos claims, even allowing for their superior motivation. The maximum distance which they might have covered heavily armed, maintaining battle formation, and still fit for close combat is about 200 yards (cf. Donlan and Thompson 1976, 341). So somewhere in the interval between the battle and Herodotos' telling of it, exaggeration has overlaid reality. The crucial factor for the present investigation, however, is the widespread acceptance of the death-defying charge which, irrespective of its precise basis in truth, promoted the belief that the Athenians not only violated logic by charging at an army greatly superior to their own, but also, by gazing upon the Persians in their frightful Persian attire, did what no other Greek army had ever done previously. The Persian 'panickers' themselves became panic-stricken. Conventional reality was therefore turned on its head.

It is not too fanciful, perhaps, to suggest that the cult of Pan, the god of panic, was introduced into Athens as a way of explaining how *phobos*, which we might appropriately render as panic, descended not upon the vastly outnumbered Athenians, as logically it ought to have done, but instead upon the vastly superior Persians. If this is correct, and it has to be reiterated that there is no explicit link in Herodotos' narrative between Pan and the flight of the Persians, the god's intervention may serve as a metaphor for the morale or spirit among the Athenian troops and their commander, a factor of incalculable importance in determining the outcome of battles.[4]

Herodotos does not describe the mood of the Athenians just before the two armies engaged, but given the outcome of the battle it is virtually certain that they were nourishing a quite extraordinary degree of insouciance at the parlousness of their condition. If so, and I can think of no alternative explanation for their victory, the reconstruction which I propose is this. Although the Athenians were initially plunged into the depths of despair when they learned that they would have to fight without the Spartans, this same circumstance later filled them with an irrational sense of elation. By way of parallel, we may recall the speech which Henry V delivers to his army before the battle of Agincourt in

---

[4] To quote the early-nineteenth-century French philosopher called Joseph de Maistre (1850, 37; cited in Berlin 1967, 53) who lived in St. Petersburg at the time of the Napoleonic invasion of Russia in 1812: 'Although an army of 40,000 men is physically inferior to one of 60,000, yet if that first army possesses more courage, more experience and more discipline, it will be able to defeat the other, since it has more vitality and less mass (*plus d'action avec moins de masse*), and this is what we find on every page of history.'

Shakespeare's play of that name where, far from lamenting the fact that he is heavily outnumbered by the French, the king almost goes so far as to regret that his army is not in fact smaller (*Henry V* Act 4 Scene 3):

> If we are mark'd to die, we are enow
> To do our country loss; and if to live,
> The fewer men, the greater share of honour.
> God's will, I pray thee, wish not one man more ... .
> No, faith, my coz, wish not a man from England:
> God's peace! I would not lose so great an honour,
> As one man more, methinks, would share from me
> For the best hope I have.

Could it be that Miltiades, who happened to be the supreme commander on the day the battle was fought, brought off a similar rhetorical *tour de force* minutes before the engagement, by demonstrating that the absence of the Spartans, rather than justifying despondency, was actually a cause for celebration?[5]

Heroic *phasmata*

One powerful indicator that the Athenian army was in an abnormally heightened sensory condition is the report of sightings of phantoms or apparitions (*phasmata*), which are recorded in a variety of sources. Plutarch (*Thes.* 35.5), for instance, tells us that many Athenians 'thought that they saw a *phasma* of Theseus clad in armour rushing before them against the barbarians'. He does not tell us which Athenians received the vision. Perhaps it was those in the centre of the battle line where losses were heaviest. In addition, Pausanias (1.32.5; cf. 1.15.3) informs us that the people of Marathon claimed that 'the *phasma* of a man of rustic form and dress took part in the battle, which, having slain a number of barbarians with a plough, then disappeared'. From inquiry at Delphi, the Athenians later learned that their anonymous helper was a certain Echetlaios (He of the ploughshare), who was henceforth to be honoured as a hero. Since, like rustic Pan, Echetlaios was a figure who would have been 'close to the hearts of the Marathonian peasants' (Jameson 1951, 57), it is readily comprehensible why he, too, would have been credited with an appearance on the field of battle.

Finally, Herodotos (6.117.2-3) relates that a certain Epizelos son of Kouphagoras claimed that a giant hoplite appeared to him during the

---

[5] The appearance of a supernatural being before a military action is well-documented in antiquity. Julius Caesar's momentous decision to march on Rome in 49 BC was allegedly provoked by the sudden appearance of 'a being of wondrous size and beauty who sat and played on a reed', urging him and his army to cross the Rubicon. The epiphany thus explains (and justifies) how Caesar was able to resolve his doubts and take the fateful and irreversible step of initiating the Civil War (Suet. *JC* 32).

battle with a chin so large that it overshadowed his shield. The hoplite, also described as a *phasma*, passed by and killed the man standing next to him. As a consequence Epizelos lost the sight of both eyes, although he had not been stabbed or shot, and so remained for the rest of his life. No theory is offered as to the hoplite's identity, but he was presumably a hero fighting on the enemy side. The reason why Herodotos ignores all the other instances of supernatural intervention in the battle is perhaps due to his personal disbelief. He may have made an exception in Epizelos' case because no other explanation could be found for his blindness.

Powers of time and place

Phasmata functioned as visible participants on the battlefield, wielding their swords and their ploughshares, whereas Pan's intervention was perhaps more subtle and more pervasive – he stood for a collective spirit shared by all the army in some measure. No less pervasive influences were what we would identify as environmental factors, including the weather, the time of year, and the positions taken up by both sides before battle commenced.

Before engagement the polemarch Kallimachos made a vow in the name of the Athenian Demos to sacrifice to Artemis Agrotera as many goats as the number of Persian dead on the battlefield. Though the polemarch himself died, the Athenians honoured his vow posthumously by instituting a token annual sacrifice of 500 goats, since they did not have a sufficient number to match the 6,400 Persian dead. Nearly one hundred years later, they were still discharging their vow, as Xenophon confirms (*Anab.* 3.2.12). Although there is no allusion to Artemis Agrotera's intervention in surviving accounts, the goddess surely made a significant contribution, not least because her festival, which fell on Boedromion 6, became the foremost victory celebration of Marathon (Plu. *Mor.* 349e). This may be due in part to the fact that the battle was fought at a time of year when her protective aura was particularly keenly felt. Possibly, as well, its outcome depended in some way upon the presence of the moon, with which Artemis was closely identified.[6]

The belief that the gods fought alongside the Athenians at Marathon was given visible expression in the painting of the battle displayed in the

---

[6] Hammond (1968, 39f.; 1988, 511) attractively suggests that Artemis Agrotera may have been credited with immobilising the Persian cavalry, who for some unknown reason, though present at Marathon, played no part in the conflict. Each night the cavalry were taken to a watering-place and brought back to the camp around moonset. According to Hammond's theory, the lateness of moonset on the morning of the engagement may have prevented them from returning in time for the battle due to a miscalculation on the part of their grooms.

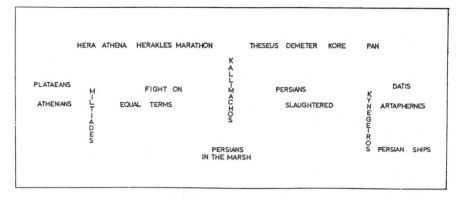

Fig. 6. Tentative reconstruction of the placing of figures in the picture of the battle of Marathon exhibited in the Stoa Poikile. From E.B. Harrison, *AJA* 76 (1972).

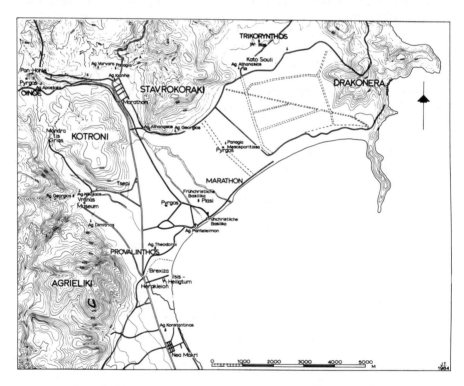

Fig. 7. Map of the plain of Marathon. From J. Travlos, *BTAA*.

Stoa Poikile or Painted Stoa which was erected in the Agora in *c.* 460, where the eponymous hero of Marathon, Theseus, Athena, Herakles and the hero Echetlaios were depicted in combat with the invaders (Paus.1.15.3; Fig. 6). The inclusion of Herakles is particularly interesting because it was in his precinct at Marathon that the Athenians pitched camp before the battle, and in another at Kynosarges that they took up position afterwards, following their spectacular dash back to Athens (Hdt. 6.108.1, 116). The coincidence is surely too striking to be accidental. Although strategic considerations may have been to the fore in the decision to pitch camp in the Marathonian Herakleion, situated as it was on the main road between Marathon and Athens and so blocking the Persian advance, the determination to stick with the hero a second time was undoubtedly based on an appreciation of services previously rendered. Athens had fought and would fight again under his protection. The power of a hero no less than that of a deity was experienced most strongly in a sanctuary, and Greek as well as Roman armies habitually exhibited a marked preference for taking up a position close to a national shrine (e.g. Plu. *Arist.* 11.7). Herakles' association with northeast Attica was, moreover, extremely close, for it was the demesmen of Marathon according to local legend who first acknowledged him as a god (cf. Paus. 1.15.3, 1.32.4). Of particular interest in this connection is the discovery of an inscribed *stêlê* or pillar (*IG* I³ 3 = *SEG* XXXIV.1) from the southern part of the plain of Marathon dated to the early fifth century which refers to the re-organisation on Panattic scale of the four-yearly games in honour of Herakles. The decree may well have been passed shortly after the battle in frank acknowledgement of Athens' indebtedness to the local hero-god. In the immediate aftermath to the battle the Herakleia festival even attained Panhellenic renown (cf. Vanderpool 1948, 335f.).

The presence of both Theseus and Athena at the battle is also likely to have been occasioned in part by their intimate association with northeast Attica. Though no Theseion as such has been identified in the region, Theseus is said to have rendered help to the people of Marathon by killing the bull which was ravaging their district. A precinct of Athena, who possibly received worship under the cult title Hellotis, is known from an inscribed boundary stone which was found about half a mile from where the battle was fought (Soteriades in *PAE* [1935] 90; cf. Hom. *Od.* 7.80).

The Athenians also gave credit to the leading role which the Persians played in their own downfall. Retribution was the due reward for the barbarians' overweening confidence, duly meted out to them by the goddess Nemesis, its personified essence, whose cult, established by the beginning of the fifth century at the latest, was located a few miles to the north of Marathon at Rhamnous (*SEG* XXXIV.39). As Pausanias (1.33.3) reports, the insolence of the Persians had reached such baroque heights that they brought along with them a piece of Parian marble for the purpose of fashioning a trophy 'as if the battle was already won'. The sculptor Pheidias subsequently used it to carve a statue of Nemesis. In accordance with the best principles of Greek tragedy, the Persian defeat was thus partly self-inflicted. By arousing the anger of a goddess 'most implacable to men who display hybris', the barbarians scored a notable own-goal.

The Marathonian war dead

Besides heroic and divine intervention, a further explanation for the victory was the fact that the men who laid down their lives were regarded, spiritually speaking, as larger-than-life. Pausanias (1.32.4) reports that at night even in his time horses could be heard neighing and men fighting, as if a ghostly sound-track was being played over and over. He adds:

> No one who ever went there deliberately has ever seen anything distinct, but the anger of the *daimones* does not overtake those who have not heard about it and encounter it by chance.

The *daimones* or spirits in question, the 192 Athenian dead, were buried at the spot where they fell. Over them was heaped a great mound known as the Soros on which were set *stêlai* bearing their names listed by tribe. In addition, a cenotaph was perhaps erected in the Kerameikos on the west side of Athens, as if to guarantee that their beneficent presence would be felt in the Asty as well as at Marathon. Some time afterwards the dead were awarded heroic honours and a sacrifice was instituted, to be performed annually at the Soros under the auspices of the polemarch 'on behalf of those who died in the cause of freedom' (*IG* II¹ 471.26f., as emended by Koehler; cf. [Arist.] *AP* 58.1).

Neither before nor afterwards did the Athenians award such distinctions to their war dead. The fighters of Marathon were in a class of their own. Thukydides (2.34.5) says that they were granted these unique privileges because their countrymen 'deemed their valour to be outstanding'. That is perhaps something of an understatement. When else, as Aristeides (*Panath.* 108 = 202D-203D) reports, did a dead man, slain by Persian arrows, leap to his feet and start frightening away the enemy 'like an immortal' – or rather like some ghastly scarecrow from Hades? The fact is that the Athenians conceived these men to be heroes in the exact, technical sense of the term. We can sense something of the indomitable pride which was felt by the *Marathônomachoi*, as those who survived the battle were called, from Aristophanes' portrayal of them in his plays (*Wasps* 1081f.; *Acharn., passim*). Eloquent, too, of their unique honour is the anecdote that the poet Aeschylus left instructions in his will that his tomb should record no other information than that 'he had as witnesses to his valour both the grove at Marathon and the Persians who landed there' (Paus. 1.14.5).

Pan arrives in Athens

Herodotos tells us (6.105.3):

> When their affairs had recovered the Athenians believed Pheidippides' story and built a shrine (*hiron*) to Pan under the Acropolis and sought to

propitiate him (*hilaskontai*) with yearly sacrifices (*thusiêisi epeteioisi*) and a torch-race (*lampadi*), because of his message.

The shrine in question is almost certainly to be identified with two hollows containing votive niches situated close to the northwestern end of the Acropolis (Fig. 8 and Plate 11). From Herodotos' wording it would seem that the Demos was initially inclined to be somewhat sceptical about the alleged epiphany, and only later, perhaps having had time to subject Pheidippides' testimony to rigorous scrutiny in the light of their extraordinary victory, gave it their blessing, so to speak, and accepted the god into the community (cf. Bovon 1963, 225). Conceivably the delay was due to the fact that the decision was only reached after prolonged wrangling. Even so, the fact that the Athenians as a whole were credited with the building of the shrine suggests that we are dealing with a public cult established with the backing of the Demos.

Although no name other than that of Pheidippides is mentioned in connection with the cult's foundation, the god presumably had powerful advocates among those who wished to commemorate not only the victory itself but also, hardly less important, the controversial decision to fight at Marathon which preceded it. We have already noted that both Kallimachos and Miltiades made dedications connected with Phei-

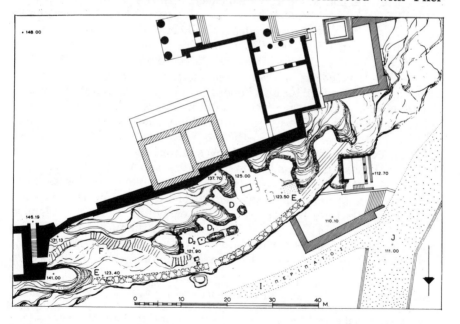

Fig. 8. Plan of the northwest slope of the Acropolis showing the cave of Pan. D = shrine of Pan; E = Pelargikon; F = stairway to Acropolis; I = Peripatos; J = Panathenaic Way. From J. Travlos, *PDA*.

dippides' mission to Sparta, and this fact suggests that the cult of Pan enjoyed the support of Athens' top military brass. No doubt it was crucial. As a peasant and a foreigner, Pan surely had to face considerable opposition from the conservative right. An odd alliance was probably formed between the Athenian high command and the peasants of Attica, and it was this constituency which supported his petition most vigorously. Whether Pan's fellow Arkadians took any part in their god's introduction into Athens is entirely possible but unproven. Pausanias (8.54.6) tells us that in later times a sanctuary of Pan was erected at the exact spot where 'Athenians and Tegeans both assert that Pan appeared to Pheidippides and spoke to him'.[7]

No priest of Pan is mentioned in any of our sources and it is quite likely that none existed. Probably the god was served by a pluralist, that is to say, by a priest who administered rites on behalf of more than one deity. This hypothesis is strengthened by the modest size of his Acropolis sanctuary, which was devoted in part to the worship of the Nymphs. The Nymphs may even have ceded a small area of their cave to Pan on condition that their priest overseered Pan's cult. Little else is known about its organisation. Lukian (*Double Indictment* 9-10), who reports that Pan received the modest sacrifice of a castrated goat, would have us believe that the god was sorely displeased with the treatment which he received from the Athenians. It has been suggested that the decision to honour Pan with a torch-race reflects an effort to recreate the context of Pheidippides' run (cf. Parke *FA*, 172f.). On a recently published Attic black-figure *kylix* or mixing-bowl which is contemporary with Marathon the god is depicted as a fleet-footed runner, torch in hand, like a contestant in the race in his own honour (Plate 12; cf. Simon 1976, 19-23).

Archaeological evidence for the cult of Pan in Attica bears out perfectly Herodotos' claim that it was only after the battle that the god became officially incorporated into the Athenian pantheon. The worship of Pan has been detected in a number of caves throughout Attica, notably at Marathon, Eleusis, Phyle on Mount Parnes, Vari on Mount Hymettos, the Piraeus, Mount Pentelikon, Daphni and on the banks of the Ilissos River in Athens. Yet in none have any dedications been found dating to the period from the Late Bronze Age to the early-fifth century (Orlandos 1958, 21; Travlos *PDA*, 417). Likewise no Athenian vase-painting depicting the goat god is earlier than the battle (Brommer 1956, 956f.). Cuttings for steps and walls which have been found in the Acropolis cave

---

[7] In a forthcoming article Fred Cooper identifies economic links between Athens and Arkadia as an important motive behind the establishment of Pan's cult. Observing that the first influx of silver into Arkadia occurs around the beginning of the fifth century, he plausibly suggests that this represents payment from timber of which Athens was soon to become a major importer for the construction of her triremes. He concludes, 'By establishing a religious bond with Arkadia the Athenians assured themselves of continued commercial interests in that part of the world.' I am most grateful to Professor Cooper for allowing me to see a copy of his article in draft form.

probably also belong to this period (Judeich *Topog.*[2], 303).

Even so, it is highly improbable that the worship of Pan was completely unknown in Attica before 490. Many of the caves in which he took up residence, including as we have seen the one on the Acropolis, were already sacred to the Nymphs, whose cult flourished in the Archaic period and to whom countryfolk felt much felt closer than to the mighty gods of Olympos (Fuchs 1962, 245). Several myths testify to Pan's close association with the Nymphs. He was said to be the son of Aither and the nymph Oinoe. His love for the nymph Echo was a popular theme in pastoral poetry. Yet another nymph, Erato, was said to have been his prophetess in days of yore when he gave out prophecies (Paus. 8.37.11). The decision to grant him house-room in sanctuaries devoted to the Nymphs was therefore uncontroversial, and the process of accommodating him therein may well have begun around the beginning of the fifth century. After 490, however, it accelerated, to the mutual advantage of both parties, as we see from the fact that the cult of the Nymphs was prosecuted with increased vigour from the mid-fifth century onwards, notably in connection with parents' concern for the welfare of their children, an area in which these minor deities exercised an important influence.

With Artemis, too, Pan enjoyed a close and fruitful association. In Euripides' *Iphigeneia in Tauris* (ll. 1125-7) he attends upon the cult statue of Artemis as it is conveyed by ship to Attica, his pipes marking time for the rowers. Even more significant is the fact that miniature mixing-bowls of a type known as *kratêriskoi* depicting scenes connected with the cult of Artemis have been discovered in Pan's cave near Eleusis (Plate 15). Since Artemis herself played a major part in the battle, her priesthood would have been in a strong position to back Pan's claims to public worship.

The prior existence of a cult of Pan in the Attic countryside is entirely consistent with Herodotos' account. Pan had complained to Pheidippides that he lacked '*epimeleia*' from the Athenian state. His protest does not exclude the possibility that he was already receiving worship from countryfolk in the outlying regions of Attica. What the god and his adherents were seeking in 490 was surely a level of recognition which had been previously denied to them. We are dealing with a cult which was lobbying for enhanced prestige, rather than one which was seeking initial entry. That, too, as we have seen, may have been the case with Herakles, whose prestige was also enhanced after the battle. Very likely the same is true of the hero Echetlaios, a rustic *daimôn* invoked at the ploughing season in order to ensure a good crop in the spring, who is henceforth credited with a military capability as well.

The tradition of Pheidippides' encounter with Pan on the rugged hilltops of Mount Parthenion later inspired a number of copycat sightings of Pan in the domesticated landscape of Attica, as is indicated by a series of votive reliefs which depict the dedicator in the company of the goat god and the Nymphs. It is noteworthy that whereas humans are only two-thirds the height of the gods on such reliefs, Pan is almost invariably smaller than his divine companions, further evidence of his approach-ability and nearness to mankind (cf. Robertson *HGA* I, 375; Fuchs 1962, *passim*).

Conclusions

A noteworthy feature of the Athenian explanation for the victory of Marathon is its pronounced emphasis on gods and heroes associated with the Attic countryside. More strikingly, the gods and heroes who are credited with intervention in the battle, namely Artemis Agrotera, Athena, Herakles, Echetlaios, Marathon himself, Pan and Theseus, were all in some measure local figures associated primarily with Marathon deme, so much so that Theseus was actually depicted on the painting in the Stoa Poikile as 'coming out of the earth' (Paus. 1.15.3). Incontestably this was a victory achieved not merely *at* but also *by* Marathon, which is to say, by the spirits inhering in its fields and hills. One of the incidental consequences of the battle may have been to emphasise Marathon's status as an important religious centre, since these cults were all indigenous to her soil.

The establishment of a state-sponsored cult of Pan came at an important turning-point in the history of Athenian religion, since Pan's request for enhanced prestige coincided approximately with the era when the Demos was perhaps just beginning to exercise independent authority in matters of religious innovation (see further ch. 5). From the evidence of iconography, Borgeaud (1988, 160; cf. Fuchs 1962, 244) has suggested that the sanctuary of Pan on the Acropolis functioned as 'the model (or point of reference) for the caves dispersed outside the city'. It may also have served to impose a certain uniformity upon the worship of the Arkadian god, thereby enabling a centralised authority to extend its influence upon the outlying districts of Attica.

Without relinquishing his links to those outlying districts, Pan, by virtue of the fact that he was admitted into the heart of Athens, now became partially urbanised, a phenomenon which exactly paralleled the experience of many country-dwellers in this same period, as the Asty and Piraeus port began to act as a magnet for a rural population which was increasingly being drawn to these urban centres in search of employment. Pan's establishment on the Acropolis therefore provides incidental yet telling proof of a large influx of Athenians from the Chora or countryside into the Asty in the 490s and 480s, as well as for the fact that their religious needs were being accommodated. Like other minorities, particularly the numerous ethnic groups which gravitated towards Athens and the Piraeus in the later-fifth and fourth centuries, this rural population achieved integration by being granted the privilege of worshipping its own gods in its own distinctive way.

Pan's arrival on the Acropolis had a profound impact upon his status throughout the Greek world, since soon afterwards his cult was established in Sicily, Italy, Boiotia, Macedonia and Asia Minor (cf. Brommer 1956, 954). No less a poet than Pindar composed an ode in Pan's honour not long before 474 after the god had been sighted singing one of his paeans on the road from Helikon to Kithairon (fr. 95 Maehler, *T*; cf. Haldane 1968, 20f.). As happened later in the case of Asklepios, acceptance in Athens thus served as a springboard for the god's conversion into a Panhellenic deity, although there is no evidence that the cult was ever directly exported from Athens.

Irrespective of the true facts, the battle of Marathon became in the re-telling Athens' most heroic victory, the keenest possible test of the physical, mental and moral qualities of her fighting stock. It could easily be overlooked that all it did ultimately was to buy time until the Persians returned a decade later with a vengeance. Easily overlooked, too, was the contribution made by her Plataian allies and liberated slaves. And because moral qualities were incorporated into the myth which the battle generated, that myth gave free rein to Athens' own sense of cultural and racial superiority, which in turn was founded on the belief in her unique enjoyment of divine favour (above p. 9).

The intervention attributed to the gods at Marathon offers perhaps the most complete explanation in Greek history of a military victory won against all odds. As such it serves as a valuable object lesson for the variety of ways in which human life is subject to divine influence at moments of crisis. In the language of religion the victory at Marathon was accomplished by the uncommon valour of the *Marathônomachoi*, by Persian hybris, and by the interventions of gods and heroes. All of this is merely another way of saying that it was due to the extremely high morale and discipline of the Athenians, the over-assurance of the Persians, the peculiarly advantageous seasonal and climatic conditions, and the fact that the Athenians were fighting on home ground for everything which they owned. Who won the battle of Marathon? The gods and heroes of Athens. Or, if you prefer, an extraordinary concatenation of circumstances favourable to the Athenian side. It is ultimately a matter of perspective.[8]

---

[8] Christian Habicht has drawn my attention to the fact that Pausanias' description of supernatural occurrences connected with the repulse of the Gallic attack on Delphi in 279 BC, in which the Athenians also took a leading part, is closely modelled on the account of the battle of Marathon, notably in its references to the part played by a local hero called Phylachos (10.23.2) and Pan (10.23.7-8). Cf. C. Habicht, *Untersuchungen zur politischen Geschichte Athens im 3. Jhr. v. Chr.* (Munich 1979), 87-94.

3

Themistokles and the Cult of the Intellect

Either in the autumn of 481 or else in the spring of 480 the Athenians sent two sacred ambassadors called *theopropoi* to Delphi to inquire what to do in the face of an imminent invasion by the Persian army under the command of its king Xerxes, come to avenge the defeat at Marathon. Their situation was little short of desperate. Athens was indefensible by land. The only viable course of action, as the politician Themistokles realised, was to evacuate the entire population and risk a naval engagement with her as yet untested fleet which had been built on his recommendation just two years earlier. As the price for survival, in other words, Themistokles was proposing that the polis, including its temples and ancestral tombs, be abandoned to destruction. So great was the repugnance felt by the majority of the citizenry towards this prospect that they simply did not want victory on these terms (Plu. *Them.* 9.4).

The double consultation at Delphi

Herodotos (7.140-4), who is our only source for the embassy to Delphi, provides us with an unusually circumstantial account of what at first sight might be regarded as a somewhat trivial event, peripheral to the main concerns of his narrative. He tells us that after performing the customary rituals (*ta nomizomena*) in the forecourt of the sanctuary, which included the payment of a fee and the sacrifice of a goat (e.g. Plu. *Mor.* 437ab), the *theopropoi* entered the *megaron* or sanctum where consultations were held and sat down. Before they had an opportunity to put their question to the god, however, the Pythia, a woman named Aristonike, delivered the following dire prediction in twelve lines of hexameter verse:

> Wretched men, why do you sit here? Fly from the remotest dwellings of your land and the topmost peaks of your wheel-shaped polis. For neither its head, nor its body, nor the tips of its toes or fingers remain firm, nor is its middle part left, but all is ruined. A conflagration, in combination with ruthless Ares who drives a Syrian chariot, brings it to its knees. He will destroy many other fortresses and not only yours. Many temples belonging

64

to the immortals he will give over to devouring fire, ones which now stand dripping with sweat and quaking with fear. From their topmost crests black blood, envisaging the necessity of distress, pours. Go forth from this sanctuary and open your heart to evil.

Herodotos tells us that the two envoys, hearing these terrible words, judged their situation to be 'very grave'. That is surely putting it mildly. Not to put too fine a point upon it, it must have cast them into the depths of despair. Rarely if ever in Delphi's history had Apollo delivered a less equivocal pronouncement of doom. Such, moreover, was the god's absolute conviction in Athens' imminent destruction – for how else can we interpret the Pythia's behaviour? – that he delivered his prophecy without waiting for the petitioners to put their question to him first.

Matters did not rest here, however. After the *theopropoi* had withdrawn from the *megaron* and were pondering what to do next, a certain Timon, son of Androboulos, whom Herodotos describes merely as 'a very eminent Delphian', advised them to re-enter the shrine carrying suppliant branches and request a second oracle (7.141.1).

Although we know little about the way in which Delphic policy was determined, Herodotos' account would seem to indicate that a minority of Delphians, Timon among them, advocated a policy of resistance to Persia and that this faction, whatever the exact nature and extent of its political clout, had sufficient influence to induce the god to 'think again' when confronted with a particularly intransigent pair of suppliants. We do not know whether Timon acted on his own initiative or had been primed in advance to intervene on behalf of the *theopropoi* in the event of an unfavourable response. Either way, secret negotiations probably took place behind the scenes, resulting in a compromise between Timon and the party which urged submission to Persia. Accordingly the *theopropoi* came forward a second time into the *megaron* – perhaps later the same day – and prayed to the god as follows (7.141.2):

Lord Apollo, deliver some better oracle (*chrêson ... ameinon ti*) concerning our homeland and show your respect for these suppliant branches which we bear as we approach; otherwise we will not depart from your holy of holies (*aduton*) but remain in this place until we die.

We are told that the god consented to their prayer – threat of polluting his sanctuary would perhaps be a more accurate way of describing it – and that Aristonike delivered a second oracle, again in the form of a twelve-line hexameter poem (7.141.3-4):

Pallas Athena cannot propitiate Olympian Zeus, even though she prays with many utterances and profound wisdom. But I make this pronouncement to you, which I have fixed firm in adamant. When everything else has been captured which the boundary marker of Kekrops and the summit of divine Kithairon hold between them (i.e. all Attica), broad-ruling Zeus shall give a wooden wall to the Thriceborn (i.e. Athena), and it alone shall never be destroyed but shall bless you and your children. Do not peacefully await the cavalry and great army of infantry that is coming from the mainland, but turn your back on it and withdraw. On a day yet to come you will stand against them. O divine Salamis, you will bring death to women's sons either at the moment when Demeter is scattering or when she is coming together.

Though hardly favourable, this utterance was rather less bleak than its predecessor and as such provided grounds for cautious optimism. In Parke's (1967, 104) words: 'The Delphic authorities had given the ambassadors the barest minimum.' The *theopropoi* duly wrote the oracle down and made their way back to Athens.

Despite the irregular circumstances surrounding the so-called 'double consultation', the incident is undoubtedly based on historical fact. Although the Pythia usually adhered to the principle of petition response (i.e. refrained from utterance except in response to a specific question), Plutarch, who served as a priest at Delphi for 'many Pythiads' (*Mor*. 792f) and so knew what he was talking about, confirms that she 'was accustomed to prophesy spontaneously, even before the question is put to her' (*On Garrulousness* 28 = *Mor*. 512e). While we might expect Delphic procedure to have changed somewhat in the six-hundred-year interval between Herodotos and Plutarch, Herodotos also gives other examples of spontaneous prophecy (1.65.2; 5.92b). It is worth noting as well that in the version of the myth of Oedipus preserved by Herodotos' contemporary Sophokles in the *Oedipus Tyrannos*, the poet has Apollo pre-empt a petitioner's inquiry in order to achieve his spectacular dénouement (*OT* 788-93). When Oedipus is about to ask the god who his real parents are, he is so stunned by the revelation that he will kill his father and marry his mother that he departs from the sanctuary having omitted to establish their true identity. In sum, there is every reason to suppose that Herodotos' narrative is consistent with contemporary Delphic practice and that in certain situations the mere presence of a particularly luckless petitioner in his sanctuary provoked a spontaneous outburst from the god.

Besides, as Parke and Wormell (1956, I p. 170) point out, 'No forger would have perpetrated such a mistake as to show Apollo induced to change his mind about one of the most important events of Greek history' – particularly, we might add, since Delphi is the most likely source for the story (cf. Waters 1985, 80). Although there is no good parallel in Greek history for a double consultation, the exceptional circumstances under which it took place should caution us from assuming that it is a fabrication (cf. Evans 1982, 24). Even if we accept its historicity unreservedly, however, we are not, of course, obliged to believe that the oracles' wording is also genuine. Indeed it is in the highest degree unlikely that a presumably uneducated peasant like Aristonike could have produced twenty-four lines of hexameter verse at a moment's notice. Herodotos or conceivably some other party has surely embroidered the two oracles, just as the historian regularly embroidered the speeches which he incorporated into his narrative.

But why did Apollo change his mind – or at least modify his tone – if that is the right way to put it? Ostensibly the god yielded at the insistence of the *theopropoi* themselves, who under the guise of suppliancy threatened to die and pollute his sanctuary unless he supplied them with 'some better oracle'. To our way of thinking 'some better oracle' may sound like a piece of theological doublethink, but not so to the Greeks. The conviction that it was possible to evade or at least defer fulfilment of an unpopular oracle was at least as old as Homer. When, for instance, the Trojan seer Polydamas interpreted the sight of an eagle dropping a monstrous snake from its talons as a portent that the Trojan army should refrain from advancing against the Greeks, Hektor called him a coward and dismissed his explanation with the words, 'One omen is best, to fight for our country' (*Il.* 12.243). The oracle's fulfilment was duly postponed, thanks in part to Hektor's determination and resourcefulness.[1] As Nock has observed (1972, 542), 'An omen was not so much an indication of inevitable destiny as a token of luck or an endorsement of policy'. In fifth-century Athens there actually existed established procedures for averting an unfavourable dream, and perhaps as well for warding off evil omens (cf. Dodds 1973, 183).

Although Herodotos does not reveal the identity of the Athenian who put the proposal to consult Delphi on the agenda of the Ekklesia, the credit should undoubtedly go to Themistokles, since it was he who had everything to gain from the god's support and virtually nothing to lose from his opposition. Plutarch lends circumstantial evidence in favour of this theory by stating that Themistokles 'brought forward' oracles to persuade the people after reasoned argument had failed (*Them.* 10.1).

There are, however, no grounds for assuming that the second oracle was invented by Themistokles. As Evans (1982, 27) points out, ' "a wooden wall" and a vague mention of Salamis ... were slender supports for a naval strategy. Both oracles were defeatist in tone; the second differed from the first only in that it added a note of ambiguity.' In other words, if the oracle was a fake, it is surprising that Themistokles was not able to come up with a less equivocal endorsement for his policy of resistance at sea. He surely gambled on the hope of winning the god's support for his unpopular proposal in the certain knowledge that if Apollo withheld it both he and his proposal were doomed. The fact that the god

[1] Justly celebrated, too, is the clever ruse of Lucius Junius Brutus, the founder of the Roman Republic, who, upon receiving with two of his companions an oracle to the effect that whichever of their number kissed his mother first should hold supreme authority in Rome, laid immediate claim to the title by prostrating himself and kissing the earth, 'the common mother of all things' (Li. 1.56.9-13).

generally counselled surrender in the face of the Persian advance is a sure sign of Themistokles' political courage – or else his desperation. Such a bold initiative was entirely in character. What most impressed Thukydides about the politician was his ability to come up with a ready and effective solution to a crisis (see below p. 73). Never did he display his talents to better advantage than in the weeks leading up to the battle of Salamis.

It must also be emphasised that Herodotos nowhere suggests that the *theopropoi* resorted to bribery. His silence on this issue is all the more telling in view of the fact that he does not refrain from reporting actual instances and unproven allegations of bribery elsewhere in his narrative. He asserts, for instance, that the Spartan king Kleomenes bribed the Pythia to declare that his rival Demaratos was illegitimate (6.66), and, closer to home, that the powerful Alkmaionid *genos*, after being driven into exile by the Peisistratids, allegedly bribed Delphi to pressure the Spartans to help liberate Athens (5.63, 90.1; cf. 6.123.2). At the worst, therefore, the Athenian *theopropoi* were guilty of procedural irregularity, since having obtained one pronouncement from the god, they ought perhaps to have taken their place at the back of the oracular queue. In view of the fact that the first response which they received was unsolicited, however, it is quite possible that their request was still in order.

Deconstructing Delphi

Upon their return to Athens the *theopropoi* made their report to the Ekklesia, though for tactical reasons they probably suppressed all mention of the first oracle. In any event most of the ensuing debate seems to have been taken up with trying to decipher the meaning of the phrase 'wooden wall'. The older generation understood it to be a reference to a wooden palisade which in former times had protected the Acropolis and maintained that Delphi was urging upon them the defence of that holy rock. Others, Themistokles possibly among them, although Herodotos has not yet mentioned him by name, interpreted the wall as an allusion to the stout timbers of Athens' fleet and claimed that the gods were urging them to prepare for a naval battle (Hdt. 7.142; cf. Plu. *Them*. 10.1).[2] The problem for those supporting the latter view was that the last two lines of the second oracle – 'O divine Salamis, you will bring death to mothers'

[2] The fact that Themistokles is not specifically credited with interpreting the wooden wall to mean the fleet but only with the elucidation of 'O divine Salamis, etc.' is taken by Evans (1982, 28) as evidence that he was not in fact present when the debate began and only returned from the Isthmus when it was already in full swing. Evans further asserts that it was the *chrêsmologoi* who interpreted the phrase correctly, but this is not entirely accurate. What Herodotos asserts is that 'others' (in distinction to the older generation, *hoi presbuteroi*) understood it in this way and that the *chrêsmologoi* 'took the verse to mean that if they prepared for a naval battle near Salamis they would be defeated'.

sons, etc.' – suggested that if they fought in the straits of Salamis they would be soundly beaten. This was the opinion of the professional interpreters of oracles or *chrêsmologoi*, who were so convinced of the inevitability of a naval defeat that they actually called for the permanent abandonment of Attica and the founding of a new polis elsewhere (Hdt. 7.143.3).

The *chrêsmologoi* would certainly have had their way, had it not been for Themistokles who argued with great ingenuity and subtlety that the 'death' referred to in the oracle was not one that would *afflict* Athens but rather one which she would *inflict* upon her enemies. He did so by pointing out that the oracle did not describe Salamis as 'hateful' or 'destructive', as logically it ought to have done if something evil were being foretold, but rather as 'divine', which suggested that a naval engagement in the straits would result in a favourable outcome. Themistokles' interpretation ultimately won the day over his professional rivals and the decision was taken to fight the Persians at sea. Those who refused to accept it barricaded themselves inside the Acropolis and were subsequently slaughtered (Hdt. 8.51.2). Herodotos (9.13.2; cf. Thuk. 1.89.3) reports that after the battle the Persian general Mardonios, before withdrawing from Attica, 'burnt Athens, and then overthrew and destroyed any wall or house or temple that was still standing'. The archaeological evidence fully bears out this picture of total devastation. One of the few survivors from the catastrophe was the venerable olive-wood statue of Athena, which, in view of the fact that it is referred to in later documents (e.g. *IG* I³ 474.1), was evidently removed for safe-keeping before the Persian descent into Attica.

Themistokles' interpretation was bold and imaginative, but entirely in keeping with the principles of oracular exegesis which required that the interpreter should make sense of the whole oracle. It was here that the *chrêsmologoi* had failed and Themistokles had succeeded. In the best scholarly tradition he had resolved an otherwise insoluble crux. Oracles invariably left much to the judgement of individuals, and the human factor, that is to say, what the recipient himself injected into Apollo's meaning, was integral to their interpretation. 'Know thyself', the famous rubric inscribed on the sanctuary wall at Delphi, warned the petitioner that without self-knowledge he or she would profit little from a consultation (cf. Plu. *On Garrulousness* 17 = *Mor.* 511ab). An oracular text, as Derrida might have put it, was not primarily a means of communication between author and recipient, but an independent object into which the recipient himself had to put whatever meaning best made sense. There was, in sum, no transcendental signified, no truth in the absolute sense, and no Apollo as author of determinate meaning. Signifier and signified, oracle and recipient, were part of the same floating discourse. Apollo was not in the business of handing out life's answers on a plate. Deconstructionists would have felt entirely at home in Delphi. Besides all this, there existed a good recent precedent for not jumping to the obvious conclusion when destruction was being forecast: king Kroisos of Lydia, having learned that he would destroy a great empire if he marched against Persia, had characteristically failed to take note of the possibility that it might be his own (Hdt. 1.53.3).

Although it was the deciphering of the oracle which displayed Themistokles' formidable intellect at its keenest and upon which the decision to fight finally depended, this was by no means the only piece of good advice which he gave in connection with the battle of Salamis. It was also he who proposed a decree recalling all Athenian exiles in order to prevent his rival Aristeides from offering his services to the barbarians (Plu. *Them.* 11.1); by a cunning trick prevented the Greek fleet from withdrawing to the Isthmus of Corinth as many of the other generals recommended the night before the battle (12); and finally, succeeded by his intimate knowledge of weather conditions in engaging the Persian fleet just at the time of day when a sea breeze arose, causing their tall ships to roll badly (14.2).

Human sacrifice

A source of unknown date informs us that just before battle commenced Themistokles was prevailed upon to sacrifice three Persian prisoners who were 'very beautiful in appearance, strikingly attired and wearing gold jewellery', said to be the sons of the Great King's sister (Phanias of Lesbos fr. 25 Wehrli[2] = Plu. *Them.* 13). This pre-battle sacrifice was allegedly conducted in honour of a god called Dionysos Omestes (Raw-eater). Though revolted by the deed, Themistokles is said to have gone along with it under intense pressure from the army and on the recommendation of a seer called Euphrantides, who claimed that this most potent form of sacrifice would bring salvation and victory to the Greeks.

The anecdote is unlikely to be historical, both because of the improbability that such important prisoners had been captured before the battle, and because of the total lack of external evidence for an Attic cult of Dionysos Omestes. It none the less paints a convincingly bleak picture of the mood of dejection in the Greek camp just before the battle took place, when not for the first time a crisis of nerve was resolved by Themistokles. Confronted with fear and despondency, he succeeded, if not by means of human sacrifice then perhaps by some other desperate remedy, in converting it into anger and blood-lust. The sudden change in mood may therefore have been remarkably similar to that experienced by the Athenian army before Marathon. The only other deity besides Dionysos Omestes who is known to have received pre-battle sacrifice is Artemis Agrotera, to whom, interestingly, the Athenians also sacrificed at Marathon (cf. Henrichs 1981, 219f.).

Powers of weather, place and time

Salamis, like Marathon, was won by the Greeks against superior odds, and its success was similarly attributed to supernatural agency. Herodotos (7.189.1) tells us that a few months earlier, while the Persian fleet was beached at Artemision in Thessaly, the Athenians 'called upon their son-in-law Boreas', who obligingly responded to their appeal by sending a northeast wind to destroy 400 of the enemy's ships, thereby narrowing the odds in favour of the Persians by a considerable margin. The storm god was known in Attica before 480, having in 492 unleashed his fury upon Dareios' fleet near Mount Athos on Chalkidike in northeast Greece (Hdt. 6.44.2-3), close to his homeland (cf. Hom. *Il.* 9.5, cf. 23.229f.; Ibykos fr. 286.9 *PMG*). It was in 480, however, that he was provided with a sanctuary in Athens beside the Ilissos River, at the spot where he was believed to have abducted Erechtheus' daughter Oreithyia and evidently in recognition of services rendered (Plate 14; Paus. 1.19.5). A lost play by Aeschylus entitled *Oreithyia* (fr. 281 *N²*) may actually have been performed at the inauguration of the cult (cf. Simon 1967, 118). The god's popularity at this date is further indicated by the fact that the myth was told in a contemporary poem of Simonides (fr. 534 *PMG*).

Both instances of Boreas' alleged intervention point up Athens' increasing preoccupation with the sea during this period. It was in 493/2 that work on the fortifications around the Piraeus began, an initiative predicated on the conviction that Athens' future lay at sea, and at Salamis twelve years later that her new navy, funded from the profits accruing from a new silver strike at Laurion, so spectacularly justified its existence. Nor should we overlook the fact that northeast Greece was becoming an area of increasing strategic importance for Athens, both as a source of timber for her fleet and as an important staging post on the route to the Black Sea region upon which her growing population was becoming increasingly dependent for grain (cf. Agard 1965, 245f.). It was hardly surprising, therefore, that the Athenians should at this time give tangible expression to their political and economic interests by honouring the god, his homeland and its people, in much the same way as they had honoured Pan a decade earlier.[3]

As at Marathon, where the tutelary gods of place played a leading part in the outcome of the battle, so at Salamis much was seen to depend upon

[3] Boreas was also in receipt of cult at Thourioi and Megalopolis, where the circumstances leading to his introduction were remarkably similar to those which prompted his entry into Athens (cf. Ail. *VH* 12.61; Paus. 8.36.6). Whether the sea-god Poseidon was also rewarded at this time is less certain. Since the earliest surviving evidence of his presence on the Acropolis is an inscribed *perirrhantêrion* or vessel for lustral water dated 460-450 (Raubitschek, *DAA*, 384), L.H. Jeffery (in Binder 1984, 21f.) has suggested that his Acropolis cult was not founded until after the battle of Salamis and that the depiction of the contest between Athena and Poseidon on the west pediment of the Parthenon in fact celebrates its inauguration (but cf. above p. 31).

the gods of the local islands. At daybreak on the day of battle an earthquake occurred which prompted the Greeks to pray to their gods and 'to call upon (*epikalesasthai*) the Aiakidai, the heroes of Salamis and Aigina, to be their allies'. To give more substance to their prayer, a ship was dispatched to the neighbouring island of Aigina to fetch the group – presumably, though this is not actually stated, in the form of their cult images. The ship made a timely reappearance, evidently with the heroes on board, just as Themistokles was giving his sailors the order to embark (Hdt. 8.64, 83.2; cf. Plu. *Them.* 15.1). How it succeeded in slipping undetected through the enemy lines is not revealed, though this feat would undoubtedly have bolstered Athenian confidence before the battle commenced, just as did the secret sacrifice performed to the heroes Periphemos and Kychreus before the Athenian attack on Salamis in the time of Solon (above p. 37). After the battle a Phoinician trireme was dedicated to the heroes' father Aias in recognition of the services which he had rendered to their cause (Hdt. 8.121.1).

Gods of time also contributed to the victory. Plutarch (*Mor.* 349f) states that Mounychion 16 was henceforth dedicated to Artemis Mounychia because 'on that day the goddess shone with a full moon upon the Greeks as they were conquering at Salamis'. As was the case at Marathon, it is not altogether clear how the full moon affected the result. Conceivably the light which it shed the night before the battle enabled the Greeks to obtain valuable information about the disposition of the Persian fleet. Plutarch claims that near panic had broken out among the Peloponnesians (*Them.* 12). Had it not been for Themistokles, who in the night dispatched his old tutor to Xerxes with the message that his master wanted to defect and urged the king to take all measures to prevent the Greek navy from escaping, the allies might well have abandoned their posts altogether. Xerxes took the bait and ordered his crews to remain at their oars on the lookout for any movement among the enemy fleet. Could it be that the moon revealed to the Greek high command the futility of attempting a withdrawal? The goddess, who already had an impressive sanctuary on the summit of Mounychia Hill overlooking Salamis, was rewarded for her patriotic support by the establishment or upgrading of the Mounychia festival, at which she was annually presented with offerings of small round cakes known as *amphiphontes* (shining on all sides). According to Plutarch the shiny appearance of the cakes symbolised the light which she provided for the Greeks. As goddess of both time and place, we may assume that Artemis' contribution to the victory was second to none.

The fact that the battle coincided with the celebration of the Eleusinian Mysteries – as indicated by the reference in the second oracle to it taking place 'either at the moment when Demeter is scattering or when she is coming together' – is evidently the reason why an Athenian called Dikaios, while crossing the Thriasian plain between Athens and Eleusis, saw a dust cloud coming from Eleusis from which there arose the Iacchos hymn as traditionally sung by celebrants in the procession, signalling that divine help was on the way (Hdt. 8.65; Plu. *Them.* 15.1). In addition, a number of soldiers claimed that they saw the image of a woman urging on the Greek fleet (Hdt. 8.84.2), while others witnessed the Salaminian hero Kychreus in the guise of a serpent (Paus. 1.36.1). Pan, too, is credited with intervention at the battle (Aes. *Pers.* 447-79, cf. S. *Ajax* 695; Sud. *s.v. haliplanktos*). Since Salamis was in a sense the naval equivalent of Marathon, and since his patron Artemis made a major contribution to the outcome of both battles, the latter's presence is entirely unsurprising.

Themistokles' genius

Later writers were fascinated by Themistokles' personality. In a remarkable homage to his intellectual prowess, Thukydides, his greatest admirer, writes (1.138.3):

> Themistokles was a man who displayed an unmistakable natural genius; in this respect he was quite exceptional, and beyond all others deserves our admiration. Without studying a subject in advance or deliberating over it later, but using simply the intelligence that was his by nature, he had the power to reach the right conclusion in matters that have to be settled on the spur of the moment and do not admit of long discussions (*di'elachistês boulês*), and in estimating what was likely to happen, his forecasts of the future were always more reliable than those of others. He could perfectly well explain any subject with which he was familiar, and even outside his own department he was still capable of giving an excellent opinion. He was particularly remarkable at looking into the future and seeing there the hidden possibilities for good or evil. To sum him up in a few words, it may be said that through force of genius and by rapidity of action this man was supreme at doing precisely the right thing at precisely the right moment. (tr. R. Warner)

A man of genius indeed – however we define the word. One of Thukydides' main points is that intellectual ability of this calibre is inborn rather than acquired. Either you have it or you don't. Others offered different explanations. His intellectual performance at the time of Salamis constituted such a brilliant demonstration of the application of creative intelligence that the only possible explanation for it, at least according to the proud possessor of that creative intelligence himself, was that he had been inspired by a divinity. We know that because shortly after the battle Themistokles established a sanctuary in honour of Artemis whom, to quote Plutarch (*Them.* 22.1), 'he called Aristoboule (Of the first-rate counsel) on the grounds that he' – notice the presumptuous use of the masculine – 'had given absolutely first-rate advice to the polis and to the Greeks.'

Plutarch does not tell us precisely what was the first-rate counsel which

Themistokles gave to the Athenians, but elsewhere in his writings he provides confirmation of the fact that it was connected with the decision to fight at Salamis (*Malig. Hdt.* 37 = *Mor.* 869 cd):

> If there are any Antipodeans, as some people allege, living beneath the earth, I imagine that not even they have failed to hear of Themistokles and of his advice (*bouleuma*). For he advised the Greeks to fight at sea before Salamis and he established (*hidrusato*) a temple to Artemis Aristoboule in the deme of Melite, when the enemy had been defeated.

The entry of this brilliant *bouleuma* into the head of Themistokles apparently belongs to that category of divine intervention which E.R. Dodds labelled monitions, a form of psychic intervention resulting in 'a departure from normal human behaviour whose causes are not immediately perceived' (1951, 13). A psychological explanation for the phenomenon was first proposed by Nilsson (1924, 374f.), who connected it with the susceptibility to sudden changes in mood experienced by the Homeric heroes, a characteristic which he identified as 'labile psychic equilibrium' (*psychische Labilität*).[4]

It is uncertain whether Artemis Aristoboule effected the entry of the *bouleuma* into Themistokles' head by enhancing his natural powers of discernment and deliberation, or by temporarily abolishing and suspending them altogether. Both explanations have merit. The experience of a monition in connection with an omen had, moreover, good Homeric authority and this circumstance may help us better to fathom its nature. In the *Odyssey* (15.172f.), while Menelaus is pondering upon the significance of a portent which has just appeared in the sky, his wife Helen anticipates him, claiming that she is going to interpret it 'as the gods put it into my heart and as I think it will be fulfilled'. I suggest that Helen's attribution of her interpretation to a fusion of native intelligence and divine inspiration neatly exemplifies how the Greeks most typically interpreted the mechanism by which an extraordinary idea takes up residence inside the human brain.[5] One thing is certain, however, if we take Themistokles at his word: he was evidently endowed with the kind of personality which is inherently susceptible to divine influences.

To sum up, Themistokles' monition, which we, with scarcely greater understanding of the cognitive process involved, might describe as a brainwave, enabled him to perceive the significance of an oracle whose

---

[4] Examples include passages which describe the transfer of energy from god to man, as, for instance, where a god is said to have 'breathed (*empneuse*) great power' into a hero (*Il.* 15.262), 'put (*thêke*) might into his heart' (21.145) or 'injected (*embale*) great strength' (21.304).

[5] Also instructive is Homer's admission of his own mental deficiency in his introduction to the so-called Catalogue of Ships (*Il.* 2.488-92): 'I could not recall nor name the people, even if I had ten tongues, ten mouths, an untiring voice and a heart of bronze, did not the Olympian Muses, the daughters of Zeus who wields the aegis, recall to my mind all those who came to Troy.'

successful decoding had thwarted even the experts. That at any rate was what Themistokles wanted the Athenians to believe and perhaps – can we disprove it? – actually did believe himself. Indeed it is just possible to argue that Themistokles' action in establishing a shrine to the source of his monition was a gesture of humility, as if he were saying 'I wasn't responsible for this oh-so-brilliant notion, a goddess was', and perhaps in public he actually *did* try to argue it that way. To outsiders, however, it looks like an expression of almost naked self-worship. This seems to be what his fellow-citizens thought, too, for Plutarch observes that Themistokles 'gave offence to the majority (*tous pollous*)' in setting up the shrine. Although we have no information concerning the organisation of the cult of Artemis Aristoboule in this period, it seems clear from this remark that it was not state-sponsored. Probably it was a hereditary priesthood reserved exclusively for members of Themistokles' own *genos*. But either the Athenians would not or they could not do anything about Themistokles' foundation and his alleged association with Artemis Aristoboule. What I mean is that either they actually did believe, some of them at any rate, that Themistokles really had had a brainwave and that this brainwave could not be explained in any other way, or else they could not prevent the establishment of the new cult because they lacked the constitutional and legal powers to do so. Or both.

The circumstances surrounding the foundation of the cult of Artemis Aristoboule were not unique. Interestingly, a remarkably similar story is narrated by Plutarch (*Arist.* 11.5-8) about a Plataian commander called Arimnestos who, on the eve of the battle of Plataiai fought against the Persians a year later, dreamt that Zeus Soter (Saviour) provided him with the correct interpretation of an oracle from Delphi relating to the forthcoming engagement. As conventionally interpreted, the oracle appeared to be urging withdrawal from Boiotia to Attica, by promising victory to the Greeks on condition that they do battle 'in the plain of the Eleusinian Goddesses'. Thanks to Zeus' revelation, however, Arimnestos was able to persuade his colleagues that the plain in question was not the famous one near Eleusis but a lesser-known one close to Plataiai itself, and in consequence of this interpretation the Greeks secured another resounding victory.

Why Artemis? Why Aristoboule?

By what deductive process did Themistokles arrive at the conclusion that his monition was due to Artemis Aristoboule? One obvious possibility is that Artemis already had a close association with his family. Pausanias (1.26.4) reports that he saw a bronze statue of Artemis Leukophryene (White-browed) on the Acropolis, which had been dedicated by the sons of Themistokles. However, the only reason which Pausanias gives for the dedication is that Leukophryene was held in honour in Magnesia in Asia

Minor where Themistokles spent his final years after being exiled from Athens. The anecdote, in other words, does nothing to establish any connection with the deity before the battle.

Another, more urgent reason why Themistokles might have identified this goddess as his source of inspiration is that Artemis Mounychia, who, as we have noted already, was worshipped on the summit of Mounychia Hill, was credited with intervention just before the naval engagement took place. Possibly Themistokles deemed it appropriate that another Artemis should have involved herself in his deliberations, just as her namesake had assisted in the execution of his plans. The existence of a close connection between Artemis Mounychia and Artemis Aristoboule is indicated by the fact that the sanctuaries of both deities have yielded examples of *kratêriskoi*, miniature mixing-bowls which are exclusive to the cult of Artemis, suggesting that their ritual practices bore a strong family resemblance (Plate 15).

There are obvious reasons, then, why Themistokles would have felt beholden to Artemis, but what made him dub her Aristoboule? Why the coupling of the goddess with this virtually unknown epithet? It may not be accidental that a close relative of Themistokles' presumed patron, a divinity who went under the title Artemis Boulaia (Counsellor), had a cult in the Agora probably in the vicinity of the Tholos where the presidents of the Council met. Perhaps it was the presumptuous echo of 'Boulaia' in the epithet 'Aristoboule' that caused such offence to the majority. Many Athenians must have felt that Themistokles was trying to upstage the state's own goddess, by appropriating for his own personal use her brighter and more dynamic counterpart. It may have seemed that he wanted to intimate that his own counsel was more effective than the collective wisdom of the Demos, the Boule, or even the Areopagus. In the light of recent events, such a suggestion might have seemed too true for comfort. Incidentally, a late inscription relating to the repair of sacred buildings in the Piraeus contains a reference to '(the shrine of) ... -*kanes* which Themistokles set up before the battle of Salamis' (*IG* II² 1035.45; cf. Paus. 1.36.1). Culley's (1973, 154) plausible restoration of '*Athenas* (or *Artemidos*) *Herkanês* (Of the fenced enclosure)' should perhaps be taken as an allusion to the oracle of the wooden wall. If this is correct, there must also have existed 'a cult of the intellect' in the Piraeus parallel to that in the Asty and perhaps established at the same time. And if so, no wonder the Athenians were fed up to the back teeth with their divinely inspired counsellor.

The sanctuary of Artemis Aristoboule in Melite

Plutarch (*Them*. 22.1-2) tells us that Themistokles set up a shrine to Artemis Aristoboule 'near his own house', and that it contained a small statue or portrait (*eikonion*) of the politician 'which suggested that he not

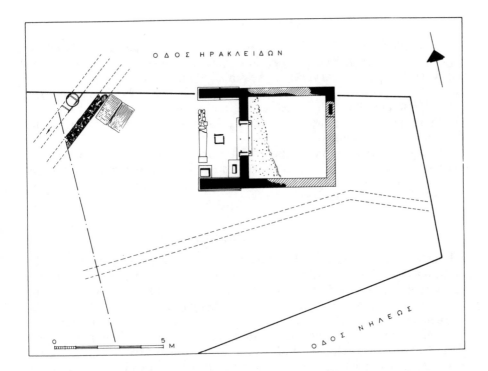

Fig. 9. Plan of the shrine of Artemis Aristoboule in Melite. From J. Travlos, *PDA*.

only possessed a heroic soul but that he also was a hero in outward appearance'. The worship of this deity continued, though not without interruption, into the second century AD. The biographer concludes by stating, not perhaps without a pinch of sarcasm, that the shrine 'is now where the public officials chuck out the bodies of those who have been executed, along with the clothing and nooses of those who have been hanged.'

Remains which came to light in 1964 just west of modern Theseion Square in central Athens in the ancient deme of Melite almost certainly belong to the shrine which Themistokles, who was himself a Melitean, founded (Fig. 9 & Plate 17). The building, which is a mere 3.6m square with a porch 1.85m in depth, is one of the most modest sanctuaries so far discovered in Athens. Its construction has been dated from a group of black-figure *kratêriskoi* to the period immediately following the Persian Wars. Soon after completion the sanctuary was abandoned and fell into ruin, evidently as a result of Themistokles' fall from grace and exile in *c.* 471/0. This was not the end of the story, however. In *c.* 395, when the Athenians rebuilt the fortifications around the Piraeus which they had been forced to pull down at the end of the Peloponnesian War and once again committed themselves to a naval role, Themistokles' reputation underwent rehabilitation and this is reflected in the refurbishment of

Aristoboule's sanctuary. A fragmentary inscription dated *c.* 330, which was set up by the demesmen of Melite, praises a certain Neoptolemos son of Antikles for his services to Artemis 'when Chairylle was priestess' (*SEG* XXII.116.5). It was surely Neoptolemos who paid for the refurbishment. The cult, which was administered by the deme, may have been revived in part to promote the interests of Melite through the vehicle of its most famous son.

Archaeological evidence supports Plutarch's testimony that the temple remained in use until Roman times. The fact that it housed a portrait of Themistokles may indicate that it came to serve as his hero-shrine as well (cf. Wycherley, *Stones*, 192).

Themistokles and religion

What kind of a man introduces a new goddess in order to celebrate the luminosity of his own mind – or, as we should perhaps more accurately phrase it, in order to immortalise the fact that he has been chosen as the inspired vehicle of the divine afflatus? Wholly removed as we are from the Greek experience of the divine, we may suspect the worst. Since we ourselves have no difficulty in 'seeing through' Greek religion, we expect an astute politician like Themistokles to be no less quick off the mark and to exploit it accordingly. Is that opinion justified? In my view, it is not. Given the way in which divinity impacted upon human affairs in the Greek world, no cynical manipulator of religion, least of all one who was living at the time of the Persian Wars, could have survived in politics for long.

There is, moreover, good evidence to suggest that Themistokles took an active interest in religion in contexts where his own political advantage may not have been the predominant factor in his calculations. For instance, he paid out of his own pocket for the rebuilding of the Telesterion at Phlya in northeast Attica which had been destroyed during Xerxes' invasion (Plu. *Them.* 1.3). His interest in the sanctuary was perhaps due primarily to the fact that his own *genos*, the Lykomidai, administered it (cf. Deubner, *AF*, 69-70; Toepffer, *AG*, 209). Some years later during his exile the Persian satrap of Upper Phrygia hired some Pisidians to assassinate him at a place called Leontokephalaion or Lion's Head in Magnesia (*Them.* 30). Shortly before Themistokles' arrival at the village, however, the Mother of the Gods appeared in a dream and warned him as follows: 'Themistokles, keep away from the Lion's Head, lest you encounter a lion. In return for this favour, I ask that you give me your daughter Mnesiptolema as my handmaid.' Themistokles escaped with his life and in gratitude to the goddess duly erected a temple to the Dindymian Mother of the Gods. Given the nature of his personality, it is difficult to believe that his gratitude was anything but heartfelt and sincere.

According to Plutarch the cult of Artemis Aristoboule is merely one of a number of instances of the harnessing of religion by Themistokles in connection with the battle of Salamis. He tells us (*Them*. 10.1):

> Themistokles, despairing of persuading the multitude by human reason, brought before them daimonic signs (*sêmeia daimonia*) and oracles, like someone setting up a machine (i.e. for a *deus ex machina*) in a tragedy.

As an example of these 'daimonic signs' Plutarch cites Themistokles' assertion that 'the goddess Athena had abandoned the Acropolis and was leading her people to the sea'. He demonstrated this by the fact that the sacred snake, which lived on the Acropolis in the temple of Athena Polias, had refused to eat any food (see above p. 22). The comparison between the politician and a playwright who devises a way of providing an otherwise insoluble plot with a somewhat botched ending does at first sight suggest the manipulation of religious sentiment for political ends. But is that what Plutarch intends? Elsewhere he states (*Numa* 4.8):

> There is nothing absurd in the ... account which is given of Lykourgos, Numa and their like, namely that since they were handling multitudes that were hard to control and hard to please, and introducing sweeping innovations into their constitutions, they claimed (*prosepoiêsanto*) to have a reputation for divine aid, to the salvation (*sôtêrion*) of those very people before whom they assumed the posture (*eschêmatizonto*).

Here as in the previous passage Plutarch's words are ambiguous. It is not clear whether he is using the verbs '*prosepoiêsanto*' and '*eschêmatizonto*' in a pejorative or merely neutral sense. The tenor of his remark, however, particularly his use of the noun '*sôtêrion*', which carries strong religious overtones, rather suggests that he endorses such behaviour. Plutarch wrote a number of essays about Delphic antiquities, including *On the Decline of Oracles* and *On the Delphic E*. Had he wished to be critical of Themistokles' use of oracles, he had plenty of opportunity to do so. In sum, Themistokles' action most appropriately belongs under that nicely nuanced category of 'pious fraud'.

It is evident, moreover, that Plutarch greatly admired Themistokles for his courage, resourcefulness and intelligence (cf. especially *Them*. 3.2, 4.1 and 11.1). Although he repeatedly insists upon the politician's excessive ambition and arrogance (cf. 3.1, 5.2 and 18.1) and indicates that the building of the shrine to Artemis Aristoboule was a major reason for his fall from power, he does not instance this action as an example of that ambition nor does he suggest that this was one of the devices by which Themistokles aimed at self-aggrandisement. What is perhaps more to the point is that in his essay entitled *The Malice of Herodotos* Plutarch cites Herodotos' treatment of Themistokles as a specific example of the way in which the latter falsified facts, in this case by downplaying the great man's achievements and crediting him with deceitfulness and trickery (37 = *Mor*. 869c-f). Given his own devotion to the gods, it is extremely unlikely that Plutarch would have hastened to Themistokles' defence if he had suspected him of manipulating religion purely for his own advantage.

More significantly, because his testimony is much closer to the events which he describes, Herodotos never suggests that Themistokles' attitude towards the gods was in any way improper. The historian was in Athens at a time when the factional feuding which led to his exile was still rife, and the hostility which his name aroused in the 460s is very much evident in his repeated insistence upon Themistokles' mercenary outlook (cf. Starr 1962, 323). As we have seen, however, not even in his account of the double consultation at Delphi does Herodotos suggest that Themistokles was acting irregularly. For what it is worth, his final picture of Themistokles shows the latter awarding credit for the victory to the gods and heroes who, in his own words, 'were envious at the prospect of Asia and Europe having a single king, and in particular one who was impious and wicked' (8.109.3).

Conclusions

Themistokles had been arguing for ten years that Athens' strength lay at sea. The current crisis provided him with a heaven-sent opportunity to prove it. He had every reason to be properly deferential to the mysterious forces which activated his brain cells, not least because the opportunity to realise his vision had time and again nearly slipped through his fingers. The Athenian Demos very nearly didn't build a fleet with the money from the silver mines at Laurion. Weeks before the battle it very nearly decided not to face the Persians at sea. On the night before the battle the Greek fleet very nearly abandoned Athens altogether by withdrawing south to the Isthmus of Corinth. Minutes before the order to engage was given it may have experienced yet another crisis of nerve. Alone of all the Greek commanders it was Themistokles 'who worked from the unquestioning assumption of a Greek victory' (Green 1970, 164). In sum, few victories in the history of human conflict have depended more upon the intelligence and resolve of one man.

The part played by the gods in surviving accounts of the Persian Wars affords a valuable insight into how Athenians explained their deliverance from foreign oppression. To what extent these accounts tallied with the truth is not my chief concern, though there can be little doubt that what has been preserved is 'a drastic simplification of the intricacies of a complicated situation so as to create an easily remembered story' (Starr 1962, 321). No matter. The point is this. We cannot hope to understand how the Athenians won unless we give proper attention to how they *thought* they won. How many Athenians would have attempted to explain the Persian rout other than with reference to the power and goodwill of the gods?

Even so, divine intervention alone was only a part of it. The gods help those who help themselves. Herodotos surely got the formula right when he wrote (7.139.5):

> It was the Athenians second to the gods (*meta ge theous*) who were responsible for rousing the Greeks who had not yet gone over to the Persian side and for repelling the Great King. Not even the terrifying oracles from Delphi could persuade them to abandon Greece, but they stood firm and resisted the invader when he came against them.

Intervention is not the same as interference. 'I have come from heaven to stay your anger, *if perchance you will obey me*,' says Athena to Achilles at the beginning of the *Iliad* (1.207f.), when the latter is about to plunge his sword into Agamemnon's liver. In other words, only if Achilles is the kind of person who is capable of taking advice will he respond to a goddess's appeal. Similarly, Themistokles would not have had his 'brainwave' if he did he not possess the kind of brain cells which are capable of lateral thinking. On the eve of the battle of Salamis Homer's vision of divine intervention is still intact. Thukydides and Periklean rationalism are apparently light years away.

4

Theseus' Old Bones

In August 479 near the town of Plataiai on the northern Attic border the Greek alliance delivered the *coup de grâce* to the Persian invasion force, thereby finally laying to rest the threat of foreign domination. According to Plutarch (*Arist.* 21) the alliance now formulated a policy intended to guarantee the continuation of concerted military action against the Persians. A communal cult of Zeus Eleutherios or Liberation was established with a quadrennial festival known as the Eleutheria, its management placed in the hands of the Plataians who, in return for the gift of sacrosanctity, were obliged henceforth to sacrifice to the god 'on behalf of all Greece'. Tradition records that on the very same day that the battle was fought the allies went on to the offensive and secured a naval victory in Persian waters off the west coast of Karia near Cape Mykale.

Kimon and the oracle

This moment of unprecedented Greek unity was not destined to endure long. Just two years later Athens withdrew from the alliance as a gesture of protest against Sparta's lacklustre performance as its leader and became the head of a newly constituted confederacy of Ionian states. The Delian Confederacy, so-called from the fact that its administration was centred upon a shrine of all Ionians on the island of Delos, was committed to the task of fighting the Persians 'until iron should float' (Hdt. 1.165.3; cf. [Arist.] *AP* 23.5). Its first military success under the Athenian general Kimon was the capture of a Persian fort at Eion on the River Strymon in northeast Greece in 476/5.

Later the same year according to the narrative provided by Plutarch (*Thes.* 36; cf. *Kim.* 8.6),[1] the Athenians received instructions from Apollo

[1] Podlecki (1975, 141f.), who points out that Plutarch provides only the date of the oracle and not that of its implementation, is in favour of lowering the date of the capture of the island and transfer of the bones towards 470, on the grounds that Kimon's 'triumphal enshrinement of the national hero then gains added point as one of the last attacks against the popularity of Themistokles' (see further p. 87). Cf. also J.D. Smart, *JHS* 87 (1967) 136f., who dates the return of the bones to 469/8. As Barron (1972, 20 n. 4; cf. 21 n. 7) points out with reference to Thuk. 1.98.1-2, however, it is 'hard to suppose that a newly founded

'to recover the bones of Theseus and, after giving them honourable burial, to watch over them (*entimôs par'hautois phulattein*)'. The bones in question were said to be languishing on Skyros, the largest island in the northern Sporades, where Theseus had sought refuge at the end of his life after being driven out of Athens by the pretender Menestheus. The hero had gone there hoping to win the support of Lykomedes, its local king, but while standing beside a steep precipice had slipped and fallen to his death or, according to another version, was deliberately pushed over by his host, who hoped by this crime to win the favour of Menestheus.

The task of recovering Theseus' bones represented a considerable challenge, since the occupants of the island, a piratical people known as the Dolopians, were famous for their 'unsociability and savagery'. Not long beforehand they had robbed some Thessalian merchants and thrown them into prison. The merchants managed to escape, however, and successfully pleaded the case for the return of their confiscated goods before the Amphiktyonic Council, which had charge of Delphic affairs. It is reported that Kimon's military expedition was actually launched at the invitation of the robbers themselves, after they had failed to persuade the rest of the Dolopians to return the plunder (*Kim.* 8.3-4). The Athenians succeeded in capturing the island, expelled the Dolopians, and then populated it with settlers of their own, as a result of which action the Aegean henceforth 'became free' (*Kim.* 8.5).

The oracle had not divulged the location of the burial spot, but Kimon, being 'ambitious (*philotimoumenos*)' to discover the grave, was assisted in his archaeological endeavours by an obliging eagle 'which pecked and tore with its talons at a place resembling a burial mound'. Thanks to what is described as a divine monition (*theiai tini tuchêi sumphronêsas*), somewhat similar perhaps to the one granted to Themistokles by Artemis Aristoboule, Kimon realised that this must be the tomb of Theseus. Accordingly he began excavating and immediately discovered 'the remains of a man of exceptional height, with a bronze spear and a sword lying alongside'. The size of the bones would have provided confirmation of the fact that their possessor had been a man of outstanding physical strength and was a hero. On returning to Athens with the precious remains on board, he received a rapturous reception from his countrymen, who laid on lavish processions and sacrifices 'as though Theseus himself were returning to the city'.

Incidentally, it is not recorded whether the Dolopians fought to retain possession of the bones. Very likely their potency had been overlooked by their erstwhile custodians. What Kimon actually dug up is, of course, anyone's guess. It has even been suggested that it may have been the bones of some prehistoric animal. It is perhaps significant, however, that Skyros had once been an important and wealthy Mycenaean outpost,

---

military alliance could have remained inactive for almost a decade'.

which, due to its remoteness, had been left relatively unscathed when
that civilisation finally collapsed. Judging from the large quantity of gold,
jewellery, weapons and armour which came to light in the last century
largely as a result of illegal excavations, the island must have contained a
number of rich Mycenaean tombs and quite possibly Kimon simply
plundered one of these. The expulsion of the Dolopians from Skyros
provided the Athenians with an ideal opportunity to establish a public
cult in Theseus' honour, since Greek hero worship operated from the
premiss that a hero's physical remains were invested with a supernatural
power which could be activated most effectively through blood-sacrifice
conducted at the grave.

The transfer of a hero through exhumation and re-burial was by no
means unprecedented in the Greek world. Some eighty years previously
the Spartans had retrieved the bones of Orestes from Tegea in Arkadia
(Hdt. 1.67-68), following this achievement up a few years later with the
removal of the bones of Orestes' son Tisamenos from Helike in Achaia
(Paus. 7.1.8). Herodotos, who provides a highly detailed account of the
former episode, concludes it with the statement (1.68.6), 'Henceforth,
whenever Sparta and Tegea went to war, Sparta invariably got the upper
hand.' It seems highly probable, therefore, that both these actions were
connected with the expansionist policy which Sparta was then pursuing,
the aim of which was to achieve domination over the whole Peloponnese.
The return of Theseus' bones served a somewhat similar aim, for it
demonstrated that the Athenians had now acquired the capability to
retrieve their national hero from a region which had previously been
inaccessible to them. It is hardly an exaggeration to state that Theseus'
repatriation thus served as a metaphor for his countrymen's recently
acquired naval supremacy, since Athens was now posing as the leader of
a maritime alliance.[2]

Why, we may ask, was Kimon ambitious to discover Theseus' grave?
Plutarch does not tell us, and as usual in Greek history when it comes to
trying to establish a basis for the affective link between sponsor and
petitioning deity we are left to forge that link for ourselves. Quite aside
from the obvious prestige which he would have earned from this
spectacular feat of daring *per se*, Kimon had a personal interest in
Theseus' welfare. The fact that Kimon was the son of Miltiades, that
Miltiades was the architect of the victory at Marathon, and that a
phasma of Theseus joined ranks with the Athenians in the battle can

---

[2] The use of archaeology to foster a new form of national identity and self-awareness is, of
course, a familiar concept in the modern world. Notable examples include the
commemoration of the heroic defence of Masada in the Jewish Revolt against the Romans in
AD 70-73, which was brought to popular consciousness by the excavations conducted at the
site by Yigael Yadin in the 1960s; and the celebration under the Shah of Iran of the 2,500th
anniversary of the foundation of Persia by Cyrus the Great, the splendour of whose reign
was revealed by the excavation of Persepolis. On both, see Lewis (1975, 4-9).

hardly be a coincidence. Quite apart from all this, Kimon was at this moment in dire need of a strategy for reminding his countrymen of the debt which they owed to his father. Barely one year after the battle of Marathon Miltiades had been prosecuted by the Demos for launching an unsuccessful attack on the island of Paros, and he had died in disgrace soon afterwards. Without denying Kimon any loftier motives, the promotion of the cult of Theseus was thus a way of polishing up the family's tarnished image, a necessary pre-condition to Kimon's own political rise. Its effective value as a propaganda ploy is proven by Plutarch's claim (*Kim.* 8.6) that the recovery of Theseus' bones was the chief reason why the Demos felt well-disposed towards Kimon, and by the frequency with which he held the elective office of generalship over the next few years. Kimon may even have wished to be identified in the public eye as a second Theseus (cf. Barron 1980, 2). The similarity between hero and general would indeed have been striking. Just as Theseus had rid the roads leading to Attica of monsters and bandits, so his spiritual heir now drove out the lawless elements from a sea which Athens was poised to convert into her backyard.

Kimon's championship of Theseus may also have been intended in part as a response to Themistokles' promotion of the cult of Artemis Aristoboule (cf. Metzler 1966, 10; Podlecki 1971, 142f.). There is other evidence to suggest that Kimon mobilised religion to combat his rival's political influence. It is possible, for instance, that he undertook the restoration of the sanctuary of the Two Goddesses at Eleusis after its destruction by the Persians as a way of counteracting the prestige which Themistokles had earned by restoring the Telesterion at Phlya (above p. 78). If the desire to upstage Themistokles constituted some part of the motive behind Kimon's action, he certainly succeeded. Two years after the battle of Salamis Themistokles' influence was already beginning to wane. By 470, the probable year of his ostracism, it had been eclipsed. One of the consequences of this political re-alignment was that it would be the hoplite battle at Marathon, and not the naval one at Salamis, which Athenians would look back on as their supreme victory over the barbarian (cf. Vidal-Naquet 1967, 296). Not until the outbreak of the Peloponnesian War forty years later did Salamis once again assume in the popular imagination the status of one of Athens' foremost victories (cf. Thuk. 1.73.2).

In sum, the recovery of Theseus' bones was a carefully orchestrated drama which owed something to private and national interest, whatever it owed to instinctive piety. Not only did the action have major implications for the future direction of Athenian policy, but it also served as a theatrical yet highly effective bid for political consensus at a period in Athenian history when faction was rife.

The life of Theseus

Our knowledge of the life of Theseus derives principally from Plutarch's biography, supplemented by references in such writers as Thukydides, Apollodoros and Diodorus Siculus, and by representations in Greek art. Plutarch's account is itself a compilation of numerous different testimonies culled chiefly from the Atthidographers, notably Hellanikos, Kleidemos, Philochoros and Demon. Since Plutarch frequently alludes to more than one version of the same story, it is clear that even among the Atthidographers disagreement abounded as to the precise 'facts' of the hero's life.

Although we do not know exactly when the various episodes recounted by Plutarch were grafted into the chronological sequence of events which he has handed down to us in the form of a pseudo-historical biography, it is abundantly clear that some incidents were invented in direct response to the experience of the Persian War period, that others originated in Athens' distant or more recent past, and that a further element may not have made its appearance until the late-fifth or even the fourth century. What is vital to appreciate at the beginning of this inquiry is that Theseus' original claims to Athenian citizenship were dubious at best, since his birthplace was Troizen on the Saronic Gulf. The hero's killing of beasts and brigands who waylaid travellers on the road from Troizen to Attica, a subject which becomes popular in art after *c.* 510, may reflect the desire to strengthen his claims to Athenian citizenship (Boardman 1972, 58). Before *c.* 510, however, he was a figure of very minor importance in Attica as compared with his great rival Herakles, on whose life his own deeds and career were deliberately and self-consciously modelled.[3]

In order to comprehend something of the excitement generated by the prospect of his return in *c.* 476/5, our task here must be to identify those parts of Theseus' biography which had been fabricated by 480 at the latest, under the reasonable assumption that the arrival of his bones coincided with the moment when a number of vital threads belonging to the saga had already been woven into a telling and effective skein. For the warmth of his welcome surely testifies to the extent to which myths linking the hero to Athens had been successfully disseminated in the course of just a single generation.

Theseus' most celebrated heroic exploit, the slaying of the Cretan Minotaur, which incidentally is the only episode in his life commonly represented in Athenian art before *c.* 510, has roots which extend back to the earliest substratum of Greek mythology in the Late Bronze Age (Plate 16). The hero's rape of the under-age Helen and the daughters of the

---

[3] Plu. *Thes.* 6.7: 'Theseus admired the prowess of Herakles, dreaming at night of his heroic deeds and being roused and stirred by day with the intention of doing likewise.' Cf. 25.4 (Theseus institutes the Isthmian Games 'in emulation of Herakles') and 29.3 (the expression 'This is another Herakles!' is applied to him).

outlaws Kerkyon and Sinis, and his attempted rape of Persephone, are also likely to be very ancient. Embarrassing though these sexual escapades must have been for those who were seeking to endow their patron with all the finest characteristics of Athenian national life, they were evidently too well-known to be expunged from the record. So the best that could be done in the circumstances was to minimise their offensiveness by providing them with a spurious legitimacy (e.g. Plu. *Thes.* 26.1, 31.1; see below). It is already possible to detect evidence of a less than condemnatory attitude towards the hero's sexual misconduct in a marble sculpture dated *c.* 500-490 which depicts Theseus' abduction of the Amazon Antiope. The work, a fragment from the pediment of the temple of Apollo Daphnephoros at Eretria on Euboia which commemorated a victory of the Athenians and Eretrians over the Boiotians and Chalkidians, may have been executed by an Attic artist (Hdt. 5.77.1-2). It is striking that Theseus' heavily tarnished reputation as a serial sex offender apparently in no way diminished the ardour of his welcome in Athens.

To judge from his immense popularity on Attic vases from the last quarter of the sixth century onwards, it was in this period that Theseus began to be identified as the epitome of an emergent and self-conscious Athenian nationalism, as a result of which he acquired an actuality as a mythical figure which far outshone that of the illustrious but much more shadowy Attic kings Kekrops and Erechtheus. A critical gap in the record is whether it was in the time of Peisistratos or Kleisthenes that Theseus was first portrayed as the author of the synoecism. In our present state of knowledge all that can be safely inferred is that there are grounds for arguing in favour of both periods, since both leaders had good reason to wish to identify themselves with a hero who was credited with such a visionary achievement.

Theseus' celebrated rout of the Amazons is likely to have been modelled upon the Persian invasion of Attica of 480/79. There was, after all, an obvious analogy. Just as the rape of their queen Antiope brought the Amazons to Attica, so Athens' participation in the Ionian revolt brought the barbarians to Attica (cf. Boardman 1982, 8 and 14). Later the story appears to have been re-worked to accommodate Theseus' more statesmanlike image. Plutarch (*Thes.* 26.1-2) informs us that various authorities including Philochoros (*FGrH* 328 F110) reported that Antiope was not actually abducted by Theseus, as the majority of writers claimed, but presented to him as a 'reward', though Plutarch himself was rightly sceptical of this patriotic attempt to whitewash the national hero.

It is conceivable that the version of Theseus' death at the hands of Lykomedes was inserted into the Theseus saga around the time of the return of his bones as an item of contemporary political propaganda. Since Themistokles was a member of the Lykomed *genos*, of which Lykomedes was himself the founder, the point of the story may have been to suggest that Themistokles' own loyalty to Athens was less than dependable (Plu. *Them.* 1.3; cf. Connor 1970, 162). Plutarch's form of words (*Kim.* 8.5) – 'Kimon learned that ancient Theseus, son of Aigeus and an exile from Athens, fled to Skyros where he was murdered by Lykomedes' – suggests that this version of his death may not have been common knowledge. Possibly the ancedote may have been invented at this time further to justify the naval assault on Skyros.

The image of Theseus as a proto-democrat does not demonstrably predate the final quarter of the fifth century, although its origins may well be earlier. His ambivalent characterisation in Euripides' *Suppliants* (produced in *c.* 420) as a monarch who magnanimously conferred upon his people the right to vote but retained unrivalled authority over their decisions heralds the beginnings of this trend (ll. 349-53):

> I desire the whole polis to approve this decision. Since I wish it, it will approve it. By putting forward my reasons, however, I shall meet with a more favourable response from the Demos. For I made the Demos sole monarch when I set free the polis and gave equal votes to all.

A similar picture of Theseus as an enlightened monarch is found in Sophokles' *Oedipus at Kolonos* (produced in 401), where the Athenian snorts derisively at Kreon (ll. 406-8):

> Did you suppose that my polis is enslaved or bereft of men and that I am as of nothing?

The implication to be drawn from both these plays is that Theseus invested his subjects with a limited degree of popular power, while maintaining overall control of the political process through force of his charismatic personality. The much bolder assertion that Theseus actually introduced democracy by abolishing the monarchy may be an invention of the Atthidographer Androtion in the mid-fourth century (cf. Ruschenbusch 1958, 408-15).

It should be abundantly clear from this discussion that in shaping the hero's career glaring contradictions in chronology were not an inhibiting factor. Or rather the overriding point is that in what was still essentially an oral culture such contradictions could be easily overidden by more immediate, political considerations. Can we believe that the Athenians of the Classical period were really taken in by such a heady confection? Without doubt, the answer has to be in the affirmative. As Pausanias (1.3.3) pointed out, it was hardly plausible that Theseus' descendants would have managed to retain the throne for four generations after the death of Menestheus if their father had been the founder of Athenian democracy. And yet the implausibility was accepted. Pausanias' explanation for the credulousness that surrounded the myth of Theseus ran as follows: 'Lots of people tell lies because they're ignorant of history and put their faith in stories which they heard in their infancy and in choruses and tragedies.' Thukydides, we automatically assume, would have agreed.

Or would he? While Thukydides, as we shall presently see, set about exposing the fraud which lay behind the nationalistic myth of the Tyrannicides Harmodios and Aristogeiton, he never questioned the historicity of Theseus nor tried to undermine his legendary achievements. I strongly suspect that the reason why Theseus could not be unmasked even by the hypercritical Thukydides was because his biography, even more than that of the Tyrannicides, was the creation of what Veyne has called 'a sincere forger' (1988, 103). In other words, the saga of Theseus was integral to Athenian national identity, in a way that the claims made about the Tyrannicides were not to the same degree.[4] It hardly matters who actually perpetrated the forgery because we are dealing with a cultural production in the exact sense of the term; that is to say, with one in which the entire citizen body connived. After all, as a noted historian has observed, getting its history wrong is part of being a nation.

Theseus' rise to prominence

The recommendation from the Delphic oracle that Athens should recover the bones of Theseus did not, of course, come out of the blue. As mentioned already, Theseus' popularity from the last quarter of the sixth century onwards is indicated by a profusion of vase-paintings depicting various episodes in the Theseus saga. Possibly as well the composition of an epic poem known as the *Theseïs* dates to this period, testifying further to his pre-eminence. Our knowledge of it is slight, however, and it has even been suggested that it may have been merely a serio-comic version of the hero's pranks (Arist. *Poet.* 1451a 19-21; cf. *IEG* II, p. 61). The fact that by the end of the sixth century the hero had come to be regarded as the property of the entire citizen body was perhaps the main reason why he was not selected as one of the eponymous heroes of the ten newly formed Kleisthenic tribes.[5] Theseus' national standing was surely too high to permit him to be appropriated by any fraction of the Demos. Logic, too, demanded that the hero who was responsible for the unification of Attica should not personify one of its sub-divisions.

A hero's status in myth is one thing; his importance in cult quite another. Whatever form the worship of Theseus had assumed in the sixth century (see below), it was his appearance on the battlefield of Marathon which chiefly alerted the nation's conscience to his claim for public

[4] An oral tradition, which is preserved in Ar. *Lys.* 1150-6, acknowledges the debt which the Athenians owed to the Spartans in expelling the tyrant Hippias.

[5] Theseus' family, by contrast, is strongly represented among the eponymous heroes, in the person of his father Aigeus and his son Akamas.

devotion. Clearly it was very much in the interests of an aspirant to the title of national hero to be seen to be putting a safe distance between himself and the Peisistratid tyranny which in the person of the aged Hippias was seeking re-instatement from a Persian victory, particularly if that aspirant had once enjoyed Peisistratid support. Not long after Marathon appear some of the earliest surviving sculptural representations of the deeds of Theseus, executed on the metopes of the treasury which the Athenians erected at Delphi (Paus. 10.11.5; Plates 19-21). It is noteworthy not only that his deeds are accorded equal prominence to those of Herakles, but also that in one metope he is actually granted the distinction of a personal audience with Athena, a privilege which had previously been reserved exclusively for Herakles (cf. Boardman 1982, 5).

One of the most important factors in Theseus' rise in the 470s was the powerful backing of the sea-god Poseidon who shortly after the beginning of the fifth century began to challenge Aigeus, the Attic king, for the honour of being the hero's father. The earliest allusion to this version of Theseus' paternity occurs in a hymn to Apollo which was composed in *c.* 484-470 by Bacchylides of Keos (*Dith.* 17, Maehler *T*). Its subject is Theseus' descent to the depths of the sea in defence of his claim to be the son of Poseidon. Bacchylides relates how Minos sailed to Athens to select his own victims for the Minotaur and on the way back made advances to one of the Athenian girls. Incensed by the king's behaviour, Theseus proclaimed that he, too, could boast of a god for his father. In response, Minos called upon Zeus to send a flash of lightning to prove that he was Zeus' son. This the god duly did. The king then hurled his gold ring into the sea and challenged Theseus to dive in and rescue it in order to prove that he was the son of Poseidon. The hymn continues (ll. 90-132):

> The swift-prowed ship sped on. Blowing a gale from the stern, Boreas urged it onwards. The band of young Athenians trembled when the hero leapt into the waves and tears poured from their gentle eyes in anticipation of a grim conclusion.
>
> But dolphins who inhabited the sea were swiftly bearing great Theseus to the palace of his father Hippios (an epithet of Poseidon as lord of steeds). He reached the abode of gods and there beheld with awe the daughters of blessed Nereus. A radiance as of fire gleamed (*lampe*) from their beautiful limbs and fillets of woven gold were entwined in their hair. With dainty feet they rejoiced in the dance.
>
> He saw his father's beloved wife, august, ox-eyed Amphitrite in her lovely abode. She threw around his shoulders a purple mantle (?) and upon his curly hair she laid a magnificent diadem dark with roses, which crafty Aphrodite had once given her as a wedding gift. Nothing which the gods (*daimones*) will is beyond the belief of mortal men possessed of sense.
>
> He then appeared before them at the ship's narrow stern. Alas, how he disappointed the Knossian king's dark imaginings when, undrenched, he emerged from the deep, a wonder to all. The divine gifts gleamed (*lampe*) upon his limbs. The maidens seated on the bench raised a joyful shout, with

newborn courage the sea resounded, and the youths sung a paean with lovely voice. God of Delos, may your heart be cheered by the Kean chorus and may you grant that good fortune be dispatched to us from the gods.

The theme of Theseus at the court of Poseidon and Amphitrite becomes popular in Attic red-figured pottery from *c*. 500 onwards (Plate 22). The existence of close links between Theseus and Poseidon is further demonstrated by the fact that they both received honours on the eighth day of every month. Theseus is also credited with founding the Isthmian Games, which were celebrated in his father's honour (Plu. *Thes.* 25.4). The intimacy of their relationship is undoubtedly a reflection in part of their shared interest in the fortunes of Athens' navy. Just as the return of Theseus' bones laid the foundations for Athens' claims to sovereignty over the Aegean, so the goodwill of Poseidon was destined to underpin its subsequent successes.

Theseus as a religious innovator

The fabrication of the Theseus saga enabled a number of important incidents from Athens' mythical past to be fused into an organic unity around the person of the hero, whose exploits later furnished the *aition* for the introduction of numerous cults and festivals connected with his deeds of heroism. To list a few examples, the altar of Zeus Meilichios beside the Kephissos River was most famously remembered in legend because it was here that Theseus purified himself after killing a number of brigands, one of whom, Sinis, was his kinsman (Paus. 1.37.4). The Hekalesia festival, in honour of Zeus Hekalos, originated from a vow which an old woman named Hekale made to that god for his safe return before he went to do battle with the Marathonian bull (Plu. *Thes.* 14.2). The Kybernesia festival commemorated Nausithoös and Phaiax (17.6), the helmsmen who steered his ship to Crete. The cult of Aphrodite Epitragia was instituted in honour of the goddess who acted as his guide on the Cretan venture (18.2), while the Oschophoria and Pyanepsia festivals celebrated its successful accomplishment (23.2-3, 22.4). Finally, the Panathenaia and Synoikia festivals celebrated the synoecism (Plu. *Thes.* 24.3-4, cf. Paus. 8.2.1; Thuk. 2.15.2), as, too, did the cults of Aphrodite Pandemos (Common) and Peitho (Persuasion), the latter being aspects of the co-operative and democratic ethic upon which the polis was founded (Paus. 1.22.3). Paradoxically, Theseus was also the unwitting agent of religious innovation initiated by others in response to his own misdeeds, as in the case of the Anakes, the twins Kastor and Pollux, whose worship was introduced into Athens by the usurper Menestheus in order to appease their anger following Theseus' abduction of their sister Helen (Plu. *Thes.* 32-3).

One of the most intriguing aspects of Theseus' impact upon Athenian religion is his championship of the cult of Herakles. In Euripides' play *The Madness of Herakles* (ll. 1325-33), produced in *c.* 417, Theseus cordially invites Herakles to settle in Athens and issues the following solemn promise:

> I will give you a home and a portion of my wealth. All the gifts I have from the people of Athens by virtue of the fact that I saved fourteen youths by slaying the bull of Knossos, I give to you. Everywhere throughout the land consecrated precincts or *temenê* have been apportioned to me. These, so long as you live, shall be named after you. When you die and go to Hades, all Athens will grant you honour with sacrifices and monuments of stone.

The *aition*, despite its inherent improbability, appears to have commanded general assent. According to Philochoros (*FGrH* 328 F18 in Plu. *Thes.* 35.2) Theseus made this offer to Herakles for having secured his release from prison where he had been thrown after attempting to rape Aïdoneus' daughter (Plate 18). In gratitude, he

> consecrated (*kathierôse*) to Herakles all the *temenê* which the polis had previously allocated to himself, and called them 'Herakleia' instead of 'Theseia', with just four exceptions.

The *aition* was presumably invented, perhaps not much earlier than the date of Euripides' play, as a way of explaining one of the most puzzling cruxes in all Athenian religion, namely why there was such an abundance of shrines dedicated to Dorian Herakles in Attica, compared with only four to 'Athenian' Theseus. If it contains any truth at all, it is best interpreted as an inversion of historical reality. When Theseus was rising to prominence in the second half of the sixth century, it is not inconceivable that the priesthood of Herakles agreed to provide him with temporary accommodation in a few of the many sanctuaries which their own hero already possessed. As happened on other occasions, however, the new entrant eventually came to overshadow and perhaps in some cases even to oust his rival. So the myth kept alive some memory of the original pact.

The rise in Theseus' fortunes at the expense of Herakles perhaps owed something to the growing tide of anti-Spartan sentiment in the early 470s. Herakles was quintessentially a Peloponnesian hero. What Athens now needed was a hero whose attachment was undivided and whose loyalty could not be in doubt. The decline in Herakles' fortunes was neither irreversible nor total, however. On the contrary, he continued to be a figure of front-rank importance in Attic cult, as is proven by the fact that just after the mid-fifth century his labours were assigned pride of place on the metopes that adorned the front wall of the Hephaisteion, while the exploits of Theseus were relegated to its sides.

In the eyes of his countrymen Theseus ultimately came to be one of the most creative religious geniuses which their city ever produced. Yet the truth or otherwise of the assertion that the cults which he instituted shared a common ancestry is ultimately less fascinating than the necessary inference that those same cults, most of which were extremely venerable, either consented or saw it in their best interests to ascribe their origins to the initiative of Theseus. Nothing in fact speaks more eloquently of the shadowy nature of Athenian religious history before the 470s than the impact which the person and deeds of this latecomer were able to make upon it.

Theseus' unique place in Athens' religious evolution did not, however, depend solely upon the links which his priesthood succeeded in forging with some of Athens' most respected cults, important though these links were. He it was as well who 'entrusted to the Eupatridai the role of having knowledge of divine matters, filling the magistracies, teaching the laws, and being expounders of religious matters' (Plu. *Thes.* 25.2); he, in other words, who gave form and substance to practice and belief, by systematising what had previously been inchoate.

The cult of Theseus

Although we do not know for certain whether Theseus was worshipped as a hero in Attica before the arrival of his bones, we are probably dealing with a pre-existing private cult which now for the first time achieved civic recognition, as seems also to have happened to Pan after the battle of Marathon. The existence of an ancient cult of Theseus is assumed by Plutarch (*Thes.* 23.3; cf. 12.1), who alludes to the establishment in the hero's lifetime and on his own initiative of a *temenos* and sacrifice. Its management was entrusted to a *genos* known as the Phytalidai, who provided Theseus with hospitality when he first arrived in Attica from Troezen. Without doubt the Phytalidai would have been ardent promoters of the public cult in the 470s. The victims which they sacrificed to him were supplied by members of those households which had been required to furnish the human tribute for the Minotaur (*Thes.* 12.1). A 'tax (*telos*) of five drachmas for the Theseion' (*Hesperia* 5 [1936] 401.134), whose existence we first learn of in a fourth-century document, was perhaps levied upon these same families (cf. A.D. Nock in Schlaifer 1940, 237). The tax can hardly have been levied on the whole citizen body since the average rate of pay for an Athenian, at least in the fifth century, was less than a drachma per day. Leading support is also likely to have come from north-east Attica, with which the hero had close mythological ties, even though no Theseion has so far come to light in this region. Finally, the insertion of the Theseia into the Athenian sacred calendar on Pyanopsion 8, a date close to other festivals associated with the hero including the Oschophoria and Pyanopsia, must have taken place with the consent of the various priesthoods in charge of these festivals, whose co-operation and agreement would have been vital. There is nothing to indicate that the Demos interfered with the traditional privileges of the Phytalidai when it took over the management of the cult of Theseus, although it may have required the *genos* to submit an account of its ritual practices for formal approval, as probably happened in other cases as well (see below p. 102).

The Theseion in the Asty, which housed the hero's bones, has never come to light, but it is thought to have been situated a short distance southeast of the Agora (Plu. *Thes.* 36.2; Paus. 1.17.2; cf. Barron 1972, 21). It is certainly not the imposing building on the west side of the Agora now identified as the Hephaisteion, which for a long time was known as the Theseion on the grounds that the metopes along its sides depict Theseus' exploits. Very little is known about the sanctuary's appearance, though we should probably be correct in picturing it as a fenced or walled enclosure containing an elaborately decorated tomb. Its walls were adorned with paintings depicting scenes from the hero's life by Mikon and Polygnotos, the foremost muralists of their day. Judging from the fact that the 600 members of the Boule occasionally met here in the first century BC (cf. *IG* II² 1039.2f.), the dimensions of the enclosure must have been considerable. A poem by Melanthios praises Kimon for adorning at his own expense 'the temples of the gods and the Kekropian agora with deeds of the demigods' (*Kim.* 4.6; *IEG* II, p. 80f.), which may include the Theseion. Of the other three Theseia mentioned by Philochoros, one was situated on Hippios Kolonos about a mile north of the Asty, another was in the Piraeus, and the third was probably located inside the Long Walls which joined the Asty to the Piraeus.

By the end of the fifth century Theseus' presence in the Agora had become ubiquitous. He was depicted in paintings housed in the Stoa Poikile and Stoa of Zeus (Paus. 1.3.3), on a terracotta tile displayed on the Royal Stoa (1.3.1), and on the metopes along the sides of the Hephaisteion. At an unknown date a statue of the hero was set up close to the spot where the temple of Ares stood in Roman times, beside that of his rival Herakles (1.8.4).

The cult of the Tyrannicides

Theseus' elevation to the rank of state hero coincided almost exactly with the promotion of a cult in honour of Harmodios and Aristogeiton, who had unsuccessfully attempted to overthrow the Peisistratid tyranny in 514. It is justifiable, therefore, to look for ideological parallels between the two cults.

The facts are these. In the wake of the restoration of democracy in 510, and allegedly in the same year as the expulsion of the kings from Rome (Pln. *HN* 34.9.17), the Tyrannicides were honoured with a pair of commemorative bronze statues executed by Antenor, one of the leading

Attic sculptors of his day. When Athens was sacked by the Persians in 480, these statues were among the loot removed by Xerxes and shipped back to Susa. In *c.* 477, just about the time when Theseus' bones were being returned to Athens, the original pair was replaced with a new group by the sculptors Kritios and Nesiotes, which stood in the centre of the Agora (Pl. 23). The marble plinth supporting the sculptures bore a couplet which was ascribed in antiquity to the epigrammatist Simonides (cf. Hephaistion *On Metres* 4.6; *Agora* I no. 3872):

> Verily the light shone upon the Athenians
>> when Aristogeiton and Harmodios slew Hipparchos.

Harmodios and Aristogeiton are the first heroes known to have been honoured in Athens with publicly commissioned statues made of bronze, a costly and prestigious material. Not until the fourth century was a like distinction conferred again (Dem. 20.70; Pln. *HN* 34.9.17). Their prominent location, combined with the fact that so little time elapsed between the removal of the first pair and their replacement, testifies to the high honour in which they were held. Such, in fact, was the continuing gratitude felt towards the Tyrannicides by their fellow-countrymen that in the second half of the fifth century their oldest living descendants were granted the right of dining in the prytaneion (or town hall) at public expense, an honour which was reserved for the greatest benefactors of the Athenian state (*IG* I² 77.5f.). In all probability, their grave on the road leading to the Academy served as the focus for their cult, which was supervised by the polemarch himself ([Arist.] *AP* 58.1).[6]

Though the Tyrannicides were not the first contemporary Athenians to be awarded heroic honours in this manner – the Marathonian war dead were heroised perhaps over a decade earlier – they were the first to be individually identified as heroes. Their heroisation in fact anticipates a trend which was to become common in Athens from the fourth century onwards when not merely heroic but also divine honours were awarded to public benefactors. Even so, both Herodotos (5.55 and 6.123) and Thukydides (6.54-9; cf. 1.20.2) allege that the establishment of their cult was a blatant example of the re-writing of Athenian history for patriotic and self-seeking ends. Thukydides' objections are threefold. He points out first that their victim was not in fact the tyrant Hippias, but rather the tyrant's younger brother Hipparchos. Secondly, their action was inspired not by a yearning for democratic freedom but by a private grudge (*di'erôtikên lupên*) against a rival lover. It seems that Hipparchos had

---

[6] It is doubtful whether the Tyrannicides had a hero-shrine in the Agora, since public decrees conferring similar honours on later benefactors of the Athenian state frequently stipulate that their statues should be set up 'not beside Harmodios and Aristogeiton'. Obviously this injunction would have been redundant if a proper precinct had been assigned to them.

made sexual advances towards Harmodios, who was Aristogeiton's lover, and when rebuffed had responded by publicly insulting Harmodios' sister. While others in the conspiracy may have had more lofty aspirations, the Tyrannicides themselves were motivated by nothing more lofty than a straightforward desire for revenge. Lastly, the murder of Hipparchos did not lead to the overthrow of the tyranny, which actually endured for another four years, but rather to an increase in its repressiveness. In the course of his furious diatribe against the falsification of historical fact, Thukydides produces not a single shred of evidence to prove that he is right and others are wrong, but restricts himself to issuing a simple categorical imperative (cf. Veyne 1988, 10). It is as if the myth of the Tyrannicides is simply to be replaced by the myth of the Expert Historian.

As Braudel (1980, 129) has remarked: 'A *laudator temporis acti* is never without ulterior motives relating to the present.' Whatever the facts about the contribution made by the Tyrannicides to the overthrow of the tyranny, it is undeniable that their cult, like that of Theseus which it strongly resembles in its patriotic flavour, provided the Athenians with a most serviceable instrument with which to primp themselves upon their indomitable self-reliance and indissoluble attachment to democracy. Both legends contained an anti-Spartan bias, the Tyrannicide legend by presenting a direct challenge to the claim that it was the Alkmaionid *genos* which, with help from the Spartans, was instrumental in ridding Athens of the tyranny, the legend of Theseus by incorporating the story of a Spartan assault upon Athens (Plu. *Thes.* 32-3; cf. Podlecki 1966, 129-35). Though it is ultimately futile to speculate whether the Tyrannicide cult was promoted by the same political lobby as the one which canvassed the interests of Theseus or by a different one, there are some grounds for suspecting that these were rival foundations, and moreover that the Alkmaionidai supported the cause of Theseus, particularly in view of their influence over the oracle at Delphi, where Theseus' deeds were prominently depicted on the Athenian treasury.

Conclusions

Irrespective of Theseus' significance for the Athenians before 476/5 and irrespective of the use which had or had not been made of him in the sixth century by those seeking to legitimate political and constitutional change, it was the return of his bones, in combination with his re-worked image as a political visionary, which provided the primary justification for the establishment of a public cult in his honour, as is amply borne out by Plutarch's observation that the Athenians welcomed the bones 'as if Theseus himself were returning to the city' (Plu. *Thes.* 36.2). As generally happened at the time of the introduction of a new cult, the physical entry into the community of the god or hero, the allocation of a shrine, and the establishment of cult formed part of a unified set of arrangements.

The worship of Theseus is perhaps best understood as an offshoot of the type of cult which commonly developed around the historical founder or *oikistês* of a Greek colony, since his legendary life-story gave coherence and credibility to the belief that the defining features of the early-fifth century Athenian state, namely its freedom from foreign domination, its centralised unity, its cults and its popular sovereignty were the creation of a single genius, much in the same way that a colonial foundation was impressed with the distinctive personality and acts of its historical founder. As Malkin (1987, 189) notes, 'With the death of the oikist, the foundation process comes to an end.' Likewise by interring Theseus in or at any rate very close to the very heart of Athens, Kimon was in effect claiming Theseus as the state's *oikistês*.[7]

As a general rule the return of the bones of a hero of national importance, coinciding as it did with a moment when the state in question was assuming a more active and aggressive foreign policy, served to symbolise a newly acquired spirit of national pride and self-determinism. The city's protector was brought into the midst of the city. What could be more comforting or more apt? The sense of well-being was millennial in its implications. Through the founder's re-burial the city experienced its own rebirth.

In contrast to the Panhellenic cult of Zeus Eleutherios, which served to perpetuate a universalist ideal, namely Greek unity in the face of a common enemy, the cult of Theseus was, like most hero-cults, a reflection of strictly localised political aspirations. Theseus now became the pre-eminent symbol of the rising tide of Athenian nationalism, a tide which was destined within a single generation to transform Athens into a ruthless imperial power exercising an iron fist over those same states which initially looked up to her as the leader of a free alliance against foreign oppression. He thus perfectly symbolises the reaction against common Hellenic purposes which the Persian Wars had momentarily fostered.

From the variety and antiquity of the cults and cult practices which became associated with the name of Theseus, it is abundantly clear that his meteoric rise to prominence was no miracle, but due rather to the mobilisation of quite extraordinarily broad support for his claim to the title of national hero. Indeed no other Athenian hero, perhaps no Athenian deity, enjoyed such extensive nor such powerful connections. At what date these links were forged is impossible to determine, but even if some of them postdate the return of his bones, the fact that Poseidon agreed to acknowledge him as his son and that he could be portrayed alongside Herakles on the Athenian treasury at Delphi proves that

---

[7] A modern analogy of an *oikistês* cult of (till recently) comparable political significance is that of Lenin as founder of the USSR, which Stalin instituted in 1930 by preserving his embalmed corpse under glass in a granite mausoleum in Red Square.

already in the 470s he enjoyed very powerful support.

Yet despite his national standing, Theseus was no copybook hero or cardboard symbol of patriotic pride. The hero who delivered his subjects from subservience to a foreign power also had a penchant for under-age girls, in consequence of which he exposed his country to the peril of a foreign invasion. Ironically – it can hardly have been intentional – his accomplishments and failings thus provided the Athenians with an exact paradigm of their own complex and ambivalent moral posture in the Greek world in the aftermath to the Persian Wars, more precisely from the mid-450s onwards when they began to convert the Delian Confederacy into an instrument of their own policy and will. There is nothing inherently peculiar about the fact that a national symbol should be cast in such a morally ambiguous role.[8] Not all societies feel the need to present themselves to the outside world as shining examples of moral rectitude. A collective mentality which could accept Perikles' proposition (Thuk. 2.63.2) that 'the empire which you rule is a tyranny' was clearly capable of accommodating a national hero who happened to be a child-molester. Besides which, Theseus' sexual escapades afforded proof of his superabundant virility, a quality in which his countrymen might even have taken a certain robust pride.

The irony in Theseus' identity is nowhere more striking than in the fact that his tomb became 'a place of refuge for household slaves and all those of humble estate who are fearful of others more powerful than themselves' (Plu. *Thes.* 36.2). If some high-minded Athenians were moved to dwell with smug self-righteousness upon their state's resemblance to the positive aspects of their national hero in the mid 470s, they would have had good reason to reflect upon his negative attributes during the half-century that lay ahead.

---

[8] We may compare the image of Theseus with the ambivalent symbolism surrounding the portrayal of John Bull as the quintessential Englishman by Gillray and other political caricaturists at the time of the Napoleonic Wars. See R. Paulson, *Representations of Revolution: 1789-1820* (New Haven and London 1983), 190.

5

Transfiguration and the Maiden

For the fifty-year interval between the end of the Persian Wars and the eve of the Peloponnesian War there is no record of any god of consequence achieving official recognition in Athens. Instead, Athens' religious system was given what might be described as a kind of spiritual face-lift, inasmuch as profound changes took place in relation to existing religious practices. The leading player was the virgin goddess Athena, who symbolised Athens' grandiose political aspirations.

The stability of the Athenian pantheon was due to several factors. First, after the violent upheavals on both the human and divine planes caused by the experience of the Persian Wars, an era of conservatism and re-trenchment was perhaps inevitable. Secondly, this was a period undistinguished by any dramatic turn of events of the kind that could warrant a major revision of the religious system.[1] In addition, Athens' attachment to Athena, which from the synoecism onwards was arguably as close as that felt by any Greek community to a single deity, became even stronger in the second half of the fifth century. An increasing fascination with the national deity was thus another factor which may have contributed to the stabilisation.

For a number of reasons this period was none the less critical for Athens' religious development, due partly to the Demos' growing interest in all matters religious, partly to the influence of the sophistic movement, which challenged and undermined traditional belief, and partly to Athens' conversion into an imperialist power, which not only stimulated the Demos to seek religious sanctions to justify its new status, but also placed at its disposal vast financial resources for the commissioning of ambitious public works. In the sense that this half-century witnessed a

[1] The only supernatural intervention in battle which is recorded for this period has to do with an anonymous 'half-deity' (*hêmitheos*), who is said to have opposed the Athenians when they fought unsuccessfully against the Boiotians at Koroneia in 447. See W. Peek, *Griechische Vers-Inschriften* I (Berlin 1955), no. 17. For discussion and further bibliography, see Pritchett (*GSW* III, 26). As Pritchett points out, the 'official nature' of the war memorial commissioned by the Demos is a powerful argument in favour of the belief that this constituted the generally accepted explanation for Athens' defeat, rather than a *post eventum* explanation on the part of a single, possibly unrepresentative individual.

dramatic shift both in the direction of established cults and in the control of religious practice, what took place may aptly be described as a transfiguration.

In the Archaic period religious authority, including, most crucially, the authority to sanction the introduction of new gods, is likely to have been invested primarily in the archonship and the Areopagus. Although the Areopagus may well have continued to exercise some residual control in this department so long as Athens remained pagan, in 487 the power of this body became fatally weakened by a law which made election to its ranks consequent upon sortition. It will be my contention that from this date onwards the Demos was on its way to becoming the chief arbitrator in all matters pertaining to religion. Whether its appropriation of religious authority came about gradually or all at once is not clear. What seems undeniable, however, is that by *c.* 432 at the latest, when the cult of Thracian Bendis was established under state patronage, all the necessary machinery had passed into its hands.

Following the constitutional reforms of *c.* 462 associated with the names of Perikles and Ephialtes which converted Athens into a radical democracy, the Demos became the personification of a religious spirit which embodied, more comprehensively than ever before, the will of the whole citizen body. Given the tenor and tendency of the age, it was inevitable that this will should express itself in religious innovations which reflected Athens' military and imperialistic ambitions and successes. What follows is an attempt to outline the stages by which the Demos' control over religious innovation was made increasingly apparent and the specific form which that control took.

The decree of the Praxiergidai

Although we lack any example of cult innovation which conclusively proves that the Demos had by now begun to acquire outright control over decisions involving religion, a number of decrees survive which argue convincingly in favour of this hypothesis. The earliest in the series, which almost certainly dates to the 450s (*IG* I^3 7), outlines the duties of a *genos* known as the Praxiergidai whose members were entrusted with the solemn task of attending to the sacred olive-wood statue of Athena Polias.[2] Their duties were performed in the month of Thargelion at two rituals known as Plynteria (Washing) and Kallynteria (Cleaning). Two

---

[2] Deubner's notion (*AF* 21 n. 2; cf. Parke *FA* 152-5 and Simon *FA* 46-8) that the Praxiergidai carried the statue down to the coast and gave it a ritual scrub down in salt water has recently been challenged by I.B. Romano ('Early Greek cult images and cult practices', pp. 127-34 in R. Hägg, N. Marinatos and G.C. Nordquist (eds.), *Early Greek Cult Practice* (= *Proceedings of the Fifth International Symposium at the Swedish Institute at Athens*, 26-29 June 1986 [Stockholm 1988]). Romano (p. 131) is of the opinion that the Plynteria relates specifically to the washing of the garments of the goddess, not to her cult statue.

months later on Hekatombaion 28, the traditional date of Athena's birthday, the Praxiergidai clothed the statue in a new *peplos* or embroidered woollen garment, a ceremony of the utmost solemnity which formed the climax to the Panathenaia festival. It is hardly an exaggeration, therefore, to state that this *genos* was in charge of rituals of unparalleled sanctity and importance conducted on behalf of the foremost deity of the Athenian state. The decree outlining their duties reads as follows:

> The Council and the Demos [resolved]. In the [...] prytany, | [...] was secretary, [on the motion of ...]. | In the matter of the requ[est of the Praxiergidai] that they | inscribe [the oracle of the g]od and the for[mer
> 5 decree] on a [stone] *stêlê* and [erect it on the Acropolis] || [be]hind the ancient temple. [Let the *pôlêtai* (literally 'sellers', i.e. officials who organised contracts for public works) | author]ise payment. The money [for the inscription] is to come | from the goddess (i.e. Athena) in accordance with ancestral practice (*kata ta patria*). [The *tamiai* (treasurers)] of the goddess and] the *kôlakrêtai* (literally 'thigh-collectors', i.e. junior financial officials) are to give [them (i.e. the *pôlêtai*)
> 10 the money] ... . || Apollo sanctioned (*echrêsen*) [the following] n[omima (rules) for the Praxiergidai:] | when they put the *peplos* [on the goddess and perform the preliminary sacrifice | to the Moir]ai (Fates), Zeus Moiragetes (Leader of the Fates) and Ge (Earth) .... | [The following] are the *patria* of the Prax[iergidai] ... [six lines missing] ...
> 20 For the month of Thargelion the temple is to be sea[led off until the t]ritê (i.e. 28th) | on which the archon is to hand over the keys (i.e. of the temple) | to the Praxiergi[dai] ... so that they can dress the statue in ... A fine of [... is to be imposed on those who fail to comply with these regulations].

If we accept the plausible restoration of *n[omima]* in line 10, together with a suggestion by Ostwald (1986, 147) that the rules in question constitute changes in cult practice which are quite distinct from the *patria* of line 13, then the primary purpose of the decree would seem to have been to promulgate important modifications in the robing ceremony which are here being introduced in accordance with a recent oracular pronouncement from Apollo (cf. l. 4). Precisely what these modifications might have been is unclear, since the inscription is illegible at this point. Its secondary aim appears to have been to put on permanent record, very likely for the first time, certain responsibilities and practices which had since time immemorial been invested in the Praxiergidai, such as their temporary custody of the keys of the temple in which the statue was housed. If the restoration '28th' (l. 21) proposed by Lewis (1954, 20f.) is correct, the *patria* in question are likely to have been connected with the Plynteria, which was performed on Thargelion 25 (Plu. *Alk.* 34.1). A possible interpretation of these lines, then, is that the Praxiergidai had just two days to prepare the statue for public display after its annual refurbishment before the doors of the temple were once again re-opened at the beginning of Skirophorion, the month preceding Hekatombaion.

We know nothing about the circumstances which led to the passing of this decree. One suggestion is that it was prompted by a dispute between the Demos and the Praxiergidai concerning the latter's prerogatives, which Apollo had been called upon to resolve (cf. Ostwald 1986, 148). More plausibly, however, we are dealing with 'an implied assertion by the Demos that even the oldest privileges depend on the will of the people' (Lewis 1954, 19); in other words, that all religious usage came within its sphere of influence. It is a reasonable assumption that up till now the Praxiergidai, like all other Attic *genê*, had exercised a rather free hand in the way they conducted their rituals, being entitled to introduce whatever modifications they liked and whenever they saw fit, though presumably always in consultation with an oracular source and the Areopagus. By *c.* 460 onwards, however, all changes in procedure had to be vetted and approved by the Demos, which now subjected ritual activity conducted in its name to close scrutiny. We can go further. It may even have been the Demos' intention through the vehicle of this decree to serve notice that henceforth *particularly* the oldest privileges, even those belonging to a major *genos* with charge of the prime deity, ultimately depended upon its assent.

The priesthood of Athena Nike

Further evidence of intervention by the Demos in the running of what was possibly a gentilician cult is provided by a decree (*IG* I³ 35 = *ML* 44 = *SEG* XXXI.9) dated *c.* 448, which laid down regulations regarding the appointment ([*kathista*]*sthai*) of a priestess of Athena Nike by allotment 'from all Athenian women (*echs Athenaion hapa[sôn]*)'. The decree states further that the priestess was to receive an annual salary of 50 drachmas, together with the legs and hides of animals slaughtered in public sacrifices. Since there exists evidence for a cult of Athena Nike on the Acropolis from as early as the middle of the sixth century (above p. 39), it is more likely that this decree was regulating changes in the procedure by which the priestess be selected than actually creating a new priesthood.[3]

If an independent priesthood did exist before 448, it may have been hereditary within an unknown *genos*, which now found itself divested of its privileges. Although there exists no comparable example from this period of a democratic takeover of a gentilician cult, the phenomenon is attested in later times. As we have already seen, the cult of Artemis Aristoboule, which was almost certainly reserved within Themistokles' own *genos* when first instituted, had passed into the control of the deme of Melite by the time it was revived in the mid-fourth century. Similarly, the

---

[3] It is just possible, however, that the cult of Athena Nike had previously been administered by the priestess of Athena Polias, with whom Nike had close links (see below p. 106), and that now, owing to pressure of business, she relinquished this duty to an independent priesthood.

cult of the healing god Asklepios, initially a private foundation, later received state patronage and a democratic priesthood (below p. 128).

A state takeover of a private cult – if that is what actually happened – might have been prompted by a variety of motives, not all of them manifestations of officiousness or high-handedness on the part of the Demos. One possible explanation is that the Demos deemed it inappropriate and undemocratic to leave the cult of a somewhat militaristic deity in private hands. Another is that the Demos' interest in the goddess may have been prompted by a desire to upgrade her status and dignity. To judge from a further injunction in the same decree to provide a door to the shrine and at some future date build a temple and marble altar, it is safe to conclude that before the state took control Nike's sanctuary was extremely rudimentary, consisting of little more than a piece of consecrated ground with a humble poros altar. There appear to be other occasions when the state injected public monies into a cult in order to win the favour of its deity, which was judged to have become critical to the welfare of the citizen body (see below p. 111). Public patronage was, after all, a god's best guarantee of continuous funding at an adequate level.

Re-affirming Marathon

From around the middle of the fifth century onwards, or perhaps a little before, the Demos commissioned an impressive series of monuments which served to underline and re-affirm Athens' continuing pride in her victory over the Persians at Marathon. The earliest of these monuments was a permanent commemorative trophy in the form of an Ionic column made of white marble, which was set up on the field of battle perhaps around the time of the formation of the Delian League in 478.[4] The location of the monument is not known for certain, but it perhaps stood in the marsh where Persian losses were heaviest, just as the Soros marked the spot where Athenian casualties were heaviest (Paus. 1.32.5). The new trophy was evidently intended to replace the temporary one which had been set up immediately after the battle made from a hewn-down tree trunk and ornamented with armour and weapons captured from the enemy. A palpable reminder of the fact that the glory of this victory was indeed imperishable, it served to enliven the memory of Athens' finest hour.

Probably in *c.* 460 a painting of the battle was put on display in the Stoa Poikile or Painted Stoa at the northwest corner of the Agora, which also

---

[4] As Lucy Meritt (forthcoming) points out, the choice of an Ionic column to commemorate the Persian defeat may have been dictated partly as a compliment to the Ionian Greeks and partly by a desire to point up Athens' role as their protector against their Persian oppressors.

Fig. 10. The northwest corner of the Agora in the late fifth century BC (view from the southeast). Top left: Stoa Basileios or Royal Stoa; top right: Stoa Poikile or Painted Stoa; foreground: Leokorion. From H.A. Thompson, *Agora*[3].

housed other representations of Athens' most celebrated military achievements (Fig. 10; Paus. 1.15.3). The artist appears to have been given explicit instructions about how to execute his commission: the fourth-century orator Aischines (3.186) tells us that the Demos refused permission for the name of Miltiades to be inscribed on the picture, though it did allow him to be depicted 'in the front rank urging on his soldiers', an honour which was not granted to any of the other nine generals who participated in the battle. The influence of Kimon is surely to be seen behind 'the full, perhaps even excessive credit' which was accorded to Miltiades for his part in securing the Athenian victory (Connor 1970, 162), even though the fact that his father's name could not appear in the picture must have been something of a disappointment to him. Since the painting would have made a major contribution to the dissemination of the official version of the battle (cf. Wycherley 1953, 29), there are obvious reasons why an ambitious politican would have wished to ensure that his father received his full measure of recognition.

Other contemporary works celebrating the victory include a colossal bronze statue of Athena by Pheidias, which was erected outdoors on the Acropolis in the mid-450s. Known in later times as the Athena Promachos or Front-rank (cf. schol. on Dem. 22.13), this statue was paid for by the booty which had been captured from the Persians. From

Pausanias' claim (1.28.2) that the tip of Athena's spear and the crest of her helmet were visible to sailors as they approached the Piraeus from the direction of Sounion, it has been estimated that the work must have been over eighteen metres high (cf. Robertson *HGA* I, 294). A temple of Eukleia (Glory), known only from a brief reference in Pausanias who describes it as 'a dedication from the Persians who landed at Marathon' (1.14.5), may also have been erected at this time (cf. Boersma *ABP*, 62f.).

Finally, there can be little doubt that the construction of the Parthenon was also part of the same initiative. The previous temple on the site, begun shortly after 490 as a thank-offering for the victory, had been destroyed by the Persians in 480/79. The scenes of mythical battles adorning the metopes of the new building, which included representations of the Greeks fighting Trojans, Greeks fighting Amazons, Lapiths fighting Centaurs, and gods fighting giants, were unambiguously intended to invite comparison with the victory of the Athenians over the uncivilised invaders from the east. Whether the architectural sculpture of the Parthenon also contained a contemporary allusion to the battle is a matter of continuing controversy. Boardman (1977, 39-49) has suggested that the famous cavalcade of horsemen and chariots which runs around the outer wall of the cella was intended to evoke the memory of those who fought and died at Marathon, here seen participating in their last Panathenaia, which had been held just six weeks before the battle. Omitting from his count the drivers of the chariots, Boardman has calculated that the cavalcade consisted of 192 horsemen; exactly the same number as those who fell in the battle itself, in other words. Given the fragmentary condition of the frieze, however, any count is inevitably somewhat impressionistic.

The re-affirming of Marathon in this public way was not just a nostalgic throwback to Athens' finest hour. On the contrary, it may have been a way of massaging the national ego at a time when that ego was feeling distinctly battered, consequent upon a disastrous expedition to Egypt in *c.* 450. Certainly it was prompted by a practical need to justify Athens' continuing leadership of an anti-Persian alliance at a time when the pressure upon her to disband the alliance, following a probable peace with Persia in 449, was becoming intense.[5] Athens was in effect reminding her allies, herself and the world at large, first of the need for continuing vigilance and secondly of how much was owed to her for preserving the freedom of Greece. As in 490, so now in the 440s she alone could offer protection, should the peace with Persia prove only temporary. The overriding message conveyed by the imagery of the Parthenon, in

[5] The so-called Peace of Kallias, like that of the Oath of Plataiai, is mentioned neither by Plu. *Per.* nor by Thuk., and its authenticity was later challenged by Theopompos. Its date is disputed even by those scholars (now the majority) who accept it, some placing it in 449, others as early as *c.* 468. See Stadter (1989, 150f.) for a summary of the opposing views. For Thuk.'s silence, see R.A. Moysey (*AHB* 5.1&2 [1991]30-5).

other words, was the necessity for an effective deterrent. In the fourth century Athens' orators would return to Marathon when seeking justification for the reconstruction of the empire, promoting this patriotic and imperialistic message through the vehicle of the funeral oration (cf. Loraux *Invention*, 155-71). In Periklean Athens, more spectacularly and more eloquently, this same patriotic and imperialistic message was broadcast visually.

The religion of imperialist Athens

From the 450s onwards the Athenian state increasingly came to see itself as dependent upon the exclusive patronage of Athena, who now began to symbolise not only Athenian military success but also the Athenian imperialist will to dominate over the Aegean. By a natural extension of her role as guardian of all Attica, Athena also came to be perceived as the tutelary deity of her empire. In other words, the goddess was both Nike and Arche, Victory and Empire, to the extent that she now began imperialistically to overshadow her fellow Olympians as never before, with the possible exception of Demeter.

The evidence for this claim is the following. First, it was Athena who now became the principal beneficiary from the funds which flowed into the state's coffers as a result of the tribute exacted from the allies. Following the transfer of the league treasury from Delos to Athens in 454, it was she who replaced Apollo as the divine custodian of its funds and who now received one-sixtieth of the tribute as *aparchai* or 'first fruits' for her pains. Secondly, among the various temples which were constructed both in the Asty and in the Attic countryside from *c.* 448 onwards, not only was the most magnificent, the Parthenon, dedicated in her honour, but two others were also consecrated to Athena and another deity jointly, namely the Hephaisteion in the Agora and the temple of Ares in Acharnai.

In addition, the Demos adopted a number of initiatives clearly intended to encourage her allies to identify their interests more closely with those of their imperial mistress. The Panathenaia, for instance, increasingly assumed the character of a festival which was celebrated by Athens and her empire jointly – and with irresistible logic, too, since the Aegean was in effect becoming an extension of Attic territory. A fragmentary inscription probably dating to the late 450s, whose primary function was to lay down regulations regarding the installation of a democratic council in Erythrai, a city on the Lydian coast, following an unsuccessful attempt on the latter's part to secede from the league, marks the beginning of this trend (*IG* I³ 14.3ff. = *ML* 40). Although its precise details are irrecoverable, it is clear that the opening section of the decree imposed certain obligations upon the Erythraians in regard to the celebration of the Panathenaia – obligations which have been rightly described as representing 'an early stage in the conversion of an Athenian into an Empire festival' (ML, p. 91).

Just how seriously the Athenians regarded allied participation in their premier festival is indicated by a decree which was moved by a certain Kleinias a few years later. The main purpose of his legislation was to tighten up regulations regarding the collection of the tribute. Contained within the decree, however, was the following stern warning (IG I³ 34.41-3 = ML 46):

> If anyone breaks the law (adikei) in regard to the sending of the cow and the [panoplies], there will be indictments (grapheis) and [punishment (zêmian)] against him in the same way (viz. as if it were an offence regarding payment of tribute).

It is an obvious inference that at some date previously a requirement had been imposed on the allies to present a cow and a suit of armour to the goddess at the Panathenaia. The fact that the failure to discharge this duty was treated as an offence of equal gravity to that of defaulting on the tribute indicates the high symbolic value of these items.

Athens and her allies were in effect members of one and the same religious community. Or so Athens would have her allies believe. There are other telling signs of the harnessing of religion for imperialistic ends. Either in the 450s or 440s a cult of 'Athena mistress of Athens (Athêna Athênôn medeousa)', the imperialist equivalent of Athena Polias but apparently packaged for export only since no traces of the cult have been detected on Attic soil, makes an appearance in allied territory, notably on the islands of Samos and Kos, and at Chalkis on Euboia, where boundary stones have been found which prove the existence of her consecrated precincts. Although the circumstances surrounding the introduction of this cult are unknown, the initiative probably came from Athens, since a spontaneous outburst of loyalist sentiment from the allies is hardly to be expected at a time when Athens' ambitions were becoming more naked and giving ever greater rise to allied concern (cf. Meiggs AE, 297). In brief, the cult is likely to have been a further mechanism by which the Demos sought to concentrate the minds of her recalcitrant subjects upon her sovereignty at a time when they were becoming increasingly rebellious.

Athena was not the only deity to be appropriated in this way. Towards the end of the Archidamian War in c. 422 a decree was passed requiring the Athenians 'in accordance with ancestral practice and the oracle from Delphi' to offer first fruits to the Two Goddesses. The decree further stipulated (IG I³ 78.14-18 = ML 73 = SEG XXXVI.12) that:

> The allies are to offer first fruits on the same terms (viz. as the Athenians). The poleis are to appoint collectors of grain after whatever fashion it seems to them that the grain will most efficiently be collected. When it has been

collected, let them send it to Athens. Those bringing it should hand it over to the *hieropoioi* (or performers of sacred rituals) of Eleusis at Eleusis.

The enlisting of the Eleusinian Mysteries in the service of Athens' foreign policy goals may be interpreted as an extension of the Two Goddesses' increasingly Panhellenic importance in this same period. Probably early in their history, if not from their inception, the Eleusinian Mysteries had addressed spiritual needs which transcended the narrow boundaries of Greek particularism. Whereas most cults collected around themselves closed communities which debarred aliens and outsiders, initiation into the Mysteries was available to all who spoke Greek, independent of sex, social status or ethnic background. Given the tremendous increase in their popularity in the Periklean era, as dramatically indicated by the construction of yet another new and enlarged Telesterion in the 440s (Fig. 11), the spiritual edge which Athens enjoyed over all other Greeks by virtue of her control over their management may well have proved a more subtle and effective weapon in her efforts to strengthen her leadership over the alliance than did the conversion of the Panathenaia into an imperialistic cult.

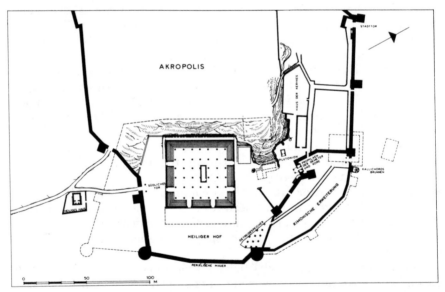

Fig. 11. The Periklean telesterion. From J. Travlos, *BTAA*.

Evidently Athenian aspirations extended beyond the confines of her empire, as the following notice to the Eleusinian priesthood contained in the same decree suggests (ll. 24-6):

Let the *hierophantês* (literally 'revealer of sacred objects') and the *daidochos* ('torch-bearer') at the Mysteries invite (*keleueto*) the Greeks to offer first fruits according to ancestral practice and the oracle from Delphi.

What was the motive behind such an injunction? A vaguely articulated hope of achieving spiritual hegemony? Or simply a pious desire to promote the Goddesses for their own sake? Whatever the answer, the Demos evidently did not count on eliciting much of a response, for the decree discreetly adds (ll. 30-6):

> The Boule is to announce to all the other Greek states, wherever it seems possible, in what manner the Athenians and their allies are offering first fruits, not ordering them but inviting (*keleuontas*) them if they wish to offer first-fruits, according to ancestral practice and the Delphic oracle. If anyone brings any first fruits from these poleis, the *hieropoios* is to receive them in the following manner ... .

The Periklean building programme

In a speech which he delivered in the 340s the orator Lykourgos (*Against Leok.* 81; cf. D.S. 11.29.3) tells us that just before the battle of Plataiai in 479 the Greek combatants had sworn an oath

> not to re-build any of the temples burnt and destroyed by the barbarians, but to let them remain (viz. as they are) as a memorial to future generations of the impiety (*asebeia*) of the barbarians.

The authenticity of the oath was already doubted in antiquity by the fourth-century historian Theopompos (*FGrH* 115 F 153). The possibility cannot be ruled out that it was invented as a way of explaining and justifying a state of affairs which had in reality been brought about not by religious scruples but by Athens' economic prostration at the end of the Persian wars. Even so, it would be somewhat extraordinary if the Athenians made the oath up altogether, not least because oath-taking itself was regarded with grave solemnity.

Sometime after the conclusion of the probable peace with Persia, a decision was taken on the initiative of Perikles to rescind the so-called oath of Plataiai and use the tribute money paid by the allies in part to finance a costly and ambitious programme of rebuilding. It is noteworthy that in the speech which Plutarch (*Per.* 12) puts into the mouth of Perikles on this occasion the latter does not allude to any desire to honour or gratify the gods, either because this motive did not figure in his calculations or because it was so obvious that there was no need to remark upon it. Perikles merely asserts that the rebuilding will bring the city 'everlasting fame', as well as providing a source of income for a large and perhaps otherwise unemployed body of workmen. We catch a glimpse of the wonder and amazement generated by the project from the following editorial comment by Plutarch (*Per.* 13.1-2):

Men thought that each of the works would require many generations to complete it, but all of them were fully completed in the heyday of a single administration.

The first temple to be built was the Hephaisteion, which stands on the hill called Kolonos Agoraios overlooking the west side of the Agora. In view of the fact that no earlier building existed on this site, however, technically speaking it should not be seen as initiating the Periklean building programme proper, whose precise aim was to rebuild what had been destroyed by the Persians, but as preceding it. The Hephaisteion is the best preserved of all Greek temples and was dedicated jointly to Hephaistos and Athena as god and goddess of metal-working and handicraft. Hephaistos' rise to prominence in a district where bronze- and iron-working foundries have come to light during recent excavations affords palpable proof of the increasing importance of Athens' industrial workers from the mid-fifth century onwards, as well as of her vastly increased industrial output. The god's promotion thus closely parallels the rise in importance and wealth of that element in the citizen body which operated under his patronage and protection. It is also striking that the festival which was celebrated in the god's honour was either introduced or more likely remodelled in 421, contemporary with the resumption of building activity which had been interrupted by the outbreak of war a decade earlier (cf. *IG* I³ 82).

It was the Acropolis, however, which with full appropriateness claimed prime attention from Perikles' builders and which now rose spectacularly from the ashes. The earliest project to be undertaken was the Parthenon, followed a decade later by the construction of a monumental gateway known as the Propylaia on its western extremity. Among other architectural works which were probably planned in the 440s as part of the overall conception of a fully restored Acropolis, though not actually begun until some time later, should be included the temple of Athena Nike, which was erected on top of the Mycenaean bastion at its northwest corner, and the Erechtheion, which lies a short distance to the north of the Parthenon. Perikles' builders were hardly less active in the Attic countryside. A temple to Ares and Athena was set up in the deme of Acharnai close to the northern border of Attica, another to Poseidon was built at Sounion at its southernmost tip, and a third to Nemesis at Rhamnous on the northeast coast. All three are believed to be the work of the so-called Hephaisteion architect (cf. Dinsmoor 1941).

State funding of cults

To the years immediately preceding the outbreak of the Peloponnesian War dates evidence for the imposition of taxes upon the citizen body in order to fund a variety of state cults. A cult in the Piraeus, for instance, which up till now had been supported wholly by voluntary contributions, received from *c.* 432 onwards an income which was funded from a compulsory levy paid by shipowners upon the completion of each sea voyage. The state also agreed to provide up to 500 drachmas towards the building of a shrine to the same god, the remaining cost to be borne by voluntary subscription (*IG* I^3 130; cf. Lewis 1960, 189-94). Although the identity of the cult is not preserved, a likely beneficiary of this financial package is Apollo Delios. Athens must have gravely offended Apollo when she removed the league treasury from his jurisdiction in 454. She would, moreover, have had particular reason to fear his disfavour as war with Sparta appeared more and more inevitable in the late 430s, not least in view of the god's publicly stated and unconditional preference for the Peloponnesian side (Thuk. 1.118). A cult of Apollo, perhaps Pythios, was also awarded a subsidy in the same period from an annual tax imposed on cavalry, hoplites and archers (*IG* I^3 138). Finally, we also hear of an embarkation tax levied on passengers and a 2 per cent tax charged on exports and imports passing through the Piraeus. The latter tax was used to subsidise the running of the cult of the Anakes, the protectors of sailors, whose accounts were henceforth to be the object of public scrutiny by examiners and assessors (*IG* I^3 133 = *SEG* X.59). Since the Anakes were actually Spartan heroes, it is just conceivable that the promotion of their cult was also in part a response to premonitions of war, being intended to neutralise the twins' age-old antipathy towards Athens for Theseus' abduction of their sister Helen (see above p. 91).

These few inscriptions hint at a far more extensive and detailed system of the financing of public cults than we presently have knowledge of, as well as at what appears to have been a desperate last-minute bid to secure the goodwill of gods and heroes whose loyalty to Athens was questionable at best.

The entry of Bendis

Probably on the eve of the outbreak of the Peloponnesian War a public cult of Thracian Bendis was established in the Piraeus (Plate 26). The *terminus ante quem* for the goddess's arrival is 429/8, as is indicated by the appearance of the first two letters of her name in the treasury accounts of the Other Gods for that year (*IG* I^3 383.143). Detailed regulations regarding the public worship of Bendis are preserved in a decree of the Demos which was found in the vicinity of her sanctuary on the southwest slope of Mounychia Hill in the Piraeus (*IG* I^3 136). Though continuing uncertainty about the date of the decree, which is variously assigned to the period between 432/1 and 411, prevents us from knowing for certain whether the cult was state-sponsored at the time of its entry in *c.* 432 or only became so later, there are grounds for assuming that it was public from the start. That is because if the goddess initially entered

Athens in a private capacity, then we might expect that her Thracian worshippers, who very likely constituted the cult's main clientèle at the outset, would have been obligated to obtain the right to own land and a shrine (*enktêsis gês kai oikias*) as a pre-condition to worship. Certainly this requirement was enjoined upon the sponsors of foreign cults in the fourth century (cf. *IG* II² 337). Yet there is no evidence to indicate that this is what happened.

The Bendis decree provides important testimony for the authority of the Athenian Demos in matters pertaining to religious innovation. Though fragmentary, it appears to lay down conditions for the appointment of a priest who is to be democratically elected 'from all Athenian men (*[ex Athena]iôn hapantôn*)' (l. 30), in the same way as the priestess of Athena Nike was to be elected 'from all Athenian women' (see above). It also contains a reference (ll. 22, 27) to the offering of first-fruits to the goddess, as well as to an all-night festival or *pannuchis*, to which Plato alludes at the beginning of the *Republic* (1.328a). While interest in the public cult of Bendis appears to have been on the decline by the end of the fourth century, private sanctuaries of the goddess were later established both in the Asty and at Laurion in southeast Attica for the benefit of foreigners and slaves, many of whom were Thracians.

One of the most fascinating questions raised by the introduction of Bendis is how a semi-barbarian goddess succeeded in gaining entry into Athens in the first place.[6] No *aition* relating to Bendis has survived in our sources nor is there any hint as to the identity of the group which championed her cause first in the Boule and later in the Ekklesia, where the merits of her case must have been debated at considerable length, given her outlandish background as a quintessentially barbarian goddess and the general ignorance of the populace of her claims to worship. Despite the silence of our sources, however, there can be little doubt that Bendis' entry represents a remarkable though by no means unique example of the influence of foreign policy on domestic worship, as Nilsson (1951, 45-8) correctly surmised. Thukydides (2.29.4) informs us that at the time of the outbreak of the Peloponnesian War Athens attached considerable importance to the formation of an alliance with the Odrysian Thracians. In the event her expectations were seriously misplaced, for although the Thracians supplied her with mercenaries throughout the war, the formal alliance brought no tangible benefits. Yet this in no way alters the fact that the establishment of a cult in honour of Bendis would have been perceived at the time as a highly effective way of consolidating a military partnership, particularly in view of the fact that Bendis' status among the Thracians was such that she effectively personified their military might. Throughout Greek history religious and

---

[6] A.D. Nock, *Conversion* (Oxford 1933), 18, somewhat provocatively states, 'There was nothing more revolutionary (viz. in Bendis' entry) than there was in the introduction of the potato and tobacco into England from America.'

1. The Acropolis from the northwest. View from the Hill of the Nymphs, showing the Areopagus in the foreground.

2. Black-figure *hydria* depicting an epiphany of Athena in the form of an owl perched above an altar, third quarter of the sixth century.

3. Attic kylix, *c.* 460–450, depicting Nike acclaiming a schoolboy who has won a lyre-playing contest.

4. Panathenaic prize amphora, *c.* 560–550. Inscribed 'From the games at Athens' and 'Nikias made me'.

5. The so-called Olive Tree pediment, *c.* 570.

6. Detail of Plate 5.

7. The so-called
Bluebeard pediment,
second quarter of the
sixth century.

8. Pediment depicting
Herakles wrestling with
a Triton, second quarter
of the sixth century.

9. Pediment depicting the apotheosis or introduction of Herakles on to Olympos, *c.* 570. From
left to right: Zeus, Hera, Herakles and Hermes. The missing figure in the gap between Hera
and Herakles should be Athena, who is leading on the hero.

10. Bell krater by the Pan
Painter depicting Pan pursuing
a goatherd, *c.* 470.

11. The cave of Pan at the northwest corner of the Acropolis.

12. Tondo of a black-figure *kylix* depicting Pan as a runner, *c.* 490.

13. Portrait herm of Themistokles from Ostia. Roman copy of Greek original dated to the second quarter of the fifth century.

14. *Oinochoê* by the Pan Painter depicting Boreas abducting Oreithyia, dated *c.* 480–470.

15. *Kratêriskoi* as used in the cult of Artemis.

16. Interior of a red-figure *kylix* depicting Theseus killing the Minotaur in the tondo and performing other heroic exploits in the outer ring, *c*. 480.

17. The excavations of the shrine of Artemis Aristoboule.

18. Red-figure *lêkythos* or oil-flask
which depicts Herakles helping
Theseus to rise from a throne of rock to
which he has become attached in
Hades (cf. Plu. *Thes.* 35), *c.* mid-fifth
century.

19. The Athenian Treasury at Delphi, *c.* 490–480.

20. Metope from the Treasury: Theseus and Athena.

21. Metope from the Treasury: Theseus fighting an Amazon.

22. Red-figure *kylix* signed by Euphronios as potter and ascribed to Onesimos as painter, depicting Theseus being welcomed by Amphitrite into Poseidon's underwater palace, *c.* 500–490.

23. Roman copy in marble of the Tyrannicides. The original was executed in bronze by Kritios and Nesiotes, *c.* 480.

24. Roman copy in marble of a portrait of Perikles. The original was executed by Kresilas in the second or third quarter of the fifth century.

25. Votive relief from the Piraeus depicting Asklepios, 329/8 BC. A bearded Asklepios is in the centre, leaning on a staff. On the right is Bendis, wearing a Phrygian hat. On the left are two worshippers. In the recessed panel at the top left, half-size, are Hermes holding a cornucopia, the three Charites (or Nymphs) and Pan holding his flute.

26. Votive relief in honour of Bendis depicting a team of victors in her equestrian relay race offering her a libation, c. 400–350.

27. Roman copy in marble of a portrait of Sokrates. The Greek original was probably made at the end of the fifth century.

28. Head of Asklepios from Milo, possibly fourth century.

29. Athena's sacred olive tree beside the Erechtheion on the Acropolis.

30. The place in the rock where Poseidon is said to have struck the Acropolis with his trident.

military partnerships were one and the same. When, for instance, the Persian king Xerxes offered an alliance to the Athenians after the battle of Salamis, the latter coolly informed him (Hdt. 8.144.2) that there was no prize on earth capable of tempting them to betray their 'Greekness' (*to Hellênikon*), a characteristic which they then went on to define as not only sharing the same blood and language, but also as recognising 'the same cults, sacrifices and religious outlook (*theôn hidrumata te koina kai thusiai êthea te homotropa*)'. The incorporation of a foreign deity into another state's pantheon was, in effect, the ultimate diplomatic compliment which one state could pay to another. Bendis' entry at the level of state-sponsored deity thus affords powerful proof of Athens' desire to appropriate Thracian military might and goodwill, and correspondingly of her perceived dependency on that alliance in the forthcoming conflict.

It would be interesting to know what arguments *pro* and *contra* were advanced in the Boule and Ekklesia on the occasion when the question whether to admit this barbarian goddess into the state pantheon appeared at the head of the agenda. It is surely inconceivable that the sponsors of the new goddess, whoever these may have been, argued their case wholly along secular lines. So how did they justify the need for her inclusion among the prestigious gods of state? We can easily enough comprehend the conditions which created the need; far less easily can we comprehend how political advantage interacted with a genuine desire to acknowledge formally the reality and beneficence of a previously unacknowledged foreign goddess. And yet I believe that we should be thinking in terms of just such an interaction. To assume that the Athenians established the cult of Bendis merely as a bait to hook the credulous Thracians, on the basis that Greek religion was only an extension of diplomacy carried on by other means, is tendentious in the extreme. Very likely Bendis received important assistance in her candidacy from Artemis, with whom the Thracian deity had a natural affinity and with whom she could conveniently be identified (cf. Fol and Marazov 1977, 23). What strengthens the probability of a link is the fact that Artemis Mounychia had a sanctuary on Mounychia Hill in close proximity to the Bendideion. The unqualified support of this priesthood might well have made a considerable difference to the outcome of the debate.

To the best of our knowledge Bendis' application was not fortified by the report of an epiphany or by the claim that the goddess had already benignly intervened in Athenian affairs. It would seem therefore that Athens was under no obligation, so to speak, to propitiate her with sacrifices and offerings. Does this constitute evidence of the fact that the Demos considered itself to be in such a parlous military condition in *c.* 432 that it waived its customary insistence upon proof of a deity's goodwill when debating the merits of her application? Was Bendis' introduction, unlike the other cults which we have so far considered, not an *ex post facto* response to divine favours already received, but anticipatory of divine favours yet to come? It should be noted that the latest date for which we have testimony relating to the cult of Bendis is 261/0 BC. It is just possible, therefore, that all interest in her had ceased long before the encyclopaedists and others had begun to cull *aitia* from the lost works of the Atthidographers, and that hers has simply disappeared from our records.

The plague

Perikles' death, and with it the demise of the transfiguration of Athenian religion over which he had presided, occurred shortly after the outbreak of the Peloponnesian War in 428. There is a tragic but fitting irony in the fact that his own death and that of his children came about in direct consequence of the strategy which he himself initiated, namely that of abandoning the Attic countryside and confining Athens' entire population inside the city walls. Although plagues were a common enough occurrence in the ancient world, the level of virulence that accompanied this particular epidemic was unlike anything previously experienced in living memory. The pestilence first assailed Athens in 430/29 and continued to rage, with brief intermissions, until the winter of 426/5 (Thuk. 2.47.3, 3.87.1-3). Such was the enormity of its impact that it undermined the foundations of Athenian piety, as is repeatedly insisted upon by Thukydides, who takes a certain grim satisfaction in the spectacle of a religious system for which he has little respect in complete disarray. He writes (2.47.4):

> All the supplications which people made at sanctuaries, all the consultations which they had at oracular shrines – everything in fact which they tried, proved useless, and in the end they gave up trying, overcome by the evil.

And again (2.53.4):

> Neither the fear of the gods nor the laws of men restrained anybody. For with regard to the former they observed that people were perishing in the same way whether or not they demonstrated piety (*sebein*), and with regard to the latter no one expected that he would live long enough to be called to justice to pay the price.

Although Thukydides confines himself to describing how the Athenians responded to the disaster in their private worship, its impact upon public religion must have been no less cataclysmic. We know that the state continued to make dedications after military victories and, at least in some of the plague years, to celebrate the City Dionysia and Lenaia, and we know as well that plays were performed on such occasions (Mikalson 1984, 219). But what of less prestigious festivals? A general scaling down of all forms of religious activity in the plague years seems inevitable. There may even have been some festivals which, either because of the impracticality of holding them now that Athens was effectively under siege or because of shortage of funds, were temporarily suspended altogether.

Conclusions

Any hypothesis regarding a radical change in the traditional system of the ordering of religious affairs in line with Athens' democratic revolution such as proposed here should be advanced only very tentatively, first because we have so little evidence for the entire preceding period, and secondly because the copious information provided by inscriptions published in the name of the Demos inevitably lends an *appearance* of increased control over the day-to-day workings of Athenian religion, whereas in reality it may merely be symptomatic of any transfer of power from an unaccountable aristocratic body to an accountable democratic one. The Demos was under an obligation to promulgate all its decisions however trivial, whereas the Areopagus, which may have taken a no less active interest in the minutiae of religious observance, was not. Even so, the evidence points strongly towards the conclusion that it now came to acquire a unique dominance over the handling of religious affairs, comparable to its control over the assembly and lawcourts.

Let us take an example. The cult of Artemis Aristoboule introduced by Themistokles had, as we have seen, 'given offence to the majority'. That 'majority' was, of course, the Demos. My suspicion is that if Themistokles had tried to introduce his goddess twenty years later, he would have been thwarted because the indications are that by this time the Demos had arrogated to itself outright control over the introduction of new gods. Whether the Demos also laid down a precise set of conditions which had to be met by the petitioning party in order for a new cult to be awarded state recognition is a yet more speculative area of investigation.

The conclusion seems irresistible that the Demos utilised religious worship for the furthering of its foreign policy. The community of allies over which Athens presided could be identified as such precisely because it owed devotion to the same set of deities, just as the military partnership with Thrace was strengthened by the entry of Bendis at the rank of state deity. There was nothing inherently sinister or cynical in such an arrangement. Political and social upheavals were invariably predicated on comparable changes in the religious landscape, as we have seen in the case of the eponymous heroes of the ten Kleisthenic tribes. In domestic as well as in foreign policy, a state's gods were deeply implicated in the advancement of its aims.

6

Asklepios and his Sacred Snake

The entry of the healing god Asklepios (Plate 28) into the Piraeus in the late 420s not only constituted an important new addition to the Athenian pantheon but also heralded a radical shift in the religious outlook of the whole community, since previously magical healing had been largely confined to hero shrines of limited, local importance. Now for the first time in Greek history, however, sickness and its cure became the exclusive concern of a personage who was soon destined to become a major god. The phenomenon is exactly paralleled by the rise of the Hippokratic tradition of medicine, and in Athens at least by the first appearance of public physicians, both of which events have their origins in the third quarter of the fifth century. Initially administered by the members of its founder's family, the cult of Asklepios was immediately able to command such a large following that within twelve months of its arrival in the Piraeus a second shrine had been established on the Acropolis. By about the end of the fifth century, moreover, it seems that the sanctuary in the Piraeus had been awarded state patronage.

Thanks to the survival of copious epigraphic material relating to Asklepios' entry and installation in Athens, we are able for the first time in the course of this investigation to re-construct in fairly precise detail the stages in the adoption and promotion of a new god.

Asklepios' origins

We know very little about the cult of Asklepios before its arrival in Athens. Like other healers whom he ultimately came to overshadow, the future god almost certainly began his career as a physician hero with an exclusively local clientèle. Homer (*Il.* 2.729-32) depicts him as an ordinary mortal, the ruler of a region in Thessaly which incorporated the towns of Trikke, Ithome and Oichalia, and father of Machaon and Podaleirios to whom he bequeathed the secrets of the healing art. In myth he is a somewhat shadowy figure, which lends testimony to his 'lateness'. Only the circumstances surrounding his birth and death were well-known, an early version of which appears in Pindar's *Pythian Ode* 3 where he is identified as the son of Apollo, a deity who is also closely associated with healing, and a mortal woman called Koronis. The story goes that Koronis betrayed Apollo and that when the god discovered her deceit he slew her, although he snatched her unborn child from the flames of her funeral pyre. In later life Asklepios' skill was such that (ll. 47-53):

> All who came to him sick with festering sores, or with limbs wounded by shiny bronze or by far-hurled stones, or with bodies that were wasting from the scorching summer or chilly winter, he loosed and delivered from their assorted aches and pains, attending some with soothing spells, making others drink comforting potions, or wrapping their limbs all round in bandages, or setting them back on their feet through surgery.[1]

Asklepios was eventually struck by Zeus' thunderbolt for having accepted a fee to resurrect one of his patients from the dead, his punishment perhaps serving as a painful reminder of the necessary and inevitable limits of medical expertise (ll. 54-8). It is perhaps not too fanciful to suppose that his all-too-human past and death, far from disqualifying him from medical practice, actually contributed to his skill and bedside manner.

The earliest evidence for the worship of Asklepios found anywhere in the Greek world – whether as hero or god at this date is unclear – is provided by a bronze *patera* or shallow offering bowl from Epidauros in the northeast Peloponnese, which was dedicated to the god by an otherwise unknown Mikylos. The dedication has been dated by its letter forms to the beginning of the fifth century (*IG* IV² 1.136; cf. *LSAG* 180). Asklepios' origins were a matter of controversy even in antiquity. On the strength of Homer's testimony, Strabo (*Geog.* 9.5.17 = C437) maintained that 'the earliest and most famous temple' was established in Trikke. Delphic Apollo, on the other hand, who should perhaps be given some credit for knowing the facts about his son's birthplace, granted priority to Epidauros (Paus. 2.26.7). In the present state of our knowledge it is quite impossible to determine which region has the more powerful claim (cf. Ziehen 1892, 195-7; Holtzmann 1984, 864). What is undeniable, however, is that it was Epidauros which took the initiative in diffusing the cult of Asklepios throughout the Mediterranean.

Asklepios was not the first healer to be worshipped at Epidauros. That distinction belongs to an obscure personage called Maleatas or Maleatis, who was already receiving cult in a sanctuary overlooking the well-preserved fourth-century theatre on the slopes of Mount Kynortion long before there is any evidence for Asklepios at the site. It seems likely

---

[1] As these lines reveal, in principle at least there was no conflict between conventional and mystical healing in the Greek world – spells and surgery were complementary not adversarial aspects of the same *technê* or discipline.

that the principal sanctuary at Epidauros was initially dedicated either to Apollo alone or to Apollo and Asklepios jointly. By the fifth century, however, Apollo had been completely ousted by his son. A similar situation evolved at Corinth where Asklepios, again an interloper at a sanctuary of Apollo, eventually took over his father's practice completely (Roebuck 1951, 154). In both instances it would be interesting to know whether Apollo's priestood was entirely happy with this arrangement. It hardly seems likely that matters should have turned out thus without some protest from the host establishment. What seems certain, however, is that in the early phase of Asklepios' career Apollo provided invaluable backing for his son. It should not be overlooked that Thessaly, which claimed to be his birthplace, lay in close proximity to Delphi.

For the first half of the fifth century, and possibly rather longer, the worship of Asklepios was confined to the northeast Peloponnese, largely due to the fact that Epidauros lay in the direct line of fire between Sparta and Athens at a period of protracted hostilities. The only other Asklepieion known to have been founded earlier than the one in the Piraeus is that on the island of Aigina, to which there is a brief allusion in Aristophanes' *Wasps* (1. 122f.). Since the play was produced in 422, the *terminus ante quem* for the sanctuary is barely one year before the god's triumphant entry into the Piraeus.

The Telemachos Monument

The arrival of the cult of Asklepios in Attica is described on the shaft of a monument which was erected in the god's sanctuary on the south slope of the Acropolis (*IG* II^2 4960; Fig. 12). Known today as the Telemachos Monument, in deference to the initiative taken by a certain Telemachos in promoting the Attic cult, this sheds valuable light upon the process by which the god and his divine entourage were conveyed to their new home:

[......] when he (i.e. the god) came up from Zea on the occasion of the Great Mysteries, he was conveyed to the El[eusinio]n and having [summoned] his sn[ake] from its home (or from his house) he brought it hither in Telemachos' [chariot]. At the same time Hyg[ieia] arrived, and in this way the whole [sanctuary (*hieron*)] was established [during the archonship of Astyphilos of Kydantidai (420/19)]. Archonship of Archeas (419/8): at this time the Kerykes (Heralds) contested their entitlement to the land (*chôrion*) and [prevented] certain plans from being implemented. Archonship of An[tiphon (418/7)] ... at this time ... . [Archonship of Euphemos (417/6)]: at this time ... . built ... . [Archonship of Charias (415/4)]: at this time ... this wooden gateway. Archonship of [Teisa]ndros (414/3): at this time repairs were carried out to the wooden gateway and the other things [connected with the rites] were set up nearby (or in addition). [Archonship of Kleokri]tos: [the ground was planted with trees and] all the sanctuary (*temenos*) was put into order ... .

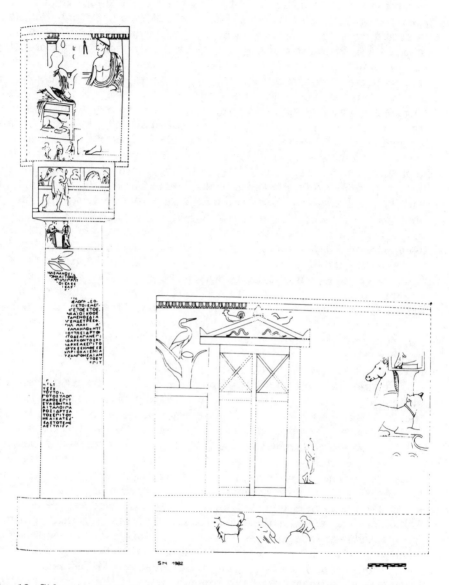

Fig. 12. Sides A and B (lower *pinax* only) of the Telemachos Monument as reconstructed by L. Beschi.

The monument was crowned by a double *pinax* or rectangular tablet which was illustrated with scenes connected with the worship of the god. According to the reconstruction by Beschi (1967, 381-436; 1983, 31-43), the lower *pinax* on Side B appears to depict Asklepios' arrival by sea, as is indicated by the prow of a ship which is just visible on the extreme right (Fig. 12, B). To the left of the ship are a pair of closed doors probably belonging to the *enkoimêtêrion* or incubation chamber. In such a building the sick passed their nights in the hope of being visited by the god in a dream and receiving instructions about how to be cured. The upper *pinax* on Side A shows Asklepios standing beside a seated female figure who is probably his daughter Hygieia. Medical instruments, such as are commonly found in Asklepieia, hang on the wall behind. To this should perhaps be joined a fragment in Verona (not shown in the reconstruction) depicting a standing, bearded figure only two-thirds the size of the deities, perhaps to be identified with Telemachos (cf. Beschi 1982, 39f. with fig. 8). He raises his right hand to the pair in a typical gesture of homage.

The monument indicates that Asklepios was conveyed by ship from Epidauros to Attica, where he disembarked at Zea port in the Piraeus probably in 421/20. He was no doubt accompanied by a large retinue of Epidaurian personnel whose task was to ensure that his installation was accomplished with due propriety and that the new priesthood entrusted with the management of his cult had been correctly instructed in Asklepian ritual. It is not altogether clear whether his initial status was that of hero or god, though later he was certainly worshipped as a god. An impressive sanctuary which lay on the east side of Zea port at the foot of Mounychia Hill now became his permanent home.

Following an interval of perhaps less than a year after his disembarkation at Zea, Asklepios, now upwardly mobile in both senses of the term, was conveyed to the Asty in Telemachos' chariot, even though no sanctuary had yet been consecrated for his use in the upper city. Although we do not know what relationship henceforth existed between the two cult centres, it is at least possible that whereas the Zea Asklepieion was a branch establishment or *aphidruma* founded under the auspices of Epidauros, that in the Asty was an *aphidruma* of Zea. Certainly the scenes depicted on Sides A and B of the Telemachos Monument suggest that the two were closely linked together, and it is quite possible that Telemachos was himself responsible for establishing them both. That a 'duplicate' cult was set up in the Asty before the completion and perhaps even before the acquisition of a permanent home for the god is a measure of the urgency, even of the desperation that attended his arrival.

The inscription on the Telemachos Monument records that when Asklepios moved to the Asty he was accompanied by his daughter Hygieia, the personification of health. It is tempting to interpret this as a symbolic reference to the impact which the god had already made upon the well-being of the citizen body. His daughter's presence at his side would have been particularly appropriate in *c.* 420 in view of the fact that the plague, which had been ravaging Athens for almost a decade, abated when the refugees from the countryside left their cramped and unhygienic quarters in the Asty and returned to their farms following the conclusion of peace (see further below).

The sacred snake

Like all such installation ceremonies, the purpose of the god's disembarkation at Zea was to give palpable reality to that community's appropriation of the god's favour. All transfers of cult required the acquisition of a symbol of the deity's physical presence whether in the form of a human actor playing the part of the god, an animal which was his familiar, a cult statue, or even, as in the case of the Mother of the Gods, a large stone. Without that symbol and without the ritual attending its entry, the link between god and community could not be forged. From descriptions of his reception elsewhere, it is no surprise to learn that Asklepios was accompanied by his sacred snake, which was thought to embody his healing power. Wherever Asklepios went, there, too, went his snake. Or perhaps the snake *was* Asklepios through some mystical equation which defied rational explanation or logical analysis. When, for instance, Asklepios was conveyed to Sikyon by a woman called Nikagora probably about a decade after his arrival in the Piraeus, he did so, Pausanias (2.10.3) tells us, 'in a cart drawn by two mules ... in the likeness of a serpent'. Again, when the Romans sought to acquire an image or *signum* of Asklepios in response to a plague which broke out in AD 292, the Epidaurians complied by dispatching by boat a snake 'in which his *numen* (or godhead) was thought to reside' (Li. *Periocha* 11; cf. Val. Max. 1.8.2, Ov. *Metam.* 15.626-744). The reptile in question was yellowish in colour and seems to have been peculiar to the region around Epidauros (Paus. 2.28.1). The intimate association between snakes and medicine was based in part on the snake's ability to undergo annual renewal by sloughing off its old skin (cf. schol. *ad* Ar. *Plout.* 733), which served as an apt metaphor for the regenerative and restorative powers of medicine; and part on the fact that medicinal herbs are produced in the earth, the abode of chthonic beings such as snakes (Küster 1913, 133).

Belief in the theriomorphic appearance of a god was by no means exclusive to Asklepianism. On the contrary, theriomorphism represents a very ancient strand of Greek religion, one which was overlaid but never entirely supplanted by anthropomorphism. A sacred reptile known as the household snake or *oikouros ophis* lived in the precinct of Erechtheus on the Acropolis. So closely was this creature identified with the person of Athena that its loss of appetite before the battle of Salamis could be interpreted as evidence that the goddess herself was abandoning the citadel (Hdt. 8.41.3). In the present instance we cannot know whether the Athenians regarded Asklepios' familiar merely as a symbol of his divine grace or as his actual theriomorphic incarnation. Possibly the physician and snake represented complementary images of the healing art. Their intimate partnership is made visibly explicit in a celebrated votive relief from Oropos in northeast Attica which depicts the hero Amphiaraos tending the dedicant's shoulder just as a real physician would do, while a snake licks the affected part as the same dedicant sleeps.

Telemachos and Epidauros

Although there is no hint as to why Telemachos decided to become the founding father of Athenian Asklepianism, there is little reason to doubt that his motives were entirely personal. In all probability either Telemachos or a close relative of his experienced the god's healing power at Epidauros, and this moved him to establish the cult in his home town. The experience of a mystical cure by a private individual may have been the leading factor in the spread of Asklepianism throughout the Greek world. The Asklepieion at Pergamon, for instance, was founded by a certain Archias, son of Aristaichmos, who was healed at Epidauros after spraining his ankle in a hunting accident (Paus. 2.26.8). Likewise the one at Halieis in the Argolid was established by a certain Thersandros after he had undergone a cure at Epidauros (Kutsch 1913, 20f. no. 33). In none of these instances is there the least evidence of any political motive.

It would be instructive to know whether the entry of Asklepios reflects an entirely spontaneous and unprompted outburst of religious devotion on the part of one individual or whether it was the product of conscious and deliberate planning by a self-interested and ambitious Epidaurian priesthood. There can be no denying that Epidauros had much to gain from the dissemination of the god's cult in terms of both prestige and wealth. *Iatreia* or healing fees were a highly profitable source of income for any sanctuary operating under licence from Asklepios, so to speak, and it is possible that offshoots from the mother sanctuary were under an obligation, moral or otherwise, to contribute a percentage of their earnings as a fee for operating in the god's name.[2]

On balance, however, it seems unlikely that Epidauros was already actively proselytising in the fifth century, first because there is no

[2] This was certainly the case by the middle of the fourth century, as we learn from an inscription from Epidauros listing all the *theôrodokoi* or 'receivers of sacred ambassadors'. The sacred ambassadors in question were dispatched to Asklepieia throughout Greece for the purpose of collecting funds for the maintenance and improvement of the mother sanctuary (*IG* IV² 94). Such was the god's popularity in the second century AD that over 320 Asklepieia are known to us both from texts and excavations, though the real figure was undoubtedly much higher. Cf. J. Beaulieu, *La religion romaine à l'apogée de l'Empire* I (1935), 30 n. 1. See further Holtzmann (1984, 865).

evidence of any embellishments to the mother sanctuary at this date such as might have been expected as the result of its increased wealth, and secondly because the earliest Asklepieia may have exercised more freedom over the conduct of their affairs and the disposal of their income than did later foundations. This is hinted at by the varied ways in which records of the god's miraculous cures are preserved at different sanctuaries. Only at Epidauros did grateful patients set up lengthy inscriptions recording their cure in minute detail (*IG* IV² 1.121-4).³ In the Asklepieion at Corinth, also an early foundation, it was customary to leave dedications in the form of the affected part of the body, whereas in the Asty and at Zea patients set up *ex-voto* reliefs illustrating visitations by the god, a type of dedication rarely found at Epidauros (cf. van Straten 1974, 178).

The Eleusinian connection

As the Telemachos Monument indicates, Asklepios' subsequent transfer from Zea to the Asty was facilitated by the hospitality of the Two Goddesses who provided the god with temporary accommodation in the City Eleusinion alongside the Panathenaic Way, a short distance northwest of the Acropolis. Since the Eleusinion was one of the few sanctuaries not to have been occupied by refugees during the Archidamian War (Thuk. 2.17.1), it was an obvious, perhaps even an inevitable choice. Even so, this arrangement testifies to the existence of close links between Asklepios and Eleusis.

Other evidence points strongly in the same direction. The fact that Asklepios' transfer coincided with the celebration of the Mysteries, as stated in the inscription on the Telemachos Monument, is a further indication of the extent to which the Eleusinian priesthood was prepared to put its services and its ceremonial at the disposal of the new cult. Acknowledgement of Asklepios' indebtedness to the Two Goddesses is further revealed in a legend which survives only in a second-century AD source but whose origin may be much older to the effect that the god actually underwent initiation at Eleusis in a ceremony which was staged exclusively for his benefit 'because he had arrived too late from Epidauros for the Mysteries' (Philostr. *VA* 4.18). Whether he consented out of deference to his Eleusinian hosts or in payment for their services is unclear.

In commemoration of this historic event the Athenians established an annual festival known as the Epidauria, which was held on the anniversary of Asklepios' installation in the Asty either on Boedromion

---

³ I readily concede the point, mentioned by a reader, that the cures in question 'may well have been fabricated by the Epidaurian priesthood as propaganda for sanctuary and cult'. What I am concerned with here, however, is merely the striking difference in fashion between Epidauros and other early Asklepieia.

17 or 18. The festival became incorporated into the structure of the Great Mysteries and provided mythic justification for the initiation of those who arrived after the ceremony had begun. As we have already seen, processions frequently functioned as a re-enactment of a deity's first entry into the community, their purpose being to perpetuate and revitalise the physical and spiritual bonds binding deity to community. The Epidauria did that and much more, for it permanently bound the destinies of two cults together. As such, it represents a highly impressive gesture of confidence on the part of one of Athens' most venerable cults in this, the newest addition to her pantheon. Another festival in honour of the god known as the Asklepieia was celebrated six months later in Elaphebolion (March/April). Like the Epidauria, it, too, was closely linked in the calendar to an older and highly prestigious festival, namely the City Dionysia. As Parke (*FA*, 65) has observed, 'The whole arrangement suggests the conscious planning of a careful priesthood working in harmony with the authorities of Athens.'

It is abundantly clear that there existed close links between Asklepios and the Two Goddesses, even to the extent that the worship of Asklepios may have been modelled in part on Eleusinian cult practice. Correspondences include the following: both incorporated mystic rites known as *teletê*, the knowledge of which was confined to initiates (Paus. 2.26.8; [Arist.] *AP* 56.4). Both had priests who bore the title *hierophantês*, 'revealer of holy objects'. A drink consisting of wheat, honey and oil, which the sick drank in honour of Asklepios' daughter Hygieia, contained the same ingredients as the *kukeon* or sacred potion which was drunk by Eleusinian initiates. Before incubation in an Asklepieion the sick were required to undergo purification by sacrificing a piglet, as, too, were initiates at Eleusis. At Epidauros a temple was erected to the worship of the Two Goddesses. Likewise there are traces of a cult of Demeter at Epidauros. A votive relief from the Asty Asklepieion, which depicts the god in the company of Demeter and Kore being hailed by six male figures, possibly members of the medical profession, testifies further to the strength of the attachment (*IG* II² 4359; cf. Aleshire 1989, 94f.).

Ideologically as well as procedurally the two cults were closely related. The Eleusinian Mysteries incorporated the idea of healing, just as the cult of Asklepios had an eschatological aspect. The Two Goddesses were apparently capable of working miraculous cures, as for instance in the case of a blind man who recovered his sight in time to witness the sacred procession from Athens to Eleusis, while Asklepios was credited with attempting to resurrect the dead. The last words of Sokrates – 'Krito, we owe a cock to Asklepios. Pay and do not forget it' (*Phd.* 118a) – appear to ascribe to the divine healer the miraculous capability of effecting for his worshippers a painless departure from this life.

Sophokles Dexion

A late tradition which is not mentioned in the Telemachos Monument reports that the dramatist Sophokles put his 'house' or *oikia* at the disposal of Asklepios when the god first arrived in the Asty. Sophokles' gesture was so admired by his fellow-countrymen that upon his death the poet was awarded heroic honours and given the name Dexion (Receiver) in gratitude for the rôle which he played in promoting the new cult (*Et. M. s.v. Dexiôn*).

The spectacle of the poet playing host to a snake has not found total support among scholars. The German scholar Körte (1896, 287-332) proposed that the *oikia* in question should be understood as an allusion to the Amyneion, the sanctuary of the healing hero Amynos (Defender) located on the south side of the Acropolis, over which, quite possibly, Sophokles presided as priest (see below). According to this interpretation what the poet did was to set up an altar to Asklepios within the Amyneion while the god was awaiting a permanent home on the Acropolis. Körte's hypothesis is strengthened by the fact that the Amyneion, which lay a short distance from the future Asklepieion, has yielded decrees dating from the mid-fourth century onwards which were passed in the name of the *orgeônes* (members of a religious association) of Amynos, Asklepios and Dexion (e.g. *IG* II^2 1252-3, 1259). Although Sophokles' own name does not appear on any inscription found in the sanctuary, the anonymous *Life of Sophokles* (11), which was composed in the first century BC, states, 'He also held the priesthood of Alon (or Halon), the hero who was nurtured by Cheiron after Asklepios'.[4]

In view of the fact that the poet was known to have written a paian in the god's honour commemorating his reception in Athens (cf. *IG* II^2 4510), we cannot ultimately dismiss the possibility that the anecdote was fabricated by Hellenistic writers as a way of accounting for Sophokles' interest in the cult. But the precise amount of historical truth behind the tradition is not the main issue here. What does matter is the belief which underpins it. Fictional or otherwise, this anecdote provides an interesting example of the heroisation of a 'culture hero'; that is to say, of a hero who, like Theseus, pioneered a major improvement in the welfare of the community, in this case by improving its health. Given the nature of Asklepios' expertise, it would have been entirely appropriate to award the poet heroic honours, particularly if the god faced severe obstacles upon his arrival in the Asty (see below).

---

[4] Ingenious as Körte's suggestion is, there are in fact parallels for the reception of a god in a private house. Xenainetos of Opos, for instance, records how a Thessalonikan woman called Sosinika put her house at the disposal of the Egyptian gods Sarapis and Isis, presumably while a permanent sanctuary was being prepared for them elsewhere (*IG* X.2.1 255, above p. 15; cf. also *IG* II^2 4969.2, cited below p. 129).

Asklepios' dispute with the Kerykes

While Asklepios occupied temporary lodgings in the City Eleusinion, Telemachos was presumably busy acquiring a permanent sanctuary for him on the southern slope of the Acropolis. The latter's eventual success in installing the *parvenu* god under the shadow of this hallowed rock represents a quite remarkable religious *coup*. Since the Acropolis was by this date crammed with sanctuaries, however, it was virtually inevitable that his precinct would encroach on property that was already sacred to some deity or another. Not surprisingly, the priesthood of Asklepios soon found itself embroiled in a boundary dispute with that of its erstwhile hosts and sponsors, the Kerykes, an influential *genos* whose members were responsible for the administration of the Eleusinian Mysteries.

The precise nature of the dispute is not recorded, but the most likely explanation is that the borders of the god's sanctuary trespassed upon land enclosed by the Pelargikon, a fortification wall which was originally constructed in Mycenaean times and whose occupation was warned against by a pronouncement from Delphi (Thuk. 2.17.1; cf. Luc. *Pisc.* 42; Fig. 8). What increases the likelihood is that a year or so earlier a seer called Lampon had proposed the following rider to the decree, discussed earlier, regulating the offering of first-fruits at Eleusis (*IG* I^3 78.54-9 = *ML* 73; see above p. 107):

> Let the basileus lay down the boundaries regarding the sacred places (*ta hiera*) in the Pelargikon, and in the future let no one erect altars in the Pelargikon without permission from the Boule and the Demos. Let no one cut out stones from the Pelargikon or remove earth or stones. If anyone breaks the law, let him pay a fine of 500 drachmas and let the basileus arraign (*esangelleto*) him before the Boule.

Although the rider does not state explicitly that the onus of enforcing this regulation is to be borne by the Kerykes, this is a reasonable inference in view of the fact that the decree itself concerns the worship of the Eleusinian goddesses. It is a clear testimony to the popularity and influence of the new god and his supporters that the quarrel was ultimately decided in favour of the Asklepian priesthood and not that of the Kerykes, who must have represented a very formidable force in Athenian religion. Given the intimate nature of the ties that existed between the two cults, however, it is unlikely that their relationship was permanently marred by the outcome of the dispute.

The Asklepieion in the Asty

As the Telemachos Monument proudly records, the Asklepieion in the Asty was completed within the space of twelve months (Fig. 13). The speed of its construction provides yet further evidence of the god's

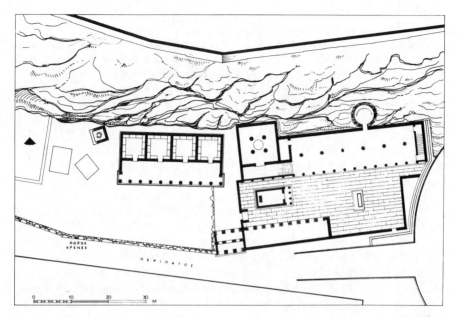

Fig. 13. The sanctuary of Asklepios on the south slope of the Acropolis in the first century AD. From J. Travlos, *PDA*.

prestige and economic resources. This is all the more remarkable in view of the fact that Athens was recovering from the effects of the Archidamian War. Over the next few years a number of minor improvements were made to the *temenos*, including the landscaping of its garden. It is at this point that the inscription breaks off. The earliest building to be erected may have been an Ionic stoa, dating perhaps as early as 420, which is located on the western terrace. Attached to the rear of the stoa are four square rooms whose internal arrangements indicate that they functioned as dining rooms or *hestiatoria* for cult personnel or visiting dignitaries. Since the stoa straddles the northern return from the polygonal wall demarcating the Pelargikon, this may have been the cause of the dispute between Asklepios and the Kerykes (cf. Travlos *PDA*, 127).

The western wall of the Ionic stoa lies a few metres from a sacred spring which, to judge from the large number of votive reliefs discovered in the area, was originally sacred to the Nymphs. All Asklepieia were located near a source of fresh water, since water played an indispensable part in the healing process. It may well have been the easy availability of fresh water which primarily commended the choice of this site to Telemachos. As commonly happened elsewhere, the priesthood of the Nymphs no doubt extracted a fee for the use of their water by the devotees of the new cult. An encircling wall was erected around the spring at the same time as the construction of the Ionic stoa, partly as a mark of respect to the original inhabitants of the site, and partly to demarcate the limits of Asklepios' territory.

The earliest identifiable temple remains which have come to light were found on the eastern terrace and date to the fourth century. It is extremely doubtful whether any such structure existed previously. No temple is alluded to in the Telemachos Monument and since Greek cult was performed *al fresco* temples were inessential to the act of worship, serving primarily to house votive offerings and cultic apparatus. Even at Epidauros the god functioned adequately without a permanent home for well over a century (cf. Burford 1969, 32). All the arrangements in the Asty sanctuary are likely to have been somewhat provisional until the turn of the fourth century, when work began on the ambitious two-storey Doric stoa on the eastern terrace (cf. Aleshire 1989, 27f.).

At the time when Asklepios' popularity reached its peak in the second half of the fourth century, the boundaries of the Asty Asklepieon extended for a distance of about 80 metres from the retaining wall of the theatre of Dionysos, which defined its eastern border, towards the future Odeion of Herodes Attikos to the west. The sanctuary consisted of two terraces to east and west of a passage connected to the so-called Peripatos pathway which encircled the Acropolis. In the earlier, much more modest form provided for it by its founder, however, it was probably less than half that size.

From private cult to state cult

The first priest of the Asty cult was almost certainly its founder Telemachos, whom Kirchner identified with Telemachos, son of Theangelos, of the deme of Acharnai (*PA* 13561), on the somewhat tenuous grounds that a certain Thea[ngelos] served as priest of Asklepios in the fourth century. An inscription found in the Asty Asklepieion, which Beschi (1967/8, 412) attributes to the Telemachos Monument, states that Telemachos 'was the first to erect the shrine and altar to Asklepios' (*IG* II² 4961). Nothing else is known about him other than the self-evident fact that he must have been extremely wealthy. He was probably an Athenian; an alternative suggestion, that he belonged to the Epidaurian priesthood, has no foundation, even though it must be conceded that foreigners are known to have pioneered the entry of new gods (see above p. 18). Initially both the Asty and Zea cults were privately organised, as is proved by a set of regulations which Telemachos himself drew up regarding sacrifices to be conducted on behalf of the god and a coterie of 'altar-sharers' who were granted accommodation inside the Asty sanctuary (*IG* II² 4355). Had Asklepios' cult been under state control at this time, these regulations would have needed authorisation from the Demos.

The next priest of the Asty Asklepieion who is known to us by name was Thea[ngelos], who, if we accept Kirchner's identification, would presumably have been the founder's great-grandson, given the usual Greek

practice of naming sons after their grandfathers. An inscription (*IG* II²
4963) which dates to the first half of the fourth century records his
munificence as follows:

> In Thea[ngelos' priesthood the entire *temenos*] was surrounded [with an
> enclosure wall (*sêkos*)] and ... was accomplished and the offering table
> (*trapeza*) [was set up], which the doers of sacred deeds (*hieropoiountes*)
> provide (i.e. with meat and other sacrificial foods) for Asklepios.

The Asklepieion in the Asty does not seem to have been awarded state
patronage until around the middle of the fourth century. A decree of this
date from the Asty, which may possibly be connected with its
reorganisation as the result of a generous gift from a certain Demon,
reads as follows (*IG* II² 4969):

> The god (i.e. Apollo) pronounced to the Athenian Demos [to dedicate] the
> house (*oikia*) of Demon and the [ga]rden [attached to it] to Asklepios and to
> make Demon [his priest]. Demon, son of Demomeles, of the deme of Paiania,
> a priest, [dedicated] both the *oikia* and garden [at the behest of the god], and
> the Athenian Demos ga[ve (i.e. him) the priesthood] of Asklepios in
> accordance with the ora[cle].

Demon apparently agreed to donate his house and garden as a source of
income to the sanctuary on condition that he was awarded the priesthood.
After due consultation with Delphi, the Demos agreed to his terms. It
may have been this act of generosity which made the change from private
cult to state cult financially viable, particularly in view of the fact that the
decree was contemporary with the Social War, a period when Athens
experienced very acute economic difficulties and when the funding of
public cults was giving rise to serious concern (see above p. 23).
Henceforth the names of the priests of Asklepios appear on dedications
together with their demotics, suggesting that the priesthood was now
being awarded for an annual term only (e.g. *IG* II² 4351-4; cf. Aleshire
1989, 14f.). After Demon retired or else died, the method of appointment
was perhaps by sortition rotating in tribal cycles, as was certainly the
case by the early third century (e.g. *IG* II² 1163. 2f.).

By contrast, the Zea Asklepieion appears to have come under the
control of the state by the early fourth century, according to a public
decree found in the Piraeus so dated by Kirchner (*IG* II² 47.23-31 = *LSGS*
11):

> The Demos resolved. Athenodo[ros] proposed. In the matters raised by
> Euthydemos, the priest of Asklepios, the Demos has decreed as follows. In
> order that the preliminary sacrifices (*prothumata*) may be offered and that
> the other sacrifices take place on behalf of the Athenian Demos in
> accordance with the expert religious opinion of Euthydemos (*ha exêgêtai
> Euthu[d]ê[m]os*), the priest of Asklepios, the Demos has decreed that the

superintendents (*epistatai*) of the Asklepieion should offer the preliminary sacrifices (*prothumata*) in accordance with the expert religious opinion of [Eu]thydemos, (*sc.* funding the sacrifice) from the money derived from the mine ... .

It is the specific reference to the Demos in the first line of the inscription which indicates conclusively that we are dealing with a public cult, though we do not, of course, know whether this document marks the occasion when it first became public. Henceforth the sacrifices which had to be performed to the god before his intervention could be sought were to be conducted 'on behalf of the Demos', and not as presumably before merely on behalf of the cult's founder and his descendants. Whereas previously the sanctuary at Zea had been administered and financed privately, now it became the object of close monitoring by the Athenian Demos. In return for public funding, Asklepios was expected to assume responsibility for the welfare of the entire community, as is indicated by the wording of the prayers which accompanied sacrifices conducted in his honour.

Euthydemos, who proposed the change, proferred his expert opinion both as *exêgêtês* or expounder of sacred law and as priest of Asklepios. He was the first to make the preliminary sacrifices in the manner ordained by the Demos, as we learn from another inscription (*IG* II^2 4962 = *SIG*^{3} 1040 = *LSG* 21) which was dated by Kirchner to the beginning of the fourth century. The fact that Euthydemos performed both roles no doubt ensured that the changeover went through smoothly. Since this would have needed the approval of an oracle, he was presumably consulted in his capacity as *pythochrêstos exêgêtês* or 'Delphic interpreter', an official who was selected by Pythian Apollo probably from a list of nominees which had been submitted by the Demos (cf. Pl. *Laws* 6.759c-e). It has been suggested that the purpose behind the state takeover was to give more importance to the Piraeus cult (cf. Sokolowski on *LSGS* 11), but it may also have been connected with the devastation inflicted upon the economy of the port at the end of the Peloponnesian War. Perhaps it was now that a 'tax (*telos*) of one drachma to Asklepios' was first levied upon the citizen body to help fund the cult (*Hesperia* 5 [1936] 401.142) and in particular to cover the fees of public physicians who operated inside the sanctuary (cf. *IG* II^2 772.9f. with Schlaifer 1940, 241 n. 1).

Asklepios and the plague

Of all the cults which we have investigated up till now, that of Asklepios stands alone in lacking any apparent political dimension whatsoever. What, then, was the explanation for his popularity? The obvious answer is that the cult was established primarily in connection with the plague which broke out in Athens in 430. There are other indications of the extreme anxiety which was generated by the epidemic among the population at this date. One is that in the 420s the Athenians can be detected tending with particular diligence those cults which were believed to be capable of providing immunity against infection. A sanctuary at the northwest corner of the Agora, for instance, plausibly identified as the Leokorion and allegedly set up in commemoration of the daughters of Leos who gave their lives in order to deliver Athens from an earlier plague, shows signs of special attention from *c.* 430 onwards after a period of neglect (cf. Thompson *Agora³*, 89; 1978, 101f.). A shrine of Herakles Alexikakos, whose cult epithet refers to his capacity to ward off the evil connected with illness, was also founded in the deme of Melite at this time. Such was its importance that it was provided with a statue by Ageladas, a leading sculptor of his day (cf. schol. *ad* Ar. *Frogs* 501; Travlos *PDA*, 274f.).

It is noteworthy, too, that the Athenians made a number of gestures at this time which were specifically intended to appease Apollo, the god of purification, whose favours had proved so unforthcoming during the epidemic. Plague is the physical antithesis of purity, and in 430 the Athenians had good cause to fear that the god, gravely offended by their recent behaviour, was himself the author of the current epidemic (cf. D.S. 12.58.6; see above p. 114). Upon the outbreak of war they had been compelled to violate the sanctity of their temples and hero-shrines and use them as living quarters for the refugees from the Attic countryside (cf. Thuk. 2.17.1). Many, too, unable to conduct proper funerary ritual on behalf of each family member who perished as a result of the plague, resorted to 'shameless methods of burial', which would have been wholly inadequate for containing the pollution of the dead (Thuk. 2.52.4). As a way of countering Apollo's wrath, in the winter of 426/5 the Athenians purified the sacred island of Delos, Apollo's birthplace, by exhuming and removing all burials from the island and transferring them to neighbouring Rheneia, simultaneously decreeing that no births or deaths should henceforth take place on Delos (Thuk. 3.104.1-2). They also revived on a grand scale an ancient Ionian festival known as the Delia which was held in honour of Apollo and Artemis. This latter initiative was either intended as a thank-offering for final deliverance from the plague or else constituted a pious hope that relief was on the way (Thuk. 3.104.2-6; D.S. 12.58.6-7).

There are, however, certain objections to the theory that Asklepios' entry was directly connected with the plague. One is this: if the first epidemic broke out in 430, then why did the Athenians wait ten long years before availing themselves of his services? Secondly, Pausanias (1.3.4) specifically claims that the god who came to the salvation of the Athenian people was a previously unrecognised deity called Apollo Alexikakos (Averter of Illness), who acquired this title 'because in accordance with an oracle from Delphi he stayed the plague which afflicted Athens at the time of the Peloponnesian War'. Neither objection is particularly compelling. It must have been obvious to everyone that even if Apollo Alexikakos had rendered useful service on this occasion, his intervention hardly amounted to an unqualified success in view of the fact that the epidemic reduced Athens' population by perhaps as much as a third. Few therefore would have disagreed with the proposition that the services of a more effective saviour be enlisted for the future. The reason why Asklepios initially established himself in Zea may well have been due to the fact that the Piraeus was the first region in Attica to fall victim to the epidemic (Thuk. 2.48.2). Given the density of its population, coupled with its dependency on easily polluted wells, the incidence of contagious and infectious diseases is likely to have been higher here than anywhere else in Attica. Furthermore, it is perfectly possible that the goodwill of Asklepios was enlisted not at the time of the plague but only after it had abated, as an *ex post facto* measure intended to prevent a similar disaster in the future. Finally, we must also give appropriate weight to the sheer impracticability of trying to install the cult of a foreign deity during wartime. The transfer of Asklepios' cult to Athens was surely the result of prolonged consultation with the Epidaurian priesthood, a condition which could only have been met after the restoration of peace.[5]

Other healing cults in Attica

Although we might expect Asklepios to have taken considerable business away from pre-existing healing cults in Attica, his arrival seems if anything to have had the opposite effect. Far from eclipsing his rivals, the god seems actually to have contributed to an increase in their practices. Evidently there were enough aches and pains to go around. Besides, it is hardly to be expected that all the sick of Attica would have been able to travel either to Athens or the Piraeus and remain there, possibly indefinitely, awaiting a cure.

Before Asklepios' entry into Attica the most prominent healing sanctuary belonged to Athena Hygieia, whose cult was also situated on the Acropolis. It would be fascinating to know what attitude the priesthood of this goddess adopted towards the new god. Did it see Asklepios as complementing their own goddess's medical skills or as setting up a rival practice? Admittedly prevention is not the same thing as cure, and it is possible that Hygieia, as her title suggests, was entrusted primarily with the continued well-being of the healthy, rather than with ministering to the sick, as suggested, for instance, by the *Orphic Hymn to Hygieia* (68.13) which bids the goddess 'Keep away the

---

[5] Mikalson (1984, 220) attractively suggests that the Athenian attack on Epidauros in the first year of the Peloponnesian War (cf. Thuk. 2.56.4) may have been an abortive attempt to appropriate the god's grace – by force. This, however, assumes that there was already considerable public interest in the cult at this date, for which there is no other evidence.

cursed pain of evil disease'. Even so, her cult appears to have been one of the principal casualties from the rise of Asklepios, in view of the fact that no dedication to the goddess has been found later than 420. Given Hygieia's familial relationship with Asklepios, it may be that the god's professional concern included preventive as well as curative medicine.

Another prominent healing figure was the *hêrôs iatros* or 'hero physician' who in a variety of guises was venerated at various sites including the Asty, where he was later identified as Amphilochos; Marathon, where he was known as Aristomachos; Eleusis, where he went under the name of Oresinios; and Rhamnous, where he was known as Aristomachos and later supplanted by Amphiaraos. The largest Attic healing sanctuary, however, was that of Amphiaraos at Oropos, who is first attested in Aristophanes' lost play *Amphiaraos* which was produced in 414 (cf. Kearns *AH*, 18).

We should note that the success enjoyed by Asklepios both in the Piraeus and the Asty was not confined to these two centres. An inscription dated to the first century AD bids 'farmers and locals to sacrifice to the twin deities (viz. Asklepios and Hygieia) in the manner prescribed by religious law' (*IG* II² 1364). A chance find such as this hints at the possible existence of an extensive network of sanctuaries dedicated to the god and his entourage throughout Attica, as well as to the continuing importance of the cult into the Christian era.

Finally, those Athenians who had the leisure and wealth to do so may still have preferred to make a pilgrimage to Epidauros rather than to rely on a local manifestation of the god. One such patient was the politician Aischines, who journeyed to Epidauros when suffering from a boil on the head. His cure, which fell somewhat short of the miraculous, took three months (*AP* 6.330; Herzog 1931, no. 75).

Conclusions

Asklepios' rapid rise to prominence in the Greek world provides a classic example of the speed with which an upwardly-mobile cult was capable in favourable circumstances of attaining a truly Panhellenic ascendancy. It also furnishes further evidence of the way in which Athens not only took the initiative in hosting a foreign, originally localised deity, but also acted as a powerful catalyst for that deity's absorption Greece-wide. Athens was not, we should note, the only polis to admit Asklepios into her midst in this period. Aigina certainly, and possibly Corinth and Sikyon, instituted cults before the end of the fifth century. What probably counted most for the future of Asklepianism as a Mediterranean-wide religion, however, was the god's arrival in Athens, coupled, we might add, with the strong support which he received from Delphi and Eleusis.

A feature of the worship of Asklepios which sharply distinguishes it from conventional Greek religion is that it was concerned with the needs of the individual rather than those of the state. One of the most absorbing questions which can be asked in relation to the rise of Asklepianism is whether it actually sanctioned a new concept of self, and in so doing offered an antidote to conventional, polis-centred religion. Much of what we know about its *modus operandi* points to this general conclusion. Of all the gods, it was Asklepios, arguably, who came closest to challenging the polytheistic basis of Greek religion and who in consequence was destined to pose the most serious challenge to Christianity. It is perhaps for this same reason that the early Christians were so ruthlessly efficient in destroying his sanctuaries.

The sick who spent the night in Asklepios' sanctuary undergoing incubation were by definition a random cross-section of the citizen body, united only in the fact that they suffered from a varied assortment of illnesses and injuries. Indeed the fact that human misery could now be perceived as the proper concern of a major deity may be regarded as symptomatic of an increasing self-preoccupation on the part of the Greeks in general. Since, moreover, a cure was normally revealed to the incubant in a dream in which either the god or his sacred snake appeared and spoke directly, suppliants of Asklepios may be said to have routinely enjoyed a type of personal relationship with their god which in other cults was highly exceptional. What we are probably witnessing, then, is the emergence of a wholly new attitude towards both illness and the gods. It may have been in direct response to Athens' experience of the plague that her people, no longer regarding health as the normal condition of the corporate citizen body, invoked the assistance of a god who was prepared to bestow his favour upon a section of humanity whose very feebleness and incapacitation would have precluded it from meriting the attention of his more venerable and illustrious colleagues.

The growth in the cult of Asklepios at the beginning of the fifth century exactly parallels the growth of a tradition of systematic medical inquiry in the Greek world. Now for the first time investigations were being conducted into the causes and treatment of disease. Now, too, attempts were being made to elevate medicine from mere *magganeia* or magic to the status of a *technê* or rational discipline. The reason why Asklepios and medical science make a simultaneous appearance is due wholly to their complementarity. Sickness and its cure were now being identified for the first time as legitimate and self-contained areas of professional and divine concern.

It is interesting to note that there is a striking consistency in the iconography exhibited by statues of the god throughout the Greek world. Almost invariably Asklepios is depicted bearded with a serene expression on his face, either seated or leaning on his staff around which his snake entwines itself. This uniformity may have been due in part to the powerful, centralised control exercised by the Epidaurian priesthood, who sought in this way to maintain their unchallenged dominance over the worship of their god. But it may also be regarded as an extension of the belief held by medical practitioners that the human body is subject to a single set of governing principles.

7

Sokrates and the New *Daimonia*

In February 399 an indictment was brought against the philosopher Sokrates (Plate 27) on the double charge of impiety and corrupting the young. Radical democracy had been restored just four years previously, after a brief period of tyrannical government following Athens' defeat at the end of the Peloponnesian War. There can be no doubt whatsoever that Sokrates' prosecutors were politically motivated, the accused being a convenient scapegoat on which to hang a large share of the blame for Athens' recent internal upheavals. Not only was he openly contemptuous of democracy, but he also numbered among his closest associates and pupils Kritias, a leading member of the so-called Thirty Tyrants who terrorised Athens from 404 to 403, Charmides, one of their principal henchmen, and the traitor Alkibiades, whose desertion to Sparta in the final years of the war was arguably a leading factor in Athens' defeat (e.g. Aischin. 1.173; Xen. *Mem.* 1.2.12). The prime instigator of the proceedings appears to have been Anytos, a moderate democrat and fanatical opponent of the sophists, who had been largely instrumental in achieving a general amnesty for those of oligarchical persuasion after the overthrow of the tyranny. Presumably because the pursuit of a private vendetta by a politician who was peddling a comprehensive policy of reconciliation would have gravely undermined the latter's credibility, Anytos took a back seat at the trial, leaving a fourth-rate poet called Meletos to put his name to the affidavit. A person of this name is also known to have prosecuted the orator Andokides for impiety a few months earlier, and it is not improbable that they are one and the same. Nothing of any note is known about the third prosecutor, whose name was Lykon.

The charges against Sokrates

The trial of Sokrates is of major importance for the present inquiry since one of the counts against the accused was that of 'introducing new *daimonia*'. So far as we know, this was the first occasion in Athenian history that anyone had ever been prosecuted for a crime of this nature. Unprecedented though the charge was, however, the existence at this

136

date of a statute requiring proposals for the introduction of new gods to be submitted before the Ekklesia for approval is entirely consistent with what we have identified as the Demos' growing conviction, born of past experience and its own high-handed behaviour, that religious innovation was politically too sensitive an issue not to be in its own hands.

The most trustworthy source for the wording of the charge is the third-century AD writer Diogenes Laertios (2.40), who claims to be citing verbatim from a Roman writer called Favorinus, who in turn claims to have seen a copy of the affidavit in the Metroön in the Agora which functioned as a public archive:

> Meletos, son of Meletos, a demesman of Pithos, has brought this charge and lodged this affidavit (*tade egrapsato kai antômosato*) against Sokrates, son of Sophroniskos of Alopeke. Sokrates has broken the law (*adikei*) by not acknowledging (*ou nomizôn*) the gods whom the state acknowledges and introducing (*eisêgoumenos*) other new daimonic beings (*hetera kaina daimonia*). He has also broken the law by subverting (*diaphtheirôn*) the young. The penalty should be death.

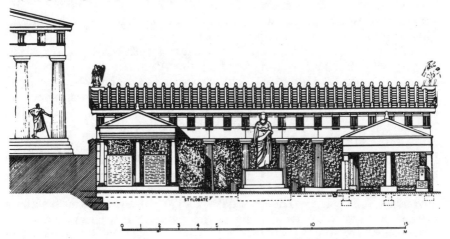

Fig. 14. The Stoa Basileios on the west side of the Agora where Sokrates faced his pre-trial hearing. From M.L. Lang, *Socrates in the Agora* (Princeton, New Jersey, 1978).

As Sokrates' alleged offences primarily came under the general heading of *asebeia* or impiety, Meletos was required to file his affidavit before the *archon basileus* in the Stoa Basileios at a pre-trial hearing, somewhat similar to an arraignment, called an *anakrisis* (Fig. 14). The purpose of this hearing was to determine whether the prosecution's case merited sending the accused to trial. Having determined that it did, the *basileus* recorded the plea of the accused, took written depositions from the witnesses, who could not be cross-examined in court, and fixed a date for his trial in the Heliaia, the popular court empowered to hear cases involving impiety.[1] Sokrates pleaded not guilty to all changes.

Definition and origins of *asebeia*

Asebeia, impiety, was not heresy. Heresy in a sense analogous to the definition provided by the *Oxford Dictionary of the Christian Church* (*s.v.*), namely 'the formal denial or doubt of any defined doctrine of the Catholic church', did not exist among the Greeks, for the simple reason that their religious system was too chaotic and disorderly to permit a synthesis of belief along dogmatic, Christian lines. Rather, *asebeia* covered a multitude of offences against the gods, one's parents, one's native land and the dead – with the emphasis firmly on behaviour and not belief. The word, or rather its adjectival equivalent, first makes an appearance in the work of the sixth-century poet Theognis of Megara, who urged his friend Kyrnos to 'Respect and fear the gods, for this prevents a man from doing or saying anything that is *asebê*' (l. 1179f.).

We do not know for certain when *asebeia* first found its way on to the Athenian statute books nor what range of offences it included when it did. The third-century AD philosopher Porphyry (*Abst.* 4.22 p. 268.23-6 T) would have us believe that Drakon, a legendary lawgiver of the sixth century BC, passed a law instructing the Athenians 'as a group (*en koinôi*) to honour the gods and local heroes in accordance with ancestral practice'. However, the existence of a statute holding the populace collectively responsible for a specific code of behaviour is totally inconsistent with Athenian law, which observed the principle of individual guilt, quite aside from the fact that such a regulation would have been impossible to enforce. Moreover, the only two recorded instances of the violation of religious law by individual Athenians before the Peloponnesian War period are of a very different character from that envisaged by Porphyry. The first, dated c. 630, concerns the massacre by members of the Alkmaionid *genos* of the supporters of Kylon, when the latter were clinging in supplication to the statue of Athena on the Acropolis. In consequence of their crime, a curse was laid on the Alkmaionidai and their descendants in perpetuity.[2] Since the offence

---

[1] Although the charge of 'corrupting the young' would properly have fallen within the competence of the *thesmothetai* or judicial board in charge of proceedings in connection with non-religious offences (cf. [Arist.] *AP* 59), Sokrates' case came before the *archon basileus* because impiety was officially the more serious charge. As Derenne (1930, 146) points out, the Greeks were not so punctilious as ourselves in drawing rigid juridical distinctions.

[2] We are not told who actually uttered the imprecation on this occasion, but since the offence had been committed in the sanctuary of Athena probably it was the priestess herself, just as it was the Eleusinian priesthood who cursed Alkibiades in 415 after he had been convicted of parodying the Mysteries (Plu. *Alk.* 22.4). Both curses are likely to have been authorised by a decree or *psêphisma* of the citizen body, possibly in response to a recommendation by the Areopagus.

properly constituted an act of sacrilege or *hierosulia*, however, it is doubtful whether it came under the heading of *asebeia* at all.

The only other incident which can be cited as evidence for the existence of a law against *asebeia* before the Peloponnesian War concerns the alleged revelation by Aeschylus in one of his plays of secrets pertaining to the Eleusinian Mysteries. Aristotle (*NE* 3.1.1111a 9f. *OCT*), who is our earliest source for the incident, states merely that the poet did not know that these mysteries were not to be divulged. For further information we have to turn to Aristotle's pupil Herakleides of Pontos, who claims that the accused took refuge at the altar of Dionysos before being prevailed upon to stand trial, and that he was subsequently acquitted (fr. 170 Wehrli). Even assuming that this anecdote is historical, however, it does not provide proof of the existence of a law against impiety before 456, the year of Aeschylus' death, since the crime may well have constituted an offence against what are elsewhere described as 'the laws and institutions (*ta nomima kai ta kathestêkota*)' of the Eleusinian priesthood, rather than those of the Demos (cf. Plu. *Alk.* 22.3).

The decree of Diopeithes

Very likely *asebeia* did not become a punishable offence in Athens until *c.* 432 when the Demos passed a decree or *psêphisma* on the recommendation of a soothsayer called Diopeithes. Plutarch, who provides the earliest and indeed only testimony for the decree, says this about it (*Per.* 32.1):

> Diopeithes proposed a *psêphisma* relating to the impeachment (*eisangellesthai*) of those who do not acknowledge divine things (*tous ta theia mê nomizontas*) or who teach doctrines relating to the heavens.

Though some scholars doubt the historicity of Diopeithes' decree, the increasingly proprietary attitude manifested by the Demos towards religion in this period makes it inherently likely that a law of this kind was passed just before the outbreak of the Peloponnesian War.

Although the charges brought against Sokrates are likely to be connected with Diopeithes' decree, it is important to note that Sokrates did not face trial under the procedure known as *eisangelia* or impeachment, which Plutarch suggests was mandatory in cases of this kind. Instead his offence came under the heading of a *graphê* or indictment (cf. Pl. *Euthyph.* 2a; D.L. 2.40). If Plutarch's testimony is accurate, the distinction is not trivial, since *eisangelia* was used in the prosecution of serious offences such as treason, whereas a *graphê* covered only misdemeanours. One possible explanation for the apparent discrepancy is that Diopeithes' law had lapsed briefly in 403 at the time of the re-inscription of Athens' lawcode by Nikomachos, and that when the laws were re-instated it was re-classified under the less serious heading of *graphê*. If so, that is a bitter irony, given the outcome of the trial.

Since Sokrates' trial was politically inspired, it may be appropriate to consider the original motivation behind Diopeithes' decree. Late sources indicate that it served as a conveniently oblique way of undermining Perikles' political base by representing him as the *intime* of undesirable aliens who scoffed at Athens' laws. Its chief victims were all members of Perikles' circle, notably the philosophers Anaxagoras and Protagoras, and Perikles' mistress Aspasia. But was this the intention behind the law? In other words, was the undermining of Perikles' popularity Diopeithes' principal or even sole objective, and if so was this also the objective of the majority in the Ekklesia who voted his proposal on to their statute books? Were Diopeithes and his supporters primarily cynical political opportunists or incontinent religious bigots? And supposing for the sake of argument that their aim was at bottom political, should we then think of the Demos as their fellow-travellers, conniving in the passage of a law whose real purposes lay barely concealed beneath a superficial veneer of pietism, or as their simple-minded dupes?

Given the fact that Diopeithes was himself a professional seer, a case certainly exists for regarding him as a religious fanatic who, in the words of Derenne (1930, 21), was 'battling for the conservation of popular belief'. The prohibition against the teaching of matters relating to the heavens can then be interpreted as a direct retort to the meteorological speculations of Anaxagoras of Miletos, whose famous assertion that the heavenly bodies were no more than clods of earth amounted to a belittling of Diopeithes' professional expertise, since seercraft was premissed on the assumption that the sky is permeated with signs from the gods. The scholiasts to Aristophanes' *Birds* (l. 988) actually describe Diopeithes as 'a little crazy', though it is questionable whether their testimony is based on anything more than the bad press which Diopeithes receives in Comedy.

Whatever the exact nature of Diopeithes' motives, we are certainly not entitled to regard him as wholly destitute of religious scruples. As a prominent politician from *c.* 433 to 414, he was ideally placed to lead a counter-attack against the sophists, whose popularity may well have been declining in the years immediately preceding the outbreak of the Peloponnesian War as the city geared itself up for a showdown with Sparta. In *c.* 432 the omens were such that traditionally-minded Athenians, always in the majority, would have had every reason to feel distinctly uneasy about the blasphemous blatherings of a coterie of incoherent intellectuals. One obvious way to relieve this feeling was to furnish immediate proof of goodwill towards the gods. At no time since the Persian Wars had Athens' destiny been more dependent upon their favours. As already noted (p. 111), there is good evidence to indicate that Athens was making strenuous efforts to placate Apollo in the late 430s and 420s, and it is not inconceivable that Diopeithes' decree belonged to the same general programme of attempted appeasement, particularly in view of the fact that it constituted a defence of seercraft, over which Apollo himself held undisputed sway.[3]

Problems of evidence

The trial and execution of Sokrates is generally regarded as the most notorious crime committed by Athenian democracy and it continues today to be the subject of fierce and lively controversy. In 1989 alone three books appeared on the subject, I.F. Stone's *The Trial of Socrates*, T.L. Brickhouse and N.D. Smith's *Socrates on Trial*, and C.D.C. Reeve's *Socrates in the Apology*. Though all are illuminating in their different ways, none sheds much useful light on the charge of impiety.

In order to comprehend the full implications of the particular brand of *asebeia* with which Sokrates was charged, we should, of course, need to possess a copy of the prosecution's speech instancing the evidence upon which the complaint was based. But no such document has survived. Instead what we have are two different versions of the speech for the defence written by Sokrates' pupils, Plato and Xenophon.[4] Since Sokrates did not deliver either of them, neither should be regarded as a primary source. In view, moreover, of the reverential attitude of their authors towards the accused, neither can be assumed to be entirely free of bias. Though Plato claims to have been present at the trial himself (cf. *Apol.* 34a, 38b), he did not publish, and may not have composed, his *Apology* until about a decade afterwards. His account is therefore likely to be more contrived than the speech which Sokrates delivered impromptu on his own behalf (Pl. *Apol.* 17c; Xen. *Apol.* 8; *Mem.* 4.8.4). It is, after all, a literary artefact, and may well have been written with hindsight and a pervasive sense of tragic irony. It would hardly be surprising either if, in the light of the outcome of the trial, Plato felt moved to present his hero in a rather more uncompromising and belligerent attitude than the one which the latter actually assumed in front of his judges. Xenophon's *Apology* has much less claim to authenticity than Plato's, for its author was in Asia Minor at the time of the trial and did not return to Athens until some years later following a period of exile. Although he claims to have consulted a certain Hermogenes son of Hipponikos, also a pupil of

---

[3] Whether, as other late sources indicate, the Athenians continued to prosecute free-thinkers throughout the Peloponnesian War, their victims including the musician Damon (after 428), Euripides (before 425), Diogenes of Apollonia (*c.* 420), Diagoras of Melos (*c.* 415) and Prodikos of Keos (*c.* 400), is impossible to verify. All that can be said is that in the light of their persistent failure to elicit much support from their gods in this period, such a manifestation of intermittent collective paranoia would be entirely understandable.

[4] Xenophon's *Memorabilia* was in fact intended as a counterblast to a written attack by an 'accuser' (1.2), thought to have been a sophist called Polykrates who wrote up the prosecution's speech some years after the trial.

Sokrates, who attended the trial (*Apol.* 2, 10; *Mem.* 4.8.4; cf. Pl. *Phd.* 59b), we do not know how accurate was the report which the latter gave him nor how closely Xenophon chose to abide by it.

Since we cannot escape the influence of our two chief witnesses, however, and indeed have little with which to supplement their testimony, our best course of action will be to try to mediate between the two. As witnesses for the defence, so to speak, they both had a powerful motive for obscuring the truth about Sokrates' guilt – if indeed guilty he was. So, too, did the prosecution, for by trading in innuendo, it could hope to render the defendant uncertain of the exact source and nature of the complaints – the exact condition of Kafka's K. in *The Trial* – a technique brought to perfection by ecclesiastical courts presiding over heresy trials during the Inquisition.

'Not acknowledging the gods whom the state acknowledges'

So how did a pious Athenian 'acknowledge' a god, which were 'the gods whom the state acknowledges', and what constituted culpable negligence in this area of civic responsibility? Brickhouse and Smith (1989, 31f.) comment: 'Meletos' charge is not that Sokrates completely neglects proper religious practice; it is that Sokrates is a complete atheist.' Likewise Reeve (1989, 79) declares: 'Despite the seeming incongruity between the written charge and its oral interpretation, the real charge, the charge that Sokrates must answer, is a charge of atheism.' Stone (1989, 139), who also takes 'acknowledge' to be a synonym for 'believe', comments dismissively: 'The discussion of his religious views diverts attention from the real issues.' I want to propose here that the contrary is the case; namely that Sokrates' religious views, or more accurately his religious practices, are as much 'the real issue' as anything else.[5]

In Xenophon's *Apology* the defendant claims (*Apol.* 11) that numerous people had observed him 'sacrificing during the common festivals and on the public altars'. Likewise in the *Memorabilia* Xenophon asserts (1.1.2) that Sokrates 'had frequently been seen sacrificing both at home and on the public altars of the state'. Later he describes him fulsomely (1.2.64) as 'the most conspicuous of all men in his devotion to the gods'. Xenophon therefore counters what he evidently interprets as a charge of religious negligence with a bold assertion to the contrary, by depicting Sokrates as a man of exemplary piety and the victim of malicious and unfounded slander. In the absence of any doctrine or creed upon which to test the accused in the way that, say, Galileo was tested in the course of his trial for heresy, this was, of course, the most obvious line of defence. Piety

---

[5] It would be extremely illuminating to know how much time the prosecution devoted proportionately to the three charges in the *graphê*, but of this there is no hint at all. In Plato's *Apology* Sokrates devotes approximately as much time to the two counts of *asebeia* as he does to the charge of corrupting the young.

consisted in performing one's cultic duties, and visibility in this area was the litmus test, as these passages amply demonstrate by their somewhat strident reference to Sokrates' conspicuous participation in religious ritual. The same defence is used in lawcourt speeches dealing with cases of disputed adoption, where plaintiff and defendant habitually back up their claim to be the genuine heir of the deceased by arguing that they, unlike their opponents, have been frequently observed performing the customary practices on behalf of the dead.

Plato's Sokrates adopts a very different approach from Xenophon's. Instead of professing his faith in the traditional gods, he claims to be totally baffled by the charge. So he interrogates his prosecutor as follows (*Apol.* 26c):

> I am unable to understand whether you claim that I teach that I acknowledge there to be some gods, and that I myself acknowledge that gods exist, and that I am not a complete atheist (*atheos*)[6] in this respect, but that these are not 'the gods whom the state acknowledges' but other ones, and that this is what you charge me with, that I acknowledge other ones. Or do you allege that I do not acknowledge gods at all and that I teach this to others?

To which Meletos replies:

> That is what I allege, that you do not acknowledge gods at all (*parapan ou nomizeis theous*).

As the defendant surely intended, Meletos' reply merely serves to obfuscate matters yet further, since, in order to be consistent with his own affidavit, what Meletos ought to have replied is that Sokrates did indeed worship gods, or at least a spurious semblance thereof, namely the *kaina daimonia* referred to in the other part of the religious charge, but not the official gods of the Athenian state. This is actually what Sokrates himself points out to Meletos a little later when he accuses him of contradicting himself (27a). So why does Meletos fall into Sokrates' trap? Perhaps he was not very bright, or perhaps Sokrates temporarily tied him up in knots, or perhaps Plato merely puts a rather stupid answer into his mouth, or perhaps the details of the exchange (but not necessarily the substance) are merely a literary invention.

Unlike his counterpart in Xenophon, Plato's Sokrates makes no claim to punctiliousness in the discharging of his religious obligations. Instead

---

[6] It is impossible to know how best to translate '*atheos*' in this passage since the adjective is used to mean 'ungodly' or 'abandoned by the gods', just as frequently as 'unbelieving in the gods' (cf. *LSJ*[9]). Its earliest occurrence is in Pi. *Pyth.* 4.162 (*c.* 462) where a hero is described as being rescued from 'ungodly weapons (*atheôn beleôn*)'. As W.K.C. Guthrie (s.v. 'Atheism' in *OCD*[2]) points out, the adjective 'tended to be a term of abuse rather than a reasoned description'. In other words, little of value can be gleaned from its use in this passage.

Introducing New Gods

he asks his prosecutor if what he is implying is that he, Sokrates, does not acknowledge the divinity of Helios and Selene, the sun and moon, as the rest of mankind does (26cd). When Meletos answers that this is precisely what he means, Sokrates proceeds to mock his prosecutor for ascribing to him views held by Anaxagoras, who was charged with impiety for asserting that Helios was a glowing rock and Selene a piece of earth – crackpot theories which he, the defendant, like all sensible Athenians, finds totally ludicrous (26de). As scholars have often noted, Sokrates adopts a prevaricating attitude in order to avoid committing perjury. This in turn sends out a clear signal that the charge did not lack substance, since Plato's Sokrates is incapable of telling a falsehood.[7] As a result he is reduced to making his prosecutor look either foolish or malicious or both. In this he succeeds admirably.

In conclusion, I suggest that Sokrates was accused of neglecting to perform sacrifices and of failing to participate in state festivals. The charge, one of non-conformity in religious practice rather than unorthodoxy in religious belief (cf. Burnet 1924, 104), was fully justified, notwithstanding Xenophon's claims to the contrary.

Who, finally, were 'the gods whom the state acknowledges'. In all probability the formula denoted the publicly sponsored gods at the top end of the scale and the privately sponsored domestic ones at the bottom. The defendant was not being accused of atheism in the modern sense of the term but of a particularly offensive brand of irreligiosity, namely failing to pay his dues to the select band of gods on whose goodwill Athens' survival and prosperity depended. There may have been no shortage of atheists in late-fifth-century Athens. But Sokrates was not among their number nor was he formally so accused.[8] His crime was the neglect of civic and approved gods in fatal combination with the promotion of private and unapproved *daimonia*. And that made him far more dangerous than any atheist. The Athenian law against *asebeia* is thus comparable to the British law on blasphemy passed in 1676 and still in force today, which, to the recent anger of Britain's Moslem community

---

[7] Possibly Plato's Sokrates' alludes to Helios as a somewhat oblique way of demonstrating that he did acknowledge the gods of the Athenian state (26d). The choice of deity is at first sight somewhat odd, as Mikalson (1989, 98) points out, since to the best of our knowledge there was no official cult of Helios in Athens at this time. In view of the fact that the Greeks customarily prayed to the sun at its rising and setting (cf. Hes. *Works and Days* 339 with M.L. West *ad loc.*; Pl. *Laws* 10.887e), it is just conceivable that the defendant ingeniously chose this example in order to turn the tables on his accusers and jury alike, by demonstrating that they, too, committed the 'crime' of worshipping a god who had not been formally 'introduced'.

[8] Since Sokrates has left no writing behind, his religious views are impossible to identify with certainty. On the evidence of Plato's *Apology*, however, in addition to the conviction that he was attended by a personal *daimonion*, they included the following: belief in a single god, even though he occasionally alluded to 'the gods' (42a; e.g. 41d); uncertainty about man's condition in the afterlife (40c-41c); and respect for the utterances of the Delphic oracle (20c-22e).

in the matter of the publication of Salman Rushdie's *Satanic Verses*, serves only to protect the doctrines and rituals of the established Church of England.

What strengthens the hypothesis that the charge of neglecting the state gods was not a mere smokescreen is the fact that in 410 the Demos authorised a review of Athens' lawcode under the direction of Nikomachos and a board of secretaries known as *anagrapheis*. Part of their duty according to Lysias (30.29) was 'to transcribe the ancestral rites *(ta patria)*', which were then presumably displayed, along with the other laws, in a central archive. The review had initially been expected to take only four months, but the exercise turned out to be far more complicated and laborious than anticipated, and dragged on for six years. It was still incomplete in 403 when the Thirty Tyrants came to power and suspended the work of the commission. Nikomachos and the *anagrapheis* were re-appointed by the Demos in 403 and continued working on the project until 399 when Nikomachos was accused of malfeasance.[9] Sokrates therefore stood trial at a time when the Demos was seeking to establish the extent and limits of its religious obligations, which, it is safe to say, had grown increasingly complex and confused over the years.

We can therefore be confident that the jury would have paid extremely close attention to the charge of 'not acknowledging the gods whom the state acknowledges', since Sokrates' alleged crime not only constituted a test case for the validity of the newly published codification, but also presented a challenge to the authority of the democratically appointed commission, and thus by implication to the newly restored religious authority of the Demos itself.

'Introducing other new daimonic beings'

Scholarly opinion is divided about whether the *daimonia* of the second charge should be interpreted as an adjective with *pragmata* or some such word understood (i.e. 'introducing new daimonic practices') or as a noun (i.e. 'introducing new daimonic beings'). Reeve (1989, 75f.), for instance, takes *daimonia* to be a reference 'not to a daimonic thing ... but to the doings of a *daimôn*, to its utterances, visitations and pronouncements', while Brickhouse and Smith (1989, 34) render 'new divinities'. For our purposes, however, the distinction is of little importance, since the introduction of a new *daimonion* would necessarily have entailed the introduction of new religious practices as well, whereas, conversely, the

---

[9] It is sometimes alleged that in his first term of office Nikomachos was concerned with secular laws and in his second with sacred ones (e.g. Clinton 1982, 34f.). This is disputed by Robertson (1990, 66) who argues that the date of compilation of the sacrifices to which Lysias refers was 'any time between 410 and 401'. Some fragments from the *stêlai* inscribed in 410-404 indicate that they included at least a summary account of ritual expenditures (*IG* I[3] 239-41; Robertson 1990, 57).

existence of new religious practices implied, if it did not necessitate, the existence of a new *daimonion*. According to Brickhouse and Smith (1989, 34) the charge against Sokrates was one of introducing 'new entities that are not real divinities at all', their argument being that if the new entitities were 'real', his action would have been 'a boon to the city'. As this book has demonstrated, however, new gods and their sponsors were by no means assured of a warm welcome when they petitioned for entry into a Greek community, and Athens was no exception.

Scholars are virtually unanimous in their belief that the basis for the charge was Sokrates' well-known guiding spirit or prophetic voice, although there was sufficient disagreement both before and during the trial to provoke discussion. In Plato's *Euthyphro* (3b), for instance, when Sokrates is discussing the charge with a sacred expounder or *exêgêtês*, who is therefore an expert in such matters, the latter comments:

> It's because you say that the *daimonion* comes upon you from time to time (*sautôi hekastote gignesthai*). So, on the grounds that you are innovating in religious matters (*kainotomountos sou peri ta theia*), Meletos lays this charge against you and comes to court in order to excite prejudice against you, well knowing that matters of this kind can be misrepresented before a mass of people (*tous pollous*).

Plato alleges that Sokrates made the following confession at his trial (*Apol.* 31c):

> A certain divine or daimonic something comes upon me (*moi theion ti kai daimonion gignetai*), which in fact Meletos makes a travesty of in his indictment.

Xenophon, too, suggests that it was his *daimonion* which got the philosopher into trouble, though he expresses his opinion somewhat cautiously. He writes (*Mem.* 1.1.2-3):

> The gossip was that Sokrates claimed that the daimonic (*to daimonion*) communicated to him (*heautôi sêmainein*). It was especially from this circumstance, in my opinion, that the charge of introducing new daimonic beings arose.

Later writers take the same view. The Jewish writer Josephos (*Ap.* 2.263), for instance, observed scornfully:

> Sokrates was condemned to death by taking a dose of hemlock not because he betrayed his city to the enemy or committed temple robbery, but because he swore new oaths and claimed – surely as a joke as some say – that something daimonic gave signs to him (*ti daimonion autôi sêmainein*).

No other instance of this charge is recorded in Athenian history and it is possible that the phrase 'new daimonic beings (or practices)' was inserted into the affidavit in place of the more regular 'new gods' because of the notoriety of Sokrates' divine sign (Mikalson *APR*, 66). Why then 'beings' in the plural? There are, I suspect, basically two reasons. First, the charge of introducing a plurality of divinities is obviously more impressive than that of introducing only one; and secondly, it enabled the prosecution to build on the popular misconception of Sokrates as a religious freak. In Aristophanes' *Clouds*, for instance, Sokrates requires his pupils to worship the fictional deities Chaos, Clouds and Tongue (ll. 423-6), and conceivably there may have been some recollection of this characterisation in the jurors' minds. Many Athenians, as Plato's Sokrates ruefully observes, were quite unable to distinguish between objective testimony on the one hand, and their own preconceived image of the accused on the other.

Sokrates' divine sign is designated *to daimonion* only twice in Plato (*Euthyph.* 3b5; *Theait.* 151a4). Elsewhere it is referred to as *to daimonion sêmeion* (the divine sign), *to tou theou sêmeion* (the sign of the god), *to eiôthôs sêmeion* (my customary sign), *hê eiôtheia moi mantikê* (my customary oracle), and simply *phônê* (voice). As this terminology implies, the sign merely took the form of an admonishing voice. Nowhere is there any suggestion that his *daimonion* ever appeared to Sokrates in anthropomorphic guise. It is also highly significant that it is never called a *daimôn*, a word which roughly translates as 'guardian spirit', even though that concept was well-known in Plato's day (cf. Burnet 1924, 16). A major problem confronting all efforts to determine the character and identity of Sokrates' voice, as Kierkegaard observed (1841, 158) in his doctoral thesis, is that *to daimonion* by itself 'is neither simply adjectival in such a way that one must complete it by understanding *ergon, sêmeion* (deed, sign) or something similar, nor is it substantive in the sense that it designates a special or unique being'. As a result of our semantic quandary, we are incapable of establishing whether the *daimonion* had any objective reality external to Sokrates, or whether it functioned as a temporary manifestation of his own eccentric personality.

To comprehend its nature more fully, we must again consult our witnesses for the defence. Xenophon writes (*Mem.*1.1.3-4):

Sokrates was not 'introducing' anything new (*ouden kainoteron eisephere*), any more than do those who, practising (*nomizontes*) divination, make use of flights of birds, oracular utterances, chance occurrences and sacrifices (i.e. at which they examine the entrails of the victims). Persons of this kind do not believe that the birds or the people whom they meet by chance know what is useful for those seeking oracular guidance; rather they believe that the gods, through these agents, communicate (*sêmainein*) these signals; and that was what Sokrates himself acknowledged (*enomize*). But whereas the majority claim that it is the birds or the people whom they meet that dissuades them or prompts them, Sokrates said exactly what (or how?) he understood (*hôsper egignôsken, houtôs elege*). For he asserted that the daimonic (*to daimonion*) communicated (*sêmainein*). He prophesied to many of his friends to do or not to do something, on the signalling (*prosêmainontos*) of the *daimonion*.

Xenophon seems to be saying that Sokrates' *daimonion* functioned as a private oracle which granted him foreknowledge on a random and indiscriminate basis. The only difference between Sokrates and a professional soothsayer would appear to be that whereas the latter used his expertise to interpret coded signs as messages from the gods, the former received communications from the divine in the language of everyday utterance.[10] So Xenophon's line of defence amounts to the claim that Sokrates was just like anyone else who practised seercraft, except for the fact that he was more straightforward about the way in which the gods communicated with him. As with the previous charge, therefore, the author would have us believe that the accused was the victim of misrepresentation.

From the kind of expressions which Plato puts into Sokrates' mouth, such as 'a certain divine or daimonic something comes upon me', it seems that he, on the other hand, took the *daimonion* to be his master's susceptibility to falling into a peculiar psychological state during which he was in direct contact with the divine. The function of such 'encounters' was wholly negative: they invariably served as a deterrent, often in quite trivial contexts (cf. *Apol.* 40a). As Vlastos (1989, 1393) points out, however, we are hardly justified in assuming that the *daimonion* constituted a 'divine revelation' in the exact sense of the term (viz. 'disclosure of knowledge to man by divine or supernatural agency', *OED*), since Plato's Sokrates never suggests that his voice is a substitute for reason, but merely a supplement. In Burnet's (1924, 17) words, 'It served to justify certain instinctive reluctances of which he was unable to give a clear account.'

From the Demos' point of view, however, Sokrates' *daimonion* as depicted by Plato was anything but innocuous, since, like its recipient, it harboured, or at least was thought to harbour, crypto-oligarchical leanings. This emerges at the trial where, in response to the allegation that he never offered any advice in the Ekklesia while always acting the busybody in private, Sokrates asserts (Pl. *Apol.* 31cd) that his refusal to participate in politics was specifically prompted by his sign. Four years after the overthrow of a bloody tyranny the proposition that a gentleman should not soil his hands by taking part in the running of his country

---

[10] I take the sentence 'Sokrates said exactly what (or how?) he understood' to be a reference to the communicative mode employed by his *daimonion*, though it is just conceivable that it is intended as an allusion to Sokrates' idiosyncratic terminology (rather than to his idiosyncratic powers).

would have been offensive enough. But for its most outspoken critic to profess that he had received a divine injunction expressly ordering him to stay out of the political arena would have aroused violent opposition. No wonder that the jury made an uproar when Sokrates spoke of his divine sign in court, 'some in disbelief, others jealous of the fact that he received greater favours from the gods than they' (Xen. *Apol.* 14).

There were sound religious reasons, too, for regarding the *daimonion* of Plato's Sokrates with the gravest suspicion, first because it made its communications exclusively to one individual, secondly because it demonstrated not the slightest interest in the welfare of the rest of the citizen body, and thirdly because it could be contacted without recourse to the traditional channels of communication between man and god, namely sacrifice, votive offering, prayer and so on. It is no exaggeration to state that by substituting 'something completely abstract for the concrete individuality of the gods' (Kierkegaard 1841, 160), Sokrates was undermining three of the basic tenets of Greek religion.

It is important to note that the defendant was not accused of introducing *false* gods. An Athenian jury had no part in determining the entitlement to worship of the *daimonia* concerned. There are obvious reasons why this was the case. To have brought a charge pertaining to the introduction of false gods would have exposed the prosecutor and his community to possible reprisals from the *daimonia* concerned, while also involving the court in pronouncing upon issues beyond its competence to assess. It follows from this that Meletos and his fellow prosecutors were not engaged in a doctrinal or theological conflict with the accused but a purely procedural one. Their task could not have been more straightforward. They merely had to demonstrate to the jury's satisfaction that Sokrates had invoked a divine being (or beings) which had no place in the established canon of public and private gods. No proof was actually needed of the allegation that Sokrates had 'introduced' his *daimonion*, since, according to the presuppositions of Greek religion, it was impossible to worship a god unless that god had been properly introduced. That he had invoked such a being, Sokrates himself did not deny, however Xenophon tried to fudge the issue.

The charge of introducing new daimonic beings, like that of failing to acknowledge the state gods, would have been of immediate and topical concern to the Demos, since the Peloponnesian War had witnessed the introduction of several foreign cults into Athens. As we have seen, two of the earliest in the series were Bendis and Asklepios. While the decision to admit these foreigners is unlikely to have been particularly controversial, given their obvious and immediate benefits to a hard-pressed population, the entry of others aroused considerable hostility among nation-alistically-minded Athenians. The cult of the Thraco-Phrygian Sabazios, for instance, which was admitted a year or two before Asklepios, was pilloried for its orgiastic and ecstatic practices in no fewer than four

Aristophanic comedies. In one play Sabazios and other foreign trash are brought to trial and unceremoniously kicked out of Athens (cf. Cic. *Laws* 2.37), a spectacle which would have afforded valuable group therapy for the poet's audience, many of whom were no doubt fed up with playing host to a sundry assortment of divine ne'er-do-wells.[11]

Epilogue

Three other possible examples of illicit religious innovation are known to us from later times. In *c.* 350 a foreign *hetaira* or prostitute by the name of Phryne was charged with 'introducing a new god and assembling *thiasoi* of men and women' (Euthias fr. 1 Müller = Ath. *Deipn.* 13.590d-591f; cf. Hypereid. fr. 60 *T*). The outcome of the trial is unknown. Then in 324 the orator and politician Demades was fined ten (or according to another version one hundred) talents 'because he introduced (*eisêgêsato*) Alexander as a god' (Ath. *Deipn.* 6.251b; cf. Ail. *VH* 5.12). A final instance is reported in the case of a priestess who was executed by the state apparently because of her participation in *thiasoi* organised by Aischines' mother Glaukothea (Dem. 19.281). Josephos (*Ap.* 2.267-8) has this to say about the case:

> They executed Ninos the priestess because someone accused her of initiating foreign gods (*xenous emuei theous*). This was prohibited by law and the punishment laid down for those who introduced a foreign god was death. Those who observed such a law clearly did not acknowledge (*enomizon*) that the gods of other peoples were gods. Otherwise they would not have begrudged themselves the pleasure of having more gods.

Josephos has garbled the facts. First, Ninos merely took part in rituals from which her office as priestess automatically debarred her – she did not initiate anything new; secondly, death was not the statutory punishment for introducing new gods, as we see in the case of Demades; and thirdly, the Athenians were certainly not backward in acknowledging that 'the gods of other people were gods', as this investigation has demonstrated. The fact that they later acquired the reputation for being hostile to new gods was no doubt due in part to the notoriety surrounding the trial and condemnation of Sokrates.

---

[11] Incidentally, Sabazios and his worshippers remained the butt of cheap humour for well over half a century. In order to blacken his rival's reputation, Demosthenes (18.259-60) conjured up a picture of Aischines' mother performing a concoction of unsavoury rites connected with the worship of Sabazios. Not until *c.* 350 did the Athenians, allegedly in obedience to an oracle, finally desist from mocking the god (schol. on Dem. 18.259-60). Many foreign cults may have faced similar abuse and mockery in their early days, of the kind commonly reserved for the new boy on the block.

Conclusions

Stone (1989, 139) remarks: 'It was the political, not the philosophical or theological, views of Sokrates which finally got him into trouble.' I have tried to demonstrate that the very opposite was the case, that the religious counts against Sokrates as much defined him as a traitor as did the charge of being the teacher of anti-democrats like Kritias, Charmides and Alkibiades. The Demos' power had been recently restored after an oligarchical rule of terror. It needed to re-establish its authority. The charge against Sokrates, whatever the actual substance of it, was not trivial. Indeed it impinged directly upon the current concerns of the Demos, as witnessed by Nikomachos' review which, in the course of establishing a comprehensive list of Athens' religious obligations, had authoritatively and definitively determined the identity of 'the gods whom the state recognises'. Sokrates' religious outlook presented a challenge to the very concept of Athenian democracy, which operated on the principle that it and it alone had the right to determine who should be worshipped and in what manner.

The philosopher had defied the Demos in a manner that was reminiscent of Themistokles, though his crime, ostensibly at least, was much less offensive than that perpetrated by the politician. Unlike Themistokles, he did not seek to establish a shrine in honour of his personal *daimonion* with himself or a member of his family assuming the office of priest. He merely acknowledged a special kind of divine intervention in his private life. Themistokles had eventually been driven into exile, partly no doubt because of his high-handed behaviour in religious matters. By demanding the death penalty for Sokrates, the prosecution was underlining the fact that his behaviour was subversive of democracy and contemptuous of popular belief.

Although we do not know the exact size of the jury which tried Sokrates, Plato (*Apol.* 24e) tells us that a majority of sixty found him guilty as charged and that the prosecution proposed death as the penalty. When the defence was called upon to propose its penalty, however, Sokrates did not recommend exile, which the jury might have preferred as a way of getting him rid of him without assuming responsibility for his death. Instead he further antagonised them by suggesting that his punishment should take the form of free meals in the prytaneion for the rest of his life. A second ballot was taken, whereupon eighty more jurors cast their votes in favour of the death penalty than had previously voted for his conviction (D.L. 2.42). It is a serious indictment of the Athenian legal system that eighty jurymen were able to vote for Sokrates' execution who had already pronounced him innocent of all the charges. If Sokrates was guilty, and according to the letter of the law he indubitably was, all the more culpable were those rancorous and irate Athenians.

8

The World of the Athenian *Aition*

It is possible that every Attic cult, festival and ritual ultimately came to possess its own *aition* or foundation legend explaining the circumstances which led to its introduction. An *aition* served as a cult's *raison d'être*. It legitimated the rites which were conducted in its name by providing the priesthood who conducted it with a justification and warrant of antiquity for why it did what it did, in what might be described as 'the tense of a metaphysical present' (Connerton 1989, 43).[1]

While it is probably true that every *aition* offers 'a faithful transcript of the action and the mood of the worshippers' (Robertson 1985, 240), as historical documents purporting to provide an accurate and trustworthy explanation of the origins of religious usage, they are of distinctly limited value and sometimes ignored in studies of Greek religion. With the notable exception of Pheidippides' encounter with Pan, few *aitia* are demonstrably as old as the cult or ritual itself, many are likely to have been invented or embellished in the fifth century or later, and all are indeterminate in origin. Their significance, however, and it is not an inconsiderable one, resides chiefly in the light that they shed upon the type of conditions which according to the preconceptions of Athenians living long after the event were imagined to have prevailed at the time when their respective cults or rituals were instituted.

We do not know for certain when such justifications became commonplace. A Panhellenic desire to furnish a circumstantial explanation for the origins of the Olympian dynasty is detectable from around the beginning of the seventh century through the medium of the

---

[1] Connerton is actually discussing the festivities which were held annually on November 8 in Nazi Germany in commemoration of the sacrifice of the sixteen original martyrs or 'blood witnesses' of National Socialism who died in the 1923 Putsch. Invidious though the comparison is, it may be suspected that the ceremonies held on that day, which included a march from the Munich Bürgerbräukeller to the Feldherrnhalle 'along a route marked by burning torches, to the accompaniment of funereal music, the tolling of bells, and the slow recital of the names of all those killed since 1919 in the service of the party', corresponded both in emotional appeal and structure to those, say, commemorating the Tyrannicides and the Marathonomachoi. The Nazi ritual is aptly described by Connerton (p. 42) as a 'pagan passion play drenched in borrowed religious vocabulary'.

so-called Homeric hymns. Whether this impulse was mirrored on the local level in connection with the origins of polis cults at this same date is, however, far from evident. Not until the rise of Attic tragedy in the fifth century does concrete evidence exist for a distinctly Athenian interest in *aitia*, though we should note that many important legends, like those woven around the name of Kekrops, are not actually attested before the fourth (cf. Philochoros *FGrH* 328 F94-8, with Jacoby). Whatever their precise connection with the cults and rituals which they sought to explain, it is likely that *aitia* attained increased importance in the fifth and fourth centuries when competitiveness among the members of Athens' pantheon was perhaps on the increase, engendered in part by the dramatic rise in Athens' metic population, a phenomenon which in turn gave rise to the entry of numerous foreign gods who represented the interests of Athens' numerous ethnic minorities.

The setting of most foundation legends is a period of history prior to the establishment of the community's most venerable rites and institutions – or to put it in the language of mythology, the period before the Olympian regime had achieved 'its final and permanent configuration' (Clay 1989, 12). This was the so-called Age of Heroes, who are described by Hesiod as a race of just and noble demi-gods (*Works and Days* 156-69; cf. Hdt. 3.122.2). In this era gods and heroes intermingled freely and even enjoyed sexual relations together, fostering in consequence the nigh-interminable series of offspring which the poet records in his *Catalogues*. At the end of the Trojan War such intimacy became a thing of the past. Odysseus' polite but firm rejection of Calypso's offer of immortality – on condition that 'you stay here with me and guard my household', as the nymph puts it in her rather quaint, old-fashioned way (*Od.* 5.208) – may be interpreted as sounding its death-knell. In the drab, post-heroic universe which followed and which we ourselves currently inhabit, the Age of Iron, human existence became discontinuous with the divine. The gods withdrew from fellowship with mankind and intervened less frequently in their affairs, though they continued to provide occasional assurances of their support by means of epiphanies at moments of crisis. But the memory of that older, jointed universe was nurtured and kept alive through myths about their former comings and goings which were situated in the Greek landscape with topographical exactitude. In the historical era the physical and inhabited world was pervaded with the erstwhile presence of deities and heroes whose close attachment to place was commemorated in legend and celebrated in cult.

The study of Athenian *aitia* is, and was in antiquity, an inexact science, as the bewildering array of variants which cluster around what appears to be a single foundation legend amply prove,[2] and what follows is an

---

[2] The survival of apparently contemporaneous variants of the *aition* relating to the Arkteia festival at Brauron, for instance, raises the intriguing possibility that doubts about the explanation of its origin may even have existed within the same sanctuary (cf. Sale 1975, 273 and 280).

attempt to provide a simple introduction to a highly complex field of inquiry. For that reason I do not list the numerous variants of *aitia* which are preserved in different sources. Given the difficulty which existed within the same community in establishing an authorised version of a myth, we can readily appreciate that in the Greek world at large the task must have been virtually impossible. Just to give a couple of examples of the kind of complications that existed, the fragmentary *Hymn to Dionysos* rejects five locations which claimed to be Dionysos' birthplace, before giving approval to mythical Nysa. Likewise there were no fewer than twelve regions of Greece which vied with each other for the dubious privilege of having provided the setting for the rape of Persephone (cf. Richardson 1974, 148-50). Even in Eleusis itself two different locations were proposed, quite apart from other candidates in Athens, including the Pnyx and the Acropolis (cf. Jacoby commentary on Phanodemos *FGrH* 325 F27). Internal inconsistency was the very life-blood of Greek aetiology, and rivalry at every level gave it special flavour.

It can be argued that all literary genres create worlds within worlds. Whether we are dealing with the Christian Gospel, the medieval *chanson de geste*, the Shakespearean sonnet, or the modern detective thriller, each functions strictly in accordance with its own internal code of laws and its own circumscribed sense of reality. Each presents an extremely unified, essentially enclosed and highly eclectic view of the world. I tentatively propose that the Athenian *aition*, though hardly a genre in the exact sense of the term, acknowledges at least four different impulses behind any decision to establish a new cult or ritual, although I am not suggesting that these categories were prescriptive for the authors concerned nor that they were mutually exclusive. I would identify these four impulses as follows:

(1) guilt at having committed an offence which gravely offended the dignity of a deity;
(2) gratitude and relief at having escaped an impending catastrophe;
(3) wonder at a deity's epiphany or at a heroic exploit;
(4) pride in a community's cultural advance.

The *Hymn to Demeter*

The earliest surviving example that is relevant to this investigation is the Homeric *Hymn to Demeter*, which describes the origin of the Mysteries of Demeter and Kore at Eleusis. As an explanation of the introduction of a Panhellenic rather than a purely Attic cult, its *aition* is unique among those we shall be considering. In view of the fact that the hymn contains no reference to Athens, it is often argued that it must have been composed by an Eleusinian poet some time before the Athenians took over the management of the cult around the middle of the sixth century (above

p. 43). Although the vexed question of authorship is extremely important for a full understanding of how the cult became integrated into the Athenian state, that is not our main concern here.

In contrast to other Homeric hymns, notably those to Apollo and Hermes, and the fragmentary hymn to Dionysos, its subject is not the birth and upbringing of a new deity – birth being a convenient metaphor by which to express the introduction of a new cult. Rather, it is the emergence of a new joint cultic entity, namely the Two Goddesses, Demeter and Persephone as mother and child, whose indissoluble and perpetual union was fittingly expressed in Greek by the dual form of the noun, '*tô theô*'.

The story goes as follows: in sorrow at the loss of her daughter Persephone, who has been secretly abducted by Pluto, lord of the underworld, Demeter abandons Mount Olympos and goes in search of her. She arrives at Eleusis, where, disguised as an old woman, she offers queen Metaneira her services as a midwife and is duly hired. But the latter suspects her of malpractice and incurs the goddess's anger. Whereupon Demeter reveals herself to the queen in all her glory and instructs the Eleusinians to build a temple in her honour. Famine sweeps the earth, threatening the destruction of the entire human race. Demeter rejects Zeus' appeal for her to return to Olympos – and thus by implication to restore the natural order. Eventually Pluto agrees to release Persephone, and Demeter and Persephone are re-united on Olympos. Zeus proposes a compromise agreement and the famine abates. The hymn ends as Demeter explains her holy rites and awful mysteries to the kings of Eleusis.

Put in the simplest terms, an upheaval on Olympos produces a natural disaster on earth which leads to the establishment of a new cult. The hymn thus presupposes that an act of outrage and violence which has been perpetrated by one Olympian deity against another justifies and demands an appropriate response from mankind. But although the royal house of Eleusis is required to make atonement for the fact that Demeter was slighted by Metaneira when she sojourned in the queen's palace, this humanly perpetrated affront to the goddess' dignity is incidental to the main thrust of the narrative. Likewise the temple and rites which Demeter orders to be instituted by the Eleusinians on her behalf have no discernible effect upon her depressed spirits. On the contrary, it is her fellow Olympians who ultimately and alone succeed in assuaging her grief, by making practical concessions in recognition of her maternal instinct and in compensation for having connived in Pluto's brutal act. Henceforth, as a result of Zeus' unequal but equitable dispensation, Persephone's favours are to be divided between her mother and her husband, who are awarded two-thirds and one-third of her time respectively. A solution is thus worked out on the basis of a barter agreement which requires both parties to compromise.

By adopting a dual perspective, that is to say, by inviting his audience to consider religious innovation as it impinges upon both the divine and human planes of existence, the author has created an evocative image for the inevitable adjustment and re-alignment, on Olympos as well as on earth, which accompanies all religious change. Both gods and men are required to modify their behaviour towards the sorrowing Demeter as a new order of divine precedence is established (cf. Clay 1989, 207f.).

Euripides

One of the earliest Athenian writers to evince what may be described as a somewhat scholarly interest in *aitia* is Euripides, who frequently introduced a foundation legend at the end of his dramas in part as a way of commenting upon the relevance to contemporary Athenian society of Athens' mythical past. Excluding his *Kyklôps* and *Alkêstis*, which are both satyric plays, only *Trojan Women* among his surviving tragedies demonstrably omits a prophecy relating either to cult or to cult-related nomenclature (cf. Barrett 1964, 412). *Helen*, for instance, contains an *aition* relating to the cult of Helen at Sparta, *Herakleidai* to the hero Eurystheus at Pallene, *Madness of Herakles* to cults of Herakles throughout Attica, Hippolytos to *Hippolytos* at Troizen, *Ion* to the heroes of the four pre-Kleisthenic tribes, and *Medea* to the cult at Corinth established in commemoration of Medea's killing of her own children. Perfunctory though such prophecies may seem to a modern audience, their value and significance for the poet's contemporaries should not be underestimated. An Euripidean *aition* provided an essential link between the events which the audience had just witnessed on stage and the origin of rituals which this same group was performing to that day, since it was an instrument by which contemporary reality could be represented as a logical consequence of the past.

In some plays Euripides was probably utilising material of immemorial antiquity concerning the cult whose introduction constituted the climax and conclusion of his drama. In others, however, he was almost certainly inventing or at any rate adding the finishing touches to what was perhaps ultimately destined to become the definitive explanation of a cult's origin. For we cannot wholly exclude the possibility that Euripides may upon occasion have composed the endings of his plays on the recommendation of a priesthood or some other interested party. In his lost play *Erechtheus*, for instance, which contains an *aition* relating to the origins of the Erechtheion and which was probably written when work on that building was in progress, the poet makes a striking departure from the tradition preserved in the *Hymn to Demeter* (l. 154) by ascribing a Thracian, instead of Eleusinian, origin to Eumolpos, the eponymous founder of the Eumolpid *genos* and foe of Athens. As Parker has observed (1986, 203), it is difficult to conceive that Euripides 'had no semblance of authority for changing a war against Eleusinians into a war against Thracians, and so transforming one of the most honoured religious families of all Greece into descendants of a barbarian war-lord' – though the particular source of that authority eludes us.

Given the fact that the poet wrote some eighty-eight tragedies in all, Euripides' impact upon Athenian and to a lesser extent non-Athenian aetiology can hardly be over-estimated. His fellow dramatists show rather less interest in foundation legends, though they do not eschew them altogether. Notable examples include the establishment of the cult of the Semnai at the bottom of the Acropolis in Aeschylus' *Eumenides*, and Oedipus' attainment of heroic status in the deme of Kolonos in Sophokles' *Oedipus at Kolonos* (see below).

The Atthidographers

Most of the *aitia* which have come down to us were recounted by the Atthidographers, the seven local historians of Athens who flourished for a period of about one hundred and fifty years from the end of the fifth century to just before the middle of the third. The Atthidographers evidently saw it as their duty to systematise the varied, often contradictory traditions about the monarchic period of Athenian history with a view to enhancing Athens' sense of national identity at a time when that identity was experiencing crisis and eventual eclipse. The earliest *Atthis* was written by Hellanikos of Lesbos and published in *c.* 404/3. The first Athenian to attempt such a history was Kleidemos, who wrote around the middle of the fourth century. He was followed, in probable sequence, by Androtion, Phanodemos, Demon and (of unknown date) Melanthios. The last Atthidographer was Philochoros, whose seventeen-volume work, incomplete at the time of his death, breaks off around the time of Athens' surrender and loss of independence at the end of the Chremonidean War in *c.* 261. All these works have mainly perished, except for excerpts and paraphrases preserved in Plutarch, in lexicographical writings, and in scholia on Aristophanes and the orators, these latter compiled in the late-Roman and Byzantine periods.

In view of the fact that at least three of the Atthidographers held religious offices, it is possible that the group as a whole had a vested interest in the claims of Attic mythology and the origins of Athens' most venerable cults which went beyond mere academic rivalry. We know, for instance, that Kleidemos was an *exêgêtês*, that Phanodemos was appointed *hieropoios* to the Pythaïs at Delphi in 330, and that Philochoros was a 'seer and inspector of victims', a *mantis* and *hieroskopos*. Obsessed as they were by chronology, it was their somewhat dubious accomplishment to provide an era date, usually in the form of the reign of an Attic king, for every myth or legend which they described. Jacoby (1949, 144), whose monumental study of Atthidography still remains the standard reference work on the subject, went so far as to claim that 'dating ... is the most important point for the Atthidographers'. The extent to which the Athenians as a whole concerned themselves with the order of their kings is unclear. We are in no position, in other words, to assess the impact of their writings upon the religious sensibilities and beliefs of the general populace. While giving all due weight to the worthy effort made by these learned men to standardise and systematise Attic mythology, we should ourselves, of course, firmly resist the temptation to fashion it into anything resembling a logical system of belief to which all worshippers were obliged to subscribe, there being nothing comparable in Greek religion to an explicit theology controlled and handed down by a centralised priestly authority. Ritual, after all, does not depend on theology for its effectiveness.

Pausanias

Finally, there is the second-century AD traveller Pausanias, the first book of whose *Description of Greece* is devoted to the sights and monuments of Attica, many of which he illustrates with a myth of origin. Since Pausanias did not invariably take at face value the reports of the anonymous antiquarians and guides who served as his informants at the various temple-sites he visited, his approach to his material tends to be somewhat eclectic. For instance, after noting that there were two different legends regarding the origins of the cult of Aphrodite Ourania in Attica, the 'official' state version and another promoted by the deme of Athmonon, Pausanias sagely comments, 'The claims (*legousi de*) of the polis frequently differ radically from those of the demes' (1.14.7). In so doing, he establishes what might be termed the first law of aetiology, which is that even in the same polis rival supporters of the same god or hero touted rival *aitia*, in the same way that rival Attic playwrights dramatised and promulgated rival versions of the same myth. More strikingly, in a later book he comments, 'Even the Argive guides (*exêgêtai*) themselves know that not all the stories they tell are true; yet they stick to them because it is not easy to persuade the general public to change their opinions' (2.23.6). Presumably what he means by this is that it was not necessarily in the guides' own interest to substitute what they understood to be the truth for the much-loved fictions which the public expected and wanted to be told.

Atonement

The most dramatic scenario presented by Athenian *aitia* is a fourfold schema involving petition, rejection, reprisals and atonement. A god petitions for entry into a community, is rejected in a highly insulting manner, either to his face or in the person of his intermediary, and then seeks revenge, most typically by inflicting famine or disease (*limos* or *loimos*) on those who have treated him disdainfully. The community in question, which now finds its existence threatened, hastens to make amends by instituting a cult of atonement. The ritual which it re-enacts on an annual basis can be interpreted as a continuing attempt to appease the god for the original insult. The dominant psychological drive behind the cult thus consists of a potent combination of guilt and fear. A typical example concerns the entry of Dionysos Eleuthereus (see above p. 42). The scholiast to Aristophanes' *Acharnians* (l. 243) provides the following account of his initially cool reception and its consequences:

> Pegasos of Eleutherai – Eleutherai is a polis in Boiotia – came to Attica with the statue (*agalma*) of Dionysos. The Athenians did not receive (*edexanto*) the god with honour (*timê*), but he did not depart from those who took this decision without exacting a price. For the god became enraged and a disease struck the private parts of the males and the illness was incurable. As they were helpless in the face of the disease, which proved stronger than any human magic and skill, sacred ambassadors (*theôroi*) were hastily dispatched to consult the god (viz. Apollo). When they returned they said that the only cure was this, namely if they should introduce (*ei ... agoien*) the god with all due honour. Being persuaded by these reports the Athenians fashioned phalluses privately and publicly, and with these they venerated (*egegairon*) the god in memory (*hupomnêma*) of their illness.

The exaction of terrible reprisals from those who rejected the god on his first application into their community features prominently in Dionysiac myth throughout the Greek world. Whatever the precise facts about Dionysos' origins, about which we shall never have more than a hazy outline, scholars are undoubtedly right to assume that such stories represent 'an echo, frozen in memory, of a concrete and very real history' (Detienne [1989], 6, citing Erwin Rohde). The reality underlying such legends would seem to be that the god faced extreme opposition upon his entry into Greece and that this opposition was matched, if not exceeded, by the violence of his adherents, who secured a leading place for their god primarily by resorting to brute force. Very similar is the *aition* relating to the cult of the Mother of the Gods in the Agora. It is surely no coincidence that both Dionysos and the Mother of the Gods had origins which probably lay ultimately in Asia Minor and that their worship was ecstatic in nature. The degree of hostility which they both aroused may in part have been a consequence of their utter dissimilarity to traditional Attic cult. The fourth-century AD emperor Julian (*Or.* 5.159a) recounts this version of the goddess' entry into Athens:

> The Athenians are said to have treated the Gallos (title of a priest of the goddess) contemptuously and expelled him since he was introducing new gods (*ta theia kainotomounta*), because they failed to appreciate the value (*chrêma*) of the goddess, and how she was honoured by them under the

name of Deo, Rhea and Demeter. Then followed the wrath of the goddess[3] and the appeasing of it. For the priestess of the Pythian god (i.e. Apollo) ... ordered them to propitiate (*hilaskesthai*) the wrath of the Mother of the Gods. The story goes that the Metroön was established as a consequence, this being where the Athenians used to keep all their official documents.

It hardly needs pointing out that *aitia* associated with cults of atonement are anything but paradeigmatic for the study of religious innovation in Classical Athens. In Dionysos' case they owe their peculiarity to factors which are specific to the god's unique identity, most important of which was the existence of lingering doubts throughout antiquity as to whether he was Semele's son by Zeus or by an ordinary mortal (cf. Eur. *Ba*. 26-30). Secondly, and quite irrespective of the fact that the god's name already appears on Linear B tablets of Mycenaean date, Dionysos was habitually perceived as the archetypal divine outsider, the latest born and least integrated of the Olympian twelve (e.g. Hdt. 2.145.4). Thirdly, he appears to have fostered, if not directly encouraged, a type of exclusive relationship with his followers which, as we have already seen, was alien and indeed inimical to the basic spirit of Greek polytheism. The civil strife occasioned by his irruptive entry into Thebes as depicted in Euripides' *Bacchai*, for instance, is made possible by the fact that his worshippers constituted a standing army, ready to match violence with violence and embark upon a holy war under the military dictatorship of their god. As Dionysos himself states (ll. 45-52, cf. 789-91):

> Pentheus now wages god-war (*theomachei*) against my person and thrusts me from his libations and neglects me in his prayers. Therefore I shall prove to him and to all Thebans that I am a god ... . If Thebes tries to force my Bacchai from the mountains with violence and arms, I shall marshal my maenads and do battle.

The action of Euripides' drama thus wholly revolves around the issue of the strength of opposition to Dionysos' claims by a temporal authority. As we further learn, the god, who is to be his own advocate, is to undertake his war with no more inspiring nor lofty aim than that of revenging himself upon his aunts for doubting the claim put forth by his mother Semele that she had been impregnated by Zeus (ll. 26, 41). Dionysos, in other words, is primarily embroiled in a family feud, and a particularly unedifying and unsavoury one at that. Irrespective of the benefits which accrue to mankind from Dionysism – which Euripides certainly does not

---

[3] Precisely how the goddess manifested her wrath is not indicated but she probably unleashed disease or plague upon the recalcitrant Athenians. See P. Garnsey, *Famine and Food Supply in the Graeco-Roman World* (Cambridge 1988), 192f. and P.Y. Forsyth (*AHB* 4.4 [1990] 75-8) for the plausible suggestion that the Magna Mater, the Roman equivalent of the Mother of the Gods, was introduced into Rome from Asia Minor in 204 in response to disease and famine.

omit to mention in the course of his play – the establishment of the cult is achieved in consequence of a successful private and personal crusade waged by the god purely in defence of his own honour or *timê* (cf. 321). Pentheus' rejection of Dionysos' divinity is thus essentially due to a failure of intellect, rather than to any ungodliness, immorality or impiety. The issue of faith does not enter into it because neither Thebes nor Pentheus is to be offered any choice in the matter. This is no take-it-or-leave-it cult. Dionysos will 'force' people to wear the livery appropriate to his religious rituals (l. 34), and Thebes will learn 'whether it wishes it or not' what it means to neglect his worship (l. 39f.). Once the god has scored his inevitable victory, he will move on 'to some other land' (ll. 48-50).

For all these reasons Dionysos' claim to worship as presented in the *Bacchai* poses a challenge as much to the political and social order of the polis, as to its religious system. By contrast, the cults which we have been investigating sought not to overhaul, far less to annihilate the existing social and political order – arguably the achievement of Dionysos at the end of the *Bacchai* – but rather to give clarity and focus to a previously unidentified interest group within that order. Notwithstanding the fictionalised nature of Euripides' description, it must be conceded that the image of an irate god stalking the margins of the polis, ready to unleash his fury upon those who deny his claims to worship, remains a potent and haunting symbol of precisely how much was at stake in matters pertaining to religious innovation.

It is pertinent to inquire whether a god who was initially rejected or who received a less than wholehearted welcome would have functioned as obligingly as one who was greeted with open arms, so to speak. Let us consider the case of Poseidon, of whom, following his defeat at the hands of Athena for the guardianship of Attica, Aristeides (*Panath.* 41f.; cf. Plu. *Mor.* 741a) writes:

The god withdrew, but did not end his love (*erôs*). Poseidon and Athena's subsequent behaviour afforded no less proof (*sêmeia*) of the zeal and honour which the Athenians enjoyed from both. For she granted to the city superiority in wisdom, while he granted to it superiority in naval battles ... indeed I think surpassing any who at any time or place have fought and won battles at sea.

Notwithstanding Aristeides' comforting assurances, the possibility cannot be ruled out that a certain degree of wariness on the part of both deity and community would have permanently marred the relationship. Is it frankly conceivable that Poseidon, hardly a god to let bygones be bygones, as we see from the vendetta which he wages against Odysseus in the *Odyssey*, would have meekly accepted the judgement passed against him and not have felt lingering resentment towards those who were responsible, albeit indirectly, for delivering his most celebrated snub?

The myth of his flooding the Thriasian plain in pique at his defeat proceeds from a more robust and, arguably, more realistic appreciation of the hazardous consequences of offending an Olympian deity (below p. 164).

Gratitude and relief

The second category has to do with religious activities established in response to a crisis which had nothing to do with the ill-will or anger of the gods. The activities which the crisis called forth were presumably believed to contain an inherent potency capable of overcoming the original evil and were repeated perhaps partly to expiate the original terror and partly to prevent a similar recurrence in the future.

Characteristic of this group is the *aition* associated with the establishment of the Choës or Pitcher festival, which was celebrated in honour of Dionysos Limnaios. It should be noted that the *aition* does not explain the entry of Dionysos Limnaios into Athens but merely the reason for the introduction of a new ritual in his honour. The origins of the ritual were traced back to the aftermath of the Trojan War when the polluted matricide Orestes arrived in Athens from Delphi on Apollo's bidding seeking expiation for his crime. Phanodemos (*FGrH* 325 F11 in Athen. *Deipn.* 10.437cd) provides us with the following description:

> Demophon the king established the festival of the Choës in Athens. When Orestes arrived in Athens Demophon wanted to receive him, but was unwilling to let him approach the sacred rites or share the libations, since he had not yet been tried. So he ordered the sacred things to be locked up and a separate pitcher (*chous*) of wine to be set before each person, saying that a flat cake would be given as a prize to the one who drained his pitcher first. He also ordered them, when they had finished drinking, not to put the wreaths with which they were crowned on the sacred objects because they had been under the same roof as Orestes. Instead each one was to twine them around his own pitcher and take the wreaths to the priestess at the precinct in Limnai, and then to perform the rest of the sacrifice in the sanctuary. From that day hence the festival has been called Choës.

In this instance there is no threat of divine retribution because no offence has been committed against the dignity of any god. The community found itself imperilled merely because it was harbouring a potential source of virulent pollution. In other words, the ritual which is instituted recalls an occasion when Athens successfully overcame the threat of a murderer's pollution. Under the guidance and direction of her king, a strategy was devised which both enabled her people to entertain a deadly pollutant and prevented his pollution from seeping into their midst. By squaring the circle, so to speak, the community resolved a seeming impossibility. The procedure proved efficacious and the city commemorated its release by re-enacting the procedure on an annual basis. But the re-enactment surely did more than that: it served as an apotropaic guarantee or at least a pious hope that Athens would never in the future be overwhelmed by this kind of evil.

It is a characteristic of such *aitia* that they conveniently explain illogical, bizarre or unconventional ritual procedures, since historical precedent is an essential and complete justification for their continuance in perpetuity. Thus, in answer to the question, 'Why at the Choës festival do Athenians drink out of individual pitchers, rather than from a communal one, put wreaths not on the sacred objects, as is the usual practice, but instead on their pitchers', the inventor of the *aition* simply replies, 'Because that's what they did when Orestes came to Athens in order to avoid polluting themselves and their sacred objects. It worked then, and it will work always.' Under this heading may be included both those cults which were established in gratitude for a deity's or a hero's military intervention, such as Pan, Theseus, Boreas and Artemis Aristoboule, and those which were upgraded in recognition of further services rendered in battle, such as Artemis Agrotera and Herakles after Marathon, and Artemis Mounychia after Salamis.

Epiphanies and heroic exploits

Any epiphany provided a necessary and sufficient justification for the establishment of a new cult because a site which had been visited by a deity became automatically hallowed and sanctified by the aura of that deity's presence. Especially venerated were those which had provided the setting for an incident in which the love, anger or grief of the gods had been powerfully stirred, as by a divine birth, a divine rape, a theomachy or a competition among their ranks for supremacy. So, too, sites where a hero had performed a mighty exploit or merely visited in the line of his professional duty became objects of veneration and cult. Plutarch's *Theseus*, for instance, constitutes *au fond* an aetiological and onomastic itinerary whose function is to lend legendary authorisation to rituals established at the places which Theseus visited in the course of his extensive wanderings throughout Greece. Many Attic sanctuaries traced their origins to the fact that such occurrences had taken place within their premises, including several of Athens' most venerable cults.

The sanctity of the Acropolis, for instance, was explained in part by the fact that it was here that the contest between Athena and Poseidon took place, the proofs (or *marturia*) of whose miraculous gifts survived in the form of Athena's sacred olive tree and a cleft in the rock caused by Poseidon's trident (Plates 29, 30). The *aition* first receives brief and somewhat cryptic mention in Herodotos (8.55). A much more detailed account is provided by the second-century AD mythographer Apollodoros (3.14.1):

They say that in the reign of Kekrops the gods resolved to take possession (*katalabesthai*) of the poleis in which each god was destined to receive individual honours (*timai*). Poseidon was the first to arrive in Attica and struck his trident at the centre-point of the Acropolis, producing a sea which men today call Erechtheis. After him Athena arrived and, having made Kekrops the witness of her act of possession (*katalêpsis*), she caused an olive tree to grow, the one which to this day is on display in the Pandroseion. When a contest arose between the two for the land, Zeus parted them and appointed judges, not as some say Kekrops and Kranaos, nor Erysichthon, but the twelve gods. In accordance with their verdict the land was assigned to Athena, because Kekrops testified that the goddess was first in planting her olive tree. Athena called the polis Athens after herself, and Poseidon, who was enraged, flooded the Thriasian plain and submerged Attica.

What is particularly interesting is that the decision to award Athena the role of *poliouchos* or 'city-holder' ultimately rested upon the evidence of a human, specifically Athenian witness in the person of king Kekrops. In another version an Athenian king acted as the judge (cf. Ail. Aristeid. *Panath.* 41). The gods do not impose themselves upon human beings but submit their claims either to divine or to human judgement. It is also significant that Poseidon was defeated not because his miracle was inferior to his rival's but because he violated the established rules governing trials of strength in the Greek world by failing to appoint any witnesses to corroborate his miracle before he actually brought it off. Athena, in other words, won not by merit but by default. The *aition* thus reflects the invidiousness of making an objective judgement between two such powerful deities and two such impressive miracles. Not the least of its purposes may have been to provide the Athenians with a reassuring explanation as to how they were spared the necessity of passing a verdict on two Olympians based exclusively on their respective merits. More fundamentally, the myth is an expression in narrative form of the high honour accorded to Athens and her people by the gods, since it demonstrates that the guardianship of Athens aroused their jealous rivalry (above p. 161).

No less sacred than the Acropolis was Eleusis, whose sanctuary, consecrated to the worship of the Two Goddesses, was believed to have been established at the spot where Demeter rested on her travels while seeking information about the disappearance of her daughter. Presumably because of her intense emotional attachment to the focal point of her grieving, Demeter instructed the people of Eleusis to build a temple and altar in her honour 'beneath the Acropolis and its sheer face, above the well Kallichoron, on a rising hill' (*h. Dem.* 270f.), this being where she first rested upon arrival. It was here, too, according to Pausanias (1.38.6), that 'The women of Eleusis first instituted a dance and sang in honour of the goddess'. The Eleusinian priesthood further claimed that Pluto had descended into the bowels of the earth at a cavernous rock which was venerated as the Plutoneion when he dragged off Persephone to be his bride, though as we have seen (p. 154) this claim by no means went uncontested in the Greek world.

Cultural evolution

The final category of foundation legends has to do with religious activities which commemorated Athens' cultural evolution. Such legends commonly tell of the inventive intervention of a god or hero which led to a decisive improvement in the conditions of communal life, whether of a technical, political or social nature, and hence to a shift from an ancestral to a modern mode of existence. In Attic myth the culture-bringer *par excellence* is Prometheus, whose numerous benefits to mankind included carpentry, mathematics, medicine, seercraft, metalworking, and much else besides (Aes. *PV* 476-506). Native Attic culture-bringers include Kekrops, Triptolemos and Theseus, whose gifts provided justification for the cults established on their behalf or, in the case of Theseus, those established by the hero himself in commemoration of his own inventiveness.

Kekrops, commonly regarded as the first king of Athens, was credited with founding the institutions of marriage and burial of the dead, and of elevating Athena to the rank of Polias. In addition, he established the Kronia festival in honour of Kronos and Rhea, whose *aition*, as related by Philochoros (*FGrH* 328 F97), places emphasis upon the need for the entire household, slaves as well as free, to participate in the gathering of crops and fruit at harvest time:

> When crops and fruit have been collected, the heads of households everywhere should eat with the slaves with whom they have endured the task of cultivating the land. For it was pleasing to the god that in recognition of their toil slaves should be honoured.

Triptolemos was worshipped because the Eleusinian king 'was the first to sow cultivatable seed' (Paus. 1.14.2). Agriculture was probably the most commonly celebrated invention in the aetiological record, not only because it denoted the change from a nomadic to a settled way of life, but also because of the constant danger of drought and famine, which promoted the fear that man's limited agricultural skill would be overwhelmed by natural disaster.

Theseus not only played a leading part in Athens' social and political evolution but also introduced religious activities in celebration of that evolution, including the Synokia festival, which commemorated the unification of Attica, as well as the cults of Aphrodite Pandemos and Peitho, which symbolised the co-operative and democratic spirit which underpinned it. In the same category should also be included the cults of the eponymous heroes of the ten Kleisthenic tribes, whose elevation towards the end of the sixth century in line with the division of the citizen body into ten artificial units had the effect of giving reality and substance to what would otherwise have been merely a sterile and lifeless administrative convenience (see above p. 43).

According to Phanodemos (*FGrH* 325 F12 in Ath. *Deipn.* 11.465a) a ritual associated with the temple of Dionysos Limnaios commemorated the occasion 'when wine was mixed with water and then for the first time drunk diluted'. Since the drinking of unmixed wine was regarded by the Greeks as a characteristic of barbarian societies (cf. Pl. *Laws* 1.637e), this civilised discovery laid the foundations of Hellenic culture. Phanodemos' fellow-Atthidographer Philochoros (*FGrH* 328 F5b) further claims that 'by drinking properly mixed wine men ceased to stand in a bent posture as they had been compelled to do by neat wine'. Thanks to Dionysos, in other words, man no longer goes on all-fours.

The *aition* pertaining to a ritual associated with the cult of Artemis Mounychia provides a justification for the substitution of human by animal sacrifice – another vitally significant cultural advance – though this might also be considered as a ritual of atonement for the killing of an animal sacred to the goddess. As narrated by the Suda (*s.v. Embaros eimi*), it reads as follows:

> After the slaughter by the Athenians of a bear which had broken into the sanctuary of Artemis Mounychia, a famine(?) ravaged Athens. The god (i.e. Apollo) prophesied that its expulsion would only come about if an Athenian sacrificed his daughter to the goddess. A certain Baros agreed to do so on condition that the priesthood should henceforth be hereditary among his own *genos*. After decking out his daughter (i.e. as a sacrificial victim) he then hid her and sacrificed instead a ram which he dressed up to resemble his daughter.

We should note that here it is a human being, not a god, who is responsible for what is in effect the non-institution of human sacrifice, even though human sacrifice had been recommended by Apollo.

The Arrhephoria

Of the multitude of *aitia* which once existed, only a handful have survived. In a few cases the loss may be due to the fact that the legend was a closely guarded secret which was known only to the priesthood concerned. Especially mysterious is the secret rite known as the Arrhephoria (or Arrhetophoria, as it is called in later sources), which was celebrated by two or possibly four Athenian girls of noble birth known as *arrhêphoroi* in joint honour of Athena Polias and Aphrodite in the Gardens. Pausanias (1.27.3) gives the following description of its ritual:

> What chiefly amazed me is something that is not generally known, and so I shall describe it. Two maidens dwell not far from the temple of Athena Polias. The Athenians call them '*arrhêphoroi*'. For a time they live with the goddess, but when the festival (*heortê*) is celebrated this is what they do by night. The priestess of Athena places on their heads some objects for them

to carry – neither she who gives them nor those who take them know what they are – and by means of a natural subterranean passage the maidens descend into a precinct within the Acropolis not far from the sanctuary of Aphrodite in the Gardens. There they leave what they are carrying and bring back something else covered up. Thereupon the Athenians release these girls and bring others in their place on to the Acropolis.

Although no ancient author provides an *aition* for this ritual, most scholars are agreed that it has to do with the legend concerning Aglauros, Herse and Pandrosos, the three daughters of Kekrops, who were given a basket by Athena containing the infant Erichthonios with a snake or snakes to guard him and placed under strict instructions never to open it (Eur. *Ion* 21-4, 271-4). In the majority of accounts Pandrosos obeyed the injunction, but Aglauros and Herse peered inside the basket and saw the snakes (Apollod. 3.14.6; Paus. 1.18.2). Terrified, these two sisters went mad and hurled themselves off the Acropolis at the point where it is steepest. It is likely that the myth of their suicide served to explain the annual descent of the *arrhêphoroi* to the sanctuary of Aphrodite in the Gardens, to which Pausanias alludes. The *aition* also made sense of what might have appeared to be an otherwise inexplicable conundrum: namely, why Pandrosos received cult on the summit of the Acropolis, whereas Aglauros was worshipped on the slopes below.

Not the least curious feature about the Arrhephoria is that its ritual was 'not generally known', as Pausanias claims. Even odder is the fact that the girls who were selected annually to be *arrhêphoroi* performed their arcane duties without, it seems, having any clear idea as to what these duties actually signified. This at any rate is the conclusion that must presumably be drawn from the fact that they did not know the identity of the objects which they were carrying on their heads. And if, as Pausanias further claims, the priestess of Athena Polias didn't know their identity either, who did? While it is conceivable that Pausanias' inquiries were somewhat perfunctory or that his informants were ill-informed, it may be that the only person in Athens privy to the secret was the *archon basileus*, the ritual father of the *arrhêphoroi*, who in his capacity as 'king' may have been entrusted with the supervision of the ceremonies which the daughters of the royal house once performed on behalf of Athena (cf. Simon *FA*, 42f.). Even so, that still leaves a problem, for if the rest of the population was left totally in the dark, what significance can the Arrhephoria have had for them?

Without inquiring into the full meaning which lay behind the practice, about which a great deal has been written in recent years, I suggest that one small part of the answer may be that mystification is a vital component in the performance of every ritual. Indeed one might argue that the power and intensity of ritual is proportionate to the degree to which its actors are excluded from a full understanding of its symbolic function. In the impulse to rationalise and explain the bizarre practices of

Athenian religion, a tendency which probably began in the early decades of the fifth century, there was perhaps a handful of rituals for which no explanation was made popularly available. This need have troubled no one. The worship of Athena was its *own* justification. After all, nothing more eloquently expressed Athena's quintessential 'otherness' compared with virtually every other cult in Attica than the fact that her cult statue had dropped from heaven.

The heroisation of Oedipus

We turn finally to the *Oedipus at Kolonos*, Sophokles' study of the infusion of divinity into a blind, bitter and frail old man. The play was written in 406/5 and performed in 401. In the four-year interval Athens had suffered defeat at the hands of the Peloponnesians. Uniquely in the entire corpus of Greek literature the drama is concerned not with the purely procedural issues to which heroisation gives rise, but rather with the spiritual and physiological journey which a hero-elect is required to undergo as he solemnly departs from this life. Its action is ostensibly concerned with Oedipus' application for shelter in Athens, which is granted when Theseus agrees to settle the wanderer in Attica with full citizen rights (l. 637). At a more profound level, however, the play constitutes a dramatised debate about the merits of Oedipus' claims to settlement· within the pantheon of divine and heroic beings who are worshipped by the demesmen of Kolonos. The two levels of meaning in which the play deals are brought into sharp focus in the opening lines when Oedipus inadvertently yet fortuitously blunders on to sacred ground close to the spot where he himself is destined to receive worship upon decease. Oedipus' search for a space in which to shelter thus becomes a powerful and evocative metaphor for his search for a point of entry into the Athenian pantheon.

When the play begins Oedipus, the epitome of pollution, is *apoptolis* (l. 208), a man without a city, a common vagrant seeking shelter. He and his daughter Antigone have arrived at the outskirts of Athens where they take refuge on sanctified ground in the deme of Kolonos. There they encounter a man of Kolonos, who informs them that they have strayed into a grove sacred to the Semnai. On hearing the name of these dread chthonic powers, Oedipus instantly recognises the fulfilment of the prophecy which was given to him long ago by Apollo and announces that he has arrived at his final resting place (ll. 84-95). He now knows that he is within hours of his death. In a formal supplication to the assembled gathering of demesmen, he declares (l. 287f.):

I have come as one who is sacred (*hieros*) and pious (*eusebês*), bearing favour for these townsmen.

What Oedipus evidently intends by this is that Athens will receive favour from Apollo in payment for cherishing a man who now enjoys the god's protection. Ironically, however, he has said more than he realises, since upon attaining heroic status he will be capable of producing favours from the grave. Soon afterwards Oedipus' daughter Ismene arrives and informs her father that a prophecy has just been delivered to his Theban countrymen from Apollo, whose import is such that they will now seek him 'dead or alive, for their safety's sake' (ll. 388-90). Oedipus' mystification (and ours) upon hearing these words is profound and he questions his daughter thus:

> O: Who could have profit from a man such as me?
> I: In your hands (*en soi*) lies their power, so they say.
> O: So when I am no more, then I am a man?
> I: For now the gods raise you, whereas before they brought you low.

Clearly Ismene's words offer no final explanation for Oedipus' life of suffering. Are we intended to regard his impending heroisation as somehow justifying the havoc which the gods have wreaked throughout his life? No statement in the entire play takes us closer to understanding this central paradox of Greek religion – how an old blind beggar who had committed terrible albeit involuntary deeds was transformed from being an abhorred and polluted outcast to a deeply desired immigrant – and yet in the end it tells us nothing other than that such a transformation *is* a paradox. The observation is reminiscent of Tertullian's on the paradox of Christ's incarnation (*De carne Christi* 5): 'It is certain because it is impossible.'

Hearing that his tomb is destined to become the focus for a cult in his honour, Oedipus looks forward with keen appetite to the day when his 'slumbering and hidden chilled corpse will drink the hot blood of my enemies' (l. 621f.). His increasing stature as the play progresses is revealed both by the steadfast conviction which henceforth informs his actions and by his clear and unimpeded vision of the vicissitudes of human life. Above all, however, it is made manifest by the access of venomous and ungovernable rage into his ravaged and enfeebled body. For it is his ability to curse his son Polyneikes without a shred of remorse or pity when the latter comes seeking forgiveness which most conclusively signals that Oedipus' withdrawal from the temporal plane is imminent or, more accurately perhaps, that his withdrawal has in effect already taken place and that what we are witnessing here is the completion of his heroisation (cf. Burian 1974, 408; Edmunds 1981, 229).

In response to the peals of thunder announcing that his final hour on earth has arrived, Oedipus urgently summons Theseus, to whom alone he reveals his intended burial place and the rituals pertaining to his cult, with strict instructions that he should pass on this knowledge 'alone to one who is chiefest (*tôi prophertatôi monôi*)' (ll. 1518-32). The play thus provides justification for the secrecy surrounding the whereabouts of Oedipus' tomb. It also explains how it came about that custody of the cult was entrusted initially to the king's eldest son and then later, after the monarchy had been abolished, to an appointed official of the state (cf. Jebb 1900, *ad loc.*).

Oedipus' leave-taking is interrupted by a mysterious voice which insistently chides him: 'Ho there, Oedipus, why are we delaying? You have been lingering too long' (l. 1627f.). In Burian's memorable words (1974, 427), 'At the moment of Oedipus' death, discord is silenced by ineffable mystery.' The striking use of the first person plural to denote hero and god in sacred union is the ultimate proof that Oedipus' spiritual transformation is now complete.[4]

---

[4] For a close analogy to the conditions surrounding the heroisation of Oedipus, cf. Eur. *Herakl.* 1026-35, where Eurystheus, a foreigner like Oedipus, will become in death the city's protector: 'Since your polis let me go and was ashamed to slay me, I will reveal to you an ancient oracle of Loxias (i.e. Apollo) which will benefit you more than you can imagine in time to come. When I die, bury me in the appointed place beside the shrine of the holy virgin of Pallene (i.e. Athena). I will be kindly (*eunous*) towards you and the saviour (*sôtêrios*) of your polis, and I will lie beneath the earth as a metic for all time, and will be implacably hostile to the descendants of these people (viz. the Spartans) when they come against you with a large army, paying back your kindness with treachery.'

Conclusions

If we carefully control every statement we make about an ancient theory or belief by reference to the evidence, if we are constantly on the watch against importing Christian or other modern preoccupations into antiquity, it seems to me that we have a slender chance of getting at the truth. Most likely we shall fail; at best we may get at that fraction of the truth which it is possible for our generation to comprehend.

Sir Hugh Lloyd-Jones.

Cults arise within and carry the meanings and values of historical contexts by which they can be understood. The history of fifth-century Athenian religion is inseparable from the history of Athenian political and social aspirations, and the centrality of religion to public as well as private life requires us to evaluate the two side by side. It has been my task here to investigate why a particular new cult was vital to the state's welfare at a specific historical moment, on the assumption that a new cult is necessarily an expression of the state's own experience of its internal and external relations. The point is well-illustrated by the story of Kleisthenes of Sikyon, who sought to ban the cult of the Argive hero Adrastos during a war with Argos by promoting at Adrastos' expense that of his deadly rival Melanippos (Hdt. 5.67). Kleisthenes even went so far as to hand over Adrastos' sacrifices and feasts to Melanippos. As Gordon (1972, 92) has put it, 'That a given innovation happens to come from outside a given culture is relatively trivial: it is more significant that an additional cult is being provided so that the religious system as a whole can continue its integrating function.' Anxiety, anger, relief, fear, hope, ambition – whatever the dominant psychological drive underlying the introduction of a new deity, it provides a valuable commentary upon Athens' collective consciousness, according to the principle that changes in the human situation brought corresponding changes in the superhuman.

The intimate link between warfare and religious innovation which has formed a thread throughout our investigation is due to at least three factors. First, war is the activity where human and divine interests most closely coincide, since the welfare of the gods is intimately bound up with the fortunes of the worshipping community. Hence the gods were rewarded after a victory with dedications and commemorative sacrifices.

171

Nowhere perhaps is the connection between military success and divine prosperity more apparent than in the enormous personal fortune acquired by Athena Polias in the period from *c*. 450-430. Secondly, war produces a very high incidence of events which are unpredictable, accidental and inexplicable. Whatever the odds on victory or defeat before battle commences, in the heat of the moment orders are not heard, equipment breaks down, leadership is weak, the weather intervenes, men lose their nerve. War is accordingly the prime human activity to scrutinise for evidence of the workings of the gods, since often the only explanation for its outcome is one which concedes the theoretical possibility of divine intervention. A final reason why battle serves as a forcing-house for the birth of new cults is that the constant danger to life and limb generates a heightened state of consciousness among combatants and non-combatants alike, thereby rendering individuals and groups especially susceptible to visions of the supernatural.

Both historically and mythologically, eras of radical religious upheaval tend to be situated either at junctures of abrupt political and social change, or at moments when the state faced an external threat to its very existence. Demographic change was also a leading cause of religious innovation, particularly in the late-fifth and fourth centuries when Athens' population of resident aliens reached its peak, since an ethnic minority sought to put down roots by establishing cults in honour of its gods. Our understanding of Athenian democracy is conventionally based upon our grasp of the political issues which dominated the first half of the fifth century. But no political decision was without religious implications. Conversely, no decision to introduce a new god was entirely innocent of the political consequences that would follow in its wake. As Nilsson (1940, 392) observed fifty years ago: 'That mythology served as a means of politics is well known and often mentioned ... Mythological claims served for the Greek states the same purpose as national claims in our days ... . It has been less noticed that the cults too were used for political purposes, especially in fusing the petty states of Attica into a unity – the state of Athens.' One might add that the very concept of Athenian democracy was also predicated on the existence of cults which sanctioned and gave the stamp of legitimacy to this unparalleled constitutional experiment.

Yet to treat Athenian religion *merely* as an extension of her political and social aspirations, and to extrapolate from it *merely* a coded commentary on Athens' relationship with herself and the outside world, is to miss half the point, because religion was not an epiphenomenon of a state's temporal aspirations. Any investigation of Athenian religion, if it is not to founder upon our own rationalising presuppositions, must give appropriate weight to the integrity of Athenian religious sensibilities. From a Christian or merely modern perspective Athenian religion appears patently fraudulent since self-interest formed an essential and indissoluble part of its *raison d'être* and *modus operandi*. It is therefore tempting to regard it as little more than a rich hunting ground for cynical, manipulative and ambitious politicians whose sole objective was to exploit a credulous and ignorant populace. Exploitation, cynicism and manipulation were indeed prominent features of Greek religion, as they have been of religious systems throughout history. What marks out this system from others, however, is that it treated worldly success as wholly commensurate with divine favour and patronage. We therefore need to acknowledge that we are dealing with a conception of the world which is entirely different from our own experience and understanding of it. It is precisely because human life was so inextricably bound up with the divine that it is so difficult to discover the underlying motives behind the introduction of a new god.

Our own tradition has made us not only intolerant but also uncomprehending of other systems of belief.[1] By dismissing a spiritual leader such as the Ayatollah Khomeini as a sinister old hand-chopper we deprive ourselves of a strategy for explaining why a quarter of a million mourners should risk being crushed to death for a glimpse of the Imam's refrigerated remains. Our inability to take the Olympian gods seriously puts us at a comparable disadvantage in undertaking a study of Greek religion, since we tend to assume *a priori* that the Olympians are and never were 'real' gods. What I have tried to do in this book, therefore, is to accord Athenian religion as much respect (reverence would be too strong a word) as I am capable of demonstrating to any system of belief which does not number me among its adherents. It may in conclusion be salutary to bear in mind that gravitation does not exist either, even if we seem to feel its effects, for Einstein's theory of General Relativity now postulates that what Newton described as gravitation is actually the consequence of a geometrical configuration which directs lesser bodies towards larger ones. Yet belief in the Olympian gods and the theory of gravitation have in their different ways assisted the human mind in accounting for its experience of the world, and the fact that they have only proved provisional in no way diminishes their usefulness. When the Greeks attributed their salvation to a new and previously unacknowledged deity, as they did constantly throughout their history, what they were doing, I submit, was not unlike discovering a new scientific formula. The goal of Greek religion, like that of post-classical physics, was at bottom relatively modest: it signified an attempt to achieve a limited understanding of the constrained randomness of Chaos.

---

[1] Cf. the excellent remarks of Neusner (1990, 273) on 'the incapacity of religions to form a useful theory of the other'.

Chronology of Athenian Religion

Epigraphical citations are to the most recent discussion known to me. Unless otherwise stated, dates based on archaeological data are taken from Travlos (*BTAA* and *PDA*), who also supplies a convenient listing of up-to-date bibliography.

c. 900	Possible date of the establishment of a cult in honour of the hero Akademos (or Hekademos) in the Academy
c. 750	The so-called 'Sacred House' and temple of Artemis Propylaia are built at Eleusis
c. 750-700	The cult of Athena Polias is established on the Acropolis. Earliest evidence of hero-cult is found at sites throughout Attica. Traces of a cult of Zeus Ombrios are found on the peak of Mount Parnes (cf. Paus. 1.32.2)
c. 750-600	Traces of definitively Athenian cults are detectable at sites throughout Attica
c. 630	Kylon and his supporters are murdered on the Acropolis. Origins of the Alkmaionid curse
c. 600	The so-called Solonian Telesterion and precinct wall are built in the sanctuary of the Two Goddesses at Eleusis. Date of the earliest temple remains at Brauron and Rhamnous
c. 594/3	Solon conducts a review of Athens' sacrificial calendar and introduces legislation intended to curb ostentatious display at funerals and post-funerary rituals
c. 570	Date of pedimental sculptures attributed to the so-called Hekatompedon ('Hundred-footer'), which is thought to have been erected on the Acropolis in honour of Athena Polias
566/5	Athletic competitions are added to the Panathenaia, possibly under the direction of Peisistratos (cf. Pherekydes *FGrH* 3 F2; schol. *ad* Ailios Aristeides 13.189.4-5 = Dindorf 3.323)
c. 560	The cult of Eurysakes and the Hero at Hale is established in the deme of Melite. Peisistratos attempts to establish a tyranny with the assistance of a woman called Phye disguised as Athena
c. 550	A sanctuary of Athena Nike is established on the Mycenaean bastion at the northwest corner of the Acropolis. A temple of Athena Sounias is built at Sounion. Archaeological traces of a branch establishment of the cult of the Two Goddesses found on the north slope of the Acropolis indicate that control of the Eleusinian Mysteries is now in Athenian hands. A temple tentatively identified as that of Apollo Proöpsios (Far-sighted) is built on Mount Hymettos

174

c. 550-525	Date of possible remains of Archaic temples of Zeus Agoraios and Apollo Patroös, found in the Agora. Earliest remains of a sanctuary on the site of the future Stoa of Zeus Eleutherios in the Agora (H. Thompson, *Hesperia* 6 [1937] 8-14)
c. 550-500	Date of construction of the temple of Dionysos Eleuthereus on the south slope of the Acropolis
c. 550-525	The so-called Peisistratid Telesterion and precinct wall are built at Eleusis
c. 546-527	Tyranny of Peisistratos
c. 546	Peisistratos purifies Delos by removing all graves within sight of the sanctuary of Apollo (cf. Hdt. 1.64.2; Thuk. 3.104.1)
c. 534	Possible date of the first performance of tragedy at the City Dionysia (*Màrmor Parium* 43; cf. U. Wilamowitz, *Homerische Untersuchungen* [Berlin 1884], 248 n.13; *CAH* III.3², 412)
c. 527-511	Tyranny of Hippias. Extensive building work is undertaken at the Academy in connection with a number of cults, notably Athena, Eros, Hephaistos and Prometheus. A torch race is now incorporated into the Panathenaia (cf. N. Robertson, *RM* 128 [1975] 285)
c. 525	The so-called 'Old Temple of Athena Polias' is built (or re-built) on the Acropolis on a site between the future Parthenon and Erechtheion
c. 520	An issue of Attic tetradrachms is minted bearing the head of Athena on the obverse side of the coin
522/1	The younger Peisistratos dedicates an altar to the Twelve Gods in the Agora and another to Apollo Pythios on the banks of the Ilissos River (Thuk. 6.54.6-7; *IG* I² 761 = *ML* 11 = *SEG* XXXI.31)
c. 520(?)	A temple of Dionysos Eleuthereus is built on the south slope of the Acropolis
c. 515	Under the direction of the sons of Peisistratos work begins on the temple of Olympian Zeus on the banks of the Ilissos River (Arist. *Pol.* 5.1313b23)
514	*Terminus ante quem* for the establishment of the Leokoreion in the Agora ([Arist.] *AP* 18.3). At Delphi the Alkmaionid *genos* rebuilds the temple of Pythian Apollo which had been destroyed by an earthquake in 548
c. 510-500	Date of the earliest surviving Athenian decree relating to the Eleusinian Mysteries (*IG* I³231 = *SEG* XXI.3)
c. 508/7	Cults are instituted in honour of the ten eponymous heroes of the new Kleisthenic tribes. Kleisthenes allows the *genê, phratriai* and priesthoods to continue to exist 'in accordance with ancestral practice' ([Arist.] *AP* 21.6)
507/6	Earliest evidence for public burial of the war dead outside Attica (Clairmont *PN* I, no. 2)
502/1	The City Dionysia receives public sponsorship
501/0	The choregic system of supporting tragedy at public expense is instituted
c. 500	A decree of the Ekklesia and Boule is passed regulating the preliminary sacrifices ([*prote*]*leia*) to be offered at the Eleusinion in Eleusis by the *hieropoioi* of the Eleusinia (*IG* I³ 5). The earliest temple of Artemis Brauronia is erected at Brauron, along with a branch establishment on the Acropolis. The earliest temple of

Poseidon is begun at Sounion. An altar of Aphrodite Ourania (Heavenly) is dedicated at the northwest corner of the Agora (Camp *Agora*, 57). The Archaic Metroön is erected in the Agora beside the Bouleuterion. The first permanent theatre is erected in the sanctuary of Dionysos Eleuthereus. A temple of Apollo Zoster is erected at Halai (Vouliagmeni). Dedications from this period provide the earliest datable evidence for a cult of Athena Hygieia on the Acropolis (e.g. *IG* I² 516)

c. 500-480 Earliest datable evidence for a cult of Zeus Parnessios in the Asty, possibly an offshoot of the sanctuary on Mount Parnes (*SEG* XXXIV.39)

c. 500-450 A temple of Dionysos Limnaios (?) is built in Athens

c. 499 Earliest epigraphic evidence for a cult of Nemesis at Rhamnous (*SEG* XXXV.24)

493/2 *Terminus post quem* for the foundation of a public cult of Zeus Soter and Athena Soteira in the Piraeus

490 The 192 Athenians who died at Marathon are buried on the field of battle and an annual sacrifice is established in their honour. *Terminus ante quem* for the establishment of a cult of Artemis Agrotera in Athens. In honour of the goddess an annual sacrifice of 500 goats is instituted in commemoration of a vow taken by the polemarch Kallimachos before the battle (Xen. *Anab.* 3.2.12)

post 490 A public cult of Pan is established on the north slope of the Acropolis (Hdt. 6.105). Traditional date for the introduction of the cult of the Marathonian hero Echetlaios (Paus. 1.32.5; cf. 1.15.3). Date of either the introduction or the remodelling of the Herakleia festival in honour of Herakles at Marathon (*IG* I³ 3; *SEG* XXXIV.1). A temple of Triptolemos is constructed in the City Eleusinion. Approximate date of the construction of a new marble Athenian treasury at Delphi (Stewart *GS*, 132; *ML* 19). A temple of Themis is erected in the sanctuary of Nemesis at Rhamnous

c. 488 The so-called Hekatompedon is demolished and work on the Pre-Parthenon begins

487/6 Comic performances are added to the City Dionysia

485/4 The so-called Hekatompedon Decree is passed regulating conduct on the Acropolis (*IG* I³ 4 = *SEG* XXIII.2)

c. 480-479 Destruction of sanctuaries on the Acropolis, in the Agora, at Brauron, Eleusis, Rhamnous and Sounion by the Persians

c. 479 The state institutes the Mounychia Festival in honour of Artemis Mounychia. Themistokles establishes a private cult of Artemis Aristoboule in the deme of Melite (Plu. *Them.* 22.1-2) and restores the Telesterion at Phlya (*Them.* 1.3). A state cult of Boreas is established on the banks of the Ilissos River (Hdt. 6.44.2-3). A sacrifice to Zeus Eleuthereus 'on behalf of all Greeks' is instituted (possibly) after the Greek victory over the Persians at Plataiai (Plu. *Arist.* 21.1). The Demos takes (possibly) the so-called Oath of Plataiai not to rebuild any of the temples destroyed by the Persians. A poros temple of Athena Nike is perhaps now built on the Acropolis. Repairs are carried out to the sanctuary of the Two Goddesses at Eleusis and work begins on the so-called Kimonian Telesterion.

	Approximate date of the construction of the Stoa Basileios in the Agora (T.L. Shear, *Hesperia* 40 [1971] 249f.; H. Thompson, private communication)
c. 477/6	Probable date of the establishment of a cult of the Tyrannicides in Athens
c. 476/5	Kimon brings back the bones of Theseus from Skyros and establishes a state-sponsored cult of the hero (Plu. *Thes.* 36). A tomb (*sêkos*) of Theseus is built in the Asty
c. 475	Approximate date of the establishment of the ceremony of public burial for the war dead, known as the *patrios nomos* (cf. Clairmont *PN* I, 13)
c. 471	Following the disgrace and exile of Themistokles, the sanctuary of Artemis Aristoboule falls into disrepair
ante *c.* 460	The Demos passes a decree regulating the Eleusinian Mysteries, which (possibly) includes the imposition of a fine of 1000 dr. on members of the Eleusinian priesthood who attempt to initiate *en bloc* (*IG* I^3 6 = *SEG* XXXIV.2)
c. 460	The Demos authorises changes in religious observances in connection with the worship of Athena Polias as supervised by the Praxiergidai (*IG* I^3 7 = *SEG* XXXVI.4). The Stoa Poikile is erected in the Agora. Probable date of the commencement of work on the temples of Apollo Delios on Delos and Athena Sounias at Sounion (H. Thompson, forthcoming). Possible date of the erection of a temple of Eukleia in the vicinity of the Agora (Paus. 1.14.5)
457	The office of *archon basileus* is opened to the *zeugitai*, the third property-owning class of Athenian citizens
c. 455	A colossal bronze statue of Athena Promachos is erected on the Acropolis (*IG* I^3 435 = *SEG* XXXV.10)
454	The treasury of the Delian League is transferred from Delos to Athens and placed in the safe-keeping of Athena, who henceforth receives first-fruits amounting to one-sixtieth of each city's tribute (*ML* 39). Work on the temple of Apollo Delios on Delos is interrupted
453-2(?)	The Demos passes a decree imposing certain obligations (not preserved) upon Erythrai regarding the Great Panathenaia (*IG* I^3 14 = *ML* 40)
c. 450	The Metroön at Agrai is built on the west bank of the Ilissos River. The tomb of Iphigeneia is reconstructed at Brauron
c. 450(?)	The Demos passes a decree requiring all its allies to send a cow and panoply to the Great Panathenaia (cf. *IG* I^3 34.41-3 = *ML* 46)
c. 449	Work begins on the so-called Periklean Telesterion at Eleusis
c. 449-447	The Demos decides to abrogate the Oath of Plataiai (if it ever took it) and to rebuild the temples destroyed by the Persians. It appoints a board of *epistatai* (superintendents) with charge over the financial running of the sanctuary at Eleusis (*IG* I^3 32)
449-444	Probable period of construction of the so-called Hephaisteion on Kolonos Agoraios
c. 448	The Demos passes a decree ordering the appointment by lot of a priestess of Athena Nike 'from all Athenian women', and the building of a temple and altar to the goddess (*IG* I^3 35 = *ML* 44 = *SEG* XXXI.9)

c. 447/6-433/2	Dates of the construction of the Parthenon (*IG* I³ 436-51 = *SEG* XXXV.11)
c. 444-440	Dates of the construction of the Classical temple of Poseidon at Sounion
440	Probable *terminus ante quem* for the completion of the so-called Periklean Telesterion at Eleusis (*IG* I³ 32 = *SEG* XXXVI.7)
c. 440-436	Dates of the construction of the temple of Ares and Athena in (probably) the deme of Acharnai
438/7	Pheidias' colossal chryselephantine statue of Athena is dedicated in the Parthenon (*ML* 54)
c. 437-432	Dates of the construction of the Propylaia on the Acropolis (*ML* 60) Dates of the remodelling of the sanctuary of Artemis Brauronia at Brauron
c. 436-432	Dates of construction of the (never-to-be-completed) temple of Nemesis at Rhamnous
ante 434	A cult of Apollo, possibly Pythios, receives state patronage (*IG* I³ 138)
434/3(?)	The so-called Decree of Kallias is passed ordaining the establishment of a new board of 'Treasurers of the Other Gods' (*ML* 58). The Treasurers of Athena henceforth inscribe annual inventories of all the dedications held inside the Parthenon
post 434/3	The cult of the Anakes receives state patronage (*IG* I³ 133 = *SEG* X.59)
c. 432	The seer Diopeithes introduces a decree concerning impiety (*asebeia*). It is possible that Perikles' teacher Anaxagoras and mistress Aspasia are put on trial, along with the sculptor Pheidias. The cult of Apollo Delios (?) at Phaleron (?) receives state patronage (*IG* I³ 130)
ante 431 or *c.* 420	Date of the construction of the temple of Demeter and Kore at Thorikos
431/0-426/5	Athens is ravaged by the plague and neglects customary religious observances (Thuk. 2.37.4, 2.53.4, etc.)
c. 430	Possible date of the authorisation of the construction of a temple of Athena Nike on the Acropolis (*IG* I³ 35 = *SEG* XXXII.2)
c. 430-420	Dates of the construction of the stoa of Zeus Eleuthereus in the Agora
c. 429/8	*Terminus ante quem* for the establishment of a publicly sponsored cult of Bendis in the Piraeus (*IG* I³ 383.143)
426/5	Delos is purified by the removal of all burials to the neighbouring island of Rheneia. The Delia festival in honour of Apollo, held on Delos, is revived (Thuk. 3.104)
c. 425/4	Approximate date of the commencement of work on a new temple of Apollo Delios on Delos, and on the temple of Athena Nike on the Acropolis. The theatres of Dionysos in Athens and Thorikos are refurbished
c. 425-400	The sanctuary of the healing god Amphiaraos is founded at Oropos
c. 422	The Demos passes a decree regulating the offering of first-fruits at Eleusis. A rider to the decree prohibits the construction of unauthorised altars in the Pelargikon area of the Acropolis (*IG* I³ 78.54-9 = *SEG* XXXVI.12). Aristophanes writes a play in which Sabazios and other foreign deities are expelled from Athens (cf. Cic. *Laws* 2.15.37)
c. 421	A sanctuary of Asklepios is established in Zea Port in the Piraeus (*IG* II² 4960). After a long interruption, work is resumed on the temple of Athena Sounias at Sounion.
421/0	A sanctuary of Asklepios is established on the south slope of the

	Acropolis (*IG* II² 4960). The Hephaisteia festival in honour of Hephaistos is either introduced or remodelled (*IG* I³ 82). Probable date of the commencement of work on the Erechtheion. Work on temples interrupted by the Archidamian War is resumed
420/19	The Epidauria festival in honour of Asklepios is incorporated into the Greater Mysteries
418/7	Earliest evidence for a sanctuary of Kodros, Neleus and Basile, probably located in the southern outskirts of the Asty (*IG* I³ 84 = *SEG* XXXVI.15)
415	The mutilation of the herms and the profanation of the Mysteries take place. Alkibiades is condemned *in absentia* for 'crimes against the goddess' (Plu. *Alk*. 22)
410-405	The Metroön is established as Athens' official archive
409-405	Period of renewed construction of the Erechtheion (*IG* I³ 474-9 = *SEG* XXXVI.36)
406/5	Possible date of the establishment of the board of Treasurers of Athena and the Other Gods (*IG* I³ 377 = *SEG* XXXVI.29). Possible date of the commencement of the transfer of precious objects and monies from Eleusis to the Acropolis (*IG* I³ 386/7 = *SEG* XXXIV.34)
c. 403-400/399	Nikomachos carries out a revision of Athens' sacrificial lawcode
c. 400	The cult of Asklepios in the Piraeus receives state sponsorship (cf. *IG* II² 47 = *LSGS* 11, as dated by Kirchner)
400	Andokides is accused of impiety
399	Sokrates is found guilty of 'not acknowledging the gods whom the state acknowledges and introducing new daimonic beings (*kaina daimonia*)', and is condemned to death

Glossary

aduton – literally 'a place not to be entered'; innermost shrine of a temple, entry to which was barred to the public

aition – legend purporting to provide the explanation for the introduction of a cult

anagrapheis – board of officials appointed to conduct a revision of Athens' sacrificial calendar

aparchai – offering of first-fruits to a deity

aphêrôizein – to heroise a dead person

archôn basileus – literally 'magistrate king'; one of the nine archons elected annually with particular responsibility for religious matters

Areopagus – hill to the west of the Acropolis; council of ex-archons who assembled on the hill with responsibility (*inter alia*) for religious matters

asebeia – improper behaviour in regard to the gods, the dead, one's parents or one's native land

Asty – the city of Athens

Atthis (pl. *Atthides*) – the name given to local histories of Athens which were written between the end of the fifth and middle of the third century BC by the so-called Atthidographers

Boule – the Council which prepared the agenda for the Ekklesia

Chora – countryside of Attica

chthonic religion – cult performed on behalf of deities connected with the earth (e.g. the Furies), the heroes and the dead

chrêsmologos – professional oracle-monger or seer

daidouchos – literally 'torch-holder'; an important priest at the Eleusinian Mysteries

daimôn (pl. *daimones*) – spirit or divinity (more general word than *theos*, 'god')

deme – village or small town; local administrative unit of the Athenian state

Demos – the citizenry of Athens (i.e. the enfranchised adult male population)

eikonion – an image displayed in a temple or shrine

Ekklesia – the Assembly of the Demos

enagismata – rites conducted annually on behalf of heroes such as Harmodios and Aristogeiton; the literal meaning is perhaps 'to put an *agos* (pollution) into food' or 'to put things which are under an *agos* into the grave'

enktêsis – grant of official permission to set up a sanctuary

epimeleia – literally 'care, attention'; used in a technical sense of the cult performed on a deity's behalf

epitheta – literally 'supplementary rites', i.e. rites believed to be recent additions to the sacrificial calendar (in distinction to *patria*)

eusebeia – proper behaviour in regard to the gods, the dead, one's parents and one's native land

exêgêtês (pl. *exêgêtai*) – expounder of sacred law

genos (pl. *genê*) – noble kin-group

gentilician – denotes a cult whose priesthood was hereditary among the members of a single *genos*

heortê – festival held in honour a deity, which often included a procession, banquets, musical or athletic events and contests (cf. J. Mikalson *GRBS* 23.3 [1982] 218)

hêrôiön – shrine consecrated to the worship of a hero

hestiatorion – dining room attached to a sanctuary for use by cult personnel and visiting dignitaries at times of festivals

hidruein – to establish a deity in his own sanctuary

hiera – sacred rites

hierophantês – literally 'revealer of sacred things'; a hereditary priest in charge of the Eleusinian Mysteries

hieron, hiron – consecrated precinct or sanctuary

hieropoioi – literally 'doers of sacred things'; officials responsible for the proper handling of religious ceremonies

hilasthai – to propitiate, seek to win favour by ritual observance

hypodechesthai – receive or entertain; hence, provide accommodation and hospitality for a new god (cf. A. Henrichs *HSCP* 80 [1976] 278 with n. 71)

kathiereusis – the official consecration of a precinct

maenad – female devotee of Dionysos

kratêriskos – miniature mixing-bowl used in the cult of Artemis

marturion – literally 'testimony, proof'; used in a technical sense of the assistance rendered by a god or hero to a community, which justified the establishment of a cult in his honour

megaron – Mycenaean palace; sanctum of a temple

naos – temple or dwelling place of a deity

nomizein – to acknowledge formally a god's entitlement to worship by ritual observance

nomizomena – literally 'customary rituals', i.e. rituals believed to be of great antiquity performed on behalf of gods and the dead

oikia, oikos – private sanctuary or place of temporary accommodation for a new god (cf. O. Weinreich, *Sitz. Heidelberg. Akad.* Phil.-hist. Kl. 16 [1919] 7)

oikistês – founder of a city; leader of a colonial venture

orgeônes – members of a cult association

pannuchis – religious ritual performed at a festival during the night

patria – literally 'ancestral rites', i.e. rites believed to be of great antiquity

peplos – the embroidered woollen robe which was used to clothe the cult-statue of Athena Polias; its removal and replacement constituted the climax to the Panathenaia

phasma – apparition or phantom, commonly of a hero

philotimia – literally 'love of honour, munificence'; frequently cited as a motive for instituting a new cult, new religious observance, etc.

phratry – literally 'brotherhood', membership of which in Classical times constituted proof of Athenian citizenship

psêphisma – resolution or decree of the Ekklesia and Boule

sêmeion – see *s.v. marturion*

sôtêr – literally 'saviour'; used in a technical sense of a deity who has delivered a community from an impending catastrophe

stêlê (pl. *stêlai*) – inscribed pillar placed on public display

Telesterion – hall of initiation

temenos – precinct consecrated to the worship of a god or hero *thambos* – the feeling of awe which is experienced in the presence of a deity

theôrodokos – receiver or host of a sacred ambassador

theopropos – sacred ambassador dispatched to a shrine outside Attica

theôria – literally 'seeing'; an official delegation dispatched to a festival held outside Attica

thesmothetai – literally 'statute-setters'; a board of six magistrates in charge of judicial matters

thiasos – religious association

tholos – circular building with conical roof believed to have particular significance in connection with the worship of chthonic deities

thusia – sacrifice conducted on behalf of a deity

timê – honour or ritual observance due to a deity

trittys (pl. *trittyes*) – third of a tribe

For discussion of the terminology of Greek cult, see Burkert (*GR*, 268-75).

Notes

Introduction: Others and the Other

2   **The unknown god.** Athens was not the only Greek city to erect an altar or altars to the unknown god(s). See the evidence collected by P.W. van der Horst, 'The unknown god (Acts 17:23)', pp. 19-42 in R. van den Broek, T. Baarda and J. Mansfeld, *Knowledge of God in the Graeco-Roman World* (Leiden, etc., 1988). Wycherley (1968, 620f.) suggests that Athens' 'unknown god' may have been a nameless hero-cult.

   Theophilia, philotheia. See Dirlmeier (1935, 57-77 and 176-93) for a full discussion. Though it is less intense than the relationship between Hippolytos and Artemis, the close affiliation (in both senses) between Ion and Apollo which Euripides explores in *Ion* is also instructive for our understanding of the links between individual and deity in a context where that individual's loyalty is put under severe pressure (cf. Yunis 1988, 121-38).

3   **Income accruing to Panhellenic sanctuaries.** For the year 408/7 the sanctuary at Eleusis received a gross yearly income of 4,299 dr. and 4 obols in initiation fees from the Great Mysteries and 46 from the Lesser, plus 500 dr. from the leasing of its land (*IG* I^2 313.145ff.). Further incidental sources of revenue accruing to sanctuaries included gifts, state subsidies, grants of access to water supply, and the sale of stone which had been quarried in sanctuary premises (for the last, see C. Ampolo, *OPUS* 1 [1982] 251-60).

5   **Teiresias.** For Teiresias and the role of seers in late fifth-century Athens, see Roth (1984, 59-69). On the high financial rewards available to seers in times of war, see Pritchett (*GSW* III, 71f.).

6   **Priestly emoluments.** Davies (1988, 378) writes: 'Priesthoods ... were a form of property, the inheritance of which buttressed other inheritable forms of property-power ... '. While this was true of certain parts of the Greek world (e.g. *LSGS* 77 for the emoluments attached to a priesthood on Chios), it does not seem to have been so of Athens. It is striking that in the case of the priestood of Athena Polias, for instance, no member of the branch of the Eteoboutad *genos* in whom the priesthood was reserved can be credited with 'even moderate wealth' (Davies *APF*, 169), even though the goddess herself was approximately five times wealthier than the Other Gods combined. For emoluments accruing to Athenian priesthoods, see Garland (*RAACA, passim*). A crass attempt to purchase the gift of conferring the Holy Spirit, whether for financial gain or some other advantage, is recorded in Acts 8:18-24 in the case of Simon whose action has been immortalised by the word 'simony'.

9   **'Infested with idols'.** On the meaning of *kateidôlos*, see Wycherley (1968, 619f.) who suggests that St Paul's perception was primarily based on the ubiquitous presence of herms (square pillars mounted with the head of

Hermes), which 'more than anything else would make him feel that at Athens idols were like trees in a wood'. For archaeological evidence relating to the topographical distribution of cults in Athens, see Wycherley (1970, 283-95).

10   'The Other Gods'. See *IG* I³ 369 = *IG* I² 324 (426/5-423/2); *IG* I³ 383 = *IG* I² 310 (429/8). For discussion, see Linders (1972). The reason for the distinction would appear to have been at least partly fiscal, the income accruing to Athena and the Eleusinian Goddesses being many times greater than that of any other god or goddess.

Genê **and phratries.** For *genê*, see the classic study by Toepffer (*AG*). Speculation regarding the number and size of individual phratries focuses upon discussion of *IG* II² 2344 (*c.* 400), which lists 20 members without demotics under the heading 'These are the *phratores* of Zeus Phratrios and Athena Phratria.' It is unclear whether this represents the total membership. Andrewes (1961, 14) is of the opinion 'that there should be many phratries, roughly speaking as many as there are *genê*', whereas Flower (1985, 235) claims 'that there were as many phratries as there were demes, say 150 for the sake of argument.' To date, the names of only six phratries are securely attested, viz. Achniadai, Dyaleis, Gleontis, Medontidai, Therrikleidai and Thymaitis. See Hedrick (1984, especially 143-50) for a detailed study. Though no doubt similar to each other in form and structure, phratries operated as independent religious associations and drew up their own regulations (cf. *SEG* XXXII.150).

Erkhia calendar. The calendar bears the title 'The Greater Demarchia' (*Dêmarchia hê Mezôn*), apparently in reference to the fact that the sacrifices which it enumerates were all conducted under the general authority of the demarch. No fewer than six different Apollos (Apotropaios, Delphinios, Lykeios, Nymphegetes, Paion, Pythios) and six Zeuses (Epakrios, Epoptes, Milichios, Horios, Polieus, Teleios) are named in the calendar. See Daux (1963, 603-34) and Mikalson (1977, 424-35) for further discussion. Incomplete deme calendars from the Marathonian Tetrapolis (*IG* II² 1358 = *LSG* 20, *c.* 400-350) and Thorikos (*SEG* XXXIII.147, *c.* 380-375) list some 20 deities apiece.

11   **Multiplicity of** *epiklêseis.* See H. Usener, *Götternamen*³ (Frankfort 1948), and, succinctly, Festugière (1954, 4) and J.M. Bremmer ('Greek hymns', p. 195 in Versnel *FHW*). Precisely which gods constituted the Olympian twelve was a matter of controversy among the Greeks, Ares and Dionysos being sometimes replaced by Hestia and Hades. Only the number itself is canonical. See further Zaidman and Pantel (*RG*, 130). Cult titles of Athena on the Acropolis include Ergane, Hygieia, Nike and Polias. Those in the Asty include Areia, Boulaia, Itonia, Phratria, Paionia, etc. In various Attic demes Athena was worshipped as Areia, Agelaa, Hellotis, Hippia, Pronoia, Skiras, Soteria, Zosteria, etc. See also R.E. Wycherley ('The Olympieion at Athens', *GRBS* 5.3 [Autumn 1964] 175-9) for a useful discussion of Zeus cults in Athens.

12   **Descent from a divine or heroic ancestor.** See Parker (1987, 194 with n. 32). Listing quadripartite divisions of Attica, Pollux 8.109 instances one such division which utilises the names Dias, Athenais, Poseidonias and Hephaistias, thereby hinting at a system whereby the population traced its ancestry from Zeus, Athena, Poseidon and Hephaistos respectively.

14   **Epiphanies.** See Pfister (1922) and Wachsmuth (1975). E. Pax (*RAC* 5 [1962] p. 838) dubs the Greeks 'the people of the epiphany', because of the frequency of this occurrence. Pritchett (*GSW* III, 19-39) provides a list of 49 military

epiphanies. The largest compendium of epiphanies in the work of any ancient author is to be found in Paus. The incident in Acts involving St Paul and St Barnabas has long been suspected of being inspired by Ov. *Metam.* 8.616-724 where Zeus and Hermes are alleged to have been received by an elderly couple in Phrygia. Yet the world of Acts is precisely one where pagans regularly mistake the Apostles for supernatural beings because of their miraculous powers, even where no parallel in Roman poetry can be found. Cf. Fox (1987, 99-101). For the characteristic features of descriptions of encounters with the divine, see Mussies (1988, 4-7) and Richardson (1974, 248). For the language, see Slater (1988, 126-30), citing H. Wankel, *Demosthenes: Kranzrede* II (Heidelberg 1976), 864. In vase-paintings as well as in literature, those witnessing a divine apparition are often depicted in a state of fright, as on a tripod *kothôn* in the Louvre by the C Painter (*c.* 570) where Paris is shown attempting to make a nimble exit stage right from Athena, Aphrodite and Hera (fig. 47 in P.E. Arias and M. Hirmer, *Greek Vase Painting*, tr. B. Shefton [London and New York 1962]). In fifth-century drama gods regularly appeared either on an upper level of the scene building or were flown in above the stage on what was known as a machine or *mêchanê*. Although such appearances are commonly dismissed by modern interpreters as 'merely' a dramatic convention, their conventionality does not necessarily argue disbelief in their reality (cf. Fox 1987, 113). Greek and Roman poets occasionally claim to have witnessed an epiphany. Horace (*Od.* 2.19), for instance, claims to have seen Bacchus. E. Fraenkel, *Horace* (Oxford, Clarendon 1957), 200, comments, 'I think Horace means what he says. He did see Dionysus ... He had only to close his eyes to see the god before him ... ', to which D.R. Shackleton-Bailey, *Profile of Horace* (London 1982), 48, sardonically replies, 'I think Fraenkel means what he says.' Epiphanies are well-attested in rural parts of the world in modern times, as in the celebrated case of the Virgin Mary who appeared to six children in Yugoslavia a few years ago. Cf. R. Laurentin and L. Rupcic, *La vierge apparaît-Elle à Medjugorje? Un message urgent donné au monde dans un pays marxiste* (Paris 1984).

16   **Paian of Isyllos.** A reference in the paian to Philip of Macedon suggests that the epiphany in question was connected with the king's attack on Sparta in 338. See Pritchett (*GSW* III, 29 n. 69).

17   **Phye.** See Connor (1987, 42-7), who rightly refrains from dismissing the event as 'mere manipulation by a cynical politician' and suggests that Herodotos' puzzlement may be due to the fact that the historian is underestimating the goodwill felt by the citizenry towards Peisistratos. In addition to Hdt., other references to the incident include [Arist.] *AP* 14.4, Kleidemos *FGrH* 323 F 15 in Ath. *Deipn.* 13.609cd, Polyain. *Strateg.* 1.21.1 and Val. Max. 1.2.2, p. 16 *T.* [Aristotle] and Kleidemos knew of sources independent of Herodotos, which suggests that the story was widely reported. For recent bibliography, see Rhodes (*CAAP*, 205f.).

18   *Mêtragyrtai.* See Semonides fr. 36 *IEG* and Hipponax frr. 127, 156 *IEG* with Burkert (1987, 35f.).

20   **Oracular authorisation.** Other examples of oracular support for religious innovation include [Dem.] 43.66, where Delphi recommends that new sacrifices be instituted in response to a portent in the sky; [Arist.] *AP* 54.6, where 'The Demos elects by lot ten performers of sacred rites or *hieropoioi* who carry out the sacrifices prescribed by oracles'; and *IG* II² 4969, which has been plausibly restored to read that Demon received the priesthood of Asklepios 'at the bidding of the god', i.e. Apollo.

22   **Erechtheion.** Literary testimony suggests that a joint cult of Athena and
Erechtheus was established on the Acropolis at a very early date (Hom. *Il.*
2.547-51; *Od.* 7.80f.). See further Travlos (*PDA*, 213f.) and Wycherley (*Stones*,
143-54).

1. Ancestral Rites

24   **Archon basileus.** For further discussion of this magistrate's religious duties,
see Rhodes (*CAAP*, 636-9) and Garland (*RAACA*, 111f.). It was the archon
basileus before whom Sokrates was arraigned (Pl. *Euthyph.* 2a; *Theait.* 210d).

25   **Continuity from the Bronze Age.** Burkert (*GR*, 43-53) provides an excellent
introduction to this difficult and complex question. As he (p. 50) points out, the
once widely held belief that the archon basileus was the successor of the
Mycenaean king was discredited by the discovery on Linear B tablets that the
king's title was '*wanax*'. For Dark Age religion, see V.R.d'A. Desborough, *The
Greek Dark Ages* (New York 1972), 278-84, who cautiously comments (p. 281),
'What we have is confined to a very few sites, is not always with certainty
demonstrable (viz. as providing evidence for cult places and practices during
the Dark Ages), and belongs almost invariably to the late Dark Ages, and
usually to the concluding phases.' See also Snodgrass (1971, 394-401). An
unconvincing case for extensive continuity across the gap of the Dark Age has
been advanced by B.C. Dietrich, *The Origins of Greek Religion* (Berlin and New
York 1974), who goes so far as to talk of 'Greek gods in Mycenaean dress' (p.
238). Coldstream (1977, 328f.) talks more prudently of 'continuity of memory'.
For Eleusis, see Snodgrass (1971, 395) and Coldstream (1977, 331f.). For the
Mycenaean *megaron*, see Travlos (*BTAA*, 92 and pls. 111-12) and Coldstream
(1977, 332). Coldstream believes that the cult must be 'at least as old as the
eleventh century', but there is a critical lack of votive deposits at the site for
the Dark Ages. For Brauron, see I. Papademetriou ('The sanctuary of Artemis
at Brauron, *Scientific American* 208 [1963] 110-20), Tomlinson (1976, 110f.)
and Travlos (*BTAA*, 191). For Hymettos, see Young (1940, 1-9), Langdon (1976,
passim) and Travlos (*BTAA*, 191). Hymettos is one of very few cult sites which
has yielded votive deposits of tenth-century date. See further de Polignac
(1984, 23f.). For the Acropolis, see Tomlinson (1976, 76f.) and Travlos (*PDA*,
52f. with bibliography on p. 55). For dedications of Late Geometric I date, see
Coldstream (1977, 128f.). For its prehistoric occupation, see Hopper (1971, ch.
1).

27   **Rise in number of dedications, etc.** See Coldstream (1977, 317-27, 332-9)
and de Polignac (1984, 23-31).

28   **Athena Polias.** Athena was commonly worshipped on acropoleis as the civic
goddess *par excellence*, notably at Athens, Sparta, Tegea, Ialysos, Kamiros,
Lindos, Emporio on Chios, Miletos, Phokaia and Syracuse (cf. Coldstream
1977, 327; Davies 1988, 377). The role may at times have placed her in
something of a quandary. In Hom. *Il.* 6.305, for instance, she is described as
'*rhusiptolis* (guardian of the acropolis)' of Troy, despite the fact that she sided
with the Greeks. The epithet 'Polias' does not necessarily connote
pre-eminence over other deities. At Argos, for instance, where there was a cult
of Athena Polias, the primary deity was Hera. In Eur. *Rhes.* 703 the Chorus
asks, 'Which do you acknowledge as your highest god (*hupatos theôn*)?', which
could be taken to imply that all poleis enjoyed a uniquely intimate relationship
with one particular deity, though this cannot be proved. With the exception of

Apollo, almost all tutelary deities were female (cf. Snodgrass 1980, 33). As Herington (1963, 63) points out, Solon (*IEG* 4) establishes a kind of hierarchy between Zeus, his favoured daughter and that daughter's favoured city.

Ionian tribes. The origin of the names of the tribes has never been satisfactorily explained. See A.S. Owen, *Euripides Ion* (Oxford, Clarendon 1939) 194-6, for the four chief hypotheses (viz. local, caste, religious or racial).

29   **Athena's connections with chthonic religion.** See Simon (*FA*, 68). For the Erechtheion as a primarily chthonic sanctuary, see N. Kontoleon, *To Erechtheion hôs oikodomêma chthonias latreias* (Athens 1949). The earliest reference to the cult of Athena Pallenis is in Hdt. 1.62.3. For further testimonia, see Solders (*AKEA*, 13f.). For the antiquity of Athena Hellotis, see Robertson (1985, 241-5), who, on the basis of similarities between the Panathenaia and Hellotia, suggests that her cult may be as old as that of Athena Polias. Athena and Poseidon shared honours in close proximity to each other elsewhere in Attica, notably at Sounion and on Kolonos Hippios. Regarding the antiquity of the Acropolis cult of Poseidon, Robertson (p. 236) notes that the god received worship in two agrarian festivals, the Skira and the Haloa (cf. Eust. on *Il.* 9.530), both of which are likely to have been important in early times.

31   **Erichthonios.** For the myth see Kearns (*HA*, 110-12, 160f.) and Robertson (1985, 231-95).

    Hero-cult. Contemporary with the Attic evidence are finds from the Argolid (Argos, Mycenae and Prosymna), Arkadia (Vasiliko), Boiotia (Thebes) Ithaca (Skala), and Messenia (Koukounara, Nichoria, Volimedia). See Abramson (1979, 5-8), Coldstream (1977, 341-57 and fig. 110), de Polignac (1984, 127-51), Snodgrass (1982, 107-19) and Whitley (1988, 178-81). The theory that hero-cult is subsequent to the circulation of epic is weakened by Hom.'s apparent knowledge of the institution (see following notes). As Coldstream (1976, 16) has remarked, 'Local heroes may have been venerated all through the Dark Age, long before the circulation of the Homeric epic ... .' It can scarcely be denied, however, that this acted as a catalyst. We may note, also, that rich burials of this period seem to show the influence of accounts of heroic burials in epic poetry.

34   **Erechtheus.** Cf. also Hom. *Od.* 7.81 where Athena is described as entering 'the well-built palace of Erechtheus'. Inevitably, these passages have been suspected of being interpolations. Robertson (1985, 255f.) takes *Il.* 2.549 to mean that the goddess installed Erechtheus 'at' (i.e. beside and not in) her temple, but this is somewhat forced. See also K. Jeppesen, *The Theory of the Alternative Erechtheion* (Aarhus 1987), for the suggestion that the Erechtheion and temple of Athena Polias were separate buildings. For further discussion of the cult and its mythology, see Kearns (*AH*, 160) and Parker (1986, 193-7). Mikalson (1976, 141-53) proposes that in its original form the Panathenaia was the annual festival of Erechtheus to which Homer alludes. It is a striking fact that there is no reference to a state festival of Erechtheus in surviving Athenian sacrificial records. For the cult-title Poseidon Erechtheus, see Eur. *Erech.* fr. 65.93f. Austin and *IG* I² 580, with Lacore (1983, 215-34) and Robertson (1985, 235f.).

    Iphigeneia. For the so-called 'grave of Iphigeneia', located southeast of the temple of Artemis Brauronia at Brauron, see Papademetriou (1955, 119; 1956, 76f.; 1957, 44f.) and Travlos (*BTAA*, pl. 74).

    Phrontis. The death and burial of Menelaus' helmsman Phrontis are described in *Od*. 3.278-85, which Abramson (1979, 8) interprets as the *aition* for a cult which already existed at the cape in the poet's day. If the cult did not exist, then it is a very reasonable assumption that one was established shortly afterwards in response to the epic. Either way, we have evidence here of a strong desire on the part of the Athenians to be connected with the personalities and events of the Trojan War cycle. The fact that there existed an early Archaic temple of Athena Sounias at Sounion is also suggestive. Might the goddess have facilitated the rise of the cult of Phrontis, just as Athena Polias allegedly promoted the cult of Erechtheus on the Acropolis? Or did these hero-cults in some way attract and sponsor the worship of the goddess? See further Picard (1940, 13), Abramson (1979, 1-19) and Kearns (*AH*, 42).

Herakles. For evidence of a possible ninth-century cult of Herakles on Mount Hymettos in the form of Geometric and Subgeometric sherds and a fragmentary inscription, see Langdon (1976, 97f.) and Young (1940, 3).

35   **Akademos.** See Stavropoullos (1956, 45-54; 1958, 5-13), Snodgrass 1982, 111f.) and Kearns (*AH*, 157). A small apsidal-ended house of Early Helladic date was fancifully identified by Stavropoullos as the hero's home.

Genesia. Cf. Jacoby (1944, 67) who convincingly argues that Solon's motive in establishing a fixed day in the calendar was to cut down the display of private grief in the capital by preventing celebrants from carrying out rites in more than one cemetery. For further discussion of funerary legislation enacted by Solon, see R.S.J. Garland ('The well-ordered corpse', *BICS* 36 [1989] 3-5).

37   **Eurysakes.** See Ferguson (1938, 15-18), Nilsson (1951, 30f.) and Garland (*RAACA*, 105). The testimonia and archaeological evidence are discussed by Wycherley (*Agora* III, 90-3) and Travlos (*PDA*, 261f.). The name derives from the 'broad shield (*sakos euru*)' of Eurysakes' father Ajax (cf. *Il*. 17.132; S. *Ajax* 574-6). The myth, which is almost certainly post-Homeric, appears in a variety of versions (e.g. Plu. *Sol*. 10.2, Paus. 1.35.2 and Hdt. 6.35). For the Eurysakeion, which also housed the cult of the nameless 'hero at Hale', see Harp. *s.vv. Melitê, Kolônetas* and Paus. 1.35.3. Ferguson (p. 16) suggests that the entry of Eurysakes may have occasioned the baptism of a pre-existing, anonymous hero-cult with the name of Eurysakes. Admittedly hero-worship usually necessitated the possession of some physical remains, but there were notable exceptions, as in the case of Oedipus (see p. 170). Athens' claim to Salamis was further bolstered by two lines in Homer (*Il*. 2.557f.) – 'Ajax brought twelve ships from Salamis and stationed them where the Athenian lines had taken up position' – which were used to demonstrate that the poet favoured Athens' ancient right of ownership.

38   **Salaminioi.** For the origins of the *genos*, see Ferguson (1938, 43-6), M.P. Nilsson ('The new inscription of the Salaminioi', *AJP* 59 [1938] 385-93), M. Guarducci ('L'origine e le vicende del *genos* attico dei Salaminii', *RFIC* 76 [1948] 223-43), Feaver (1957, 129) and Garland (*RAACA*, 87). For the cult and date of transfer of Athena Skiras at Phaleron, see Ferguson (1938, 20), Judeich (*Topog.*[2], 427) and Solders (*AKEA*, 9).

Peisistratid tyranny. For discussion of the religious edifices ascribed to this period, on whose evidence claims of Peisistratid involvement in Athenian religion are chiefly based, see C. Ampolo, *PP* 28 (1973) 271ff., Andrewes (1982, 411-15), Boersma (*ABP*, 11-27), Kolb (1977, 99-138) and Shear (1978, 1-19). It has been argued that whereas Peisistratos concentrated his building efforts in the Agora, his sons gave prominence to the Acropolis, and that this division reflects the differing political tendencies of the two generations, populist in the former instance, autocratic in the latter. But the evidence for such a division of concentrations is less than conclusive. See further Kolb (1977, 102).

39   **Panathenaia.** The oldest literary reference to a festival of Athena held in Athens is Hom. *Il*. 2.550f. – 'There in her rich sanctuary the youth of Athens propitiate her with sacrifice of bulls and rams as the years revolve' – which some scholars have suspected of being a sixth-century interpolation intended as a compliment to Peisistratos. In its early form the festival must have simply involved ritual activity in connection with the cult statue. For 566/5 as the foundation date of the games, see Pherekydes (*FGrH* 3 F2 in Marcellinus *Vit. Thuk*. 2-4.). The date is substantiated by the series of commemorative Panathenaic amphorae which begins around the middle of the fifth century. It is unclear whether Hippokleides himself played any part in the promotion of the festival. The only evidence for a link between Peisistratos and the quadrennial festival is supplied by a scholiast (Aristeid. 13.189.4-5 = Dindorf 3.323). For further discussion of the origins of the festival, see Andrewes (1982, 410f.), Davison (1958, 25; 1962, 141) and Parke (*FA*, 33f.). The Panathenaia continued to be celebrated until late antiquity, perhaps even as late as the fifth century AD, the approximate date when Athens converted to Christianity (cf. Thompson 1961, 223).

      Pedimental sculpture on the Acropolis dated *post* **570.** See Shear (1978, 3) and Boersma (*ABP*, 13). It is still unclear how many Archaic temples stood on the Acropolis. Very possibly there was only one. See Beyer (1977, 44-74) for an attempt to ascribe most of the surviving sculpture to two pediments belonging to the same building.

40   **Artemis Brauronia.** For Peisistratid property at Brauron, see [Pl.] *Hipparch*. 228b and Plu. *Sol*. 10.2 with Davies (*APF*, 452f.). The only evidence connecting the tyrant with the cult of Artemis Brauronia is circumstantial. For the branch establishment on the Acropolis, see Travlos (*PDA*, 124-6).

      Herakles. See Boardman (1972, 57-72; 1975, 1-12; 1989, 158f.). For strong objections to Boardman's proposed identification of Herakles with Peisistratos in Attic art, and hence to the theory of Peisistratos' promotion of the cult of Herakles, see Cook (1987, 167-9). For details of the Attic cult, see Woodford (1971, 211-25) and Kearns (*AH*, 166).

      Shrine of Apollo Patroös. For further arguments in favour of Peisistratid backing for the introduction of the cult, see Hedrick (1988, 206f.). Jacoby (1944, 72f.), by contrast, detected the influence of Solon.

41   **Altar of the Twelve Gods.** For discussion of the date of Peisistratos' archonship, see Davies (*APF*, 450f.). The worship of the Twelve Gods was probably imported from Asia Minor, as Burkert (*GR*, 125ff.) notes. For testimonia relating to the cult, see Wycherley (*Agora* III, nos. 363-78) and Long (1987, T14-19, pp. 62-83). The site has been identified with certainty, thanks to the discovery of a dedication (*Hesperia* 5 [1936] 358). For the archaeological remains, see Camp (*Agora*, 40f.) and Wycherley (*Stones*, 33). On the significance of non-urban cults in general, see de Polignac (1984, 31-5) who proposes (p. 35) that polis-formation accompanies the development of extra-mural sanctuaries 'at least as numerous and important in the majority of cities as urban sanctuaries could have been'.

42   **Altar of Apollo Pythios.** The dating of *IG* I² 761 (= *ML* 11 = *SEG* XXXI.31) is somewhat problematical but it should most reasonably be assigned to the period immediately after Peisistratos' archonship (cf. *ML*, p. 20). In view of the fact that no other archon is known to have made a dedicaton before 393, it has

been argued that Peisistratos' action was 'more than that of an ordinary citizen' (Lewis 1988, 294).

42   **Dionysos Eleuthereus.** Pickard-Cambridge (1968[2], 58) is reluctant to connect the god's arrival with Eleutherai's ceding of independence to Athens. Yet it is precisely political changes of this kind which foster the transplanting of a cult, there being no better way of forging an alliance between two communities than by adopting each other's gods. See further the discussion about the entry of the cult of Bendis (p. 111). For the earliest archaeological evidence for a cult of Dionysos Eleuthereus on the south slope of the Acropolis, see Connor (1989, 24-6).

43   **Olympieion.** See Wycherley (1964, 161-79, with bibliography on p. 161 n. 3) and Shear (1978, 10). Judeich's assertion (*Topog.*[2], 383) that the Peisistratid temple 'never rose above its foundations' has now been discredited by the discovery of drums of unfluted columns on the site. As Lewis (1988, 296) points out, the archaeological evidence does not tell us whether the temple was planned before or after the death of Peisistratos the elder. So far as we know, no work was carried out on it between the Archaic and Hellenistic periods. The project was resumed by Antiochos IV in 175 BC and the temple was ultimately dedicated by Hadrian in AD 132, the consequence of 'a great struggle with time' as Philostratos (*VS* 44.21 *T*) memorably observed.

    Temple of Athena Polias. See Boersma (*ABP*, 20f.) and Shear (1978, 2f.).

    Attic tetradrachms. For conflicting views about the dating of the series, see E.J.P. Raven ('Problems of the earliest owls of Athenians', pp. 40-58 in *Essays in Coinage Presented to S. Robinson* [Oxford 1968]), and P. Bicknell ('The dates of the Archaic owls of Athens belonging to Seltman's groups H & L', *AC* [1969] 175-80).

    Eleusinian Mysteries. For a succinct account of the evidence attributing Athenian interest in the Mysteries to Peisistratos, see Boardman (1975, 3-5) and Richardson (1974, 9f.). Boardman cites a fragmentary poem perhaps dated *c.* 550 (*P. Oxy.* 2622) which describes Herakles' initiation at Eleusis as further evidence of the Peisistratid connection (cf. H. Lloyd-Jones, *Maia* n.s. 19 [1967] 206-9). For the Peisistratid Telesterion, see Shear (1978, 9f.). For the sanctuary of the Two Goddesses in Eleusis, see Wycherley (*Agora III*, no. 198; *Stones*, 71f.) and Thompson and Wycherley (*Agora XIV*, 150-4). See also *IG* I[3] 231 = *SEG* XXI.3 = *LSGS* 1: fragmentary decree dated *c.* 510-500 from the City Eleusinion demonstrating Athenian involvement in the Mysteries at this date.

    Eponymous heroes. See Kron (1976, *passim*), Rotroff (1978, 205-7 with nn. 46-53) and Kearns (1985, 189-207; *AH*, 80-92). A possible explanation for the inclusion of Ajax and Hippothoön is that the list of tribal heroes was revived *post* 479 in order to accommodate 'helpful heroes from outside the Asty ... in the wake of the final victory over the Persians' (Kearns *AH*, 81, citing an idea of A.H. Griffiths). Given the political significance attaching to most of the chosen ten, Kearns is rightly sceptical as to whether the Pythia can have exercised a totally free hand in making the selection. The earliest reference to the monument of the eponymous heroes in the Agora is in Ar. *Peace* (421 BC), although the surviving monument displaying bronze statues of the ten on a long base dates only to *c.* 330 (cf. Thompson *Agora*[3], 70f.; Camp *Agora*, 97-9). It seems unlikely that there was a common Attic cult of the eponymous heroes in the Agora before the fourth century BC (cf. Rotroff, *loc. cit.*, with reference to *Agora Inventory* no. I 7475, dated 328/7 BC). For proof that the Ionian tribes continued to exist 'for ceremonial purposes' after the reforms of Kleisthenes, see J.H. Oliver ('Greek inscriptions', p. 7 in *Hesperia* 4 [1935]).

45   **Trittyes cults.** For a possible example of a trittys cult, see *IG* I^3 255 = *LSG* 11 (dated *c*. 430).

2. Pheidippides and the Magic Mountain

47   **Herodotos' testimony.** The reliability of Hdt.'s testimony is stoutly defended by Hammond (1968, 28 with n. 75), who argues that the historian 'must have consulted many veterans of the battle' who 'would be fierce and accurate critics of his account'. Fierce they might have been; their accuracy is another matter. See F.J. Frost, *Plutarch's Themistocles* (Princeton 1980), 134, who suspects that aged veterans can contribute little other than 'garrulous exaggeration, on the one hand, and pure fantasy, on the other'. Frost quotes Thuk.'s celebrated *caveat* about the unreliability of eye-witness reports of battles (7.44.1). Whether accurate or not in all its details, Hdt.'s account, being written primarily for an Athenian audience, is exactly what the Athenians themselves wanted to believe and hence *did* believe, and it is this which, for the purposes of this investigation, chiefly counts. For the detailed chronology of the period leading up to the battle, see Hammond (1988, 507f.).

    Pheidippides. The name of the runner is a matter of scholarly debate. For divergent views see Frost (1979, 159f.) and Badian (1979, 163-6). The manuscripts of Hdt. contain both names. In addition, Paus. 1.28.4, 8.54-6 and Plu. *Mor.* 862a refer to him as 'Philippides', whereas in Ar. *Clouds* we encounter the name 'Pheidippides'. For disagreements concerning the exact moment of the runner's departure to Sparta, see Hammond (1968, 34 n. 94) and Burn (1969, 119). Frost (1979, 160) grudgingly describes his achievement as 'quite a respectable run even for a professional courier'. He cites as more noteworthy that of a Plataian messenger called Euchidas who, having run from Plataiai to Delphi and back in the same day, fell down dead on the spot (Plu. *Arist.* 20.4-5). There is no earlier testimony than the late second century AD for the parallel claim that Pheidippides, after returning to Marathon, immediately took off for Athens bearing tidings of the victory, whereupon he, too, collapsed and died (Luk. *Laps.* 3).

49   **Pan and Arkadia.** For extensive discussion of Pan's Arkadian connections, see Borgeaud (1988, chh. 1 and 2) and M. Jost, *Sanctuaires et cultes de l'Arcadie* (1985), 456-75.

51   **Kallimachos' vow to Athena.** For the discovery of a winged woman (Nike or Iris) associated with an Ionic capital to which was probably attached the stone bearing Kallimachos' inscription, see Raubitschek (1940, 53-6) and Stewart (*GS*, 132 with fig. 210).

    Cave of Pan near Marathon. Excavated by I. Papademetriou in 1958, this has a narrow entrance leading to a series of large low-ceilinged rooms, exactly as Pausanias describes. See Vanderpool (1958, 321f.), Orlandos (1958, 15-22), G. Daux, ('Marathon, grotte de Pan', *BCH* 83 [1959] 587-9), Borgeaud (1988, ch. 5 n. 38) and Travlos (*BTAA*, 218 with pls. 302-3). The cave has yielded Neolithic vases and fragments of Early Middle Bronze Age vases. It was abandoned at the end of the Mycenaean era and remained unoccupied until around the time of the battle of Marathon. For a list of 30 fifth-century Athenian vases depicting Pan, see Brommer (1956, 956f.). Pan and the Nymphs continued to be worshipped alongside one another in the Marathonian cave into the Roman era (cf. *SEG* XXXVI.267, 61/60 BC).

51   **Pan's intervention in the battle.** For the prominence of *phobos* in Hdt.'s account, see Immerwahr (1966, 253f.). Cf. also Aes. *Pers.* 354 who refers vaguely to 'an avenging spirit or evil daimon (*alastôr ê kakos daimôn)*' which caused the rout of the Persians at Salamis. In the fifth century Pan shared the ability to cause sudden panic with Phobos and Dionysos. It was not until the fourth century that he acquired exclusive charge over this domain (cf. Pritchett *GSW* III, 45). For the expression *panikos thorubos* or 'confusion caused by Pan', see D.S. 14.32.3 and Plu. Mor. 192c. U. von Wilamowitz-Moellendorff, *Der Glaube der Hellenen* I (Berlin 1931), 248 n. 2, suggested that Pan came to inherit a power which originally belonged to Dionysos, but as E.R. Dodds, *Euripides Bacchae* (Oxford, Clarendon 1960), 109, has argued, Dionysos characteristically injected 'a special kind of panic – the moral and physical collapse of those who attempt to resist by normal means the fury of the possessed worshippers'.

53   **The factor of morale.** C.A. Powell ('Religion and the Sicilian Expedition', *Historia* 28 [1979] 15-31) has suggested that the opposite factor, viz what he calls 'religious pessimism', may have been a major reason for the scale of the Athenian débâcle in Sicily in 413. As Powell points out (p. 30), Thukydides' (7.79.3) suggestion that thunderstorms, which were interpreted as a sign of Zeus' displeasure, sapped the Athenian will to resist in the final days of the campaign, though largely ignored by modern scholars, convincingly explains why an army perhaps only marginally inferior in numbers to its opponent was virtually incapable of mounting proper resistance. Incidentally, we do not know even approximately the size of the Persian army at Marathon. Herodotos refers merely to 'a large and well-equipped land army' of Persians (6.95.1), as compared with 'few' Athenians (6.109, 112). Somewhat recklessly Lysias (*Epitaph.* 21) speaks of a force of 500,000 Persians.

54   **Echetlaios.** Farnell (1921, 88) writes of Echetlaios' epiphany, 'It is probably a pseudo-historic aetiological story invented to explain a name and a half-forgotten cult, and should not be regarded as proof that the cult originated in the fifth century BC.' Although there is no evidence that the Athenians consulted Delphi concerning any other matter relating to the battle of Marathon, there is no reason to assume that the oracle regarding Echetlaios is a late forgery. Like Pan, he may well have been venerated by the demesmen of Marathon from early times, becoming an official hero of the Athenian state only in 490. For sacred ploughing ceremonies performed in Attica see Plu. *Mor.* 144ab.

    Epizelos. This incident is also referred to in later sources, viz. Plu. *Mor.* 305c and Sud. *s.vv. 'Hippias'* and *'Poluzêlos'*. Immerwahr (1966, 254) suggests that Epizelos' courage in fighting on after being blinded in both eyes 'well summarises the feeling of "panic" on the part of the Athenians and the help given to them by Pan in their terror'. Cf. also Harrison (1972, 368) who interprets the apparition as 'a personification of fear, like Phobos and Deimos'. The vagueness of Herodotos' description of the incident is striking: 'I heard that in speaking about his injury Epizelos used to say something like this.' The hero is not referred to elsewhere.

55   **Artemis Agrotera.** Further proof of the goddess' importance at the battle is indicated by the fact that a waning moon behind the owl of Athena is depicted on Attic tetradrachms which were struck in the autumn of 490 (cf. C. Seltman, *Greek Coins* [London 1933] 91). For the festival of Artemis Agrotera, see Mikalson (*SCCAY*, 50) and Deubner (*AF*, 209).

56   **Marathon hero.** Plu. *Thes*. 32.4, citing the fourth-century BC philosopher
          Dikaiarchos, describes Marathon (or Marathos) as an Arkadian who fought on
          behalf of the Tyndaridai (or Dioskouroi) when they invaded Attica and sought
          to recover their sister Helen from Theseus (see p. 91). In accordance with 'some
          oracle', the hero sacrificed himself in the front line of battle in order to ensure
          victory. His courage thus epitomised the fighting spirit of the Marathonian
          dead.
57   **Herakles.** For the Herakleion at Marathon, see Soteriades (*PAE* 1935, 84ff.),
          Vanderpool (1966, 322f.) and Travlos (*BTAA*, 219, 221 with fig. 313). Its
          identification was confirmed in 1972 by the discovery of a votive inscription
          dated to the mid-fifth century (Marathon Museum no. BE 34). For the cults
          associated with the the hero at Marathon and Kynosarges, see Woodford
          (1971, 215-18). Appropriately, Herakles and Theseus also figure on the
          lēkythoi which have been recovered from the tombs of the Marathonian dead
          (cf. Clairmont *PN* I, 100).
          Nemesis. Architectural finds suggest that the earliest temple at Rhamnous
          dates to the early decades of the sixth century (Petrakos 1983, 11; 1987,
          299-302). For the later temples, see Petrakos (1983, 11; 1987, 302-5) and
          Travlos (*BTAA*, 388f.). The earliest epigraphical evidence for a cult of Nemesis
          belongs to *c.* 500 (cf. *SEG* XXXV.24), proving that the cult of Nemesis was not,
          as has sometimes been claimed, introduced into Attica as a result of the
          Persian Wars, although the assistance rendered by the goddess on this
          occasion no doubt greatly enhanced her prestige. A fifth-century inscription
          recording a dedication by a certain Lysikleides 'to this goddess here who
          occupies this *temenos* here' (*IG* I^2 828) suggests that it may have been
          unpropitious to utter aloud the name of such a dread deity. Cf. Robertson
          (1985, 245f.).
58   **Marathonian war dead.** See generally Pritchett (*GSW* IV, 126-9, 166f.). For
          the Soros, see Pritchett (1960, 140-3) and Clairmont (*PN* I, 95-8). A *bothros* or
          sacrificial pit found at the edge of the tumulus which has produced bones of
          animals and fragments of vases was evidently connected with the hero-cult.
          For the tomb of the Plataians and that of the Athenian slaves (cf. Paus. 1.32.3),
          see Clairmont (*PN* I, 99f.). For the (possible) cenotaph in the Kerameikos, see
          Wilhelm (1934, 89-118), Oliver (1936, 225-34) and Raubitschek (1940, 56-9).
          For the epigrams associated with it, see the discussions in Oliver (1935,
          193-201), *ML* 26, *SEG* XXVIII.29 and Clairmont (*PN* I, 106-11). Clairmont
          along with others believes that the lower inscribed epigram refers to Marathon
          and the upper one to the battles of 480-479. The Marathonian war dead were
          still receiving honours in the late second century BC (cf. *IG* II^2 1006.26f.).
          Other war dead in receipt of high though not heroic honours include those who
          fell at Plataia in 479 (Thuk. 3.58.4), for which see Pritchett (*GSW* IV, 174f.).
59   **Acropolis shrine of Pan.** See P. Kavvadias ('*Ta spêlaia tou Apollônos kai tou
          Panos*', *Arch. Eph.* (1897), 1-21 with pls. 1-3), Brommer (1956, 993), J.G.
          Frazer, *Pausanias' Description of Greece* (London and New York 1898), II pp.
          360ff. and IV pp. 516ff., and Travlos (*PDA*, 417 with pls. 536-9).
60   **Caves of Pan.** For a cave of Pan on Hymettos, see Men. *Dysk.* 407-9. For
          those at Daphni, Eleusis, Parnes, Pentelikon and Vari, see Travlos (*BTAA*, 177
          with pls. 235-6; 96 with pls. 105, 182f.; 319 with pls. 408-9; 329 with pls.
          416-18; 447f. with pls. 585f.).
61   **Pan and Artemis.** For the *kratêriskoi* at Eleusis, see L. Kahil ('Artémis
          attique', 127 in *CRAI* 1976). For further discussion of the association, see

Borgeaud (1988, 64f. and 156f.).

3. Themistokles and the Cult of the Intellect

64　　Date of the Athenian consultation at Delphi. Although Herodotos places this event before the meeting of the Greek states at the Isthmus of Corinth, i.e. in the spring or autumn of 481, some scholars have preferred to assign it to the interval between the abandonment of Thessaly and the battle of Thermopylai, i.e. to the spring of 480, perhaps about a month or so before the battle of Salamis (cf. How and Wells, 1912, II p. 181; Parke and Wormell 1956, I p. 169). As Fontenrose (1978, 127) points out, this compresses subsequent events into a very tight time-span. It is regrettable that Herodotos does not indicate what interval, if any, occurred between the two consultations. For further discussion, see Hignett (1963, 441-4), Hands (1965, 59f.) and Evans (1982, 24-9).

66　　Historicity of the consultation. Fontenrose (1978, 126), who includes these two oracles within his category of 'questionable responses', none the less admits that rejecting them altogether creates more difficulties than it solves, by necessitating the removal of Themistokles' interpretation of the phrase 'the wooden wall' and leaving unexplained how the anecdote arose in the first place. For a detailed discussion of Herodotos' treatment of the Delphic oracle, see Elayi (1978, 93-118; 1979, 67-151). Regarding the nature of Delphic utterance, see Roux (1976, 158f.) who suggests that the Pythia may have responded 'in Delphic dialect with rudely composed verses'.

　　　　Spontaneous prophecy. Parke (1962, 145f.) comments that spontaneous prophecy was 'a favourite motif in Delphic legend (though) none of the instances need be taken as historic.' Oddly he neglects to mention this celebrated instance in his discussion, though elsewhere he treats the double consultation as historic. The verb *'automatizô'*, which means 'to speak a prophecy without (or before) being questioned' and hence 'to prophesy spontaneously', is first used of a prophetic ill-omen uttered shortly before Philip II's death in 336 (D.S. 16.92.2), though the late attestation of the word does not prove that the phenomenon was irregular, still less that it was hitherto unknown.

67　　Unpopular oracles. See Price's remarks (1985, 151) about instances in Hdt. where oracles are either ignored (e.g. 5.89) or evaded (e.g. 5.67). Price quotes E. Evans-Pritchard, *Witchcraft, Oracles and Magic among the Azande* (Oxford 1976), 163, 'An Azande does not readily accept an oracular verdict which conflicts seriously with his interests.' Nor, evidently, did a Hektor or a Themistokles. For conflicting oracles (*chrêsmous pantoious*) to suit conflicting opinions about whether to offer battle to the Peloponnesians or shelter behind the walls in the early years of the Peloponnesian War, see Thuk. 2.21.3. For a possible example of an oracle being 're-cycled', see H.W. Parke (*ZPE* 60 [1985] 93-6) who suggests that *IG* II² 4968 may originally have begun its career as a prophecy of the Persian invasion and was later adapted for use in the struggle against Philip of Macedon. Elayi (1979a, 227-30) makes an ingenious attempt to interpret the two oracles given to the Athenians as being consistent with one other by taking 'the ends of the earth' to be a reference to Salamis (situated at the ends of Attic territory) and claiming that what the first oracle is counselling is vigorous action instead of supine resignation. It seems not to have occurred to Herodotos, his informants, the Athenian *theopropoi* or

Themistokles to interpret it in this way.

68   **Bribery of Delphi.** The incident involving Kleomenes is particularly instructive in the context of the present discussion since Herodotos reports that the Spartans managed to bribe the Pythia by suborning a certain Kobon, described as 'a very powerful man at Delphi' – an expression which is similar to the one which he uses to describe Timon. In the case we are considering, however, the influential Delphian merely advises the Athenians on a matter of tactical procedure. For allegations of oracular corruption, cf. also S. *OT* 387-9 where Oedipus accuses the seer Teiresias of prophesying for profit, and Hdt. 7.6.3-5 where the seer Onomakritos is caught forging an oracle. See further Nock (1972, 537-40).

Wooden wall. No traces of any such structure have been found on the Acropolis. It presumably supplemented the Mycenaean fortifications around the Acropolis (cf. Wycherley *Stones*, 7).

70   **Kroisos of Lydia.** See the excellent remarks of P. Green ('Delphic responses', pp. 95-8 in *Classical Bearings* [New York 1989]) concerning this incident. Green suggests that the Delphic authorities practised a kind of homespun psychology upon their clients. He writes (p. 96): 'Kroisos' character had been tested, and found wanting. He had certainly acted in excess, proving himself a classic overreacher. He had been found singularly lacking in self-knowledge ...'.

71   **Boreas.** See Agard (1965, 241-6), Bovon (1963, 223f.), Kaempf-Dimitriadou (1986, 133-5) and Simon (1967, 101-17). The myth is first represented on the chest of Kypselos, if Pausanias (5.19.1) is to be believed. One of the earliest representations of the abduction of Oreithyia in Attic art is to be found on an early red-figure *stamnos* from Brauron in Berlin, which is contemporary with the help rendered by the god in 492 (no. 2186; *ARV* p. 139). The myth does not become common in art until after 480. See Kaempf-Dimitriadou (1986, 135-8) for a complete catalogue.

72   **Artemis Mounychia.** See Palaiokrassa (1983) and Garland (*Piraeus*, 113f. and Appendix III nos. 17-22). Herodotos' (8.77.1) reference to 'the sacred shore of Artemis Chrysaoros (Of the golden sword)' in connection with the battle of Salamis is perhaps an allusion to this same Artemis. The cult is likely to have been well-established by the time of the Persian wars, particularly in view of the pre-eminent locality of the sanctuary on Mounychia Hill. For a possible epiphany of the Dioskouroi to the Aiginetans at Salamis based on the evidence of a dedication which they made at Delphi (cf. Hdt. 8.122), see Pritchett (*GSW* III, 25f.).

75   **Why Artemis? Why Aristoboule?** For a general discussion of the tell-tale signs by which individual gods could be identified, see Mussies (1988, 10-16). For circumstantial evidence pointing to a prior association between Themistokles and Artemis, see Podlecki (1975, 176f.). I have not been able to find any evidence in support of Podkecki's claim (p. 42) that while in Magnesia Themistokles 'did much to foster devotion to his patroness Artemis, under the title Leukophryene'. For Artemis Boulaia, see Wycherley (*Agora III*, 56f.). The only other reference to a deity called Aristoboule is in Porph. *Abst.* 2.54 where there is mention of her *hedos* ('abode' or 'dwelling-place') outside the city gates on the island of Rhodes.

Sanctuary of Artemis Aristoboule at Melite. For the excavation, see Threpsiades and Vanderpool (1964, 26-36) and Travlos (*PDA*, 121ff.). For the sanctuary and cult, see Wycherley (*Stones*, 91). Artemis' name is actually inscribed without any epithet on the votive pillar erected in the sanctuary by Neoptolemos. However, the modest proportions of the shrine, entirely appropriate to an essentially private cult, coupled with its location along what was almost certainly the road leading to the *barathron* (Judeich, *Topog.*², 140), provides a case for identifying her with Themistokles' goddess which in Frost's (1980, 185) words, 'only the most fervent sceptics will reject'. For lingering doubts, see Amandry (1967-8, 265-79, especially 273), who believes that the remains are those of a 'treasury'. For the possibility of Themistokles receiving hero-cult in the Piraeus, see J. Rusten (*HSCP* 87 [1983] 293 n. 15) and Kearns (*AH*, 41), citing Plu. *Them.* 32.4-5. If, as Diodoros the Topographer suggests (*loc. cit.*), Themistokles' remains were recovered from Magnesia at the beginning of the fourth century, a deliberate parallel with the recovery of Theseus' bones from Skyros might have been intended.

78   **Neoptolemos of Melite.** Neoptolemos was a man of considerable wealth, which he earned largely through silver-mining and frequently deployed in the service of religion. In addition to sponsoring the cult of Artemis Aristoboule, he gilded a statue of Apollo in the Agora, for which he was rewarded with a crown and a statue on the motion of Lykourgos ([Plu.] *Mor.* 843f), made a dedication on the Acropolis (*IG* II² 4901), and dedicated a crown to Athena (*IG* II² 1496.43f.). He also served on the board of *hieropoioi* for the Pythaïs which was sent to Delphi in 326/5 (*SIG*³ 296.4). His devotion to Apollo and Artemis is conspicuous. For his career, see Davies (*APF*, no. 10652). Interestingly his associate Lykourgos, Athens' principal finance minister in the 330s, also took a leading role as a religious innovator. Cf. S.C. Humphreys ('Lycurgus of Butadae: an Athenian aristocrat', pp. 199-252 in J.W. Eadie and J. Ober, *The Craft of the Ancient Historian: Essays in Honour of Chester G. Starr* [New York and London 1985]).

    Themistokles and religion. In his discussion of the passage where Plu. likens Themistokles to a playwright introducing a *deus ex machina*, Crahay (1956, 301) refers to the remarkable unity underlying what he calls his 'orchestration of the supernatural' at Athens during the period of the Persian Wars. He sees the Pythia as merely 'the docile instrument of the party of extreme resistance' (p. 301), Dikaios as 'undoubtedly an imaginary witness', his companion Demaratos a personage 'intended to provide the anecdote with a cachet of authenticity' (p. 304), and the fetching of the Aiakidai as a ruse intended to blunt last-minute opposition to his naval defence policy (p. 274). Finally, Crahay interprets the story surrounding the sacred olive-tree which was destroyed when the Persians burnt the Acropolis and which miraculously sprang to life the next day as 'a political fiction intended to raise the spirits of those who had sacrificed everything for (viz. his interpretation of) the wooden wall' (p. 303). I have obviously tried to present a very different picture. There also exists an apocryphal story of Themistokles arriving at Delphi in 479 with offerings of Persian spoils (Paus. 10.14.5). For the short-lived cult of the Dindymian Mother of the Gods, cf. also D.S. 14.36.4 and Str. 14.1.40 = C 647. As Frost (1980, 223) points out, the lion is symbolic of the Anatolian Mother of the Gods, since it was her familiar.

4. Theseus' Old Bones

82   **Eleutheria.** There is no other evidence for this festival in either the fifth or fourth centuries and many scholars believe that it was not founded until 338

BC. Cf. Étienne and Pierart (*BCH* 99 [1975] 67f.); J. and L. Robert (*REG* 89 [1976] 473f.). By contrast, the Athenian cult of Zeus Eleuthereus has undisputed connections with the Persian Wars. A stoa of Zeus Eleuthereus, probably built between 430 and 420, is located on the west side of the Athenian Agora and an archaic structure on the same site, which was destroyed by the Persians in 480/79, may have been dedicated to the same divinity. See Camp (*Agora*, 105-7 with fig. 79) and Thompson (*Agora*³, 79-81). Although the Oath of Plataiai is not accepted by scholars in all its details, it probably has 'a genuine core' (cf. Meiggs *AE*, 508). See further Siewert (1972, *passim*).

84   **Sparta's retrieval of the bones of Orestes and Tisamenos.** Leahy (1955, 26-38) interprets both incidents as diplomatic initiatives on the part of the Spartans which were intended to consolidate alliances with the peoples of Arkadia and Achaia (successful in the former case, a failure in the latter). The problem with this theory, as Leahy himself admits, is first that it conflicts with Herodotos' claim that the recovery of the bones of Orestes led to a military victory and not to an alliance, and secondly that it is at variance with the report that the bones were removed clandestinely. It seems preferable, therefore, to regard the transfer as primarily serving the aim of restoring Sparta's damaged morale after suffering repeated reverses during the long drawn-out war. Our knowledge of the Tisamenos cult is confined to a brief mention in Paus. 7.1.8 and we can only speculate about the circumstances which prompted its transfer to Sparta. See Kearns (*AH*, 48) for a useful discussion of the engrossing question as to whether a hero's bones were regarded as magical objects in their own right or whether they were invested with the personality and will of the individual hero.

Return of Theseus' bones. See Pfister (1909, 188-211, 510-14). One consequence of Theseus' return may have been to foster a desire on the part of the Athenians to bring home the ashes of their war dead from the battlefield and to honour them with a lavish public funeral whose institution may also date to this period (cf. Clairmont *PN* I, 14). Thus, by association with a mythic prototype, ordinary soldiers who laid down their lives for their country could henceforth partake in the lustre of heroic grandeur by becoming the '*agathoi*' or heroised dead.

Kimon's motives. See Connor (1970, 157-66) for an account of Kimon's utilisation of the Theseus myth. Rightly regarding 'mythic identification' with a hero as a perfectly acceptable method of self-promotion in ancient Greece, Connor (p. 166) concludes: 'The legends of Theseus symbolise his policy – Athenian prowess on the sea, opposition to marauders and robbers, and obstinate hostility to the barbarian invaders. And Kimon, whatever vanity or silliness we may find in him, lived this policy ... .' See further Barron (1980, 2) for the stimulating possibility that Bacchyl. *Dith.* 18.46-60 *T* 'seems to contain allusions to Kimon's father and mother, and to all three of his sons'.

86   **Life of Theseus.** The Aristotelian author of *AP*, we may note, was also among those who accepted the historicity of Theseus, crediting the hero with establishing a system of government 'deviating slightly (*mikron parengklinousa*) from monarchical power' (41.2). Likewise in Plu. *Thes.* 16.2 the author of the *Constitution of Bottiaia* is quoted as accepting as fact the payment of human tribute to Minos, though he seeks to repair the latter's tarnished reputation by alleging that the king did not kill the Athenian youths but merely kept them as his slaves. See Herter (1939, *passim*; *s.v.* 'Theseus', cols. 1045-1238 in *RE* Suppl. XIII) for a detailed treatment of the origins and

development of the Theseus legend. For its depictions in art, see K. Schefold, *Götter- und Heldensagen der Griechen in der spätarchaischen Kunst* (Munich 1978), 150-68, and Brommer (1982, passim). For discussion of the Amazon legend, see, in addition to Boardman (1982), W.B. Tyrrell, *Amazons: a Study in Athenian Mythmaking* (Princeton and London 1984), 3-13.

89   **Theseus' rise to prominence.** For divergent views about the date of Theseus' rise to Panathenian status, see Connor (1970, 143-7), Boardman (1972, 57-72) and Ostwald (1988, 324f.). Connor draws upon circumstantial evidence in order to support his claim that Peisistratos acted as Theseus' patron, notably the tyrant's alleged excision of a line from a poem by Hesiod 'to gratify the Athenians' (fr. 298 *OCT*) on the grounds that it reflected badly on his hero. Boardman argues against any Peisistratid sponsorship on the grounds that Theseus rarely figures on Athenian vases before 510 when the Peisistratids were expelled from Athens. (On the dubious wisdom of reading political allusions into the choice of subjects favoured by Athenian vase-painters, see the judicious observations of Cook [1987, 167].) Finally, Ostwald raises the possibility that the sudden interest in Theseus in Athens from 510 onwards may have been inspired by Kleisthenes' reforms, which, he points out, achieved 'a new kind of synoecism' not unlike that attributed to Theseus.

90   **Athenian treasury at Delphi.** For discussion of the date of construction and sculptural decoration of this building, see Boardman (1982, 3-5).

        Theseus and Poseidon. For evidence that Theseus and Poseidon both received honours on the eighth day of each month, see the testimonia cited by Mikalson (*SCCAY*, 19f.).

93   **Cult of Theseus.** Further evidence of the antiquity of the cult is provided by [Aristotle] who claims (*AP* 15.4) that Peisistratos held a parade 'in the Theseion' near the Acropolis when he made his third and final bid for power. Pausanias' statement (1.17.6) that the *sêkos* or tomb of Theseus was built 'after the Persians landed at Marathon ... when Kimon son of Miltiades deported the people of Skyros' is not necessarily at variance with the theory that the cult was extremely ancient, as there is no reason why a *temenos* should not have been consecrated to Theseus before the return of his bones. Kenyon's emendation of '*Thêseiôi*' to '*Anakeiôi*' is therefore unnecessary, and Rhodes's claim (*CAAP*, 210f.) that '*AP* or his source is guilty of an anachronism' unwarranted. The location, architecture and murals of the Theseion are discussed in detail by Barron (1972, 20-45). Later references to the Theseion include Hsch., *Et. Mag.* and Phot. *s.v.* The testimonia have been collected by Wycherley (*Agora III*, nos. 339-62). The Theseion served as a lawcourt, a muster hall, an election hall and, most importantly, as a refuge for runaway slaves. See further Christensen (1984, 23-32).

        For the *temenos* of Theseus on Hippios Kolonos, cf. Paus. 1.30.4 and S. *OK* 1590-4. For that in the deme of Piraeus, cf. *IG* II² 2498.3, 10 and 15f. = *SIG³* 965 = *SEG* XXXII.226, with Judeich (*Topog.*², 456) and Garland (*Piraeus*, 162f. and Appendix II no. 4). For a Theseion within the Long Walls, cf. Andok. 1.45 and *IG* II² 1035.48. For further discussion, see Jacoby (commentary on *FGrH* 328 F18) and Kearns (*AH*, 168f.). For the later cult of Theseus, see G. Bugh ('The Theseia in late Hellenistic Athens', forthcoming in *ZPE* 1990). Bugh supports the view that a new penteteric festival in honour of Theseus was established in the Hellenistic period 'to commemorate the return of Athens' old colonial possessions ... especially Skyros by the Romans at the conclusion of the Third Macedonian War in 167 BC'.

Cult of the Tyrannicides. For the date of Antenor's group, see Ostwald (1969, 132-4). For Antenor's group, see Mattusch (*GBS*, 87f.). For Kritios' and Nesiotes' group, see Brunnsåker (1955), Shefton (1960, 173-9), Wycherley (*Stones*, 73-5) and Mattusch (*GBS*, 119-21). For representations of the Tyrannicides in Attic art, see Podlecki (1966, 137 n. 53). For testimonia relating to the cult, see Wycherley (*Agora III*, 93-8). Podlecki (1966, 138) maintains that it was Themistokles who made the dedication of the replacement-statues in 477 in order 'to put the death-stroke once and for all to the patriotic pretensions of the Alkmaionids'. Had this been the case, however, we might expect such a flagrantly political gesture to have been discredited along with its author at the time of the latter's expulsion, as seems to have happened in the case of Artemis Aristoboule whose cult was abandoned. For the award of public dining-rights in perpetuity to the descendants of the Tyrannicides, see Ostwald (1951, 32-5). Kardara's suggestion (1951, 293-300) that two of the representations of Theseus which appear on a *kylix* by Kodros (BM no. E84) are 'imitated' from the Tyrannicides is an intriguing one and suggests that the artist may have been intentionally drawing an ideological link with Theseus.

Finally, to deny Harmodios and Aristogeiton *any* political motive, as Thukydides does, is patently naive. As K.J. Dover, *Thucydides VI* (Oxford, Clarendon 1965), 59, notes, 'Whatever the reason for Aristogeiton's emotion, he and Harmodios did after all plan *the overthrow of the tyranny*, not mere personal revenge on Hipparchos'.

97   *Oikistês* **cult.** See Malkin (1987, 187-266) for extensive discussion. As Malkin emphasises, a distinctive feature of the *oikistês* cult in general – including, we may note, that of Theseus from 477 onwards – is that it was not confined to an aristocratic *genos* like other forms of hero worship, but rather 'practised as the cult of the whole *polis* community' (*op. cit.*, p. 265). On mythical founders in general, see de Polignac (1984, 132-40). De Polignac (p. 133) points out that the burial of such a hero in the heart of the city was not confined to the heroes of new colonies. In some cases it took the form of the 'discovery' of a previously unknown tomb of a hero. The tomb of Ilos, mythical founder of Troy, in the Trojan plain supplies the prototype (Hom. *Il.* 10.415, 11.166f., 371f.).

5. Transfiguration and the Maiden

100   **Decree of the Praxiergidai.** In addition to Lewis' text in *IG* I³ 7 (on which my own translation is based), see also *IG* I² 80, *LSG* 15 (at odds with Lewis in some important particulars), *SEG* XIV.3, *SEG* XXV.10 and *SEG* XXXVI.4. The dating of the decree is based on its letter-forms. See Raubitschek (*DAA*, 323), Lewis (1954, 19) and Ostwald (1986, 146). Ostwald's reconstruction (pp. 145-8) of the circumstances surrounding the passage of the decree provides the basis for the present discussion.

For the Plynteria, see L. Ziehen, *s.v.* 'Plynteria' cols. 1060-5 in *RE* 21.1, Deubner (*AF*, 17-22), and Simon (*FA*, 46-8). Parke (*FA*, 152f.) wrongly states that ritual activity was conducted in connection with the colossal gold and ivory statue made by Pheidias. Only the Praxiergidai, who removed and replaced its clothing, and the *loutrides*, who perhaps bathed it, were allowed to see the olive-wood statue naked. Contrary to Plu., Phot. *s.v. Kalluntêria kai*

Pluntêria dates the Plynteria to Thargelion 29. As Mikalson (*SCCAY*, 160f.) points out, however, Phot.'s testimony is discredited by the fact that three meetings of the Ekklesia are attested for this day.

102   **Priestess of Athena Nike**. Schlaifer (1940, 260) suggests that the priestess may previously have been chosen from one of the higher property census classes, but there is no known parallel for a priesthood being restricted in this way. If no independent priesthood existed before the 440s, the goddess may have been served by the priestess of Athena Polias. Meiggs (*AE*, 136) attributes the decision to build a temple to Athena Nike to the peace with Persia, which Athens sought to represent as a 'victorious settlement'. For the archaeological remains of the temple, see Travlos (*PDA*, 148f.). That the priestess was appointed by lot is known from the epitaph of Myrrhine, the first incumbent (*SEG* XII.80). Her salary is again alluded to in a later decree (*IG* I² 25.4-8 = *ML* 71, dated 424/3), perhaps because payment had fallen into arrears.

103   **Re-affirming Marathon**. For the trophy of white marble, see Vanderpool (1966, 93-106). On permanent battlefield trophies in general, see Pritchett (*GSW* II, 256f.). For the date of the Stoa Poikile, see L.H. Jeffery, *ABSA* 60 (1965) 40f., who suggests a date before Kimon's ostracism in 462/1 on the grounds that Peisianax, its architect, was probably Kimon's brother-in-law (cf. Davies *APF*, 377f.). For testimonia relating to the stoa, see Wycherley (*Agora III*, 31-45). For the building itself, see Thompson and Wycherley (*Agora XIV*, 124-6). On the depiction of Miltiades in the painting of the battle, see Harrison (1972, 356f.). For the statue of Athena Promachos, see *IG* I³ 435 and *SEG* XXXV.10. For a critique of Boardman's arguments concerning the Parthenon frieze, see Simon (*FA*, 58-60).

106   **Religion of imperialist Athens**. For a contrary interpretation of the Samian *horoi*, viz. that they represent the strength of loyalty felt by the Samian democracy towards Athens, see Barron (1964, 35-48). There is a probable reference to the cult of *Athêna Athênôn medeousa* in a decree dated 447/6, which imposes a settlement on Kolophon following its revolt and subjugation (*IG* I³ 37.15 = *ML* 47). Estimates of the date of the decree concerning offerings of first-fruits to Eleusis range from 445 to 415, though a consensus is now forming around the late 420s. Mattingly (1974, 97) dates the decree to 425/4 and Hanson (*SEG* XXXIII.6) to c. 422.

109   **Periklean building programme**. On oath-taking, see Mikalson (*APR*, 31-8). For Perikles' justification of the programme, see Stadter (1989, 153f.) who concludes that Plu. is probably quoting a fifth-century source. For the Hephaisteion, see Camp (*Agora*, 82-7). Meritt (1975, 271) believes that the authorisation for the building of a temple and altar to Athena and Hephaistos was given in the so-called Coinage Decree (l. 18) by which Athens regulated weights and measures and enforced the use of her silver coinage upon her allies. Thompson and Wycherley (*Agora* XIV, 143) think that 'a very modest shrine' on Kolonos Agoraios may have been destroyed in the Persian conflagration. For the temple of Ares, see Camp (*Agora*, 184-7), Thompson (*Agora³*, 106-9), Travlos (*BTAA*, 1) and Wycherley (*Stones*, 84). For the temple of Nemesis, see A.T. Hodge and R.A. Tomlinson ('Some notes on the temple of Nemesis at Rhamnous', *AJA* 73 [1969] 185-92). See Robertson (1985, 245-7) for the interesting observation that Nemesis at Rhamnous was 'a deity akin to Athena'.

110   **State funding of cults**. In general, see Schlaifer (1940, 233-41). Cf. also Jameson (1980, 214-36) for a decree passed by the Demos, perhaps in c. 440, which imposed a tax on the land forces of Attica in order to pay for the upkeep of

a *temenos* of Apollo (Lykeios?).

11　　**Entry of Bendis**. Bendis is first mentioned in the work of the elegiac poet Hipponax of Ephesos (*c.* 540), where she is identified as Kybebe (or Kybele) and Artemis (*IEG* fr. 127). On Thracian religion in general, albeit with little discussion of Bendis, see Pettazzoni (1954, 81-94). The earliest reference to the goddess in an Athenian source is in Kratinos' comedy *Thracian Women* (fr. 80 in *CAF* I, p. 37), whose probable date is 442. See Nilsson (1942, 170-4) for testimonia.

6. Asklepios and his Sacred Snake

16　　**Public physicians in Athens**. The earliest secure evidence for the existence of public physicians in Athens is provided by Ar. *Acharn*. 1030 (425 BC). A fragmentary inscription dated 440-425 (*IG* I³ 164) has been interpreted as a decree awarding honours to two public physicians. Later evidence is plentiful (e.g. Pl. *Gorg*. 455b, 514d). A third-century decree (*IG* II² 772.10f.) tells us that public physicians performed a twice-yearly sacrifice to Asklepios and Hygieia in the Asty sanctuary. See further Cohn-Haft (1956, 10f.) and Aleshire (1989, 94).

　　Asklepios' origins. Earlier scholars tended to support the idea of a Thessalian homeland for the god. Cf. L.R. Farnell, *Greek Hero Cults and Ideas of Immortality* (Oxford 1921), 234-79, Thraemer (in *RE* 2 cols. 1643-55), and Ziehen (1892, 195-7). Edelstein and Edelstein (1945, 97-101, 238ff.), however, put their weight behind the claims of Epidauros.

　　Myths associated with Asklepios. See Holtzmann (1984, 863f.) for a recent discussion. Pindar's version of Asklepios' birth is a modification of Hes. fr. 50 (Merkelbach and West in *OCT*). The earliest allusion to Asklepios in Attic literature is Aes. *Agam*. 1022-4 (458 BC), which describes his death from Zeus' thunderbolt. Later fifth-century references include S. *Phil*. 1437f. and Eur. *Alk*. 3f. and 122-9.

18　　**Asklepieia older than Zea**. Sanctuaries which may be older than Zea include those at Sikyon in the Argolid, Mantinea in Arkadia and Kyllene in Elis. Their claims are based not on archaeological data, however, but on purely literary allusions to artistic works which were allegedly exhibited in their temples. Cf. Paus. 2.10.3, 8.9.1; and Str. *Geog*. 8.3.4 = C 337. For the dates of the artists in question (viz. Kalamis, Alkamenes and Kolotes), see Edelstein and Edelstein (1945, II p. 244f.).

　　Telemachos Monument. For a rather different reconstruction to Beschi's, see Mitropoulou (1975, *passim*). Mitropoulou (p. 54f.) regards *IG* II² 4963 as a fragment of a copy of the Telemachos Monument. Although the date of Asklepios' entry into the Piraeus is not preserved on the Telemachos Monument, the fact that in Ar. *Wasps* 121-3 Bdelykleon contemplates sending his father to the Asklepieion on Aigina strongly suggests that when *Wasps* was produced in 422 there was no Attic sanctuary to the god. Cf. Aleshire (1989, 7 with n. 2).

20　　**Asklepieion in Zea**. The sanctuary was excavated in the last century but the results have never been fully published. See Garland (*Piraeus*, 115-17, 208-9; Appendix III nos. 26-33 for the testimonia). Though it is likely to have been founded by Telemachos (see p. 120), we cannot assume that its priesthood was identical to that of the Asty Asklepieion. The precise relationship between the two cult centres remains unclear.

120   **Asklepios' status.** Walton (1894, 27-30) believed that Asklepios initially
           entered Athens as a hero and not as a god, citing as evidence the reference in
           Pl. *Symp.* 186e to Asklepios as the ancestor (*progonos*) of the Athenians, reliefs
           from the Athenian Asklepieion depicting death-feasts, and the existence of a
           festival in his honour known as the *Hêrôïa*. (For other possible interpretations
           of the significance and meaning of the *Hêrôïa*, however, see Girard [1881,
           51-5]). The fact that Asklepios accommodated a large entourage of
           altar-sharers (notably Maleatas, Apollo and Hermes, the dogs and the
           dog-handlers, his children Panakea, Akeso, Iaso and Aigle, and his principal
           attendant Hygieia, e.g. *IG* II² 4962) should not be interpreted as calling into
           question either his healing capacity or his divine status. It may be seen as
           recognition of the fact that healing is a co-operative enterprise which
           necessarily relies upon the services of a large number of medical personnel.

121   **Sacred snake.** For the importance of snakes in the worship of Asklepios,
           see Walton (1894, 13-16), Küster (1913, 133-7), Schouten (1967, 35-40) and
           Kearns (*AH*, 16). In the Roman period a reincarnation of Asklepios called
           Glykon is found in the form of a snake with human head and snake body. Cf.
           Thompson (*Agora*³, 268f.), and *Miniature Sculpture from the Athenian Agora*
           (Princeton 1954), fig. 79. (I am grateful to Homer Thompson for this
           information.)

123   **Eleusinian connection.** For discussion of the Epidauria and its connection
           with the Eleusinian Mysteries, see Girard (1881, 40-9). It is possible that a
           marble plaque found at Eleusis which was decorated with a pair of eyes and a
           nose was dedicated by a grateful patient who had recovered from an eye
           complaint. If so, it provides evidence for the belief in Demeter's mystical
           healing powers, on which see O. Rubensohn ('Demeter als Heilgottheit',
           MDAI(A) 20 [1895] 360-7). For doubts as to this interpretation, however, see
           van Straten (1981, 121f.). For Asklepios' power to revive the dead, cf. Aes.
           Agam. 1022-4, Eur. *Alk.* 3f., 122-9 and Virg. *Aen.* 7.765-73. In 1898 a full-size
           headless statue of Asklepios of fourth-century date was discovered about 1 km
           north of a Roman house which is believed to have been reserved for a member
           of the Eleusinian priesthood (Eleusis Museum no. 5100), suggesting that an
           Asklepieion probably existed nearby (Travlos *BTAA*, 96 with pl. 184). A
           mid-fourth-century relief from the Asty Asklepieion shows Asklepios in the
           company of Demeter and Kore (*IG* II² 4359; cf. Aleshire 1989, 94f.). For
           further correspondences between the two cults, see Edelstein and Edelstein
           (1945, 127-9), Latte (1931, 118f.), O. Kern, *Die Religion der Griechen* II (Berlin
           1926-38), 315, Farnell (1921, 244), and U. von Wilamowitz-Moellendorff, *Der
           Glaube der Hellenen* II (Berlin 1932), 474.

125   **Sophokles Dexion.** On *oikos*, *oikia* as technical terms to denote the
           residence of a god, see A. Henrichs ('Despoina Kybele' in *HSCP* 80 [1976] 278
           with n. 70). Beschi (1967-8, 422-7) claims to be able to identify a possible
           representation of Sophokles Dexion on the Telemachos Monument. There is a
           vast bibliography on the hero (cf. *ibid.*, 424 n. 4). See especially O. Walter,
           Geras Keramopoullou (Athens 1953), 469-79. Lefkowitz (1981, 84), who has
           serious doubts about the veracity of the anecdote, points out that although the
           name Dexion is attested in inscriptions dating to the second and third
           centuries AD, adults did not normally take on new names when they became
           heroised, but this objection is hardly overwhelming. Aleshire (1989, 11), who
           attempts to trace the origin of the story of the poet's involvement with
           Asklepios to the period immediately following his death, suggests that it was

'probably in reaction to this popular belief that Telemachos erected his monument with its emphasis on *prôtos* (i.e. first)'. But Telemachos would surely have needed no such provocation in order to celebrate his achievement. His own *philotimia* would have been enough. Sophokles' paean to Asklepios is preserved on a monument of the second century AD which was found in the neighbourhood of the Asty Asklepieion (Oliver 1936, 112-14).

125   **Amyneion.** See Körte (1893, 231-56; 1896, 287-332), Travlos (*PDA*, 76-8, with figs. 97-8), Mitropoulou (1975, 51) and Kearns (*AH*, 147). The trapezoidal sanctuary, which contained nothing but an altar table, was re-cleared in 1965 by J.W. Graham. Although the decrees all date to the fourth century, the sanctuary is believed to be sixth-century in origin. For dedications, see van Straten (1981, 113f.). Other inscriptions from the Amyneion referring to Amynos and/or Asklepios include *IG* II² 4365, 4385, 4422, 4424, 4435 and 4457.

126   **Dispute with the Kerykes.** Burford (1969, 51) claims that the action of the Kerykes indicates that they 'resented Asklepios' intrusion'. This seems to me improbable. The dispute was surely technical and legal, rather than ideological and personal. For the Pelargikon (literally 'Stork Building'), known also as the Pelasgikon ('Building of the Pelasgians', apparently in reference to the early inhabitants of Attica), see Wycherley (*Stones*, 7f.). J.A. Bundgaard, *Parthenon and the Mycenaean City on the Heights* (Copenhagen 1976), 147f., defines it as 'the triangle at the foot of the rock between the Klepsydra, the northwest gate and the Eleusinion'. The date of the original curse upon its occupation is not known.

    Asklepieion in the Asty. See Girard (1881, 3-21), Travlos (*PDA*, 127f., with copious bibliography) and Aleshire (1989, 7-36). For dedications made in the sanctuary, see Girard (1887, 156-69; 1878, 65-94) and van Straten (1981, 105-13). The majority of these are thought to be dated to around the middle of the fourth century. For *c.* 420 as the date of the Ionic stoa, see Martin (1944-5, 340-74). Tomlinson (1969, 116) tentatively dates the building to between 400 and 330, rejecting a date shortly after the Peloponnesian War 'on economic and historical grounds'. We should, however, give due weight to the extraordinarily rapid pace of building activity in the sanctuary, for which the Telemachos Monument provides impressive evidence.

127   **Water.** For the necessity of building Asklepieia near a water supply, see Paus. 1.21.4-5, Pln. *HN* 2.105.225 and Xen. *Mem.* 3.13.3. For discussion of the uses of water in religious ritual, see Cole (1988, 163), R. Ginouvès, *Balaneutike* (Paris 1962), 349-61 and Holtzmann (1984, 865). At the Corinth Asklepieion water appears to have been used for preliminary purification, immersion before incubation and in the treatment of certain illnesses.

128   **From private cult to state cult.** For the suggestion that Telemachos may have belonged to an important Epidaurian family, see K. Latte ('*IG* IV² 1 ed. Hiller de Gaertringen', p. 118 in *Gnomon* 7 [1931]). For Euthydemos, see Schlaifer (1940, 243f.). For Demon and his gift, see Schlaifer (1940, 241-3; 1943, 39-43) who cites other houses and gardens which were donated as sources of revenue for cults. Schlaifer believes that the Athenian cult of Asklepios was public from the start, but he fails to explain the retention of its priesthood in one family. For the persistence of family ties with the Asklepieion over generations, see *SEG* XXXII.115.

131   **Purification of Delos, etc.** Gomme (*HCT* II, 414) plausibly suggests that a further motive behind these initiatives was 'to start another international

festival, the other four being, as it happened, in Peloponnesian hands'.

132   **Athena Hygieia.** Dedications indicate that the cult of this goddess had been established on the Acropolis by the early-fifth century at the latest. See Judeich (*Topog.*², 242f.), Travlos (*PDA*, 124 and 126), Wycherley (*Stones*, 132f.) and Aleshire (1989, 12). The earliest inscription alluding to the goddess is *IG* I² 516.4, which is restored by Aleshire (n. 1) as '[*Athenai*]*an Hygieian*'. Athena Hygieia is said to have appeared in a dream to Perikles following an accident sustained by one of his key workmen (Plu. *Per.* 13.8; Pln. *HN* 22.20.44). To my knowledge no votive offerings in the form of parts of the human body have been found in connection with Athena Hygieia as they have been with other healing cults. The goddess may have stood in the same preventive relationship to health and sickness as Herakles Alexikakos (Protector against illness) and Apollo Prostaterios (Protector). See further Kearns (*AH*, 15) and Schouten (1967, 57-9).

133   *Hêrôs iatros*, etc. The site of the Asty *hêrôon* which belonged to the *hêrôs iatros* has not been discovered, though it was probably located northeast of the Agora along modern Athenas Street where two public decrees dating to the third or second century BC have come to light (*IG* II² 839, 840). Cf. also Dem. 18.129 and 19.249. For discussion of the cult, see Kutsch (1913, 48-52), Kerenyi (1960, 72-4), Wycherley (*Agora III*, no. 347; *Stones*, 193f.) and Kearns (*AH*, 171). For dedications, see van Straten (1981, 114-16). For the Marathon cult, see Kearns (*AH*, 171). For the Eleusis cult, see *IG* I³ 393 and 395. For Aristomachos and Amphiaraos at Rhamnous, see B. Petrakos (*PAAH* 1981 [1983] 127 no. 4) with *IG* II² 4452 and 4436. Votive offerings depicting parts of the human body have been found in the sanctuaries of Aphrodite on the north slope of the Acropolis and of Artemis Kalliste outside the Dipylon Gate to the northwest of the city, as well as in those of Asklepios in the Asty and the Piraeus, and in that of the *hêrôs iatros*. Votive offerings found in shrines of Roman date are reported from the sanctuaries of Artemis Kolainis, Herakles Pankrates and Palaimon on the Ilissos, and Zeus Hypsistos on the Pnyx. See van Straten (1981, 105-22) for an exhaustive list. On the comparative unimportance of healing heroes in Greek myth, see A. Brelich, *Gli eroi Greci: un problema storico-religioso* (Rome 1958) 113-18. Asklepios' failure to eclipse other healing cults in Attica is indicated by the following oracle from Delphi which is quoted in Dem. 21.52 (dated 348 BC), 'Concerning your health, sacrifice and pray to Zeus Hypatos, Herakles and Apollo Prostaterios (Protector).'

134   **Asklepios in the Christian era.** Marinos (*Life of Proklos* 12) indicates that the Asty Asklepieion was still functioning in the fifth century AD. See Aleshire (1989, 19).

The sick. Aleshire's (1989, 52-71) prosopographic analysis of all persons known to have been connected with the Asty Asklepieion reaches the unsurprising conclusion that 'the dedicants are not restricted to a few social or economic classes or to a small group of families' (p.70). Of the fourth-century dedications made in the sanctuary, 51 are by men and only 5 by women. Kearns' suggestion (*AH*, 20) that women may have been reluctant to use the new shrine because of 'greater conservatism' is not wholly convincing. Perhaps women lacked the financial resources to make costly dedications.

Complementarity between Asklepios and medical science. See Herzog (1931, *passim*) for a compendium of the cures performed at Epidauros, together with a useful commentary on the medical practices employed. For the details of temple healing, see Edelstein and Edelstein (1945, 139-213) and, more briefly, Burkert (*GR*, 267f.). For the incubation ritual, see L. Deubner, *De Incubatione* (Giessen 1899). For an entertaining parody of the ritual, see Ar. *Plout*. 653-747.

134   **Iconography of Asklepios.** See Holzmann (1984, especially 865f.) for discussion of the 'extraordinary typological poverty of images of Asklepios.' Further discussion is provided by Schouten (1967, 23-33) who comments, 'Both in posture and apparel, the Asklepios figures in Greek eyes were the ideal representation of the practising physician.'

7. Sokrates and the New *Daimonia*

136   **Anytos, Meletos and Lykon.** See Brickhouse and Smith (1989, 27f.) for a summary of all that is known about the trio. The identity of the two prosecutors who go under the name of Meletos continues to be debated (cf. Blumenthal 1973, 169-78, supplemented by up-to-date bibliography in Brickhouse and Smith, 27 n. 94). Even if they are one and the same, there are insufficient grounds for dubbing him 'a *bona fide* religious fanatic', as Brickhouse and Smith (p. 28) do. Plato (*Apol*. 23e) alleges that Meletos was angered 'on account of the poets', Anytos 'on account of the skilled workers', and Lykon 'on account of the public speakers'. For their motives, see Ostwald (1986, 472, 495 and 348).

137   **The affidavit.** On the authenticity of the text of the affidavit as quoted by Favorinus, see Derenne (1930, 139-42). No other historical example of the charge of 'corrupting the young' is known, although Isokrates (*Antidosis* 30) accuses his prosecutors of insinuating that he is guilty of this crime.

138   **The origins of the Athenian law against *asebeia*.** For the Kylonian affair and the Alkmaionid curse, see Rhodes (*CAAP*, 79-84). E. Lévy, 'Notes sur la chronologie athénienne au VIᵉ siècle. (I) Cylon', *Historia* 27 (1978) 513-21, dates it to 597/6 or 596/5. The principal accounts of the incident are those of Hdt. 5.71, Thuk. 1.126.3-12, Plu. *Solon* 12.1-3 and schol. on Ar. *Knights* 445. Other instances of priests being ordered to curse are in Li. 31.46.6 and Pol. 16.31.7. For the charge against Aes., see Ostwald (1986, 529f.) and H.G. Gottschalk, *Heraclides of Pontus* (Oxford 1980), 135f. Rudhardt (1960, *passim*) states (p. 102), 'Among the Greeks the concept (viz. of impiety) appears to be indefinitely extendable – or rather let us say more modestly that we do not know how to define it.' For a definition, see Mikalson (*APR* 1983, 91-105).

139   **Diopeithes' decree.** For Diopeithes' career, see Derenne (1930, 19-21) and Connor (1963, 115-17). He is also mentioned in schol. on Ar. *Knights* 1085, *Wasps* 380, Phrynichos fr. 9, Telekleides fr. 6 and Ameipsias fr. 10. Connor (p. 116) somewhat tendentiously characterises the seer as 'a political opportunist ... capitalising on Athenian superstition'. Regarding the historicity of Diopeithes' decree, see Dover (1975, 39f.) who concludes (p. 40), 'I am inclined to think that what Plutarch tells us about it was what the creative malice of Demetrios and the Peripatetics wished posterity to believe'. Dover (p. 24f.) provides a full list of all the testimonia relating to the prosecution of intellectuals during Sokrates' lifetime. He concludes that only the outlawry of Diagoras and condemnation of Sokrates are satisfactorily attested. As to whether Sokrates was indicted under Diopeithes' decree, see the contrary claims of Rudhardt (1960, 92), Finley (1973, 91), Derenne (1930, 223f.) and Dover (1975, 40). For arguments in favour of the witch-hunt theory, see Dodds

(1951, 189) and Momigliano (1973, 252-63; 1973a, 565f.). It has been unconvincingly debunked, though not without verve and panache, by Stone (1989, 231-47).

141   Plato's *Apology*. On the usefulness of this document as a faithful transcript of what Sokrates actually said, see Brickhouse and Smith (1989, 2-10). Their conclusion (p. 9) that 'more probably than not the Platonic version captures at least the tone and substance of what Sokrates actually said in the courtroom' does not as an article of cautious faith justify the weight which they subsequently attach to it in their discussion of the trial.

     Xenophon's *Apology*. For the lateness of this work and its unreliability as a historical account of the trial, see U. von Wilamowitz-Moellendorff ('Die Xenophontische Apologie', *Hermes* 32 [1897] 99ff.).

142   'Not acknowledging the gods whom the state acknowledges'. For the failure of Plato's Sokrates to respond directly to this charge, see Derenne (1930, 168f.). U. von Wilamowitz-Moellendorff, *Platon*[2] II (Berlin 1920), 51, justifiably taxes the philosopher with resorting to sophistry in his attempt to establish his innocence. Yunis (1988, 63 n. 10) draws an instructive parallel between the charge against Sokrates and a passage in Dein. 1.94 where Dem.'s proposal to deify Alexander is similarly presented as an offence against state religion (cf. especially the phrase *'mêdena nomizein allon theon ê tous paradedomenous'*). Earlier scholars who took the charge to be one of atheism include Tate (1936, 3-5; 1937, 3-6), who provides a useful concordance of *'nomizein theous' (vel sim.)* in Greek literature.

144   Atheists in late-fifth-century Athens. See Fahr (1969, *passim*), Henrichs (1976, 15-21) and Meijer (1981, 216-20). The most famous atheist of the period was Diagoras of Melos. Cf. Fahr (1969, 236) and F. Jacoby, *Diagoras* (Berlin 1960). For atheism in the mid-fourth century, see Pl. *Laws* 888ff.

145   Nikomachos' revision of Athenian religious law. See Clinton (1982, 27-37, especially 34f.), Ostwald (1986, 407f., 416f.) and Robertson (1990, 43-75). The supposition that Nikomachos' second term, lasting from late 403 (or early 402) to 400/399, was concerned solely with sacrificial law is based on inferences from Lys. 30.18-23, 29. It is important to emphasise that the *anagrapheis* did not themselves 'revise' or even 'publish' any laws as such. They merely collected them with the object of producing a comprehensive record. Robertson (p. 55) defines their task as 'to assemble all Athenian enactments of abiding interest – all the secular laws, as we think of them; all the ritual observances which had a claim on public funds'.

     'Introducing new daimonic beings'. For Sokrates' *daimonion*, see Guthrie (1971, 82-5). A rare dissenter from the general belief that the charge was levelled against Sokrates' 'sign' is Taylor (1932, 114f.). Cf. also Alkiphron, *Letters to Farmers* 2.8.1-2, where the writer humorously complains that his wife has become a city slicker and is 'introducing to us new gods in addition to the many we have already. Where on the farm am I to set up a shrine to the Kolides and Genetyllides? I know by report the names of some other *daimones*, but because of their number most have slipped my memory.'

8. The World of the Athenian *Aition*

154   *Homeric hymn to Demeter*. For detailed discussion of specific elements of Eleusinian ritual whose origins are accounted for in the hymn, see Richardson (1974, 211-17 and 246f.). For the importance of hymns in Greek cult, see J.

Bremmer ('Greek hymns', pp. 193-215 in Versnel *FHW*). As Clay (1989, 203) points out, discussion of the relation of the hymn to Eleusinian cult has 'indirectly impeded the study of the poem'. On the matter of authorship, Clinton (1986, 44) even goes so far as to assert that 'some aspects of the poem ... suggest that the poet's knowledge of Eleusinian matters was hardly intimate at all'. However, none of this should be allowed to obscure the fact (noted by Clay herself on p. 257) that the author unquestionably sees himself in the business of providing an authoritative explanation for ritual institutions, as we see explicitly from those passages which contain the words *'ek tou'*, *'epeita'*, viz. 'from this moment on', 'henceforth', in allusion to various examples of religious innovation (e.g. at ll. 205, 237f., 440; cf. *h. Hermes* 125f.; Hes. *Theog.* 556).

156   **Euripides' *Erechtheus*.** See further Parker (1987, 202-4). Lacore (1983, 215-34) points out that the fusion between Erechtheus and Poseidon which comes about at the end of the *Erechtheus* had no existence in contemporary cult practice and appears not to have taken root until Roman times. He dismisses it as 'a Euripidean invention' intended 'to restore serenity at the end of a patriotic drama'.

157   **Aeschylus' *Eumenides*.** Mikalson (1987) is of the opinion that the transformation of the Erinyes into Semnai, which is not previously attested in Greek literature, 'is surely Aeschylus' own creation.'

Atthidographers. Jacoby's work (1948, especially pp. 2-8, 51-70) is intended in part as a rebuttal to the notion proposed by Wilamowitz, *Aristoteles und Athen* I (Berlin 1893), 280-88, that the Atthidographers as a whole were *exêgêtai* who drew on chronicles in their keeping. For their religious activities, see further Jacoby (pp. 51-7). Earlier studies of the genre include those of von Fritz (1940) and L. Pearson ('The local historians of Attica', *TAPA* 1940 and 1942).

158   **Pausanias.** See Habicht (1985, 144-6) and Veyne (1988, especially ch. 8). Paus.' customary way of referring to his informants is either obliquely (e.g. 'a man of Mysia said' or 'an Egyptian informed me'), or by terms such as *hoi ta archaia mnêmoneuontes* (i.e. antiquarians) and *exêgêtai*. Only once (5.20.4) does he refer to a guide by name. We do not know, therefore, whether the information which his informants supplied had the authorisation, so to speak, of temple officials. Information which he ascribes to an *'exêgêtês'* clearly stands the greatest likelihood of representing the 'official' line, though it would be tendentious to assume that Paus. is invariably using this title in a technical sense (cf. *LSJ*[9] *s.v. exêgêtês* II.2).

For his religious beliefs, see Habicht (1985, 154-9). Paus. describes a fundamental change in his attitude at 8.8.3, where he seeks to resolve doubts about the historicity of *aitia* by suggesting that they be interpreted allegorically: 'When I began to write my book I regarded the Greek legends as full of foolishness, but when I reached Arkadia I came to have the following opinion about them. I reckoned that in antiquity the Greeks who were considered wise spoke in riddles rather than straightforwardly ... .'

159   **Dionysos.** The preservation of Pegasos' name in the account is interesting, given the anonymity of most instigators of new cults. Nothing is known about him other than that he was from Eleutherai and that his image was displayed in the temple of Dionysos Melpomenos (Paus. 1.2.5). It is possible that he was in receipt of heroic honours (cf. Kearns, *AH* 194). Another version of Dionysos' entry is related in schol. on Luk. *Dialogue of the Gods* 5. For Dionysos' previous

visit to Attica 'in the days of Ikarios' (Paus. 1.2.5) and his association with the deme of Ikarion where he was closely allied to Apollo, see Detienne (1989, 28-30). For the god's name (without context) on Linear B tablets from Pylos, see Burkert (*GR*, 45 and 162). For Dionysos as a perennial *xenos* (i.e. Greek but invariably perceived as coming from elsewhere), see Detienne (1989, 9-14). Dionysos is so described in Eur. *Ba.* at ll. 233, 247, 353, 441, 453, 642, 1059, 1077. For the god as war-maker, cf. also Paus. 2.23.7.

163   **The Acropolis.** For the contest for Attica and in particular the implications behind Poseidon's defeat, see Parker (1987, 198-200 with n. 54) who sees 'an implicit connection between the terrifying powers of the god (viz. as sender of storms and earthquakes), and his anger in defeat'. The myth is rarely depicted in Greek art outside Attica (cf. Robertson *HGA* I, 299). For the site of Athena's tree, see J.A. Bundgaard, *Parthenon and the Mycenaean City on the Heights* (Copenhagen 1976), ch. 11. See also R.J. Hopper, *The Acropolis* (London, etc. 1971), ch. 2, for a general account of the myths connected with the Acropolis.

164   **Eleusis.** *H. Dem.* makes no mention of Persephone's descent to Hades, possibly because of a lacuna in the text (cf. Richardson 1974, 148 and 220f.). For the Eleusinian Plutoneion as the location of the descent, see *Orphic hymn* 18.12-15. The cave in question lies under the lee of the Eleusinian Acropolis on the west side of the Sacred Way beside the Propylaia. For Kallichoron and its probable identification with the well called Parthenion (*h. Dem.* 99), see Richardson (1974, 326-8). For its location just outside the Kimonian wall at the north gate, see Travlos (*BTAA*, 91f. and 94 with pls. 154-6).

165   **Kekrops.** For his role as culture-hero, see Kearns (*HA*, 175f.); U. Kron, *Die zehn attischen Phylenheroen* (Berlin 1976), 84-103; and Parker (1986, 193, 197f.). As noted earlier, the evidence for it does not demonstrably pre-date the fourth century. For his cult on the Acropolis, cf. Eur. *Ion* 1400, *IG* I³ 474.59-63, and *IG* II² 1156.

166   **Artemis Mounychia.** For the *aition*, cf. also Eust. on Hom. *Il.* 2.732, p. 331.26; Hsch. *s.v. Embaros eimi*; Becker, *Anecdota* I, p. 444; *Paroem. gr.* I, p. 402. See further Garland (*Piraeus*, 208 with bibliography).

    Arrhephoria. The ritual has generated considerable debate. See Burkert (1966, 1-25), Deubner (*AF*, 9-17), U. Kron (*LIMC* I.1 *s.v.* 'Aglauros, Herse, Pandrosos, pp. 283-98), Mikalson (1976, 141-53), Robertson (1985, 257f.) and Simon (*FA*, 39-46). As Parker (1986, 196) points out, the story is based upon two popular folktale motifs, viz. the 'disobeyed command' and the 'good and bad sisters'. Robertson (258-61) claims that the myth of Erichthonios' birth and subsequent nurturing by Athena on the Acropolis is the *aition* for the Panathenaia.

168   **Oedipus.** For the gods and heroes of Kolonos and its environs, see S. *OK* 54-61, 668-719 and Paus. 1.30.4. They include Poseidon Hippios (Horse god), Prometheus, the Semnai, Kolonos Hippotes (Horseman), the Muses, Aphrodite Chrysanios (Of the golden rein), Athena Hippia, Peirithous, Theseus and Adrastos. As Edmunds (1981, 223 and n.8) notes, the language of Oedipus' settlement at Colonos has a definite 'cultic ring', cf. *exoikêsimos* 27, *oikêtos* 28, 39, *oikêsanta* 92, *katoikoiês* 362. On the use of *oikos* to denote a private sanctuary, see A. Henrichs, *HSCP* 80 (1976) 278 and n. 70. There were two principal traditions concerning Oedipus' death – one that he died in Thebes, and another that he was driven out of Thebes and died elsewhere (cf. Edmunds 1981, 221-38). For the Attic cult and tomb, see Kearns (*AH*, 50-2, 189, and Appendix 2). It is ultimately unclear whether Sophokles actually invented the

link between Oedipus and Kolonos. The only evidence for it in a context older than *OK* is Eur. *Phoin.* 1706f., which some scholars (e.g. E. Fränkel, *Zu den Phoenissen des Euripides* [Munich 1963], 98-100) suspect of being an interpolation. Suppliancy is a common theme in Greek tragedy, e.g. Aes. *Supp.*, Eur. *Androm.*, *Helen*, *HF* and *Supp.* On its adaptation in Soph.'s play, see Burian (1974, 408-29). On the use of the first-person plural, see Reinhardt (1979, 223) who talks eloquently of 'its terrifying yet tender kind of intimacy' which 'has no parallel in the entire range of divine voices of all ages and all religions which those who have been favoured by the gods have heard descending from heaven at the moment of their death.'

Bibliography

Reference works

ARV = Beazley, J.D. (1963) *Attic Red-Figure Vase-Painters*. 2nd ed. Oxford, Clarendon.

Bekker = Bekker, E. (1814-21) *Anecdota graeca*. Berlin.

Boersma, *ABP* = Boersma, J.S. (1970) *Athenian Building Policy from 561/0 to 405/4 BC*. Groningen.

Burkert, *GR* = Burkert, W. (1985) *Greek Religion: Archaic and Classical*, tr. J. Raffan. Oxford.

CAF = Kock, Th. (1880-8) *Comicorum Atticorum Fragmenta*. 3 vols. Leipzig.

CAH III.3² = Boardman, J., and Hammond, N.G.L. (eds.) (1982) *The Cambridge Ancient History*. Vol. III, Part 3. 2nd. ed. Cambridge, etc.

CAH IV² = Boardman, J., Hammond, N.G.L., Lewis, D.M., and Ostwald, M. (eds.) (1988) *The Cambridge Ancient History*. Vol. IV. 2nd ed. Cambridge, etc.

Camp, *Agora* = Camp, J.M. (1986) *The Athenian Agora: Excavations in the Heart of Classical Athens*. London.

Clairmont, *PN* = Clairmont, C.W. (1983) *Patrios Nomos: Public Burial in Athens during the Fifth and Fourth Centuries BC*. (= *BAR International Series* no. 161 [i]). 2 parts. Oxford.

Davies, *APF* = Davies, J.K. (1971) *Athenian Propertied Families*. Oxford, Clarendon.

Deubner, *AF* = Deubner, L. (1932) *Attische Feste*. Berlin.

DHI = Weiner, P. (ed.) (1973) *Dictionary of the History of Ideas*. 6 vols. New York.

FGrH = Jacoby, F. (ed.) (1923-58) *Die Fragmente der griechischen Historiker*. Leiden.

Garland, *Piraeus* = Garland, R.S.J. (1987) *The Piraeus: from the Fifth to the First Century BC*. London and Ithaca.

Garland, *RAACA* = Garland, R.S.J. (1984) 'Religious authority in Archaic and Classical Athens', pp. 75-123 in *ABSA* 79.

Gomme, *HCT* = Gomme, A.W. (1959-81) *A Historical Commentary on Thucydides*. 5 vols. Oxford, Clarendon.

IEG = West, M.L. (ed.) (1972) *Iambi et Elegi Graeci ante Alexandrum cantati*. 2 vols. Oxford, Clarendon.

IG = *Inscriptiones Graecae*.

Judeich, *Topog.²* = Judeich, W. (1931) *Topographie von Athen*. 2nd ed. Munich.

Kearns, *HA* = Kearns, E. (1989) 'The heroes of Attica'. *BICS* Supplement vol. 57.

Kirchner, *PA* = Kirchner, J. (1901-3) *Prosopographia Attica*. 2 vols. Berlin.

LGS = de Prott, J., and Ziehen, L. (eds.) (1896) *Leges Graecorum Sacrae*. Leipzig.

LIMC = Balty, J.C., Boardman, J., Bruneau, Ph., etc. (1981-) *Lexicon Iconographicum Mythologicae Classicae*. Zurich and Munich.

Loraux, *Invention* = Loraux, N. (1986) *The Invention of Athens*, tr. A. Sheridan. Harvard, Mass.

LSAG = Jeffery, L.H. (1961) *The Local Scripts of Archaic Greece*. Oxford.

LSG = Sokolowski, F. (ed.) (1969) *Lois sacrées des cités grecques*. Paris.

LSGS = Sokolowski, F. (ed.). (1962). *Lois sacrées des cités grecques. Supplement.* Paris.

Mattusch, *GBS* = Mattusch, C.C. (1988) *Greek Bronze Statuary: from the Beginnings through to the Fifth Century BC*. Ithaca and London.

Meiggs, *AE* = Meiggs, R. (1972) *The Athenian Empire*. Oxford, Clarendon.

Mikalson, *APR* = Mikalson, J.D. (1983) *Athenian Popular Religion*. Chapel Hill and London.

Mikalson, *SCCAY* = Mikalson, J.D. (1975) *The Sacred and Civil Calendar of the Athenian Year*. Princeton, N.J.

ML = Meiggs, R., and Lewis, D. (eds.) (1969) *A Selection of Greek Historical Inscriptions to the End of the Fifth Century BC*. Oxford, Clarendon.

N^2 = Nauck, A. (ed.) *Tragicorum Graecorum Fragmenta*. 2nd ed. revised by B. Snell. 2 vols. Hildesheim.

Nilsson, *GGR* I^3 = Nilsson, M.P. (1967) *Geschichte der griechischen Religion*. Vol. I. 3rd edition. Munich.

Nilsson, *GGR* II^2 = Nilsson, M.P. (1961) *Geschichte der griechischen Religion*. Vol. 2. 2nd edition. Munich.

OCT = *Oxford Classical Text*.

Osborne, *Demos* = Osborne, R. (1985) *Demos: the Discovery of Classical Attika*. Cambridge.

Parke, *FA* = Parke, H.W. (1977) *Festivals of the Athenians*. London and Ithaca.

PMG = Page, D.L. (ed.) (1962) *Poetae Melici Graeci*. Oxford, Clarendon.

Pritchett, *GSW* = Pritchett, W.K. (1979-85) *The Greek State at War*. 4 parts. Berkeley, etc.

Raubitschek, *DAA* = Raubitschek, A.E. (1949) *Dedications from the Athenian Acropolis*. Cambridge, Mass.

RE = Wissowa, G. (ed.) (1893-) *Paulys Real-Encyclopädie*. Stuttgart.

Rhodes, *CAAP* = Rhodes, P.J. (1981) *A Commentary on the Aristotelian Athenaion Politeia*. Oxford, Clarendon.

Robertson, *HGA* = Robertson, M. (1975) *A History of Greek Art*. 2 vols. Cambridge.

SEG = *Supplementum Epigraphicum Graecum* (1923-). Amsterdam.

Simon, *FA* = Simon, E. (1983) *Festivals of Attica*. Wisconsin.

Solders, *AKEA* = Solders, S. (1931) *Die ausserstädtischen Kulte und die Einigung Attikas*. Lund.

Stewart, *GS* = Stewart, A. (1990) *Greek Sculpture: an Exploration*. 2 vols. New Haven and London.

T = Teubner edition.

Thompson, *Agora*[3] = Thompson, H.A. (1976) *The Athenian Agora*. 3rd. ed. Athens.

Thompson and Wycherley, *Agora XIV* = Thompson, H.A., and Wycherley, R.E. (1972) *The Athenian Agora, vol. XIV: the Agora of Athens*. Princeton, N.J.

Toepffer, *AG* = Toepffer, J. (1889) *Attische Genealogie*. Berlin. (Reprinted New York 1973).

Traill, *POA* = Traill, J.S. (1975) *The Political Organisation of Attica* (= *Hesperia Supplement* vol. 14). Princeton, N.J.

Travlos, *BTAA* = Travlos, J. (1988) *Bildlexicon zur Topographie der antiken Attika*. Tübingen.

Travlos, *PDA* = Travlos, J. (1971) *A Pictorial Dictionary of Athens*. London.

Versnel, *FHW* = Versnel, H.S. (ed.) (1981) *Faith, Hope and Worship: Aspects of Religious Mentality in the Ancient World*. Leiden.

Wycherley, *Agora III* = Wycherley, R.E. (1957) *The Athenian Agora, vol. 3: Literary and Epigraphical Testimonia*. Princeton, N.J.
Wycherley, *Stones* = Wycherley, R.E. (1978) *The Stones of Athens*. Princeton, N.J.
Zaidman and Pantel, *RG* = Zaidman, L.B., and Pantel, S.P. (1989) *La religion grecque*. Paris.

Preface

Braudel, F. (1980) *On History*, tr. S. Matthews. Chicago.
Pleket, H.W. (1981) 'Religious history as the history of mentality', pp. 152-92 in Versnel (*FHW*).

Introduction: Others and the Other

Andrewes, A. (1961) 'Philochoros on phratries', pp. 1-15 in *JHS* 81.
Beard, M. and Crawford, M. (1985) *Rome in the Late Republic*. London.
Bronowski, J. (1956) *Science and Human Values*. Harmondsworth.
Brunel, J. (1953) 'À propos du transfert des cultes: un sens méconnu du mot *aphidruma*', pp. 21-32 in *Rev. Phil.* 27.
Burkert, W. (1987) *Ancient Mystery Cults*. Cambridge, Mass.
Clemen, C. (1928) 'Magoi', cols. 509-13 in *RE* 14.
Connor, W.R. (1987) 'Tribes, festivals and processions; civic ceremonial and political manipulation in archaic Greece', pp. 40-50 in *JHS* 107.
Daux, G. (1963) 'La grande démarchie: un nouveau calendrier sacrificiel d'Attique (Erchia)', pp. 603-34 in *BCH* 87.
Davies, J.K. (1988) 'Religion and the state', pp. 368-88 in *CAH IV*^{2}.
Dirlmeier, F. (1935) 'THEOPHILIA-PHILOTHEIA', pp. 57-77, 166-93 in *Philologus* 90 (= *Ausgewählte Schriften* [Heidelberg 1970] 85-109).
Ehnmark, E. (1939) 'Anthropomorphism and miracle' (= *Uppsala Universitets Arsskrift* 12).
Festugière, A.-J. (1954) *Personal Religion among the Greeks*. Berkeley, California.
Flower, M.A. (1985) '*IG* II 2344 and the size of phratries in Classical Athens', pp. 232-35 in *CQ* n.s. 35.
Fox, R.L. (1987) *Pagans and Christians*. New York.
François, G. (1957) *Le polythéisme et l'emploi au singular des mots THEOS, DAIMON*. Paris.
Griffin, J. (1980) *Homer on Life and Death*. Oxford, Clarendon.
Guarducci, M. (1974) 'L'offerta di Xenokrateia nel santuario di Cefiso al Falero', pp. 57-66 in Bradeen, D.W., and McGregor, M.F. (eds.), *PHOROS: Tribute to Benjamin Dean Meritt*. New York.
Hedrick, C.W. (1984) *The Attic Phratry*. Diss. Univ. of Pennsylvania.
Humphreys, S.C. (1975) ' "Transcendence" and intellectual roles: the ancient Greek case', pp. 91-118 in *Daedalus* Spring 1975.
Linders, T. (1972) *Studies in the Treasure Records of Artemis Brauronia found in Athens*. Stockholm.
Mikalson, J. (1977) 'Religion in the Attic demes', pp. 424-35 in *AJP* 98.
Momigliano, A. (1987) *On Pagans, Jews and Christians*. Connecticut.
Mussies, G. (1988) 'Identification and self-identification of gods in Classical and Hellenistic times', pp. 1-18 in van den Broek, R., Baarda, T., and Mansfeld, J. (eds.), *Knowledge of God in the Graeco-Roman World*. Leiden, etc.

Nock, A.D. (1933) *Conversion*. Oxford. Reprinted 1952.

Parker, R. (1989) 'Spartan religion', pp. 142-72 in Powell, A. (ed.) *Classical Sparta: Techniques behind her Success*. London.

Pfister, F. (1922) 'Epiphanie', cols. 277-323 in *RE* supp. 4.

Ranulf, S. (1934) *The Jealousy of the Gods and Criminal Law at Athens*. 2 vols. London and Copenhagen.

Richardson, R.B. (1895) 'A sacrificial calendar from the Epakria', pp. 209-26 in *AJA* 10.

Richardson, N.J. (1974) *The Homeric Hymn to Demeter*. Oxford, Clarendon.

Roth, P. (1984) 'Teiresias as *mantis* and intellectual in Euripides' *Bacchae*', pp. 59-69 in *TAPA* 114.

Slater, W.J. (1988) 'The epiphany of Demosthenes', pp. 126-30 in *Phoenix* 42.

van Straten, F.T. (1974) 'Did the Greeks kneel before their gods?', pp. 159-89 in *BABesch* 49.

Wachsmuth, D. (1975) 'Epiphanie', cols. 1598-1601 in *Der Kleine Pauly* 5. Munich.

Wycherley, R.E. (1968) 'St. Paul at Athens', pp. 619-21 in *JTS* n.s. 19.2.

—— (1970) 'Minor shrines in Ancient Athens', pp. 283-95 in *Phoenix* 24 (1970).

Yunis, H. (1988) *A New Creed: Fundamental Religious Beliefs in the Athenian Polis and Euripidean Drama* (= *Hypomnemata* vol. 91). Göttingen.

1. Ancestral Rites

Abramson, H. (1979) 'A hero shrine for Phrontis at Sounion', pp. 1-19 in *CSCA* 12.

Andrewes, A. (1982) 'The growth of the Athenian state. The tyranny of Pisistratus,' pp. 410-15 in *CAH III.3*.

Bérard, C. (1982) 'Récupérer la mort du prince: heroïsation et formation de la cité', pp. 89-105 in Gnoli, G. and Vernant, J.-P. (eds.) *La mort, les morts dans les sociétés anciennes*. Cambridge.

Beyer, I. (1977) 'Die Datierung der grossen Reliefgiebel des alten Athena-tempels der Akropolis. Mit einem Beitrag von Felix Preisshofen', pp. 44-84 in *AA* 1977.

Binder, J. (1984) 'The west pediment of the Parthenon: Poseidon', pp. 15-22 in *Studies Presented to Sterling Dow on his Eightieth Birthday*. Durham, North Carolina.

Boardman, J. (1972) 'Herakles, Peisistratos and sons', pp. 57-72 in *RA* 1972.

—— (1975) 'Herakles, Peisistratos and Eleusis', pp. 1-12 in *JHS* 95.

—— (1989) 'Herakles, Peisistratos, and the Unconvinced', pp. 158f. in *JHS* 109.

Bradeen, D.W. (1955) 'The trittyes in Cleisthenes' reforms', pp. 22-30 in *TAPA* 86.

Brouskari, M. (1980) 'A Dark Age cemetery in Erechtheion Street, Athens', pp. 13-31 in *ABSA* 75.

Burr, D. (1933) 'A Geometric house and a proto-Attic votive deposit', pp. 542-640 in *Hesperia* 2.

Calligas, P.G. (1988) 'Hero-cult in Early Iron Age Greece', pp. 229-34 in Hägg, R., Marinatos, N. and Nordquist, G.C. (eds.) *Early Greek Cult Practice* (= *Proceedings of the Fifth International Symposium held at the Swedish Institute in Athens, 26-29 June 1986*). Stockholm.

Camp, J.M. (1979) 'A drought in the late eighth century BC', pp. 397-411 in *Hesperia* 48.

Coldstream, J.N. (1976) 'Hero cults in the age of Homer', pp. 8-17 in *JHS* 96.

—— (1977) *Geometric Greece*. London.

Connor, W.R. (1987) 'Tribes, festivals and processions; civic ceremonial and political manipulation in archaic Greece', pp. 40-50 in *JHS* 107.

—— (1989) 'City Dionysia and Athenian democracy', pp. 7-32 in *Classica et Mediaevalia* 40.

Cook, R.M. (1987) 'Pots and Pisistratan propaganda', pp. 167-9 in *JHS* 107.

Davies, J.K. (1988) 'Religion and the state', pp. 368-88 in *CAH IV*[2].

Davison, J.A. (1958) 'Notes on the Panathenaea', pp. 23-42 in *JHS* 78.

—— (1962) 'Addenda to "Notes on the Panathenaea" ', p. 141f. in *JHS* 82.

Ehrenburg, V. (1968) *From Solon to Socrates*. London.

Ehrhardt, C.T.H.R. (1990) 'Cleisthenes and Eleutherae', p. 23 in *AHB* 4.2.

Farnell, L.R. (1921) *Greek Hero Cults and Ideas of Immortality*. Oxford, Clarendon.

Feaver, D. (1957) 'The priesthoods of Athens', pp. 123-58 in *YCS* 15.

Ferguson, W.S. (1938) 'The Salaminioi of Heptaphylai and Sounion', pp. 1-74 in *Hesperia* 7.

Gagarin, M. (1986) *Early Greek Law*. Berkeley, etc.

Harrison, J.E. and Verrall, M. de G. (1890) *Mythology and Monuments of Ancient Athens*. London.

Hedrick, C.W. (1984) *The Attic Phratry*. Diss. Univ. of Pennsylvania.

—— (1988) 'The temple and cult of Apollo Patroös in Athens', pp. 185-210 in *AJA* 92.2.

Herington, C.J. (1955) *Athena Polias and Athena Parthenos*. Manchester.

—— (1963) 'Athena in Athenian literature and cult', pp. 61-73 in *G&R* Supplement to vol. 10 (= *Parthenos and Parthenon*). Ed. by G.T.W. Hooker.

Hopper, R.J. (1971) *The Acropolis*. London.

—— (1971a) 'Athena and the early Acropolis', pp. 1-16 in *G&R* Supplement to vol. 10 (*Parthenos and Parthenon*). Ed. by G.T.W. Hooker.

Jacoby, F. (1944) 'GENESIA: a forgotten festival of the dead', pp. 65ff. in *CQ* n.s. 38.

Jeppesen, K. (1979) 'Where was the so-called Erechtheion?', pp. 381-94 in *AJA* 83.

Kearns, E. (1985) 'Religious structures after Cleisthenes', pp. 189-207 in P. Cartledge and F.D. Harvey (eds.), *Crux: Essays presented to G.E.M. de Ste. Croix*. London.

Kolb, F. (1977) 'Die Bau-, Religions- und Kultur-politik der Peisistratiden', pp. 99-138 in *JDAI* 92.

Kron, U. (1976) *Die zehn attischen Phylenheroen* (= *Mitteilungen des Deutschen Archäologischen Instituts*, Athenische Abteilung, Beiheft 5). Berlin.

Lacore, M. (1983) 'Euripide et le culte de Poseidon-Erechthée', pp. 216-34 in *REA* 85.

Langdon, M.K. (1976) 'A sanctuary of Zeus on Mount Hymettos', pp. 87-9, 97f. in *Hesperia* Supplement 16.

Lewis, D.M. (1963) 'Cleisthenes and Attica', pp. 22-40 in *Historia* 12.

—— (1988) 'The tyranny of the Pisistratidae', pp. 287-302 in *CAH IV*[2].

Long, C. (1987) *The Twelve Gods of Greece and Rome*. Leyden, etc.

Loraux, N. (1981) 'Cité grecque. Le mythe dans la cité. La politique athénienne du mythe', pp. 203-9 in Y. Bonnefoy (ed.), *Dictionnaire des mythologies et des religions des sociétés traditionelles et du monde antique*. Paris.

Mattingly, H.B. (1974) 'Athens and Eleusis: some new ideas', pp. 97-101 in Bradeen, D.W. and McGregor, M.F. (eds.), *PHOROS: Tribute to Benjamin Dean Meritt*. New York.

Meliades, J. (1965) 'The Acropolis in Archaic times', pp. 43ff. in *Greek Heritage* (= *American Quarterly of Greek Culture*) 2.6.

Mikalson, J. (1976) 'Erechtheus and the Panathenaia', pp. 141-53 in *AJP* 97.

Mylonas, G.E. (1961) *Eleusis and the Eleusinian Mysteries*. Princeton, N.J. and London.
Nilsson, M.P. (1951) *Cults, Myths, Oracles and Politics*. Lund.
—— (1953) 'Political propaganda in sixth-century Athens,' pp. 743-8 in *Studies Presented to D.M. Robinson*, vol. 2. Saint Louis, Missouri.
Ober, J. (1989) *Mass and Elite in Democratic Athens*. Princeton, N.J.
Ostwald, M. (1986) *From Popular Sovereignty to the Sovereignty of Law: Law, Society and Politics in Fifth-Century Athens*. Berkeley, etc.
—— (1988) 'The reform of the Athenian state by Cleisthenes', pp. 303-46 in *CAH IV²*.
Papademetriou, J. (1955) *'Anaskaphai en Braurôni'*, p. 119 in *PAA* 1955.
—— (1956) *'Anaskaphai en Braurôni'*, p. 76f. in *PAA* 1956.
—— (1957) *'Anaskaphai en Braurôni'*, p. 44f. in *PAA* 1957.
Parker, R. (1987) 'Myths of early Athens', pp. 187-214 in *Interpretations of Greek Mythology*. Ed. by J.N. Bremmer. London.
Parsons, A.W. (1943) 'Klepsydra and the paved court of the Pythion', pp. 191-267 in *Hesperia* 12.
Picard, Ch. (1938) 'La complexe Métrôon-Bouleutérion-Prytanikon, à l'Agora d'Athènes', pp. 97-101 in *RA* 12.
—— (1940) 'L'hérôon de Phrontis au Sounion', pp. 5-28 in *RA* 16.
Pickard-Cambridge, A. (1968) *The Dramatic Festivals of Athens*. 2nd ed. revised by J. Gould and D.M. Lewis. Oxford, Clarendon.
Plommer, W.H. (1960) 'The Archaic Acropolis, some problems', pp. 127-59 in *JHS* 80.
de Polignac, F. (1984) *La naissance de la cité grecque. Cultes, espace et société, 8ᵉ-7ᵉ siècles avant J.C.* Paris.
Richardson, N.J. (1974) *The Homeric Hymn to Demeter*. Oxford, Clarendon.
Robertson, N. (1985) 'The origins of the Panathenaia', pp. 231-95 in *RhM* 128.
Rotroff, S.I. (1978) 'An anonymous hero in the Athenian agora' pp. 196-209 in *Hesperia* 47.
Schrader, H. (1939) *Die archaischen Marmorbildwerken der Akropolis*. Frankfurt/Main.
Shear, T.L., Jr. (1978) 'Tyrants and buildings in Archaic Athens', pp. 1-19 in *Athens Comes of Age: from Solon to Salamis*. Princeton, N.J.
Snodgrass, A. (1971) *The Dark Age of Greece: an Archaeological Survey of the Eleventh to the Eighth Centuries BC*. Edinburgh.
—— (1977) 'Archaeology and the rise of the Greek state' (Inaugural Lecture). Cambridge.
—— (1980) *Archaic Greece: the Age of Experiment*. London, etc.
—— (1982) 'Les origines du culte des héros dans la Grèce' antique', pp. 107-19 in Gnoli, G., and Vernant, J.-P. (eds.) *La mort, les morts dans les sociétés anciennes*. Cambridge.
Stavropoullos, Ph. D. (1956) *'Anaskaphai archaias Akadêmias'*, pp. 45-54 in *PAE* 1956.
—— (1958) *'Anaskaphai archaias Akadêmias'*, pp. 5-13 in *PAE* 1958.
Thompson, H.A. (1937) 'Buildings on the west side of the Athenian Agora', pp. 1-126 in *Hesperia* 6.
—— (1961) 'The Panathenaic Festival', pp. 224-31 in *AA* 1961.
—— (1978) 'Some hero shrines in early Athens', pp. 96-108 in *Athens Comes of Age: From Solon to Salamis*. Princeton, N.J.
Tomlinson, R.A. (1976) *Greek Sanctuaries*. London.

Whitley, J. (1988) 'Early states and hero cults: a re-appraisal', pp. 173-82 in *JHS* 108.

Wilamowitz, U. von (1893) *Aristoteles und Athen*. 2 vols. Berlin.

Woodford, S. (1971) 'Cults of Heracles in Attica', pp. 211-25 in D.G. Mitten *et al.*, *Studies Presented to G.M.A. Hanfmann*. Mainz.

Wycherley, R.E. (1964) 'The Olympieion at Athens', pp. 161-79 in *GRBS* 5.3.

Young, R.S. (1939) 'Late Geometric graves and a seventh-century well in the Agora', pp. 1ff. in *Hesperia* Supplement 2.

—— (1940) 'Excavation on Mount Hymettos, 1939', pp. 1-9 in *AJA* 44.

2. Pheidippides and the Magic Mountain

Badian, E. (1979) 'The name of the runner: a summary of the evidence', pp. 163-6 in *AJAH* 4.

Berlin, I. (1967) *The Hedgehog and the Fox: an Essay on Tolstoy's View of History*. London.

Borgeaud, Ph. (1988) *The Cult of Pan in Ancient Greece*. Tr. by K. Atlass and J. Redfield. Chicago and London.

Bovon, A. (1963) 'Les guerres médiques dans la tradition et les cultes populaires d'Athènes', pp. 221-7 in *Études de Lettres* 6.

Brommer, F. (1956) 'Pan', cols. 950-1008 in *RE* Supp. 8.

Burn, A.R. (1962) *Persia and the Greeks: the Defence of the West, c. 546-478 BC*. London.

—— (1969) 'Hammond on Marathon: a few notes', pp. 118-20 in *JHS* 89.

Donlan, W., and Thompson, J. (1976) 'The charge at Marathon: Herodotos 6.112', pp. 339-43 in *CJ* 71.

Farnell, E.R. (1921) *Greek Hero Cults and Ideas of Immortality*. Oxford, Clarendon.

Frost, F.J. (1979) 'The dubious origins of the Marathon', pp. 159-63 in *AJAH* 4.

Fuchs, W. (1962) 'Attische Nymphenreliefs', pp. 242-9 in *MDAI(A)* 77.

Haldane, J.A. (1968) 'Pindar and Pan: frs. 95-100 Snell', pp. 18-31 in *Phoenix* 22.

Hammond, N.G.L. (1968) 'The campaign and the battle of Marathon', pp. 13-57 in *JHS* 88.

—— (1988) 'The campaign and battle of Marathon', pp. 506-17 in *CAH IV*^{2}.

Hampe, R. (1939) 'Ein Denkmal für die Schlacht von Marathon', pp. 168-74 in *Die Antike* 15.

Harrison, E.B. (1972) 'The south frieze of the Nike temple and the Marathon painting in the Painted Stoa', pp. 353-78 in *AJA* 76.

How, W.W., and Wells, J. (1912) *A Commentary on Herodotus*. 2 vols. Oxford, Clarendon.

Immerwahr, H.R. (1966) *Form and Thought in Herodotus* (= *Philological Monographs published by the American Philological Association* vol. 23). Cleveland, Ohio.

Jacoby, F. (1945) 'Some Athenian epigrams from the Persian Wars', pp. 157-211 in *Hesperia* 14.

Jameson, M.H. (1951) 'The hero Echetlaeus', pp. 49-61 in *TAPA* 82.

Linforth, I.M. (1928) 'Named and Unnamed Gods in Herodotus', pp. 201-43 in *California Publications in Classical Philology* 9.

de Maistre, J. (1850) *Les soirées de St. Pétersbourg*. 6th ed. Vol. 2, Entretien 7. Paris.

Meritt, B.D. (1956) 'Epigrams from the battle of Marathon, the Aegean and the

Near East', pp. 268-80 in *Studies Presented to H. Goldman*. New York.

Oliver, J.H. (1935) 'The Marathon epigrams', pp. 193-201 in *AJP* 56.

—— (1936) 'The monument with the Marathon epigrams', pp. 225-34 in *Hesperia* 5.

Orlandos, A.K. (1958) *'Marathon: spêlaion Panos'*, pp. 15-22 in *Ergon*.

Petrakos, B. (1983) *A Concise Guide to Rhamnous* (= *XIIth International Congress of Classical Archaeology held in Athens, 4-10 September 1983*). Athens.

—— (1987) *'To Nemeseion tou Rhamnountos'*, pp. 295-326 in *Philia Epê eis Geôrgion E. Mulonan*. Athens.

Pritchett, W.K. (1960) *Marathon*. Berkeley, etc.

—— (1979) *The Greek State at War. Part III: Religion*. Berkeley, etc.

Raubitschek, A.E. (1940) 'Two monuments erected after the victory of Marathon', pp. 53-9 in *AJA* 44.

Robertson, N. (1985) 'The origins of the Panathenaia', pp. 231-95 in *RhM* 128.

Simon, E. (1976) 'Ein nordattischer Pan', pp. 19-23 in *AK* 19.

Vanderpool, E. (1948) 'An Archaic inscribed stele from Marathon', pp. 335f. in *Hesperia* 11.

—— (1958) 'News letter from Greece', p. 321f. in *AJA* 62.

—— (1966) 'The deme of Marathon and the Herakleion', pp. 322f. in *AJA* 70.

Vidal-Naquet, P. (1967) 'Une enigme à Delphes. À propos de la base de Marathon (Paus. 10.10.1-2)', pp. 281-302 in *RH* 238.

Weller, C.H., *et al.* (1903) 'The cave at Vari', pp. 263-349 in *AJA* 7.

Wilhelm, A. (1934) 'Drei auf die Schlacht von Marathon bezügliche Gedichte', pp. 89-118 in *Anzeiger der Akademie der Wissenschaften in Wien*.

Woodford, S. (1971) 'Cults of Heracles in Attica', pp. 211-25 in D.G. Mitten, *et al.*, *Studies Presented to G.M.A. Hanfmann*. Mainz.

3. Themistokles and the Cult of the Intellect

Agard, W.J. (1965) 'Boreas at Athens', pp. 241-6 in *CJ* 61.

Amandry, P. (1950) *La mantique apollinienne à Delphes* (= *BEFAR* 170). Paris.

—— (1967/8) 'Thémistocle à Mélite', pp. 265-79 in vol. 4 of *Charistêrion eis A. Orlandon*. Athens.

Binder, J. (1984) 'The west pediment of the Parthenon: Poseidon', pp. 15-22 in *Studies Presented to Sterling Dow on his Eightieth Birthday*. Durham, North Carolina.

Bovon, A. (1963) 'Les guerres médiques dans la tradition et les cultes populaires d'Athènes', pp. 221-7 in *Études de Lettres* 6.

Crahay, R. (1956) *La littérature oraculaire chez Hérodote* (= *Bibliothèque de la Faculté de Philosophie et Lettres de la l'Université de Liège*, vol. 138). Paris.

Dodds, E.R. (1951) *The Greeks and the Irrational*. California.

—— (1965) *Pagan and Christian in an Age of Anxiety: some Aspects of Religious Experience from Marcus Aurelius to Constantine*. Cambridge.

—— (1973) *The Ancient Concept of Progress*. Oxford, Clarendon.

Drerup, H. (1961) 'Zum Artemistempel von Magnesia', pp. 13-22 in *Marburger Winkelmann-Programm*.

Elayi, J. (1978) 'Le rôle de l'oracle de Delphes dans le conflit Gréco-Perse d'après "Les Histoires" d'Hérodote', pp. 93-118 in *Iranica Antiqua* 13.

—— (1979) 'Le rôle de l'oracle de Delphes dans le conflit Gréco-Perse d'après "Les Histoires" d'Hérodote', pp. 67-151 in *Iranica Antiqua* 14.

—— (1979a) 'Deux oracles de Delphes: les réponses de la Pythie à Clisthène de

Sicyone, et aux Athéniens avant Salamine', pp. 224-30 in *REG* 92.

Evans, J.A.S. (1982) 'The oracle of the "wooden wall" ', p. 24f, in *CJ* 78.

Fontenrose, J. (1978) *The Delphic Oracle*. Berkeley, etc.

Frost, F.J. (1980) *Plutarch's Themistocles*. Princeton, N.J.

Green, P. (1970) *The Year of Salamis: 480-479*. London.

Hands, A.R. (1965) 'On strategy and oracles, 480/79', pp. 56-61 in *JHS* 85.

Henrichs, A. (1981) 'Human sacrifice in Greek religion,' pp. 208-24 in *Le sacrifice dans l'antiquité: Entr.Hardt* 27. Geneva.

Hignett, C. (1963) *Xerxes' Invasion of Greece*. Oxford, Clarendon.

How, W.W., and Wells, J. (1912) *A Commentary on Herodotus*. 2 vols. Oxford, Clarendon.

Kaempf-Dimitriadou, S. (1986) 'Boreas', pp. 133-42 in *LIMC* III.1.

Kirchberg, J. (1965) *Die Funktion der Orakel im Werke Herodots* (= *Hypomnemata* 11). Göttingen.

Mussies, G. (1988) 'Identification and self-identification of gods in Classical and Hellenistic times', pp. 1-18 in van den Broek, R., Baarda, T., and Mansfeld, J. (eds.) *Knowledge of God in the Graeco-Roman World*. Leiden, etc.

Nilsson, M.P. (1924) 'Götter und Psychologie bei Homer', pp. 363-90 in *ARW* 22.

Nock, A.D. (1972) 'Religious attitudes of the ancient Greeks', pp. 534-50 in *Arthur Darby Nock: Essays on Religion and the Ancient World*. Ed. by Z. Stewart. 2 vols. Cambridge, Mass.

Palaiokrassa, L. (1983) *To hiero tês Artemidos Mounichias*. Thessalonika.

Parke, H.W. (1962) 'A note on *automatizô* in connexion with prophecy', p. 145f. in *JHS* 82.

——(1967) *Greek Oracles*. London.

Parke, H.W., and Wormell, D.E.W. (1956) *The Delphic Oracle*. 2 vols. Oxford.

Podlecki, A.J. (1975) *The Life of Themistocles: a Critical Survey of the Literary and Archaeological Evidence*. Montreal and London.

Price, S. (1985) 'Delphi and divination', pp. 128-54 in Easterling, P.E. and Muir, J. (eds.), *Greek Religion and Society*. Cambridge.

Robertson, N. (1985) 'The origins of the Panathenaia', pp. 231-95 in *RhM* 128.

Roux, G. (1976) *Delphi: Orakel und Kultstätten*. Munich.

Simon, E. (1967) 'Boreas und Oreithyia auf dem silbernen Rhyton,' pp. 101-26 in *A&A* 13.

Starr, C. (1962) 'Why did the Greeks defeat the Persians?', pp. 321-32 in *PP* 17.

Threpsiades, J., and Vanderpool, E. (1964) 'Themistokles' sanctuary of Artemis Aristoboule', pp. 26-36 in *AD* 19 (A: *Meletai*).

Waters, K.H. (1985) *Herodotos the Historian*. Oklahoma.

4. Theseus' Old Bones

Barron, J.P. (1972) 'New light on old walls', pp. 20-45 in *JHS* 92.

——(1980) 'Bacchylides, Theseus and a woolly cloak', pp. 1-8 in *BICS* 27.

Boardman, J. (1972) 'Heracles, Peisistratos and sons', pp. 57-72 in *RA*.

—— (1982) 'Herakles, Theseus and Amazons', pp. 1-28 in *The Eye of Greece: Studies in the Art of Athens*. Ed. by D.C. Kurtz and B. Sparkes. Cambridge.

Braudel, F. (1980) *On History*, tr. S. Matthews. Chicago.

Brommer, F. (1982) *Theseus: die Taten des griechischen Helden in der antiken Kunst und Literatur*. Darmstadt.

Brunnsåker, S. (1955) *The Tyrant-Slayers of Kritios and Nesiotes*. Lund.

Christensen, K.A. (1984) 'The Theseion: a slave refuge at Athens', pp. 23-32 in

AJAH 9.1.

Connor, W.R. (1970) 'Theseus in Classical Athens', pp. 143-74 in Ward, A.G. (ed.) *The Quest for Theseus*. London.

Cook, R.M. (1987) 'Pots and Pisistratan propaganda', pp. 167-9 in *JHS* 107.

Fornara, C.W. (1970) 'The cult of Harmodius and Aristogeiton', pp. 155-80 in *Philologus* 114.

Herter, H. (1939) 'Theseus der Athener', pp. 244-86, 289-326 in *RhM* n.s. 88.

—— (1973) 'Theseus', cols. 1045-238 in *RE* Supp. XIII.

Hobsbawm, E., and Ranger, T. (eds.) (1983) *The Invention of Tradition*. Cambridge.

Jeanmaire, H. (1939) 'Attika: les origines rituelles de la geste de Thésée', ch. 4 in *Couroi et Courètes*. Lille-Paris.

Kardara, Ch. P. (1951) 'On Theseus and the Tyrannicides', pp. 293-300 in *AJA* 55.

Leahy, D.M. (1955) 'The bones of Tisamenus', pp. 26-38 in *Historia* 4.

Lewis, B. (1975) *History: Remembered, Recovered, Invented*. Princeton.

Malkin, I. (1987) *Religion and Colonization in Ancient Greece* (= *Studies in Greek and Roman Religion*, vol. 3). Leyden, etc.

Metzler, D. (1966) *Untersuchungen zu den griechischen Porträts des 5. Jhd. v. Chr.* Diss. Münster.

Ostwald, M. (1951) 'The Prytaneion Decree re-examined', pp. 24-46 in *AJP* 72.

—— (1969) *Nomos and the Beginnings of the Athenian Democracy*. Oxford.

—— (1988) 'The reform of the Athenian state by Cleisthenes', pp. 303-46 in *CAH IV*².

Parlama, L.P. (1984) *Hê Skuros stên Epochê tou Chalkou*. Athens.

Pfister, F. (1909) *Der Reliquienkult im Altertum*. Giessen.

Podlecki, A.J. (1966) 'The political significance of the Athenian "tyrannicide" cult', pp. 129-41 in *Historia* 15.

—— (1971) 'Cimon, Skyros and Theseus' bones', pp. 141-3 in *JHS* 91.

de Polignac, F. (1984) *La naissance de la cité grecque. Cultes, espace et société, 8ᵉ-7ᵉ siècles avant J.C.* Paris.

Raubitschek, A.E. (1960) 'The covenant of Plataea', pp. 178-83 in *TAPA* 91.

Ruschenbusch, E. (1958) *'Patrios politeia*. Theseus, Drakon, Solon und Kleisthenes in Publizistik und Geschichtsschreibung des 5. und 4. Jahrhunderts v. Chr.', pp. 398-424 in *Historia* 7.4.

Shefton, B.B. (1960) 'Some iconographic remarks on the Tyrannicides', pp. 173-9 in *AJA* 64.

Siewert, P. (1972) *Der Eid von Plataiai*. Munich.

Sourvinou-Inwood, C. (1979) 'Theseus as son and stepson: a tentative illustration of the Greek mythological mentality', *BICS* Supplement 40.

Thomas, R. (1989) *Oral Tradition and Written Record in Classical Athens*. Cambridge.

Tudor, H. (1972) *Political Myth*. London.

Veyne, P. (1983) *Did the Greeks Believe their Myths?* Paris.

Woodford, S. (1971) 'Cults of Heracles in Attica', pp. 211-25 in D.G. Mitten *et al. Studies Presented to G.M.A. Hanfmann* Mainz.

5. Transfiguration and the Maiden

Barron, J.P. (1964) 'Religious propaganda of the Delian League', pp. 35-48 in *JHS* 84.

—— (1983) 'The fifth-century *horoi* of Aigina', pp. 1-12 in *JHS* 103.

Boardman, J. (1977) 'The Parthenon frieze – another view,' pp. 39-49 in Höckmann, U. and Krug, A. (eds.) *Festchrift für Frank Brommer*. Mainz.

Connor, W.R. (1970) 'Theseus in Classical Athens', pp. 143-74 in Ward, A.G. (ed.) *The Quest for Theseus*. London and New York.

Dinsmoor, W.B. (1941) 'Observations on the Hephaisteion', *Hesperia* Supplement no. 5.

Fol, A., and Marazov, I. (1977). *Thrace and the Thracians*. New York.

von Geisau, J. (1954) 'Praxiergidai', col. 1761 in *RE* 22.

Goceva, Z., and Popov, D. (1986) 'Bendis', pp. 95-7 in *LIMC* III.1.

Harrison, E.B. (1972) 'The south frieze of the Nike temple and the Marathon painting in the Painted Stoa', pp. 353-78 in *AJA* 76.

Herington, C.J. (1955) *Athena Parthenos and Athena Polias: a Study in the Religion of Periklean Athens*. Manchester.

Jameson, M.H. (1980) 'Apollo Lykeios in Athens', pp. 213-36 in *Archaiognosia* 1.

Lewis, D.M. (1954) 'Notes on Attic inscriptions', pp. 17-21 in *ABSA* 49.

—— (1960) 'Apollo Delios', pp. 190-4 in *ABSA* 55.

Linders, T. (1975) *The Treasurers of the Other Gods in Athens and their Functions* (= *Beiträge zur klassischen Philologie*, vol. 62). Meisenheim am Glan.

Loraux, N. (1973) 'Marathon ou l'histoire idéologique', pp. 13-42 in *REA* 75.

Mattingly, H.B. (1974) 'Athens and Eleusis: some new ideas', pp. 90-103 in Bradeen, D.W. and McGregor, M.F. (eds.), *PHOROS: Tribute to Benjamin Dean Meritt*. New York.

Meritt, B.D. (1975) 'Perikles, the Athenian mint and the Hephaisteion', pp. 267-74 in *Proceedings of the American Philosophical Society*, vol. 119.

Mikalson, J. (1984) 'Religion and the plague in Athens', pp. 423-31 in *Studies Presented to Sterling Dow on his Eightieth Birthday*. Durham, North Carolina.

Nilsson, M.P. (1951) *Cults, Myths, Oracles and Politics*. Lund.

Ostwald, M. (1969) *Nomos and the Beginnings of the Athenian Democracy*. Oxford.

—— (1986) *From Popular Sovereignty to the Sovereignty of Law: Law, Society and Politics in Fifth-Century Athens*. Berkeley, etc.

Pettazzoni, R. (1954) 'The religion of ancient Thrace', pp. 81-94 in *Essays on the History of Religions*. Leyden.

Robertson, N. (1985) 'The origins of the Panathenaia', pp. 231-95 in *RhM* 128.

Roussel, P. (1943) 'À propos d'un décret attique relatif à la déesse Bendis', pp. 177-82 in *REA* 45.

Schlaifer, R. (1940) 'Notes on Athenian public cults', pp. 233-60 in *HSCP* 51.

Simms, R.R. (1988) 'The Thracian goddess Bendis', pp. 59-76 in *AncW* 18.

Stadter, P.A. (1989) *A Commentary on Plutarch's Pericles*. Chapel Hill and London.

Stockton, D. (1982) 'The death of Ephialtes,' pp. 227-8 in *CQ* n.s. 32.

Vanderpool, E. (1966) 'A monument to the battle of Marathon', pp. 93-106 in *Hesperia* 35.

Wallace, R.W. (1974) 'Ephialtes and the Areopagus', pp. 259-69 in *GRBS* 15.

Wycherley, R.E. (1953) 'The Painted Stoa', pp. 20-35 in *Phoenix* 7.

6. Asklepios and his Sacred Snake

Aleshire, S.B. (1989) *The Athenian Asklepieion: The People, Their Dedications and the Inventories*. Amsterdam.

Beschi, L. (1967/8) 'Il monumento di Telemachos, fondatore dell' Asklepieion

Ateniese', pp. 381-436 in *ASAA* n.s. 29/30.

—— (1983) 'Il rilievo di Telemachos ricompletato', pp. 31-43 in *AAA* 15.

—— (1985) pp. 16-19 in *Nuovi Studi Maffeiani: Atti del Convegno Scipione Maffei e il Museo Maffeiano*. Verona.

Burford, A. (1969) *The Greek Temple Builders at Epidauros*. Liverpool.

Cohn-Haft, L. (1956) *The Public Physicians of Ancient Greece*. Northampton, Mass.

Cole, S. (1988) 'The use of water in Greek sanctuaries', pp. 161-5 in Hägg, R., Marinatos, N. and Nordquist, G.C. (eds.) *Early Greek Cult Practice* (= *Proceedings of the Fifth International Symposium at the Swedish Institute at Athens, 26-29 June 1986*. Stockholm.

Edelstein, E.J., and Edelstein, L. (1945) *Asclepius: a Collection and Interpretation of the Testimonies*. 2 vols. Baltimore. Reprinted New York 1975.

Farnell, L.R. (1921) *Greek Hero Cults and Ideas of Immortality*. Oxford, Clarendon.

Feaver, D. (1957) 'The priesthoods of Athens', pp. 123-58 in *YCS* 15.

Ferguson, W.S. (1907) *Priests of Asklepios*. 2nd ed. Berkeley.

Girard, P. (1877) 'Catalogue descriptif des ex-voto à Esculape trouvés récemment sur la pente méridionale de l'Acropole', pp. 156-69 in *BCH* 1.

—— (1878) 'Ex-voto à Esculape trouvés sur la pente méridionale de l'Acropole', pp. 65-94 in *BCH* 2.

—— (1881) *L'Asklépieion d'Athènes d'après de récentes découvertes*. Paris.

Herzog, R. (1931) 'Die Wunderheilungen von Epidauros', *Philologus* Supplement Band 22.3.

Holtzmann, B. (1984) 'Asklepios', pp. 863-97 in *LIMC* II. 1.

Kerenyi, C. (1960) *Asklepios: Archetypal Image of the Physician's Existence*. London.

Körte, A. (1893) 'Bezirk eines Heilgottes', pp. 231-56 in *MDAI(A)* 18.

—— (1896) 'Das Heiligtum des Amynos', pp. 287-332 in *MDAI(A)* 21.

Küster, E. (1913) *Die Schlange in der griechischen Kunst und Religion* (= *Religionsgeschichtliche Versuche und Vorarbeiten* vol. 13.2). Giessen.

Kutsch, F. (1913) *Attische Heilgötter und Heilheroen*. Giessen.

Lang, M. (1977) *Cure and Cult in Ancient Corinth* (= *American Excavations in Old Corinth: Corinth Notes* no. 1). Princeton, N.J.

Lefkowitz, M.R. (1981) *The Lives of the Greek Poets*. London.

Martin, R. (1944-5) 'Chapiteaux ioniques de l'Asclépieion d'Athènes', pp. 340-74 in *BCH* 68/9.

Martin, R., and Metzger, B. (1949) 'Recherches d'architecture et de topographie à l'Asklépieion d'Athènes', pp. 316-50 in *BCH* 73.

Mikalson, J. (1984) 'Religion and the plague in Athens', pp. 423-31 in *Studies Presented to Sterling Dow on his Eightieth Birthday*. Durham, North Carolina.

Mitropoulou, E. (1975) *A New Interpretation of the Telemachus Monument*. Athens.

Nilsson, M.P. (1942) 'Bendis in Athen', pp. 169-88 in *From the Collections of the Ny Carlsberg Glyptothek* 3.

Oliver, J.H. (1936) 'The Sarapion Monument and the paean of Sophocles', pp. 91-122 in *Hesperia* 5.

Roebuck, C. (1951) *The Asklepieion and Lerna: Corinth*, vol. 14. Princeton, New Jersey.

Schlaifer, R. (1940) 'Notes on Athenian public cults', pp. 233-60 in *HSCP* 51.

—— (1943) 'Demon of Paenia, priest of Asclepius', pp. 39-43 in *CP* 38.

Schouten, J. (1967) *The Rod and Serpent of Asklepios*. Amsterdam, etc.

van Straten , F.T. (1974) 'Did the Greeks kneel before their gods?', pp. 159-89 in *BABesch* 49.

—— (1976) 'Daikrates' dream. A votive relief from Kos, and some other *kat'onar* dedications', pp. 1-38 in *BABesch* 51.

—— (1981) 'Gifts for the gods', pp. 65-151 in Versnel (*FHW*).

Thompson, H.A. (1978) 'Some hero shrines in early Athens', pp. 96-108 in *Athens Comes of Age: From Solon to Salamis*. Princeton, N.J.

Tomlinson, R.A. (1969) 'Two buildings in sanctuaries of Asklepios', pp. 112-17 in *JHS* 89.

—— (1976) *Greek Sanctuaries*. London and New York.

—— (1983) *Epidauros*. London, etc.

Walter, O. (1953) 'Das Priestertum des Sophokles', pp. 469-79 in *Geras Antoniou Keramopoullou*. Athens.

Walton, A. (1894) *The Cult of Asklepios* (= *Cornell Studies in Classical Philology* no. 3). Ithaca, N.Y. Reprinted 1965.

Walton, F.R. (1935) 'A problem in the *Ichneutai* of Sophocles', pp. 170ff. in *HSCP* 46.

Ziehen, J. (1892) 'Über die Lage des Asklepiosheiligtums von Trikka', pp. 195-7 in *MDAI(A)* 17.

7. Sokrates and the New *Daimonia*

Blumenthal, H. (1973) 'Meletus the accuser of Andocides and Meletus the accuser of Socrates: one man or two?', pp. 169-78 in *Philologus* 117.

Boegehold, A.L. (1972) 'The establishment of a central archive at Athens', pp. 23-30 in *AJA* 76.

Bonner, R.J., and Smith, G. (1930-8) *The Administration of Justice from Homer to Aristotle*. 2 vols. Chicago.

Breitenbach, H.R. (1967) 'Xenophon', cols. 1567-1928 in *RE* 2.9.

Brickhouse, T.C., and Smith, N.D. (1985) 'The formal charges against Socrates', pp. 457-81 in *JHPh* 23.

—— (1989) *Socrates on Trial*. Princeton, N.J.

Burnet, J. (1924) *Plato's Euthyphro*. Oxford, Clarendon.

—— (1924a) *Plato's Apology*. Oxford, Clarendon.

Clinton, K. (1982) 'The nature of the late fifth-century revision of the Athenian law code', pp. 27-37 in *Studies in Attic Epigraphy, History and Topography Presented to Eugene Vanderpool* (= *Hesperia* Supplement no. 19). Princeton, N.J.

Connor, W.R. (1963) 'Two notes on Diopeithes the seer', pp. 115-18 in *CP* 58.

Decharme, P. (1903) 'La loi de Diopeithes', pp. 72-7 in *Mélanges Perrot*. Paris.

Derenne, E. (1930) 'Les procès d'impiété intentés aux philosophes à Athènes au Vme et au IVme siècles avant J.-C.' (= *Bibliothèque de la Faculté de Philosophie et Lettres de l'Université de Liège*, vol. 45). Liège and Paris.

Dodds, E.R. (1951) *The Greeks and the Irrational*. Berkeley, etc.

Dover, K.J. (1975) 'The freedom of the intellectual in Greek society', p. 28f. in *Talanta* 7.

Dow, S. (1937) 'The Egyptian cults in Athens', pp. 183-232 in *HThR* 30.

—— (1953-7) 'The law codes of Athens', pp. 3-36 in *Proceedings of the Massachusetts Historical Society* 71 (= Proceedings 1953-7). Published in 1959.

—— (1960) 'The Athenian calendar of sacrifices: the chronology of Nikomachos' second term', pp. 270-93 in *Historia* 9.

Fahr, W. (1969) *THEOUS NOMIZEIN: Zum Problem der Anfänge des Atheismus bei den Griechen.* (= *Spudasmata* vol. 26). Hildesheim and New York.

Finley, M.I. (1973) *Democracy, Ancient and Modern.* London.

Guthrie, W.K.C. (1971) *Socrates.* Cambridge, etc.

Harrison, A.R.W. (1968, 1971) *The Law of Athens.* 2 vols. Oxford, Clarendon.

Henrichs, A. (1976) 'The atheism of Prodicus', pp. 15-21 in *Cronache Ercolanesi* 6.

Humphreys, S.C. (1975) ' "Transcendence" and intellectual roles: the ancient Greek case', pp. 91-118 in *Daedalus* Spring 1975.

Jackson, B.D. (1971) 'The prayers of Socrates', pp. 14-37 in *Phronesis* 16.

Kierkegaard, S.A. (1841) *The Concept of Irony, with Continual Reference to Socrates,* ed. and tr. Hong, H.V. and E.H. Princeton, New Jersey. First published as a doctoral thesis in the Univ. of Copenhagen.

MacDowell, D.M. (1978) *The Law in Classical Athens.* London.

Meijer, P.A. (1981) 'Philosophers, intellectuals and religion in Hellas', pp. 216-63 in Versnel *FHW*

Mikalson, J.D. (1989) 'Unanswered prayers in Greek Tragedy', pp. 81-98 in *JHS* 109.

Momigliano, A. (1973) 'Freedom of speech in antiquity', pp. 252-63 in *DHI* II.

—— (1973a) 'Impiety in the classical world', p. 565f. in *DHI* II.

Ostwald, M. (1986) *From Popular Sovereignty to the Sovereignty of Law: Law, Society and Politics in Fifth-Century Athens.* Berkeley, etc.

Phillipson, C. (1928) *The Trial of Socrates.* London.

Reeve, C.D.C. (1989) *Socrates in The Apology: an Essay on Plato's Apology of Socrates.* Indianapolis.

Robertson, N. (1990) 'The laws of Athens, 410-399 BC', pp. 43-75 in *JHS* 90.

Rudhardt, J. (1960) 'La définition du délit d'impiété d'après la législation attique', pp. 87-105 in *MH* 17.

Stone, I.F. (1989) *The Trial of Socrates.* New York.

Sutton, D. (1981) 'Critias and atheism', pp. 33-8 in *CQ* n.s. 31.

Tate, J. (1936) 'Greek for atheism', pp. 3-5 in *CR* 50.

—— (1937) 'More Greek for atheism', pp. 3-6 in *CR* 51.

Taylor, A.E. (1932) *Socrates.* Edinburgh. Reprinted 1953.

Vlastos, G. (1983) 'The historical Socrates and Athenian democracy', pp. 495-516 in *Political Theory* 11.

—— (1989) 'Divining the reason. Review of T.C. Brickhouse and N.D. Smith, *Socrates on Trial*', p. 1393 in *TLS* 15-21 December 1989.

Woodbury, L. (1965) 'The date and atheism of Diagoras of Melos', pp. 178-211 in *Phoenix* 19.

Yunis, H. (1988) *A New Creed: Fundamental Religious Beliefs in the Athenian Polis and Euripidean Drama* (= *Hypomnemata* vol. 91). Göttingen.

8. The World of the Athenian Aition

Barrett, W.S. (1964) *Euripides: Hippolytos.* Oxford, Clarendon.

Bruns, I. (1905) 'Die griechische Tragödien als religionsgeschichtliche Quelle', pp. 48-70 in *Vörtrage und Aufsätze.* Munich.

Burian, P. (1974) 'Suppliant and saviour: Oedipus at Colonus', pp. 408-29 in *Phoenix* 28.

Burkert, W. (1966) 'Kekropidensage und Arrhephoria', pp. 1-25 in *Hermes* 94.

Camp, J.M. (1979) 'A drought in the late eighth century BC', pp. 397-411 in

Hesperia 48.

Clay, J.S. (1989) *The Politics of Olympus: Form and Meaning in the Major Homeric Hymns*. Princeton, N.J.

Clinton, K. (1986) 'The author of the Homeric *Hymn to Demeter*', pp. 43-9 in *Opuscula Atheniensia*.

Connerton, P. (1989) *How Societies Remember*. Cambridge, etc.

Detienne, M. (1973) 'L'olivier: un mythe politico-religieux', pp. 293-306 in *Problèmes de la terre en Grèce ancienne*. Paris.

—— (1989) *Dionysos at Large*, tr. A. Goldhammer. Cambridge, Mass.

Dodds, E.R. (1960) *Euripides: Bacchae*. 2nd ed. Oxford, Clarendon.

Edmunds, L. (1981) 'The cults and the legend of Oedipus', pp. 221-38 in *HSCP* 85.

—— (1985) *Oedipus: the Ancient Legend and its Later Analogues*. Baltimore.

—— (1990) *Approaches to Greek Myth*. Baltimore.

Ermatinger, E. (1897) *Die attische Autochthonensage bis auf Euripides*. Berlin.

Finley, M.I. (1974) 'Myth, memory and history', pp. 11-33 in *The Use and Abuse of History*. London.

Frazer, J.G. (1898) *Pausanias' Description of Greece*. 6 vols. London.

von Fritz, K. (1940) 'Atthidographers and exegetai', pp. 91-126 in *TAPA* 71.

Habicht, C. (1985) *Pausanias' Guide to Ancient Greece*. Berkeley, etc.

Henrichs, A. (1981) 'Human sacrifice in Greek religion,' pp. 208-24 in *Le sacrifice dans l'antiquité* (= *Entr.Hardt* 27). Geneva.

Hester, D.A. (1987) 'To help one's friends and harm one's enemies: a study in the *Oedipus at Colonus*', pp. 22-41 in *Antichthon* 11 (1977).

Jacoby, F. (1949) *Atthis: the Local Chronicles of Ancient Athens*. Oxford, Clarendon.

Jeanmaire, H. (1951) *Dionysos: histoire du culte de Bacchus*. Paris.

Jebb, R.C. (1900) *Sophocles: the Oedipus Coloneus*. Cambridge.

Kirk, G.S. (1972) 'Greek mythology: some new perspectives', pp. 74-85 in *JHS* 92.

—— (1974) *The Nature of Greek Myths*. Harmondsworth.

Lacore, M. (1983) 'Euripide et le culte de Poseidon-Erechthée', pp. 216-34 in *REA* 85.

Lang, M.L. (1978) *Socrates in the Agora* (= Excavations of the Athenian Agora, Picture Book no. 17). Princeton, New Jersey 1978.

Lardinois, A. (1990) 'Greek myths for Athenian rituals: religion, politics and tragedy in Aeschylus' *Eumenides* and Sophocles' *Oedipus Coloneus*'. Forthcoming in *Hermeneus*.

Linforth, I.M. (1951) 'Religion and drama in *Oedipus at Colonus*', pp. 75-192 in *Univ. of California Publications in Classical Philology* no. 14.4.

McGinty, P. (1978) *Interpretation and Dionysos: Method in the Study of a God*. The Hague, etc.

Mikalson, J. (1976) 'Erechtheus and the Panathenaia', pp. 141-53 in *AJP* 97.

—— (1987) 'Religion, popular and other, in Aeschylus' *Eumenides*', James Loeb Classical Lecture delivered at Harvard in March 1987.

Otto, W.F. (1965) *Dionysus: Myth and Cult*. Indiana.

Parker, R. (1987) 'Myths of Early Athens', pp. 187-214 in Bremmer, J. (ed.), *Interpretations of Greek Mythology*. London and Sydney.

Richardson, N.J. (1974) *The Homeric Hymn to Demeter*. Oxford, Clarendon.

Robert, C. (1915) *Oidipus: Geschichte eines poetischen Stoffs im griechischen Altertum*. Berlin.

Robertson, N. (1983) 'The riddle of the arrhephoria at Athens', pp. 241-88 in *HSCP* 87.

——(1985) 'The origins of the Panathenaia', pp. 231-95 in *RhM* 128.

Rudhardt, J. (1966) 'Une approche de la pensée mythique. Le mythe considéré comme un langage', pp. 208-37 in *Studia philosophica* 26.

Rudhardt, K. (1979) *Sophocles*, tr. H. and D. Harvey. Oxford. First published in Frankfurt am Main in 1933.

Sale, W. (1975) 'Temple legends of the Arkteia', pp. 265-84 in *RhM* 118.

Thomas, R. (1989) *Oral Tradition and Written Record in Classical Athens.* Cambridge.

Veyne, P. (1983) *Did the Greeks Believe their Myths?* Paris.

Vidal-Naquet, P. (1968) 'The Black Hunter and the origin of the Athenian ephebeia', pp. 147-62 in Gordon, R.L. (ed.), *Myth, Religion and Society.* Cambridge and Paris. First published simultaneously in 1968 in *Annales ESC* 23, pp. 947-64, and in *PCPhS* n.s. 14, pp. 49-64. Page references are from Gordon 1981.

Conclusions

Gordon, R.L. (1972) 'Mithraism and Roman society: social factors in the explanation of religious change', pp. 92-121 in *Religion* 2.2.

Neusner, J. (1990) 'Thinking about "The Other" in religion: it is necessary, but is it possible?', pp. 273-85 in *Modern Theology* 6.3.

Nilsson, M.P. (1940) *Greek Popular Religion*. Columbia. Reprinted 1961.

Index Locorum

References to the pages of this book are given in bold type.

Aeschylus
  Eum. 847, **11**
  Pers. 347, **11**; 447-79, **73**
  PV 476-506, **165**
  fr. 281 *N²*, **71**
Ailian: *VH* 5.12, **150**; 12.61, **71**
Aischines: 1.173, **136**; 2.147, **30**; 3.186, **104**
Andokides: 1.111, **36**
Androtion: *FGrH* 324 F2, **31**
Apollodoros: 3.14.1, **163**; 3.14.6, **167**
Aristeides: *Panath*. 41, **164**; 41f., **161**; 108, **52, 58**
Aristophanes
  Acharn. 243, **159**; *passim*, **58**
  Birds 988, **140**
  Clouds 423-6, **147**
  Lys. 1150-6, **89**
  Wasps 119-23, **1**; 122f., **118**; 1081ff., **58**
Aristotle
  NE 3.1.1111a 9f., **139**
  Poet. 1451a 19-21, **89**
  Pol. 5.1313b 23, **43**
  [Aristotle]: *AP* 3.3, **24**; 21.6, **44, 45**; 23.5, **82**; 55.3, **13**; 56.4, **124**; 56.4-6, **24**; 57.1, **24**; 58.1, **24, 58, 95**; 59, **138**
Arrian: *Kyn*. 35, **13**
Athenaios: *Deipn*. 6.251b, **150**; 10.437cd, **162**

Bacchylides: *Dith*. 17, Maehler *T*, **90**

Cicero: *Laws* 2.37, **149**

Demosthenes: 18.259-60, **150**; 20.70, **95**; 19.281, **150**; 21.151, **20**
Diodoros Siculus: 4.39.1, **9**; 4.39.4, **19**;

11.29.3, **109**; 12.58.6, **131**
Diogenes Laertios: 2.40, **137, 139**; 2.42, **151**

Etymologicum Magnum: s.v. *Dexiôn*, **125**
Euripides
  Ba. 26-30, **160**; 34, **161**; 39f., **161**; 41, **160**; 45-52, **160**; 255-7, **5**; 321, **160**; 333-6, **7**; 465-74, **14**; 789-91, **160**
  Hipp. 84-6, **3**; 86, **14**; 104, **2**; 106, **2**; 1333, **2**; 1394, **2**; 1398, **2**; 1416-22, **3**
  Ion 21-4, **167**; 271-4, **167**; 1528f., **39**; 1575-81, **12**
  IT 1125-7, **61**; 1446-74, **14**
  Madness of Herakles 1325-33, **92**
  Supp. 349-53, **88**
  fr. 925 *N²*, **31**
Euthias: fr. 1 Müller, **150**

Hellanikos: *FGrH* 323a F2, **31**
Hephaisteion: *On Metres* 4.6, **95**
Herakleides of Pontos: fr. 170 Wehrli², **139**
Herodotos: 1.32.1, **2**; 1.53.3, **70**; 1.60.3-5, **16**; 1.65.2, **66**; 1.67-8, **84**; 1.68.6, **84**; 2.7.1. 41; 2.145.4, **160**; 3.122.2, **153**; 3.142.4, **7**; 4.95-6, **6**; 5.7, **11**; 5.55, **95**; 5.63, **68**; 5.66.1, **12**; 5.66.2, **12**; 5.67, **171**; 5.77.1-2, **87**; 5.80.1-81.1, **1**; 5.90.1, **68**; 5.92b, **66**; 6.44.2-3, **71**; 6.66, **68**; 6.105-6, **48-9**; 6.105.1, **47**; 6.105.3, **58**; 6.108.1, **57**; 6.112, **52**; 6.115-16, **52**; 6.116, **57**; 6.117.1, **48**; 6.117.2-3, **54**; 6.123, **95**; 6.123.2, **68**; 7.139.5, **81**;

7.140-4, **65**; 7.141.1-4, **65**; 7.142,
68; 7.143.3, **69**; 7.153.3, **7**; 8.41.3,
122; 8.44.2, **31**; 8.64, **72**; 8.51.2,
69; 8.55, **163**; 8.65, **73**; 8.83.2, **72**;
8.84.2, **73**; 8.109.3, **80**; 8.121.1,
72; 8.144.2, **113**; 9.13.2, **69**
Hesiod
  Th. 22f., **49**
  Works and Days 156-67, **153**; 339,
   144
Homer
  Il. 1.207f., **81**; 2.488-92, **74**; 2.547-51,
   34; 2.729-32, **116**; 6.309-11, **2**;
   8.48, **21**; 9.5, **71**; 12.243, **67**;
   15.262, **74**; 21.145, **74**; 21.304, **74**;
   23.148, **21**; 23.229f., **71**
  Od. 2.178-86, **4**; 5.208, **153**; 6.149-61,
   15; 7.80f., **34, 57**; 8.363, **21**;
   11.134-6, **4**; 13.296-9, **2**; 15.172f.,
   74; 16.184f., **16**
Hymn to Aphrodite: 100-2, **16**
Hymn to Delion Apollo: 30-50, **10**
Hymn to Demeter: 154, **156**; 270f., **164**;
  275-83, **15**
Hypereides: fr. 60 *T*, **150**

IG I²: 609, **51**; 761, **42**; 1672, **6**
IG I³: 3, **57**; 7, **101**; 14.3ff., **106**; 34.41-3,
  107; 35, **102**; 78.14-18, **107**;
  78.54-9, **126**; 82, **110**; 136, **111**;
  138, **111**; 239-41, **148**; 383.143,
  111; 474.1, **69**
IG II¹: 471.26f., **58**
IG II²: 47.23-31, **129**; 77.5f., **95**; 337,
  112; 794.4, **36**; 848.30, **36**;
  1035.45, **76**; 1039.2f., **94**; 1072.3,
  36; 1163.2f., **129**; 1252-3, **125**;
  1259; **125**; 1364, **133**; 2640, **41**;
  4351-4, **129**; 4359, **124**; 4510,
  125; 4548, **5, 20**; 4960, **118**; 4961,
  128; 4962, **130**; 4963, **129**; 4969,
  125, 129
IG IV²: 1.121-4, **123**; 94, **122**; 128, **16**;
  136, **117**
IG X.2.1: 255, **15, 125**
IG XI.4: 1299, **15**
Isokrates
  Areiopagit. 29-30, **23**
  Panath. 24, **48**

Josephos: *Ap.* 2.263, **146**; 2.267-8, **150**
Julian: *Or.* 5.159a, **159**

Life of Sophokles: 11, **125**
Livy
  Periocha 11, **121**
  1.56.9-13, **67**
LSAG: 180, **117**
LSG: 21, **130**
LSGS: 10.47-50, **45**; 11, **129**; 17, **5, 20**
Lukian
  Double Indictment 9-10, **60**
  Pisc. 42, **126**
Lykourgos: *Leok.* 81, **109**
Lysias: 26.6, **45**; 30.17, **36**; 30.29, **24**,
  145

Marmor Parium: 43, **42**
Menander: *Dysk.* 260-3, **10**
ML: 11, **42**; 18, **51**; 19, **48**; 40, **106**; 44,
  102; 46, **107**; 73, **107, 126**

Old Oligarch: 3.2, **9**
Orphic Hymn: 68.13, **132**
Ovid: *Metam.* 15.626-744, **121**

Pausanias: 1.3.1, **94**; 1.3.3, **88, 94**;
  1.8.4, **94**; 1.14.2, **165**; 1.14.5, **48**,
  58, 105; 1.14.7, **158**; 1.15.3, **40**,
  54, 56f., 62, 104; 1.17.2, **94**; 1.18.2,
  167; 1.22.3, **91**; 1.24.3, **9**; 1.26.4,
  75; 1.26.5, **30**; 1.27.3, **166**; 1.28.2,
  105; 1.32.2, **27, 30**; 1.32.3, **47**;
  1.32.4, **57**; 1.32.5, **54, 103**; 1.32.7,
  51; 1.33.3, **57**; 1.36.1, **73, 76**;
  1.37.4, **91**; 2.10.3, **12**; 2.23.6, **158**;
  2.26.7, **117**; 2.26.8, **122, 124**;
  2.28.1, **121**; 6.9.6-8, **8**; 7.1.8, **84**;
  8.2.1, **91**; 8.36.6, **71**; 8.37.11, **61**;
  8.54.6, **60**; 10.11.5, **48, 90**; 10.23,
  63
Phanias of Lesbos: fr. 25 Wehrli², **70**
Phanodemos: *FGrH* 325 F11, **162**; 12,
  166; 27, **154**
Philochoros: *FGrH* 328 F 5b, **166**; 18,
  92; 97, **165**; 94-8, **153**; 110, **87**;
  168, **36**
Philostratos: *VA* 4.18, **123**
Pindar
  Pyth. 3, 117f.; 4.162, **143**
  frr. 75.4 Maehler *T*, 11; 95, **63**
Plato
  Apology 17c, **141**; 24e, **151**; 26c, **143**;
   27a, **143**; 31c, **146**; 34a, **141**; 38b,
   141; 40a, **148**

Euthyd, 302cd, **12**
Euthyph. 2a, **139**; 3b, **146f.**
Laws 1.637e, **166**; 10.887e, **144**
Menex. 237c, **11**
Phd. 59b, **142**; 118a, **124**
Rep. 1.328a, **112**; 3.414c-e, **31**;
    4.427bc, **20**
Theait, 151a4, **147**
Pliny: *HN* 34.9.17, **94f.**
Plutarch
    Alk.22.3, **139**; 22.4, **138**; 34.1, **101**
    Arist. 11.5-8, **75**; 11.7, **57**; 21, **82**
    Kim. 4.6, **94**; 8.3-4, **83**; 8.5, **83**; 8.6,
        82, **85**
    Mor. 349e, **55**; 349f, **72**; 437ab, **64**;
        511ab, **69**; 512e, **66**; 741a, **11**,
        161; 792f, **66**; 843e, **30**; 869cd, **74**;
        869cf, **80**
    Nik. 4.1, **8**
    Num. 4.8, **79**
    Per. 8.6, **17**; 12, **109**; 13.1-2, **109**;
        13.8, **17**; 32.1, **139**
    Sol. 9, **37**; 10.2, **37**; 12, **38**; 16.3, **38**;
        25.2, **36**
    Them. 1.3, **78**, **88**; 3.1, **79**; 3.2, **79**; 4.1,
        79; 5.2, **79**; 9.4, **64**; 10.1, **67f.**, **79**;
        11.1, **70**, **79**; 13, **70**; 12, **70**, **72**;
        14.2, **70**; 15.1, **72**, **73**; 18.1, **79**; 22,
        73, **76**; 30, **78**
    Thes. 6.7, **86**; 12.1, **93**; 14.2, **91**; 17.6,
        91; 18.2, **91**; 23, **91**, **93**; 22.4, **91**;
        24.3-4, **91**; 25.4, **86**, **91**; 26, **87**;
        29.3, **86**; 31.1, **87**; 32-3, **91**; 35, **54**;
        36, **82**, **94**, **96**, **98**
Polemon: 2.41, **52**
Porphyry: *Abst*. 2.16, **4**; 4.22, **138**

Scholiast
    on Ar. *Frogs* 501, **131**
    on Ar. *Plout*, 733, **121**
    on Dem. 8.259-60, **150**; 22.13, **104**
SEG: X.59, **111**; XXI.519, 21; 541, 10;

XXII.116.5, **78**; XXIX.1205, **4**;
    XXXI.9, **102**; XXXIV.1, **57**;
    XXXIV.39, **57**; XXXVI.12, **107**
SIG^3: 1040, **130**
Simonides: *AP* 16.232, **50**
Solon: *IEG* 4.1-4, **29**
Sophokles
    Ajax 14, **2**; 92, **2**; 695, **73**
    OK 406-8, **88**; *passim*, **168ff.**
    OT 788-93, **66**
Stesimbrotos: *FGrH* 107 F9, **17**
Strabo: *Geog*. 9.5.17, **117**
Suda
    s.v. epithetous heortas, **24**
    s.v. Embaros eimi, **166**
    s.v. haliplanktos, **73**
    s.v. Hippias, **52**
Suetonius: *JC* 32, **54**

Theognis: 1179f., **138**
Theophrastos: *Char*. 16.4, **15**
Theompompos: *FGrH* 115 F 153, **109**;
    344, **4**
Thukydides: 1.20.2, **95**; 1.73.2, **85**;
    1.89.3, **69**; 1.118, **111**; 1.138.3, **73**;
    2.15.2, **91**; 2.17.1, **123**, **126**, **131**;
    2.29.4, **112**; 2.34.5, **58**; 2.38.1, **9**;
    2.47, **114**; 2.48.2, **132**; 2.52.4, **131**;
    2.53.4, **114**; 2.56.4, **132**; 2.63.2,
    98; 3.87.1-3, **114**; 3.104, **131**;
    6.54-9, **95**; 6.54.6, 41; 6.54.6-7, **42**

Valerius Maximus: 1.8.2, **121**

Xenophon
    Anab. 3.2.12, **55**
    Apol. 8, **141**; 11, **142**; 14, **149**
    Hell. 2.4.20, **14**
    Hipp. 3.2, **41**
    Mem. 1.1.2, **142**; 1.1.2-3, **146**; 1.1.3-4,
        147; 1.2, **141**; 1.2.12, **136**; 1.2.64,
        142; 4.3.16, **21**; 4.8.4, **141**, **142**

Index of Gods and Heroes

Aglauros, 38, 167
Aiakidai, 1, 72
Aias, 44
Akademos, 35
Amphiaraos, 133
Amphilochos, 133
Amynos, 125
Anakes, 13, 91, 111
Angdistis, 4
Aphrodite, 3, 4, 16, 25
Aphrodite Epitragia, 91
Aphrodite in the Gardens, 166f.
Aphrodite Pandemos, 91, 165
Apollo, 25, 66, 82, 101, 131
Apollo Alexikakos, 131
Apollo Daphnephoros, 87
Apollo Delios, 8, 10, 21, 111
Apollo Karneios, 48
Apollo Patroös, 13, 40, 42
Apollo Pythios, 42, 65, 130, 160
Ares, 11, 40, 110
Aristomachos, 133
Artemis, 2, 3, 5, 11, 40, 61, 131
Artemis Agrotera, 20, 24, 55, 62, 70
Artemis Aristoboule, ch. 3 *passim*, 20, 83
Artemis Boulaia, 76
Artemis Brauronia, 40
Artemis Leukophryene, 11, 75
Artemis Mounychia, 20, 76, 113, 166
Asklepios, ch. 6 *passim*, 1, 9, 13, 16, 17, 20, 21, 25, 34, 149
Athena, 2, 3, 4, 14, 16, 25, 29, 35, 39, 56f., 62, 81, 99, 106, 110, 138, 163
Athena *Athênôn medeousa*, 107
Athena Hellotis, 30, 57
Athena Hygieia, 17, 132
Athena Nike, 11, 39, 102f.
Athena Pallenis, 30, 40
Athena Parthenos, 30
Athena Phratria, 45

Athena Polias, 10, 11, 22, 28, 30f., 34, 79, 100-2, 166f.
Athena Poliouchos, 28, 164
Athena Promachos, 104f.

Bendis, 111-14, 149
Boreas, 71
Boutes, 22

daimonion, 14, 145-9
Demeter, 15, 40, 72, 106
Demeter and Kore, *see* Two Goddesses
Dexion, *see* Sophokles Dexion
Dionysos, 7, 11, 14, 24, 40, 139, 160
Dionysos Eleuthereus, 42, 159
Dionysos Limnaios, 162, 166
Dionysos Omestes, 70
Dioskouroi, *see* Anakes

Echetlaios, 54, 56, 61, 62
Enyalios, 24, 37
Eponymous heroes, 43f., 89, 165
Erechtheus, 22, 34, 87
Erichthonios, 31, 167
Eukleia, 105
Eurysakes, 37
Eurystheus at Pallene, 156

Ge Kourotrophos, 38

Harmodios and Aristogeiton, *see* Tyrannicides
Helios, 144
Hephaistos, 13, 22, 110
Hera, 25, 43
Herakles, 9, 19, 22, 34, 40, 56f., 62, 86, 92, 94, 156
Herakles Alexikakos, 131
Herakles at Porthmos, 38
Hermes, 17
Hermes Enodios, 13

Hermes Hegemonios, 13
hêrôs iatros, 133
Herse, 167
Hippothoön, 44
Hygieia, 120, 133

Iphigeneia, 14, 34
Isis, 15, 125

Kekrops, 22, 65, 87, 153, 163, 165
Kephissos, 20
Kleomedes of Astypalaiea, 8f.
Kronos, 165
Kychreus, 37, 72f.

Leos, daughters of, 131

Ma, 4
Maleatas, Maleatis, 117
Marathon hero, 56, 62
Marathônomachoi, 58, 63, 95, 105
Mother of the Gods, 1, 18, 45, 78, 159
Muses, 49

Nausithoös, 91
Nemesis, 57, 110
Nymphs, 20, 21, 60f., 62, 127

Oedipus, 168-70
Oreithyia, 71
Oresinios, 133
Orestes, 84, 163
Other Gods, 10, 111

Pallas Athena, 29, 65
Pan, ch. 2 *passim*, 9, 16, 18, 20, 21, 71, 73, 93
Pandrosos, 22, 38, 167
Peitho, 91, 165
Periphemos, 37, 72
Persephone, 154; *see also* Two Goddesses

Phaiax, 91
Phrontis, 33f.
Poseidon, 3, 4, 20, 22, 25, 29, 30f., 40, 90f., 110, 161, 163
Poseidon Erechtheus, 35
Prometheus, 13

Rhea, 165

Sabazios, 4, 149
Sarapis, 15, 125
Selene, 144
Semnai, 168
Sophokles Dexion, 125
Strategos, 32

theoi patrôôi, 12
Theseus, ch. 4 *passim*, 20, 22, 40, 46, 54, 56f., 62, 125, 165
Tisamenos, 84
Triptolemos, 165
Twelve Gods, 40, 42
Two Goddesses, 6, 7, 10, 14, 20, 26f., 34, 85, 107-9, 124, 154-6, 164
Tyrannicides, 24, 89, 94-6

Unknown God, 2

Zeus, 4, 16, 17, 25, 30
Zeus Agoraios, 40
Zeus Ammon, 21
Zeus Eleutherios, 7, 82, 97
Zeus Hekalos, 91
Zeus Herkeios, 13, 22
Zeus Hypatos, 22
Zeus Kronion, 11
Zeus Meilichios, 91
Zeus Olympios, 43, 65
Zeus Ombrios, 27
Zeus Phratrios, 40, 42, 45
Zeus Soter, 25, 75
Zeus Teleios, 35

General Index

Acharnai, 106
Acropolis, 9, 11, 18, 22, 28, 30, 39f., 43, 50f., 59, 102, 104, 132, 163
Aeschylus, 58, 139
Age of Iron, 153
Agora, 2, 9, 19, 32, 40f., 94f., 104, 106, 137
Aigina, 72, 118
aitia, ch. 8 *passim*, 51, 92, 112
Ajax, 2
Alexander of Abonoteichos, founder of oracle, 6
Alkibiades, 136
Alkmaionidai, *genos* of, 96, 138
allotment, appointment by, 102
Amazons, 87, 105
amphiphontes, 72
Amyneion, 125
anagrapheis, 24
Anaxagoras of Miletos, 140, 144
Anytos, Sokrates' accuser, 136
Archias, son of Aristaichmos, 122
archon basileus, 24f., 137, 167
Areopagus, 9, 19, 102
Aristonike, the Pythia, 65
Arkadia, 49f., 60
Arrhephoria, 166-8
Artemision, 71
asebeia, 137-9, 144
Asklepieion, 124, 126-8
Assembly, *see* Ekklesia
Asty, 11, 28, 42, 58, 94, 120, 126
atheists, 144
atheos, 143
Atthidographers, 36, 46, 86, 157f.

Bacchylides, 90f.
Bendideia, festival of, 112
Bendideion, 113
Boule, 19, 94
Bouzygai, *genos* of, 35

Charmides, associate of Thirty Tyrants, 136
City Dionysia, *see* Greater Dionysia
Choës, festival of, 162
chrêsmologoi, 69; *see also* seers
chthonic gods, 29f.
City Eleusinion, 21, 43, 123
Council, *see* Boule
cult-statue, 21, 168

Dark Age, 27, 35
Delia, festival of, 131
Delian Confederacy, 82, 103
Delphi, Athenian treasury at, 48, 97
Delphic Oracle, ch.3 *passim*, 20f., 29, 37, 43, 83, 89, 96, 107, 129, 144
deme cults, 10, 35
Demetrios, Ephesian silversmith, 5
Demon, priest of Asklepios, 129
Diopeithes, decree of, 139-41
Dodona, 21
Drakon, legendary lawgiver, 138
dreams, 15, 134
drought, 27

Ekklesia, 19, 67
Eleusinian Mysteries, 26, 35f., 43, 123, 139, 154
Eleusis, 26, 32, 36, 44, 133, 154, 164
Eleutherai, 42
Eleutheria, festival of, 82
Epidauria, festival of, 123
Epidauros, 117f., 120, 122, 133f.
epiklêsis, 11
epiphanies, 15-18, 48-50, 163
epitheta, ta, 23-5
Erythrai, 106f.
Epizelos, blinded Athenian, 54f.
eponymous archon, 24f.
eranistai, 11
Erkhia, deme of, 10

Erechtheion, 22, 34, 110, 121
Eteoboutadai, *genos* of, 30, 35
Euboia, 107
Eumolpidai, *genos* of, 27, 35, 156
Eupatridai, 93
Euripides, 156f.
eusebeia, 4, 8
Euthydemos, priest of Asklepios, 129f.
Euphrantides, seer, 70
exêgêtês, 130, 157

family religion, 13
famine, 27, 155, 158
foundation legends, *see aitia*

genê, 10f., 35f., 38, 43, 45, 78, 101f., 126
Genesia, festival of, 35
Greater Dionysia, festival of, 41f., 114

healing fees, 122
Helen, 74, 91, 111
Hekalesia, festival of, 91
hêmitheos, 99
Hephaisteion, 92, 94, 106, 110
Herakleia, festival of, 57
Herakleia, sanctuaries, 57, 92
hero-cult, ch. 4 *passim*, 31-4, 78
Herodotos, 47, 49, 55, 79f., 81
heroisation, 168-70
hestiatoria, 21, 127
hiera, 20, 57, 59, 76-8, 92, 126-8
Hippias, tyrant of Athens, 48, 89, 95
Hippokratic medicine, 116
Hippolytos, 2f.
household religion, *see* family religion
human sacrifice, 70, 93
Hymettos, Mount, 27

iatreia, *see* healing fees
Ilissos River, 42
impiety, *see asebeia*
Ion, 28, 156
Ionian tribes, 28, 45, 156
Isokrates, 23

Kadmos, 7
Kallimachos, polemarch, 51, 55, 59
Kallynteria, festival of, 100
Karneia, festival of, 48
katalêpsis, 29
Kerameikos, 58
Kerykes, *genos* of, 43, 126

Kimon, 7, 22, 82-6, 97, 104
kings, 30, 157
Kleinias, decree of, 107
Kleisthenes, 28, 43-5
Kleisthenic tribes, 28, 43-5, 89
Kleomenes, Spartan king, 68
Kolonos Agoraios, hill of, 13, 37
Korybantic rites, 1
Kos, 107
kratêriskoi, 61, 76
Kritias, one of Thirty Tyrants, 136
Kybernesia, festival of, 91
Kylon, assassinated by Megakles, 38, 138
Kynosarges, 57

Lampon, seer, 126
Lefkandi, 35
Leokorion, 131
Lykomedai, *genos* of, 78, 87
Lykomedes, murderer of Theseus, 83
Lykon, Sokrates' accuser, 136

Marathon, deme of, 30, 40
Marathon, battle of, ch. 2 *passim*, 85, 89, 103-6
Megakles, Alkmaionid, 38
Megarians, 37f.
megaron, 26, 64
Melete, deme of, 37, 76-8, 102
Meletos, Sokrates' accuser, 136f., 143
Menestheus, pretender to Athenian throne, 83, 88, 91
mêtragyrtai, 18
Metroön, 137
Miltiades, 47, 50, 59, 84f., 104
Minotaur, 86, 93
monitions, 74, 83
Moses, 16, 49
Mycenaeans, 25f., 31, 84

Neoptolemos, repairer of sanctuary of Artemis Aristoboule, 78
Nikias, general, 8, 21
Nikomachos, commissioner, 24, 45, 139, 145
Ninos, priestess, 150
nomizein theon, vii, 142-5

Odysseus, 16, 153
Oedipus, 66, 168-70
oikistês, 97

Olympieion, 43
Olympos, Mount, 2, 49, 155
oracles, ch. 3 *passim; see also* Delphic
    oracle
orgeônes, 11, 125
Oschophoria, festival of, 93

Painted Stoa, *see* Stoa Poikile
Panathenaia, festival of, 31, 39, 91,
    101, 105f., 108
pannuchis, 112
Parthenon, 30, 105f.
patria, ta, 23-5, 45, 101, 145
Pausanias, 158
Pegasos of Eleutherai, sponsor of
    Dionysos, 18, 159
Peisistratids, 17, 38-43, 90, 94
Pelargikon, fortification wall, 59, 126
Peloponnesian War, 1, 21, 77, 99, 111f.,
    131, 140, 149
Pentheus, 5, 160
Periklean rebuilding programme, 109f.
Perikles, 17, 100, 109
Peripatos, 126
Persian Wars, chh.2 and 3 *passim*, 1,
    17, 97, 86, 99
phasmata, 55f., 84
Pheidias, 57, 104
Pheidippides, ch. 2 *passim*, 16, 18, 152
philotimia, 7, 8
Phlya, 78
phratries, 35, 45
Phryne, *hetaira*, 150
Phye, Athenian girl who imitated
    Athena, 17
physicians, 116
Phytalidai, *genos* of, 93
piety, *see eusebeia*
Piraeus, 35, 71, 76f., 105, 111, 118, 120
plague, 114f.
Plataiai, battle of, 75, 82, 109
Plataiai, Oath of, 105, 109
Plataians, 47, 82
Plato, 141ff.
Plutarch, 79f.
Plynteria, festival of, 100f.
polemarch, 24f., 51
pollution, 131, 168
Polydamas, seer, 67
polyonomy, 11
Praxiergidai, *genos* of, 24, 100-2
priesthoods, democratic, 111

priesthoods, gentilician, 30f., 102f.
priests, priestesses, 6, 20, 30f., 60,
    102f., 128f., 156
private cults, 128
public cults, *see* state cults
Pyanopsia, festival of, 93
Pythia, Apollo's medium, 43, 64, 68
pythochrêstos exêgêtês, 130

Rhamnous, deme of, 110

sacrificial calendar, 36
Salaminioi, *genos* of, 38
Salamis, battle of, ch. 3 *passim*, 85
Salamis, island of, 37, 44
Salmoxis, founder of new cult, 5f.
Samos, 107
sanctuaries, *see hiera*
seers, 6, 126, 157
Seisachtheia, celebration of, 38
Semele, 16
Skyros, island of, 83
snakes, sacred, 22, 121f.
Social War, 23
Sokrates, ch. 7 *passim*, 21
Solon, 35-8
soothsayers, *see* seers
Sophokles, 125
Soros, mound known as, 58, 103
Sosinika, hostess of Sarapis and Isis,
    15, 125
Sparta, 47f., 53, 60, 84, 118
state burial, 45
state cults, 10, 103, 128
state funding, 110f.
Stoa Poikile, 52, 56, 94, 103f.
St Paul, 9, 17, 19
symposium, 6, 19
synoecism, 27-31
Synoikia, festival of, 91, 165

taxation, 111
Teiresias, seer, 6
Telemachos, Odysseus' son, 5, 16
Telemachos, sponsor of Asklepios, 18,
    118, 120, 122f., 126, 128
Telemachos Monument, 118-21, 128
Telesterion, 26, 36, 43
temenê, 21, 129; *see also hiera*
Tetrakomoi, 35
Tetrapolis, 35, 40
Thargelia, festival of, 25

Theangelos, son of Telemachos, 128f.
Themistokles, ch. 3 *passim*, 85, 102, 115
theophilia, 11
theopropoi, 64-8
theôria, 25
theôrodokoi, 122
theriomorphism, 121f.
Thersandros, sponsor of Asklepios, 122
Thessaly, 116
Theseia, festival, 94
Theseia, sanctuaries, 94
thiasôtai, 11
Thirty Tyrants, 136

Thracians, 111-14
Thukydides, 73, 89, 95f.
Timon, son of Androboulos, 65
trittyes, 45
trophy, 103
Trojan War, 32, 153

Virgin Mary, 29

water, use in cult, 126

Xenokrateia, sponsor of Kephissos, 20
Xenophon, 141ff.

Zea, port of, 118, 120, 123, 132

DATE DUE
